THE JAMES SPRUNT STUDIES IN HISTORY AND POLITICAL SCIENCE

*Published under the Direction of
the Departments of History and Political Science
of the University of North Carolina*

VOLUME 24
NUMBER I

———————— * ————————

Editors

ALBERT RAY NEWSOME
WILLIAM WHATLEY PIERSON
MITCHELL B. GARRETT
FLETCHER M. GREEN
KEENER C. FRAZER

JEFFERSONIAN DEMOCRACY IN SOUTH CAROLINA

By

JOHN HAROLD WOLFE, Ph.D.
Professor of History
Appalachian State Teachers College

CHAPEL HILL
———— * ————
THE UNIVERSITY OF NORTH CAROLINA PRESS
1940

TO
AILEEN COMER WOLFE
Whose Hamiltonian Industry and Jeffersonian Frugality,
Together with the James Sprunt Fund, Made the
Publication of This Monograph Possible

PREFACE

Today, when the name of Thomas Jefferson is heard so frequently, a study of Jeffersonian Democracy is particularly appropriate. A careful historical treatise of any epoch should be of some value to the reader, but some periods in history stand out because of their influence upon subsequent eras. In such potent ages there are individuals who indelibly stamp themselves upon the minds of their contemporaries and force future historians to give much emphasis to their doctrines and actions. Such an individual was Thomas Jefferson. No one can write an accurate and complete account of post-Revolutionary United States or post-Revolutionary South Carolina without giving much attention to his work and influence. Indeed, it would be folly for any historian to attempt to ignore the potency of the Jeffersonian tradition in twentieth-century American life.

As any dominant personality or influential epoch becomes farther removed in point of time, new and often erroneous opinions are associated with them. Unavoidably, the writers of each succeeding generation read something of their own present into their interpretation of the past. In order to preserve even a reasonable degree of accuracy, those who would clearly appraise any age must carefully examine the primary sources. A sincere effort has been made in this work to present Jeffersonian Democracy in South Carolina as available original sources reveal it to have been. Reliable secondary accounts, however, have also been diligently studied.

This treatise had its beginning in a brief survey of the South Carolina Federalists made by the writer while he was a student at the University of South Carolina. At that time he went far enough in his research to discover evidence which made him question the generally accepted view that the Federalists dominated South Carolina politics before 1800 and continued to be extremely influential thereafter. Later, when he was a student at the University of North Carolina, Dr. J. G. de R. Hamilton suggested that he make a study of Jeffersonian Democracy in South Carolina. While attending, about the same time, a seminar conducted by Dr. W. W. Pierson, the writer became interested in the political theories of Thomas Jefferson. These factors, given greater force by his interest in the history of his native state, caused him to begin this study. Sources were often scattered and at times fragmentary, but after diligently searching for them wherever they were and carefully examining them, the writer modestly presents the results of his labors. He takes no great delight in giving a "new viewpoint." He has tried to picture the developments as the sources revealed them to him. If he has at times differed with the findings of so respected a historian as the late Professor U. B. Phillips and others he has done so only after much thoughtful consideration. The writer would have preferred to agree with those who have done so much in the field of Southern history, but he was forced to interpret the evidence as he himself saw it.

No intense study of even a short period of history can be carried to completion without the assistance of many people. All who aided through advice or labor cannot be mentioned, as much as the writer should like to do so. Certain individuals and the attendants in certain institutions, however, must be given special recognition. The librarians and assistants of the Charleston Library Society, the College of Charleston Library, the University of South Carolina Library, the South Carolina Historical Commission, the University of North Carolina Library, Duke University Library and the Library of Congress rendered courteous and valuable service. Dr. Hamilton, already referred to, not only suggested the study but also aided and advised throughout the whole course of its preparation. Dr. A. R. Newsome and Dr. Fletcher M. Green, also of the University of North Carolina, read the manuscript, made many helpful suggestions as to content, and deserve much credit for whatever merit may be found in its organization. To Aileen Comer Wolfe, his wife, the writer is deeply indebted not only for aid and advice while he was studying and writing, but also for her untiring assistance during many hours of arduous labor in the mechanical phase of preparing the study.

TABLE OF CONTENTS

	PAGE
PREFACE	vii

CHAPTER

I. POST-REVOLUTIONARY SOUTH CAROLINA: THE
LAND, THE PEOPLE AND THE CULTURE 1

   1. The Physiography of South Carolina 1

   2. The Inhabitants and Their Culture 4

II. POST-REVOLUTIONARY SOUTH CAROLINA POLITICS:
THE CONFEDERATION AND THE STRUGGLE OVER
THE FEDERAL CONSTITUTION 14

   1. South Carolina during the Confederation: a
Summary of Political and Economic Conditions 14

   2. The Framing of the Federal Constitution 21

   3. The Struggle over the Ratification of the New
Constitution 24

III. REPUBLICAN BEGINNINGS 40

   1. Early Democratic Strivings in South Carolina... 40

   2. The First Two State Constitutions 43

   3. The Constitution of 1790 44

   4. The Continuation of Democratic Local Efforts
during the 1790's 47

   5. Initial Relations between South Carolina and the
Federal Government 54

IV. THE FRENCH REVOLUTION, THE JAY TREATY AND
REPUBLICAN SUCCESSES IN 1796 71

   1. Sympathy for France 71

   2. "Self-Created Societies" 79

   3. Opposition to the Jay Treaty 82

   4. The More Satisfactory Treaty of Thomas Pinckney 92

   5. Republican Victories in 1796 95

CONTENTS

V. TEMPORARY FEDERALIST RECOVERY, 1796-1799..... 100
1. The "X. Y. Z." Affair and the Struggle over Preparedness 100
2. The Passage of the Alien and Sedition Acts..... 116
3. Preparedness Measures in South Carolina....... 119
4. Slight Federalist Gains in 1798................ 121
5. The Continuation of the Federalist Program in the Face of Rising Republican Opposition.......... 124

VI. THE JEFFERSONIAN TRIUMPH IN 1800............. 135
1. The Nomination of Candidates................ 135
2. Campaign Methods and Practices.............. 137
3. Division among the Federalists................ 145
4. The Continued Vigor of the Campaign.......... 148
5. Republican Victories in South Carolina......... 155
6. Jefferson Finally Chosen President............. 161

VII. THE ESTABLISHMENT OF JEFFERSONIAN DEMOCRACY, 1801-1805...................... 166
1. The Principles of Jeffersonian Democracy....... 166
2. Early Appointments under Jefferson............ 168
3. South Carolina Education under Jeffersonian Democracy 171
4. The Repeal of Federalist Legislation............ 176
5. The "Geffroy Letters" and the Retirement of John Rutledge............................... 179
6. The Election of 1802 and the Establishment of the *Charleston Courier*........................ 181
7. The Purchase of Louisiana and the Interest in Florida 184
8. The Reopening of the Slave Trade............. 188
9. The Ratification of the Twelfth Amendment and Political Developments in 1804................. 194
10. South Carolina's Vote of Confidence in Jeffersonian Democracy........................ 197

CONTENTS

VIII. REPUBLICAN EFFORTS TO PRESERVE PEACE, 1806-1810 203
  1. The Independence of Williams and Sumter and the Passage of the Non-Intercourse Act......... 203
  2. The *Phocian* Letters—the Strongest Case for the Federalists 206
  3. The Election of 1806......................... 210
  4. British-French Depredations in 1807 and the Passage of the Embargo...................... 213
  5. Reform in the Basis of Representation in the State Legislature............................. 218
  6. The Embargo in Operation................... 220
  7. The Election of 1808......................... 227
  8. Further Efforts to Enforce the Embargo; the Substitution of Other Measures of Economic Coercion 232
  9. The Extension of the Suffrage and the Election of 1810............................ 240

IX. YOUNG REPUBLICANS AND THE WAR OF 1812...... 242
  1. New Vigor in Republican Leadership........... 242
  2. The Struggle for National Preparedness........ 245
  3. The Declaration of War...................... 253
  4. The Election of 1812......................... 259
  5. The First Year of the War.................... 264
  6. Republican Factionalism during the Administration of Joseph Alston............... 268
  7. Efforts of the War Party to Justify the War and Stimulate Confidence, 1813-1814............... 273
  8. Peace at Last................................ 283

BIBLIOGRAPHY 287

INDEX 299

JEFFERSONIAN DEMOCRACY
IN
SOUTH CAROLINA

CHAPTER I

POST-REVOLUTIONARY SOUTH CAROLINA: THE LAND, THE PEOPLE AND THE CULTURE

1. THE PHYSIOGRAPHY OF SOUTH CAROLINA

Against the Atlantic Ocean, between 32 and 35.2 degrees north latitude, nestled as it were between Georgia and North Carolina, lie the 30,989 square miles of South Carolina. Some parts of the state were only thinly populated even in 1816, the closing year of the period covered in this study; but, settled or unsettled, the geographical and geological nature of the whole area had already begun to affect the historical development of the commonwealth. South Carolina had long been thought of as composed, roughly speaking, of two parts—the low country and the up country. Though their importance may not have been commonly recognized there were then, as now, subdivisions within each of the two sections.

The most authoritative living student of South Carolina history has aptly said that a very detailed description of the state's soils and minerals "is the task of the geologist."[1] But, regardless of whether the historian subscribes to the tenets of the geographical interpreters of history, he must realize that his story is hardly complete without at least a brief sketch of the physical characteristics of the area discussed. We shall, therefore, survey in very broad outline the main physiological divisions of South Carolina. Of the seven sections into which the state is divided, the first four may properly be considered as lying in the low country and the sixth and seventh in the up country; the fifth is partly in both and to some extent a separate region.

[1] David Duncan Wallace, *The History of South Carolina* (New York: American Historical Society, Inc., 1934), I, 10.

There are really three parts to the first section, generally known as the coastal region: the sea islands, comprising only about 800 square miles, but stretching from the mouth of the Savannah River to Winyah Bay; the salt marshes, either on or near the islands and making up something like 600 square miles of the state's area; and finally the 300 square miles which compose the shore line north of Georgetown. Except for the almost worthless salt marshes, the soil of the islands and for some ten miles inland is a fine sandy loam with a subsoil of yellow clay and fine textured sand. Since growth of vegetation is almost completely unchecked during more than half of each year the plant life is semitropical. The palmetto, cypress, live oak and magnolia trees are found in abundance. On the islands, especially, the long, silky-fibered variety of cotton early began to thrive. The altitude is low, reaching a maximum of 25 or 30 feet on the islands; and the climate, especially near the reedy swamps, tends to be malarial. On the coast line north of Winyah the soil is hard but sandy; no marshes border the region and no islands separate it from the ocean. It is, therefore, not very valuable agriculturally. A discussion of the coastal region is incomplete without some mention of the excellent natural harbors at Savannah, Port Royal, Charleston and Georgetown and of the innumerable inlets and rivers which made inland and coastwise navigation possible. This factor was extremely important in the settlement of the region and contributed greatly to the building up of an extensive foreign and coastwise commerce, largely concentrated in Charleston. It was the coastal region and the physical division next to be discussed that formed almost completely the theatre of colonial activity.

The lower pine belt lies partly in and partly above the area of tidal influence. In the lower part of this region extensive rice fields were early located; whereas in the upper belt the abundance of long-leaf pine encouraged the development of turpentine farms. These forests were also once the pasture of large herds of cattle. The altitude rises in some places to 130 feet above sea level, and the width of the region is about fifty miles.

The upper pine belt, ranging from 130 to 250 feet in altitude and from twenty to nearly forty miles in width, contains about 5,500 square miles. Here, long-leaf pine, oak and hickory still abound. The climate was found more healthful and stimulating than that of the two lower sections; and the soil, made up of light sandy loam underlaid with clay, furnished excellent land for the growth of short staple cotton. In the upper, as in the lower pine belt, there are also much rich swamp and bottom lands.

Above the upper pine belt is the red hill region, stretching from the Savannah River through what is now Aiken, Edgefield, upper Orangeburg and Sumter counties. In the last named county almost mountainous beauty is attained in what has come to be called the High Hills of Santee.[2] Here the surface is of a heavy red clay, conducive to the growth of the hickory and the oak. This section contains the fertile ridge lands of Edgefield and considerable other very valuable agricultural soil. The elevation varies from 250 to 600 feet.

On both sides of the fall line but mostly below it lie the sand hills, ranging from 600 to 700 feet in elevation, having a maximum width of thirty miles and extending across the state and beyond in both directions. Though the land, often covered with scrubby trees, was considered until comparatively recently almost worthless for agricultural purposes, parts of the region provided healthful retreats during the hot summer months for lowland planters.

Most of the up country lies in the Piedmont region, where the masses of the white people have finally come to live. Because of its varying elevation, 400 to 800 feet, and its great irregularity of surface, careful cultivation is necessary in order to avoid erosion. Neglect often turned rich areas into ruined fields, but careful attention made parts of it among the most productive in the state. It varies in width from about eighty to ninety miles. The land is generally clay, covered with rich soil, sometimes mixed with sand and gravel. All vegetable productions of the state except rice could be grown advantageously

[2] High Hills of Santee originated as High Hills of Santé, i.e., of Health, but was later corrupted to the form given.

throughout the Piedmont section. Although the soil was not as fertile as that of the river swamps, the climate was more healthful; and very early in the nineteenth century this area became the most populous.

Finally, there is the mountainous section of South Carolina, the Alpine region. It lies in parts of what were formerly Pendleton and Greenville districts but which are now called Oconee, Pickens and Greenville counties. With an elevation ranging from 900 to 3,500 feet, the area should really be grouped with the mountain region of Western North Carolina and Eastern Tennessee. The climate is too cold and the summers too short for cotton, but grain may be cultivated to great advantage in some parts. Here a number of streams rise, whose valleys furnish almost all the tillable land of the Alpine region.[3]

2. The Inhabitants and Their Culture

The tracing of the exploration and settlement of the region now called South Carolina is hardly a part of our story. Nor is it necessary to give a detailed discussion of the origins or characteristics of the population groups that participated in the waves of migration which ultimately peopled the various sections from the sea to the mountains. Late in the seventeenth century the English, Huguenots and Jews gained a foothold along the Atlantic Coast. Everything beyond was then the back country. Gradually the early comers and others of the same nationalities who followed them set up new communities; but most of the hinterland was settled by still others who were considered foreigners by the people of the low country and who apparently so considered themselves. These later immigrants were attracted to South Carolina by the hope of greater free-

[3] A very excellent brief summary of the "Geographical Basis" of South Carolina is found in Wallace, *History of S. C.*, I, 3-10. The names of the sections and, to a great extent, the descriptions have been found valuable and usable for this study. Robert Mills, *Statistics of South Carolina* (Charleston: 1826), pp. 130-133, the work of a contemporary, has been used especially for its discussion of the Piedmont soil. William A. Schaper, "Sectionalism and Representation in South Carolina," *Annual Report of American Historical Association* (1900), I, 253-258, treats the physiography and natural resources of the state in a highly satisfactory way. A more exhaustive study is M. Tuomey, *Report on the Geology of South Carolina* (Columbia: 1848).

dom and better opportunities for comfortable living. Usually poor, they were especially interested in the abundance of cheap land. Though other groups entered the region, most of the up country was populated by Scotch-Irish and German frontiersmen from Pennsylvania, Virginia and North Carolina. Since their ingress was not through Charleston or the coast country, and since there was little communication with that region during the first decade or two, social ties did not bind the sections together. In fact, there was more frequent contact with Philadelphia and Richmond than with Charleston during the early years.

Statistics on the population of South Carolina at the close of the Revolution must be estimates and to some extent guesses. More dependable data may be found in the report of the first census conducted by the Federal Government. An examination of that document reveals that 249,073 persons were living in the state in 1790. Of these, 140,178 were whites; 1,801 were free blacks; 107,094 were slaves. The three lower districts of Beaufort, Charleston and Georgetown, often referred to as the low country, had a white population of 28,644 as compared with the 111,534 white people of the up country.

Before 1790 and for many years thereafter distinct sectionalism existed in South Carolina. The people of both the low country and the up country felt that two clear-cut societies were present. In many ways the spread of population throughout the state paralleled the Westward movement in the nation; but in one respect the similarity is not so evident. Generally, when a stranger arrived in a Western community and established himself, he was accepted as one of the group already there. A far different reception was given the frontiersmen who decided to make their homes in the South Carolina back country. They were strangers who were welcomed to the hospitality of the region but who must not expect to participate actively in its government; and, strange as it may seem, a similar attitude was held by the newcomers themselves. They were half apologetic and seemingly conscious of being of a different social group. Since they did not immediately adopt the customs and institutions of their predecessors, assimilation was more difficult when they came to outnumber the dwellers in the original communities. Gradually the up country farmers became less conscious of being intruders and began to ask for more political power. During the 1790's pamphlets and newspaper articles expressing such an attitude were common. Sometimes the language was bold; but often the writers still found it difficult to rid themselves of the feeling that they were plebeians begging privileges from a higher social class. Even though they did at times say that they *might* claim as a right the increase in political power, they continued to put their "demands" in the form of requests.[4]

Perhaps this beseeching tone was used more for the sake of policy than might appear on the surface. Although the advocates of reform did not contend that they had been oppressed, they feared the possible future abuse of power by the low country. They did not think that the state constitution adequately guaranteed their welfare, for

As it stood, it provided for the most strongly centralized and aristocratic government that could have been established under the limitations fixed by the constitution of the United States. The planters could not have wished for a better instrument of oppression if they had been inclined to injure the up country.[5]

[4] One of the most forceful statements of the up country position was that of Robert Goodloe Harper, *An Address to the People of South Carolina by the General Committee of the Representative Reform Association at Columbia* (Charleston: 1794), 42 pp. A copy is found in series 3, vol. 2, of the extremely valuable collection of pamphlets preserved by the Charleston Library Society. Replies were soon forthcoming: Timothy Ford, *The Constitutionalist or an Enquiry how far it is Expedient and Proper to Alter the Constitution of South Carolina,* first in the *City Gazette* as "Americanus," later in pamphlet form (Charleston: 1794), a copy of which is in series 3, vol. 6, of the Charleston Library Society pamphlets; and Henry William DeSaussure, *Letters on the Question of the Expediency of Going into the Alteration of Representation in the Legislature of South Carolina, as Fixed by the Constitution,* first published in the *City Gazette,* signed "Phocian," later as a pamphlet (Charleston: 1795), a copy of which is also in series 3, vol. 6, of the Charleston Library Society pamphlets. Another article favoring reform, this time less theoretical, in the form of an address by 16 senators and 56 representatives, and at least partly written by Harper was published in the *Columbian Herald* (Charleston), October 29, 1795.

[5] Schaper, "Sectionalism and Representation in S. C.," p. 423.

JEFFERSONIAN DEMOCRACY IN S. C.　　7

By the 1790's many of the separating forces had already disappeared; but South Carolinians apparently still considered themselves two distinct political peoples. This was due partly to the differences in degree of education, knowledge and refinement, but most of all to the lack, at that time, of approximate unity in economic interests. What concerned the low country most of all was security. Could the up country farmers be trusted to protect the established social order? In the 1790's the inhabitants of the lower districts still distrusted the more populous up country. Of course, it was not then certain that the black belt would cover, within a few decades, a great part of the middle section and the up country. Those who then controlled the state were afraid that a people with different interests and social outlook would deal less gently with certain peculiar institutions of the older communities. Later on, when the whole state was to be a kind of low country "writ large," changes were to come;[6] but this belongs to a later period of study.

The anthropologist would probably use different terms in explaining our problem. He would say that the South Carolina of 1790 had two distinct cultures—that of the low country and that of the up country. In shaping the trends of cultures two factors seem to be most vital—the physical and social environments or the physiography and the people. We have already seen something of the physical characteristics of the various sections of South Carolina. A brief sketch of the process of settlement has shown that people of different nationalities, different religions and different social outlooks came to inhabit

[6] This is the thesis of Schaper, "Sectionalism and Representation in S. C.," and supporting evidence seems to be ample. See especially pp. 433-452 of this work. The author does not contend that sectionalism entirely disappeared—"The great inequality in wealth which existed on the coast and formed the basis of the aristocracy never was characteristic of the up country, at least not in any such marked degree. This, taken in connection with the difference in tradition handed down from the past, was enough to keep alive a certain sectional feeling in the state. But it was no longer the free society of small farms and household manufactures of 1790 that was opposing the seaboard aristocracy. It was a younger, more democratic, slave society opposing the parent society with its grand old families, its aristocratic traditions, and its political power."—pp. 451-452.

the two main parts of South Carolina. In short, the state had been populated by different culture groups. The physiography might be expected to remain substantially the same. But would this be true of the people? In any culture there is constantly the interplay of the physical forces upon the people and of the people upon the physical forces. Were the natural features of South Carolina such as to continue the existence of these two types of civilization? Could the people bring about sufficient modifications to break down the separating forces? Or, to state it differently, could the social environment control the physical; could the active influences direct the passive? The answering of this question was to be a determining factor in South Carolina history for many a day.

While much may be done by the ingenuity of a people, the presence or absence of certain natural resources may almost predestine the cultural nature of that people. Good outlets to the sea, good soil and almost no mineral resources inevitably made the dominant interests of low country South Carolina commercial and agricultural, particularly the latter. The lack of coal and iron and the disadvantageous climatic conditions discouraged manufacturing. However, the nearness to the cotton fields, the availability of coal and iron from the mines of Alabama, Georgia and Tennessee and the mildness of its climate made the upper part of South Carolina potentially a manufacturing area long before it became so. There were, in fact, some small deposits of iron and other minerals in that section. In the days before roads were constructed and before the profits that came to be derived from cotton spread the plantation system into upper South Carolina, a system of household manufacturing with the aid of native iron, was being developed. In fact it was sometimes referred to as a "manufacturing section" in the years following the Revolution.[7]

A discussion of the culture of post-Revolutionary South Carolina must include at least a glimpse of the societies that existed in the low country and in the up country. Travelers and newcomers to a region no doubt overlook much that a closer

[7] See Schaper, "Sectionalism and Representation in S. C.," p. 258.

examiner might see, but they also observe some things that inhabitants do not or have ceased to notice. A foreign visitor in 1784 became eloquent in describing the region of Charleston.[8] "The neighborhood of Charles Town is beautiful beyond description. A road extends the distance of six or eight miles, which surpasses every thing of the kind in the world." "Several equipages are kept here. The planters and merchants are rich and well-bred: the people are showy, and expensive in their dress and way of living; so that every thing conspires to make this the liveliest, the pleasantest, and the politest place, as it is the richest too, in all America." "The large fortunes that have been acquired in this city, from the accession and circulation of its trade, most successfully have had great influence on the manners of its inhabitants; for of all the towns of North America it is the one in which the conveniences of luxury are most to be met with."[9]

When he came to the region of Camden, the traveler was less enthusiastic. Except for the rice and indigo planters the section was disappointing. "Camden is a place of considerable commerce, and is improving fast, but I do not think it meriting the pains, the fatigue and trouble, I have taken to see it, for I can discover nothing particularly remarkable either in the town, or in the country around it." The country was one continued plain and forest, with the plantations and settlements formed only upon the sides of the rivers and water courses. The inhabitants were "a feeble race, of tawney or yellowish hue, and sallow, cadaverous complexions"; but many of the rice and indigo planters in the neighborhood were "very gay and opulent." Even the Negroes were smaller and less valuable than those in Virginia.[10] The region of the Edisto was said to be noted for the "number of opulent widow ladies who reside on the banks of that river, and for the perpetual round

[8] Since most of this study deals with the period after which this town came to be called Charleston instead of Charles Town, the former is used throughout, except in quotations.

[9] J. F. D. Smyth, *A Tour in the United States of America* (Dublin: 1784), II, 52-53.

[10] *Ibid.*, I, 130-132.

of entertainments and dissipation pursued by the inhabitants of that gay settlement." The region was unhealthful and the men more exposed and intemperate than the women. This was supposed to account for the greater fatality among the males.[11]

With some of the inhabitants of the back country, the visitor was plainly disgusted. He paused to spend the night at a farm near the Catawba nation. There he found a one-room house containing only one bed, which was used by the "planter," while the traveler was given a pallet on the floor. In the latter's description of this dwelling are found such expressions as "hovel," "shelter" and "mansion of misery." He was convinced that his host must be the overseer of some wealthy Charleston planter; but when he talked with several nearby Negroes, the traveler learned that the man in question owned not only them and the land but also other plantations and more slaves. When he departed he had a feeling of contempt for this "penurious wretch" and of sympathy for the Negroes.[12] Only the climate received praise.[13]

The Charleston of 1785-1786 is interestingly described by a young man who had just arrived from the North and who was later to become prominent in the affairs of his adopted state. South Carolina's largest town had straight, generally regular but very narrow streets. On each side there were usually about four feet of pavement and brick for the pedestrians, the intervening space being in its natural state "mostly sandy and therefore disagreeable crossing the street." However, carriages made little noise passing along; and one's ears were not strained as they were in New York. There was dust sometimes. The houses were even more scattered than those in Philadelphia, permitting the "free circulation of air." Most of the buildings were of brick, though many were of wood. None of the dwellings was more than three stories while most were

---

[11] Smyth, *A Tour in the U. S.*, II, 34-35.

[12] *Ibid.*, I, 126-129. The above illustration is not given as typical or necessarily an entirely accurate description of all up country living conditions in 1784, but is intended as suggestive of the varying conditions then existing in different parts of South Carolina.

[13] *Ibid.*, II, 47.

not that high. Many, especially those of brick, could be termed "tolerably good" but they were not uniformly so. The police, he described as "pretty good."[14]

This observer was both optimistic and pessimistic.

Whatever disease this country may labour under its staples will ensure it a considerable rank in a commercial point of view —the planting interest & the various modes of lucrative business must still invite to immigration. But while the facility with which money may be made invites to population; it has a very considerable influence upon manners & customs. The inhabitants possess not that keenness & sagacity which are visible in countries more difficult to subsist in; and which tends to make them famous for ingenuity & improvements. Pleasure becomes in a great measure their study, Science but little patronized or pursued, & activity to habits of study looked upon as the retreats of the tasteless or melancholy resorts of the needy. While Science is thus in a state of degradation the art can scarcely be expected to flourish. Manufactures are neither patronized encouraged or pursued; and they seem to be perfectly content to supply themselves from foreign markets. The military art goes fast to decay; dwindling apace into empty pajeantry and artless parade. They seem willing to forget the dangers & hardships of war amidst the alluring baits of pleasure; and voluntarily to sink from the active spirit of the soldier into the effeminate spirit of luxury and dissipation. It seems strange that while they lavish so much money upon the objects of luxury they are still but illy & imperfectly supplied. A person walking thro the market would have an idea of many of the commodities being but the mere cullings from the tables of those who supply them. Flesh coarse & seldom very fat or delicate; fish in no state of perfection, always dead & sometimes stale; and all sold at exorbitant prices.[15]

At about the same time a man who was to travel very extensively throughout the United States in the years to come was writing that there was "a great dearth of religion" in Charles-

[14] Timothy Ford, "Diary of Timothy Ford 1785-1786," edited by Joseph W. Barnwell, *South Carolina Historical and Genealogical Magazine*, XIII, p. 145.
[15] *Ibid.*, pp. 203-204. It is possible that part of this criticism may be attributed to the attitude sometimes possessed by young men toward a new environment to which they go after they have reached maturity. But compare his statements with those of Asbury.

ton.[16] In 1795 he left this "seat of wickedness, not without grief and joy." He was more hopeful than he had been in 1785; and during future visits he seemed to alternate between hope and despair for the outcome of his religious endeavors in Charleston.[17] In 1786 Georgetown was also a "poor place for religion."[18]

Returning to the young man's description of South Carolina in 1785-1786, we are told that there was "but little of the spirit of education"; that ample provisions had been made for the endowment of colleges by act of the legislature in 1785, but that there was no one to "draw them forth into utility." He reported that a good many young men went to England but came back little improved and sometimes more dissipated. There was a strong connection between South Carolina and England; many were prejudiced in favor of all things English but hated England as a country, paradoxical as it may seem.[19]

Whether a man was a gentleman could often be determined by the presence or absence of a servant or servants when he was riding. It was not so in the northern part of the United States.

But so it is that in this Country a person can no more act or move without an attending servant than a planet without its satellites. If they only cross their plantation they must have a subservient follower, and if they ride out their horse might as well want a wooden leg as they the necessary equipage which is their recourse in their frequent helpless situations. And which as they advance serve as ensigns of their rank and dignity.[20]

The ladies carried "formality & scrupulosity to a considerable extreme;" a stranger made feminine acquaintances "by slow gradations interspersed with niceties & punctilios w^h often disconcert the forward & intimidate the bashful."[21] How-

[16] Francis Asbury, *The Journal of the Rev. Francis Asbury, Bishop of the Methodist Episcopal Church, 1771-1815* (New York: 1821), I, 382, under entry of February 28, 1785.

[17] *Ibid.*, II, 218; see also comments in 1808, III, 254; and those of 1812, when he wrote "Religion is not fashionable in Charleston," III, 340.

[18] *Ibid.*, I, 393.
[19] Ford, "Diary," pp. 191-192.
[20] *Ibid.*, pp. 189-190.
[21] *Ibid.*, pp. 190-191.

ever, one did meet sometimes the forward young lady "with a great flow of spirits" who talked a great deal and who even dared to intermix her words with "profanities."[22]

While travelers and newcomers saw the wealth of the planters, some of the local inhabitants knew that conditions were not as good as they seemed. Aedanus Burke asserted on the floor of the federal house of representatives that

> Though it is true, that there are men there who live in affluence, are rich in land and in servants, yet I believe they are universally in debt. This may be fairly inferred from the laws they have made to favor debtors. It would take twelve years to enable people there to pay their state and private debts; they are therefore very unable to sustain any further burthens, especially when their produce is so fallen in price as not to pay the expense of cultivation.[23]

A contemporary historian of the state thought that the Revolution was followed by a period of "disorganization."[24] Some of the planters feared both political and economic disorganization. One of them who had long been prominent in the public service of the state and nation was frightened by the rise of a democratic spirit. "Our governments tend too much to Democracy. A handicraftsman thinks apprenticeship necessary to make himself acquainted with his business. But our back countrymen are of the opinion that a politician may be born as well as a poet."[25]

Thus was post-Revolutionary South Carolina's culture agrarian and dominated by a small group of the population. In that day of political and economic flux the democratic spirit was coming in conflict with the agricultural aristocracy. Local as well as general conditions, therefore, were preparing the way for the struggle soon to develop between the established order and the forces of Jeffersonian democracy.

[22] *Ibid.*, p. 187.
[23] Joseph Gales, ed., *The Debates and Proceedings of the United States Congress* (Washington: 1834), 1st Cong., 1st Sess. (May 7, 1789), pp. 296-297. This work is hereafter cited as *Annals of Congress*.
[24] David Ramsay, *The History of South-Carolina From Its First Settlement in 1670 to the year 1808* (Charleston: 1809), II, 430.
[25] Letter of Ralph Izard to Thomas Jefferson, June 10, 1785, reprinted in *South Carolina Historical and Genealogical Magazine*, II, 197-198.

CHAPTER II

POST-REVOLUTIONARY SOUTH CAROLINA POLITICS: THE CONFEDERATION AND THE STRUGGLE OVER THE FEDERAL CONSTITUTION

1. SOUTH CAROLINA DURING THE CONFEDERATION:

A SUMMARY OF POLITICAL AND ECONOMIC CONDITIONS

This study cannot present a detailed history of South Carolina during the confederation, a complete story of the part played by her delegates in the Philadelphia convention of 1787, or a full account of the subsequent struggle in the state over ratification of the proposed federal Constitution; but all of these are parts of the background of Jeffersonian Democracy.[1]

Were the conditions in South Carolina after the Revolution

[1] Thomas Jefferson early became a prolific writer of letters. Among the recipients of missives from his pen in the years that followed the Revolution were several South Carolinians. Ralph Izard, later an ardent Federalist, carried on a very friendly correspondence with him during the 1780's. These letters, covering the years 1784-1789, may be found in manuscript form in the Papers of Thomas Jefferson, 1763-1826 (Library of Congress). Most of them have been reprinted in *South Carolina Historical and Genealogical Magazine*, II, 194-204. In vols. 30, 32, 35, 37, 38, 40, 46, 47, 48, 57 and 88 of the manuscript papers are many letters that passed between Jefferson and John Rutledge and John Rutledge, Jr. David Ramsay wrote to secure Jefferson's aid in publishing a French edition of his historical works. *Ibid.*, June 15, July 13, August 8, 31, October 12, 1785; July 10, 1786; April 7, August 4, 1787; October 8, 1788; April 12, 1790. It is of peculiar interest that these South Carolinians and most of the others who wrote to Jefferson during the 1780's later became Federalists. He did not know Charles Pinckney until later. Edward Rutledge and Jefferson formed a warm friendship during the early days of the Revolution. In the 1790's this friendship was renewed and continued until the death of Rutledge in 1800. Examples of their letters may be found in the Jefferson Papers, August 29, 1791; December 30, 1793; November 30, 1795; December 27, 1796; May 4, 19, June 24, 1797.

JEFFERSONIAN DEMOCRACY IN S. C. 15

such as to offer fruitful ground for the fertilization of the Jeffersonian ideas? If his erstwhile friends should not follow him, would others arise to supply the needed local leadership? In order to furnish a basis for the answering of these questions a brief sketch is given of the conditions during the Confederation.

The general disorganization that followed the Revolution was especially noticeable in South Carolina. The immediate outlook was dark. Land had been ravaged by war and internal strife.[2] When the British departed they carried valuable goods and slaves which the citizens of the state could ill afford to lose. Because of this loss of property and of poor crops, abnormal importation was necessary. Despite the hard times, however, many of the people were confident; and some felt that they knew the proper course to follow in alleviating their existing discomfort. The revival of trade as early as 1783 and the dire need of financial machinery resulted in an abortive attempt to establish a bank with a capital of $100,000, a sum greater than business and agriculture could then subscribe.[3]

One of the remedies early advanced by the debtors was inflation. Its supporters argued that it had been so widely used during the war, that an interruption or cessation would check recovery. Since a man's person and property were both liable to seizure for debts contracted after 1782 and since the existing conditions caused the continuation of debt-making to be almost imperative, many were less hostile to the printing of new money than would have ordinarily been the case. The opponents soon realized that they could not defeat completely all attempts of the inflationists; therefore, they concentrated on limiting the amount to be issued. Societies were organized; and the contest became heated, with the leaders of each group having at least one supporting newspaper.[4]

[2] For a description of conditions by a contemporary who had leanings toward the conservatives, see Ramsay, *History of S. C.*, II, 445-450; also Edward Channing, *A History of the United States* (New York: Macmillan, 1905-1932), III, 410-411.

[3] W. A. Clark, *The History of the Banking Institutions Organized in South Carolina Prior to 1861* (Columbia: Historical Commission of South Carolina, 1922), p. 38; and Ramsay, *History of S. C.*, II, 106.

[4] Allan Nevins, in *The American States during and after the Revolution, 1775-1787* (New York: Macmillan, 1924), pp. 526-527, says, "The

Visitors in and newcomers to South Carolina in 1784 and 1785 apparently did not consider the outlook so dark;[5] but perhaps they could not see very far below the surface. One must not be so rash, though, as to disregard utterly their accounts.

It is evident that many thought the time had come when the state government should attempt to improve the economic conditions. When the governor, in his message to the legislature in September, 1785, spoke of the scarcity of money, the inability of many to pay their debts and their liability to falling prey to aliens, several members of the assembly were ready to submit remedies. Ralph Izard thought the prohibition of the importation of Negroes for three years would help check the flow of capital from the state. Others favored stay-laws and paper money. The plan adopted was one of moderate inflation. An issue of £100,000 was to be loaned for five years, with interest, to those who could present, as security, mortgages of land valued at three times the amount borrowed or deposit in the loan office gold or silver plate of two times the value. This act obviously could not be expected to bring about immediate prosperity. Many who greatly needed aid were unable to meet the terms and it is doubtful whether anyone living forty or fifty miles from the coast secured even this small amount of relief. At any rate economic conditions did not improve noticeably by

---

paper held its value, was of great utility to the hard-pressed planters, and returned a steady revenue to the State. Such was its success that in 1789, when specie dollars were pouring into Charleston, it was preferred as being more convenient to use." However, the same writer describes as "utterly indefensible" the so-called "Pine Barren Act" of October 12, 1785, which permitted a debtor under prosecution to tender any kind of lands at two-thirds the value fixed by three independent arbiters and provided that, if the property offered exceeded the amount owed, the creditor was to give bond for the excess, payable in six months. Nevins gives as evidence for his opinion of this law the cases of a few "unprincipled" debtors who took advantage of the creditors by presenting property so far from the coast that the cost of accepting it was almost as great as the debt itself. The law was to continue only until the next meeting of the legislature, at which time it was not re-enacted. *Ibid.*, pp. 525-526.

[5] See, for example, Smyth, *A Tour in the U. S.* and Ford, "Diary," both already referred to in Chapter I.

JEFFERSONIAN DEMOCRACY IN S. C.   17

the spring of 1786. Thus, the work of the legislative session of 1785[6] had not achieved the desired results.

The report of the Camden grand jury in April, 1786, gives evidence of disorganization in business, law enforcement and communication facilities. However, there is present the note of hope; at least the members of the jury expected conditions to improve.[7] Throughout the state a similar situation prevailed. At times vigorous efforts were required to enable the money of 1785 to furnish even moderate relief. Since the statute had not made the notes legal tender, some planters and merchants declined to accept them at face value. In an effort to prevent the depreciation of the money borrowed, a group of planters met at the State House. They were addressed by merchants who placed a large portion of the blame for the depreciation on the planters because they gave more of their products for specie than for notes. After much discussion everyone pledged himself not to buy goods from anyone offering larger quantities for payment in coin. In the meantime, a more enthusiastic group at Charleston resorted to more extreme measures, organizing themselves into a society known as the Hint Club. Regular meetings were held and committees were appointed. When planters or merchants seemed inclined to aid in the depreciation of the credit-bills, members of the club's secret committee would forcibly hint to them the desirability of changing their practices. If this was not sufficient, the club was notified, and further and more effective methods were adopted.[8] Finally the debtors suc-

[6] *Journal of the House of Representatives of the State of South Carolina* (manuscript), September 26, 1785; Thomas Cooper, ed., *The Statutes at Large of South Carolina*, IV, 712. See also *State Gazette of South Carolina*, June 8, 1786. Anne King Gregorie, *Thomas Sumter* (Columbia: R. L. Bryan, 1931), pp. 217-219 gives an excellent summary of the economic conditions of the period with particular attention to the part played by Thomas Sumter.

[7] This report is reproduced in Thomas J. Kirkland and Robert M. Kennedy, *Historic Camden* (Columbia: the State Co., 1905 and 1906), II, 254-256.

[8] John Bach McMaster, *A History of the People of the United States from the Revolution to the Civil War* (New York: D. Appleton, 1911), I, 286-287. McMaster's sources are *New York Packet*, August 28, 1786, and *New York Gazetteer and Country Journal*, July 21, 1786.

ceeded in getting stay-laws enacted; but further attempts on the part of Sumter and others to expand the currency failed.[9] In some sections it was reported that people were forced to surrender their property for want of other means to pay their debts. They, accordingly, petitioned the legislature to provide some methods for the amplification of the circulating medium.[10] However, the conservatives were always strong enough to check such plans, and the petitioners were forced to resort to other methods or await general economic recovery.

Thinking that agricultural conditions might be improved through co-operation, some of the leading planters and public figures organized the South Carolina Society for Promoting and Improving Agricultural and Other Rural Concerns.[11] Agriculture was proclaimed one of the first occupations of man, "one of the most innocent and at the same time the most pleasing and beneficial of any"; it was the "parent of commerce" and the two together "form the great sources from which the wants of individuals are supplied and the principal riches and strength of every state flow. It becomes the duty, therefore, as well as the interest of every citizen to encourage and promote it."[12] The planters wished to learn about the new methods used in Europe and to introduce all foreign plants that might be suitable and profitable in South Carolina. Experimentation in methods and alternation in crops were recommended. Each member was asked to keep a written record of his efforts and the degree of his success so that everyone could find out what the others had done. In 1796 the legislature directed the commissioners of Columbia to give the society two squares of land

[9] S. C. House Journal, February 23, 1788. The legislature had voted on the previous day to appoint a committee to consider the expediency of establishing a bank.

[10] An example of one of these petitions, dated October, 1788, is found in Alexander Gregg, *History of the Old Cheraws* (Columbia: State Book Co., 1905 [reprint of the edition of 1867]), pp. 447-448.

[11] This society was formed at a meeting in the City Hall at Charleston, August 24, 1785. Its name was changed to the Agricultural Society of South Carolina on December 19, 1795. C. Irvine Walker, *History of the Agricultural Society of South Carolina*, pp. 3, 8.

[12] *Ibid.*, p. 4.

for experimental purposes; and the following year an act was passed carrying out the provisions of this resolution.[13]

In addition to its interest in agriculture, the organization was much concerned about trade and commerce. The leaders of the society and of the state[14] knew that the sale of their goods was second in importance only to their production. Beginning during the period of the Confederation, several South Carolinians corresponded with the diplomatic representatives of the United States in the interest of building up markets for the products of the state.[15]

Besides enactments of the state government, individual or co-operative self-improvement and the opening of new markets through the aid of the American ministers abroad, there was another source of possible aid—the government of the Confederation. Even though the delegates of the states in common assembly may not always have inspired confidence in America or impressed foreign governments they could at least help preserve the political and commercial advantages already possessed. At times the legislature of South Carolina was not loath to grant, at least partially, the requests of the general Congress, as is seen in the assembly's vote to grant the right of collecting impost.[16]

[13] S. C. House Journal, December 19, 1796, December 16, 1797.

[14] Many of the first officers in the society were also leading public figures. The first committeemen were William Drayton, John Matthews, John Rutledge, Charles Cotesworth Pinckney, Ralph Izard, Thomas Bee, Edward Rutledge, Aaron Loocock, and Isaac Harleston. Walker, *History of Agricultural Society*, p. 8.

[15] See letters in Jefferson Papers, November 23, 1785; May 6, 1786; February 6, May 22, July 17, November 25, 1787; January 13, March 17, June 19, July 17, December 31, 1788; April 8, September 18, 1789; May 1, 1791; September 6, 1792; May 16, 1797; June 17, 1803. It is apparent that Jefferson was sincerely interested in agricultural development and his correspondence with officers of the organization mentioned above by no means included all the letters that passed between him and South Carolinians on the subject. Examples of others are those reprinted in *South Carolina Historical and Genealogical Magazine*, II, 200-204.

[16] In announcing this decision to Jefferson, Ralph Izard wrote, "You will have heard that our Legislature has passed the 5 per cent law. Considerable opposition was given to it by some of the ablest and most respectable men of the country. It was, however, carried by a majority

Although sectional feeling was not nearly so strong as it was to become several decades later, there was an element of warning as to what might develop. Some of the Southern delegates felt that they must guard the interests of the South and the West against the commercial compromises which John Jay and other Eastern leaders were willing to make with Spain. For a time it seemed almost inevitable that the United States should relinquish temporarily the navigation of the Mississippi. Jay thought that an arrangement could be worked out without sacrificing the theoretical right of the United States to such navigation. In return for this concession advantages could be gained for Eastern commerce. To this proposal unexpected opposition developed. James Monroe of Virginia gave the most outspoken denunciation in Congress, and in his correspondence with James Madison and others he went even farther. It was the young and energetic Charles Pinckney of South Carolina, though, who placed the Southern view on a higher plane and in a less sectional tone. He stated that nature had so located the Western area that the people there must be either the friends or the enemies of the Eastern states and the outcome would depend upon the policy adopted. Nothing was to be gained by the proposed treaty that was not already possessed or to the advantage of Spain to grant. This being the case, the most likely result would be trouble between the different parts of the United States at a time when harmony was most needed. History has since justified the stand of Pinckney and his Southern colleagues.[17] Thus a South Carolina leader who is to have a very prominent part in this study aided materially in maintaining the advantages he thought the nation already had. In this he disclosed his suspicion of the Eastern commercial group but in as guarded a fashion as possible.

The attitude of the people of South Carolina toward foreign

---

of three to one; and I hope the conduct of the other States will make it unnecessary to repeal it till our public debt is paid." Jefferson Papers, April 27, 1784; also found in *S. C. Historical and Genealogical Magazine*, II, 194-195.

[17] For a clear analysis of this struggle see Samuel Flagg Bemis, *Pinckney's Treaty, A Study of America's Advantage from Europe's Distress 1783-1800* (Baltimore: Johns Hopkins Press, 1926), pp. 97-102.

nations was not at all fixed in the 1780's. They were inclined to be friendly with those that would furnish better markets for their goods. Since, in the war just closed, Great Britain had been the enemy, it was natural that many felt some grievances against her. Even one of the ardent Federalists-to-be was moved to state in 1785 that, if the reports that the British were encouraging the pirates to attack our ships could be proved, he would be willing to fight Great Britain again. However, it was a "melancholy fact" that the United States could not afford to go to war with anyone. He wrote Jefferson several times in the interest of French markets; and as late as 1787 it was his opinion that, if goods to be used in clothing slaves could be bought as cheaply in France, at least four fifths of the South Carolina planters would prefer to buy there.[18]

2. The Framing of the Federal Constitution

Some of the South Carolina leaders early advocated changing the Articles of Confederation. Henry Laurens, one of the presidents of the Continental Congress, had seriously considered moving for the calling of a constitutional convention as early as 1779, even before the Articles had been ratified.[19] The vote of the state legislature on the impost question has already been mentioned.[20] On February 15, 1786, Charles Pinckney joined with others in making a plea for more effectual methods of raising revenue. Then the following month in an effective address "by which he persuaded the New Jersey Legislature to rescind its resolution refusing to pay the federal quota, he urged the calling of a general convention to revise and amend the Articles of Confederation."[21] In 1787 the legislature of South Carolina twice recognized the need for increases in the powers of the federal government—by surrendering the state's shadowy claim to Western lands and by approving the amendment allowing the general government to regulate foreign trade,

[18] Ralph Izard to Jefferson. Jefferson Papers, June 10, 1785; April 4, 1787.
[19] David Duncan Wallace, *Life of Henry Laurens* (New York: Putman's, 1915), p. 443. [20] *Supra*, p. 19.
[21] J. H. Easterby, "Charles Pinckney," *Dictionary of American Biography*, XIV, 611.

with certain restrictions, for a period of fifteen years.[22] The legislative body of South Carolina, therefore, should have felt little surprise at the proposal that the states send delegates to a constitutional convention to be held in Philadelphia. Accordingly, on March 8, 1787, five men[23] were chosen to represent the state,

> ... they being duly authorized and empowered, in devising and discussing all such alterations, clauses, articles, and provisions, as may be thought necessary to render the Federal Constitution entirely adequate to the actual situation and future good government of the confederated States; and said deputies or commissioners, or a majority of those who shall be present, provided the State be not represented by less than two, do join in reporting such an Act to the United States in Congress assembled, as when approved and agreed to by them, and duly ratified and confirmed by the several States, will effectually provide for the exigencies of the Union.[24]

In the convention itself the delegates from South Carolina played no small part. Being men of experience and wealth, their interests as well as their patriotism were involved. On the whole they were conservative, showing at times indications of sectional consciousness.[25] Although John Rutledge, Charles Cotesworth Pinckney and Pierce Butler took active parts in the discussions and made proposals which affected the form and substance of the document finally adopted, it was the young, vigorous, aggressive and self-confident Charles Pinckney who contributed most to the Constitution of the United States. The

---

[22] *Statutes at Large,* V, 5-6. Part of the preamble to the act ceding the land states "And whereas, this State is willing to adopt every measure which can tend to promote the honor and dignity of the United States, and strengthen their federal union."

[23] John Rutledge, Charles Cotesworth Pinckney, Henry Laurens, Charles Pinckney and Pierce Butler. Laurens declined because of ill health. Why another was not chosen in his place is not certain. See S. C. House Journal, March 8, 15, 23, 1787.

[24] S. C. *Statutes at Large,* V, 4.

[25] The authorship of the clause in the Constitution intended to facilitate the recovery of fugitive slaves has been attributed to Pierce Butler. Robert Lee Meriwether, "Pierce Butler," *Dictionary of American Biography,* III, 364. Certainly the South Carolinians were among those most interested in slavery and the future of agriculture and the exports produced in the South.

JEFFERSONIAN DEMOCRACY IN S. C.

draft of a proposed Constitution submitted by him to the convention was the fullest and most carefully worked out plan received by that body.[26] Unfortunately no complete copy of the Pinckney plan has come down to us;[27] but the discoveries and reconstructions of J. Franklin Jameson and A. C. McLaughlin show that

Pinckney suggested some thirty-one or thirty-two provisions which were finally embodied in the Constitution; of these about twelve were originally in the Articles of Confederation, and of course the fact that they were restated by Pinckney in his plan may not have had material influence in securing their adoption.

It must not be assumed that we know all that Pinckney thus contributed to the fabric of the Constitution. We now know very definitely the nature of his recommendations, we know that some of them found formulation in the Continental Congress, and we know that many of them were finally embedded in the Constitution; but there were doubtless some other propositions that likewise found permanence in the work of the Convention. If mere assertion based on analogy and general proba-

[26] For what is probably the best stated case of those who claim Pinckney was virtually the author of the Constitution, see Charles C. Nott, *The Mystery of the Pinckney Draught* (New York: Century, 1908). This work by a man who had been Chief Justice of the United States Court of Claims, while it takes the extreme position, is a work of merit.

[27] In a letter to Matthew Carey, August 10, 1788, a photostat copy of which may be seen in the Library of Congress, Charles Pinckney stated that he no longer had a copy of his plan. One had been submitted to the convention and the other had been given "to a gentleman at the northward." He further said that his plan was like the one adopted except that "it proposed to give the federal government an absolute negative on all the laws of the States." One can only speculate as to who this "gentleman at the northward" was. Could he have been James Wilson, in whose papers portions of the Pinckney draft were later found? Did Charles Pinckney, subsequent to the writing of the letter to Carey, make a copy of his plan or obtain the one from the above gentleman? Was he truthful when he wrote John Quincy Adams in 1818 that he had "4 or 5 draughts" in his possession or did he send to Washington a slightly altered copy of the printed report of the committee of detail? These are questions that cannot be answered to the satisfaction of all students of this subject. A study of the other activities of Pinckney shows that he was rather vain and inclined to claim considerable credit for himself; however, as is shown in the body of this chapter, scholars are now disposed to consider Charles Pinckney among the two or three outstanding contributors to the Constitution of the United States, as it was adopted by the convention of 1787.

bility were worth while, other portions of the Constitution might be pointed to as coming from the ingenious and confident young statesman from South Carolina.[28]

3. THE STRUGGLE OVER RATIFICATION OF THE NEW CONSTITUTION

Even before the convention met in Philadelphia South Carolinians interested in changing the government were wondering what would come out of that meeting. In April David Ramsay wrote to Jefferson, "Our eyes are now fixed on the Continental Convention to be held in Philadelphia in May next." Unless an "efficient federal government" was established he foresaw such inconsistent possibilities as "an American monarch or rather three or more confederacies." Not entirely pessimistic, he thought that "in either case we have not labored in vain in effecting the late revolution for such arrangements might be made as would serve our happiness."[29] Writing in July, 1787, Laurens described the product of the convention, with few exceptions, as "infinitely better than our present Confederation." Its ratification, though, was not certain, since it must "pass through the ordeal of thirteen assemblies, and I am very sure some of them will not like it, because it is calculated to make them honest."[30] He would have preferred a legislature of one house, representatives subject to instructions and recall by their states and an absolute veto for the President; but in spite of

[28] A. C. McLaughlin, "Sketch of Pinckney's Plan for a Constitution, 1787," *American Historical Review*, IX, 740-741. McLaughlin is of the opinion that the draft sent by Pinckney to Adams in 1818 should not be severely criticized. He finds inconsistencies in numbering and in a few other details between it and the material found in the James Wilson papers; but he thinks that Pinckney may have used a different copy in 1818. See also J. Franklin Jameson, "The Federal Convention of 1787," *Annual Report of the American Historical Association, 1902*, I, 87-167. Pages 111-132 deal with the Pinckney plan. Jameson attempted to reconstruct it and evaluate its influence. He concluded that Pinckney deserved more credit than he had received but nothing like as much as he claimed in his old age. The above mentioned article of McLaughlin was written two years later than that of Jameson and based partly on it; but the former had the advantage of additional material which probably accounts for his more definitely friendly attitude toward Charles Pinckney.

[29] Jefferson Papers, April 7, 1787.
[30] Quoted in Wallace, *Life of Henry Laurens*, p. 443.

JEFFERSONIAN DEMOCRACY IN S. C.   25

the absence of these desired features he was ready to support the proposed Constitution. Christopher Gadsden, the temporarily radical Revolutionary leader who was really a conservative aristocrat, had been disappointed because the Confederation had not produced good trade conditions. To his way of thinking the trade provisions of the Constitution were particularly worthy of praise.[31]

The newspapers of the day were used by both sides. Early in December an "anti-federalist" sarcastically pointed out some of the "blessings of the proposed new government" as

1. The Liberty of the Press abolished. 2. A standing army. 3. A Prussian militia. 4. No annual elections. 5. Five-fold taxes. 6. No trial by jury in civil cases. 7. General search warrants. 8. Excise laws, custom house officers, . . . etc. 9. A free importation of Negroes for one and twenty years. 10. Appeals to the Supreme Continental Court, where the rich drag the poor from the remotest parts of the continent. 11. Elections for Pennsylvania held at Pittsburg, or perhaps Wyoming. 12. Poll taxes for our heads, if we chuse to wear them. 13. And death if we dare to complain.[32]

A "federalist" listed the "salutary consequences which will flow from adopting the federal constitution":

1. Unity and peace at home. 2. Respect and honor from abroad. 3. The total abolition of paper money. 4. A sufficient specie medium. 5. A full treasury. 6. Public and domestic debts provided for. 7. Credit established. 8. The poor and industrious eased of their present burthensome taxes. 9. Agriculture, navigation, and population encouraged. 10. A well regulated commerce. 11. Navigation act, encouraging shipping and seamen, now rotting and starving in our harbours, on account of a most unjustifiable preference for foreigners. 12. Rebellion, and civil war, not so much as understood. 13. Policy, power and spirit, to encourage virtue, punish vice, assert our rights, take possession of our territories, prevent encroachments, and repel invasions.[33]

In support of the Constitution friends of ratification quoted from Washington's "circular letter" pointing out the need for "an indissoluble union of the states under one federal head,"

[31] Letter to Jefferson, October 29, 1787, Jefferson Papers.
[32] *City Gazette* (Charleston), December 4, 1787.
[33] *Ibid.*, December 4, 1787.

"a sacred regard for public justice," "the adoption of a proper peace establishment" and the existence of friendly and peaceful relations among the people of the United States, thus making it possible for the citizens to "forget their local prejudices and policies—to make those mutual concessions which are requisite to the general prosperity."[34] At times the enthusiasm of correspondents would break forth in rhymes,[35] and some contributors wrote series of articles instead of one letter.[36]

In the meantime what had the members of the legislature been thinking about the proposed changes in the general government? On January 10, 1788, Governor Thomas Pinckney, brothers of Charles Cotesworth Pinckney, transmitted to the house of representatives a copy of the Constitution and the resolutions of the federal Congress. Although there were opponents of ratification in the legislature, they did not hope to prevent the calling of a convention. However, they did seize the opportunity to voice their opposition and attempt to have the convention meet in some town less "federalist" in tone than Charleston. Furthermore the friends of ratification wished to justify their attitude.

As might have been expected, the youthful and self-assertive Charles Pinckney began the debate. His first speech was partly historical and explanatory. In his attempt to answer possible arguments of the opposition, his manner was calm and characterized by an unusual amount of patience. Some people thought that the convention had been called to deal with commercial questions and possibly to make minor changes in the old Confederate constitution. "Whereas nothing can be more true, than that its promoters had for their object a firm, national govern-

[34] *Columbian Herald* (Charleston), December 6, 1787.
[35] *Ibid.*, December 6, 1787.
[36] An example of such a series written by a friend of ratification is the letters of "Caroliniensis" which appeared in the *City Gazette*, beginning about December 6, 1787. In the early part of April articles were contributed by "Caroliensis." In concluding his letter of April 2, the latter writer stated that "there is happily blended in the proposed plan, the energy and dispatch of a monarchical—the wisdom of an aristocratical, and the virtue and integrity of a democratical government, without the dangers and inconveniences of either."

ment."[37] The federal judiciary, he considered "the most important and intricate part of the system." Much might be expected from its unifying influence and its superiority over the state courts.[38] He had no fear of aristocracy of federal despotism; people who had such fears, according to him, were possessed with "the most childish chimeras that could be conceived." For his part, he wished the executive had greater power, but he had been made as powerful as the people would permit.[39] Pinckney had favored a bill of rights but felt that its inclusion was not essential. The general government could do only those things which were expressly permitted by the Constitution, whereas the state possessed all other powers not reserved to the people. Direct taxes would be necessary when the imports did not bring in enough revenue. The federal government must have the power and authority to use force, since force was especially necessary in a republic to prevent disunion. The most remarkable part of Charles Pinckney's long address was the admission at the close that, after all that could be said on the question, the new departure in government was an experiment, "nor was it yet possible to form a just conclusion as to its practicability."[40]

Judge Pendleton strenuously objected to giving the senate the power to be both sole legislative advisers of the President on foreign affairs and judges in impeachment proceedings.[41] Pierce Butler and Charles Cotesworth Pinckney explained how the provision in regard to foreign affairs was evolved. The placing of full treaty making authority in the hands of the President would give him excessive power or make it possible for him to be bribed by foreign governments. Since the house of representatives would be too large for the maintenance of the secrecy necessary in dealing with foreign affairs, the only other body was the senate. If the voters were not satisfied with

[37] *Debates Which Arose in the House of Representatives of South Carolina on the Constitution Framed for the United States by a Convention of Delegates Assembled at Philadelphia together with Such Notes as Could be Procured* (Charleston: 1831), p. 4.
[38] *Ibid.*, pp. 6-7.   [39] *Ibid.*, pp. 7-8.
[40] *Ibid.*, pp. 8-11.   [41] *Ibid.*, p. 11.

the senate, its membership might be changed at subsequent elections.[42]

The most persistent opponent of ratification in these debates in the South Carolina legislature was Rawlins Lowndes. In his opinion the general government was to be given too much authority over the states. He thought that the powers of the President were too great and that that office would never be filled by a person from South Carolina or Georgia.[43] Charles Cotesworth Pinckney considered the powers of the President and those of a king not worthy of analogy for the former filled an elective office and the latter an inherited one. If South Carolina and Georgia did not obtain their proper share of influence in the new government, it would be their own fault. The fact that voting was by individuals instead of by states would be an inducement for each state to keep full representation in Congress. He and John Rutledge, another delegate to the convention, assured their listeners that the dangers which might possibly arise under the Constitution would never actually materialize.[44]

According to John Julius Pringle, Lowndes was departing from his usually sound views and, in this case, becoming "extremely alarmed by a phantom of his own creation—a phantom like every other, without body or substance, and which will vanish as soon as touched."[45]

When he spoke next Lowndes paid his respects to his opponents as mostly gentlemen of the law, "who were capable of giving ingenious explanations to such points as they wished to have adopted." He warned against discarding a tested Constitution. The Confederation had carried the people through great difficulties, given the nation a place in the world and brought about the "enviable blessings of liberty and independence." The proposed Constitution had been called an "experiment." He was afraid it would be one that would bring an end to their peace and happiness. Lowndes was firmly convinced that if the new Constitution should be adopted "the sun of the

[42] *Ibid.*, p. 11-13.
[44] *Ibid.*, pp. 14-16.
[43] *Ibid.*, pp. 13-14.
[45] *Ibid.*, pp. 16-17.

Southern states would set never to rise again." Would not six of the Eastern states possess a majority in the house of representatives? Could their representatives be expected to vote against their commercial interests in favor of the agricultural South? Why had the Northern delegates opposed the importation of slaves? Why limit the trade to twenty years and why place a tax on it even before the time limit expired? He approved the law of South Carolina prohibiting importation of Negroes for three years; but he was unalterably opposed to fixing a date after which the state could not change its policy. Charles Cotesworth Pinckney was quoted as having formerly stated his opposition to the restriction of the importation of slaves so long as there remained a single acre of swamp lands in South Carolina. The argument that the commercial states had agreed to an impost would not hold for it would be passed on to the consumer. Wherein was this a reciprocal bargain? There was no alternative to government by the Eastern states according to their own interests. This Lowndes was not willing to see happen without voicing his protest. The federal Congress should not be given the power to regulate commerce permanently. This argument that only great men would be elected to positions in the general government was hardly reasonable. The time would very probably come when protesting states would be told, "go mind your own business." Lowndes apologized for going into the argument as fully as he had, since the question of ratification was to be settled by another group. His views were so different from most of his constituents that he would not be sent to the convention; consequently, he had taken the opportunity to go on record as against the new Constitution. If the convention should vote affirmatively and the document should go into operation it would then be his duty to support it.[46]

Edward Rutledge was surprised that Lowndes should prefer the Confederation to the government that would be set up under the new Constitution, for the former had really been inadequate both at home and abroad. The tax on slaves would be merely the proper impost duty. The South had nothing to

[46] *S. C. Debates on Const. for U. S.*, pp. 18-21.

fear from the commercial North.[47] Charles Cotesworth Pinckney thought that the provisions in the Constitution insured that only men of merit should ever be elected to the Presidency or the senate. It was by no means certain that slaves would not be imported after twenty years. Since the commercial states had suffered most from the separation from Great Britain it was only fair that they should be protected by turning the regulation of trade over to the federal government. Slaves could not be freed by the general government; and fugitives, under a provision of the Constitution, would be returned.[48] Jacob Read stated that the "boasted efficiency" of the Confederate congress was "farcical."[49]

In his next speech Lowndes said that so eminent were the men opposing him that he was almost ready to give up the fight. This he would do if several members who did not generally speak in public were not depending on him to express their views as well as his. The Treaty of Peace had made each state sovereign and independent; but, if the Constitution were adopted, a seat in the state legislature would be no higher than a place in a city council. One of the state's chief sources of revenue was lost with the relinquishment of the right to levy an impost. Why was the state forbidden to issue paper money? Had South Carolina not found this a safe and effective method of relieving temporary embarrassment? Jury trial was not mentioned for civil cases. Every person with whom he had talked thought that the convention had exceeded its instructions in substituting a new Constitution for the old. He recommended the calling of another convention rather than the ratification of the document before them. His opponents were challenged to reconcile the action of the convention with the statement in the Articles of Confederation that no changes should take place without the confirmation of every state.[50]

After Robert Barnwell described the Constitution as not perfect but the best that could be obtained at the time, even the erstwhile radical Commodore Gillon spoke in favor of ratification. There was no evidence that another convention could

[47] *Ibid.*, pp. 21-23. [48] *Ibid.*, pp. 23-30.
[49] *Ibid.*, p. 31. [50] *Ibid.*, pp. 31-34.

do better. It was his wish that Lowndes would come to like the new federal Constitution as well as he now did the South Carolina constitution of 1778.[51] To which Lowndes replied that he assented to the document of 1778 because it met the approval of the people. Chancellor John Matthews expressed surprise at the praise given the Confederation, since the Articles had not been ratified until 1781 and would have prevented the granting of very strong powers to Washington if they had been in operation. Competition between American and European carriers would cause charges to be reasonable.[52] Edward Rutledge argued that the delegates had not exceeded their instructions. If the East got control of trade it would mean the building up of a navy sorely needed for protection.[53] After the speech of Rutledge, Charles Cotesworth Pinckney delivered another lengthy address. The success of the Revolution had not been due to the Articles of Confederation. Another document, the Declaration of Independence, should be praised far above that one. Nothing had been said about the sovereignty and independence of the individual states in 1776. Their names were not even given in the declaration, because it was intended to impress on America the truth that the freedom and independence came through union. If the Confederation had ever been a binding compact, it had been dissolved because each state had repeatedly broken its part of the contract. This being the case it was now necessary to have a new constitution to replace the one that had thus gone out of existence.[54]

In his fifth speech Lowndes sought to clarify some of his former statements and ridicule what he considered the specious arguments of his opponents. Some gentlemen had spoken of such admirable checks having been set up as protection against tyranny. Too many checks in a political machine could end only in confusion. The new Constitution presented the "best preparatory plan for monarchical government" he had ever seen. The President would become the king, and the senate the lords. In concluding his remarks Lowndes thanked the house for listening to him so long; he hoped that the importance of the issue

[51] *S. C. Debates on Const. for U. S.*, pp. 35-40.
[52] *Ibid.*, pp. 40-41.   [53] *Ibid.*, pp. 41-42.
[54] *Ibid.*, pp. 42-49.

would furnish sufficient excuse. So great did he believe the threatening dangers to be that when his life came to a close, he wished no other epitaph than to have written on his tomb, "Here lies the man who opposed the constitution, because it was ruinous to the liberty of America."[55]

Following the last speech of Lowndes, John Rutledge made rather pointed remarks concerning what he called the former's obstinacy, in view of the fact that a convention and not the legislature would decide on ratification. He hoped that Lowndes would be a delegate in the convention and hear his fears proved groundless. Instead of the sun of the country being obscured by the Constitution, he had no doubt but that when it was adopted "the sun of this State, united with twelve other suns, would exhibit a meridian radiance, astonishing to the world."[56]

But the cutting words of John Rutledge did not prevent another from expressing his opposition. James Lincoln, an up country representative, highly praised the men favoring ratification and their arguments. He readily agreed that changes were necessary, but the more he heard about the new Constitution the more he was convinced of "its evil tendency." It would mean a change from a democratic to an aristocratic government, from local to distant rule. Was it necessary to kill in order to cure? The President might hold office so long that it would require a revolution to dislodge him. Why was the liberty of the press not guaranteed? The brief statement almost at the end of the Constitution, as if almost forgotten, concerning the obligation of Congress to maintain a republican form of government in the states was hardly an adequate safeguard for local government, since even that was dependent upon the federal government. Why was there no bill of rights? Was it intended that the President and senate would later graciously *grant* the people their rights? He expressed his great appreciation for the noble effort of Lowndes in opposing the Constitution. If anyone ever deserved the title, "man of the people," he on this occasion did.[57]

[55] *Ibid.*, pp. 49-52.　　[56] *Ibid.*, p. 52.
[57] *Ibid.*, pp. 52-55.

JEFFERSONIAN DEMOCRACY IN S. C.   33

Charles Cotesworth Pinckney discussed the question of the term of the President. If the tenure permitted had been made too short, encouragement might have been given to an overly ambitious man to overthrow the government. Also, the term might expire in an emergency when it would be inadvisable to change Presidents. As for the bill of rights, he thought it wiser not to give much attention to what was forbidden to the general government. If too much were said on that subject the theory might develop that the general government could do all things not forbidden; whereas, as it then stood, it could do only those things expressly named.[58]

The concluding speech in the debate was delivered by Colonel Mason, who thanked Lowndes for his opposition on behalf of the several gentlemen for whom he spoke. The representatives from "the country" now felt that they could go back to their constituents with the feeling that their views had been expressed.[59]

Thus after three days of discussion the house of representatives was ready to vote on the question of calling a convention. Not a single vote was cast against the motion when it was finally put;[60] but the opposition did display surprising strength in its attempt to have the convention meet at some place other than Charleston, for by the margin of only one vote, seventy-six to seventy-five, was that city chosen.[61]

In a letter to John Rutledge, Jr., who was then touring Europe, Thomas Jefferson said he was glad that enough states would ratify the Constitution to permit its benefits; but he was also glad that there was apparently enough opposition to bring about amendments that might constitute a bill of rights.[62]

Between the closing of the debate in the legislature and the meeting of the convention on May 12, the question continued to be discussed in the newspapers.[63] The articles that found

---
[58] *S. C. Debates on Const. for U. S.*, pp. 55-56.
[59] *Ibid.*, p. 56.
[60] S. C. House Journal, January 19, 1788.
[61] *Ibid.*, January 19, 1788.
[62] Jefferson Papers, February 10, 1788.
[63] See particularly the editorial in *Columbian Herald*, February 4, 1788; article signed "A Steady and Open Republican" (probably Charles

their way into print were generally favorable. This was largely due to the absence of newspapers in the up country. As pointed out in the first chapter of this study and as will be made clearer in the next, the government was still controlled by the low country, which had more power than its number of inhabitants warranted.

Unfortunately for this study the records of the debates in the convention which began its meetings in Charleston on May 12, 1788, are very incomplete. From available sources it seems that Charles Pinckney again opened the discussion. And again he dipped into history. The past and present governments in Europe were mentioned; but the speaker thought they offered few precedents for a people as free as those of the United States. They were fated to be the "first perfectly free people the world had ever seen." It was not likely that the commercial people would ever be very strong politically. There was a danger from foreign trade; but the United States, being divided from the old world, should have nothing to do with the latter's politics and as little as possible to do with its commerce. Because of their education, professional men must play an important part in the government. But most of the people were interested in the cultivation of the soil. The landed interests— the owners and cultivators of the soil—had then and he hoped would ever have the dominant influence in politics. Commerce should be encouraged only as an agent of agriculture. He expected the free governmental system to tend toward something like equality in the distribution of wealth, "with few dangerously rich or few miserably poor." The opinion was beginning to change away from the view that a republic is impossible over territory of some extent. The United States exhibited the first example of a people who calmly and deliberately changed their government in time of peace, without any compulsion from a foreign power or serious internal disturbances. No part of the country should expect to get everything it desired in a Constitution. The Revolution was fought by the states in union and the whole country should be protected by its chief govern-

---

Pinckney), in *State Gazette of South Carolina,* March 5, 1788; and the article by "Back Wood's Man" in *Columbian Herald,* March 8, 1788.

mental document, even though some slight expectations might not be realized by each section.[64]

Alexander Tweed of Prince Frederick's Parish called attention to the seriousness of the decision that must be made by the convention. Several delegates, Tweed said, had inaccurately stated that his constituents had instructed their representatives to oppose the document before them. He insisted that his mind was open and that he was perfectly willing to be convinced by either side. He realized the need for reform in the government, but he was compelled to disapprove of the dark picture that was being painted. They should not be concerned about foreign danger or domestic insurrection.[65]

Apparently there was considerable opposition to the provision forbidding the states to emit bills of credit, for another speech of Charles Pinckney dealt primarily with that subject. He stated that paper money tended to drive gold and silver out of the country. According to him South Carolina was second only to Virginia in the value of her exports. Since this sale of her products in foreign markets would continue specie would come into the state. Why then should they worry about the amount of money in circulation? There would be no need for the state to issue paper money. Such currency would only endanger the soundness of the money already in existence. The prohibition of the impairment of the obligation of contract would be a needed safeguard in commerce. A citizen of one state could trade with a citizen of another without the fear that the state would pass a law releasing its citizen from his contract. A uniform currency would encourage foreign trade. If paper money became necessary the general government could issue it. Besides there would still be foreign money of a well founded nature. Also there would no longer be the opportunity to use paper money for fraudulent purposes. A currency system would be established under which the rich and the poor would share alike. "Public as well as private confidence shall again be established; industry shall return among us, and the blessings of our Government shall verify that old, but useful maxim,

[64] *S. C. Debates on Const. for U. S.*, pp. 61-73.
[65] *Ibid.*, pp. 73-74.

that with States, as well as with individuals—Honesty is the best policy."[66]

Patrick Dollard, another delegate from Prince Frederick's Parish, strongly opposed ratification. His constituents would not accept the proposed Constitution unless it was forced upon them by arms. He paid his respects to those able gentlemen who had "ingeniously glossed over" the defects prevalent in the document. Why was there not a bill of rights? His constituents were not opposed to giving a Congress ample powers, but they were not going to surrender their birthrights to any governmental body. They recognized the ability and sincerity of the gentlemen who represented South Carolina in the Philadelphia convention, but they also knew that even such worthy men could err. He felt that there were well laid plans to set up "a monarchy or a corrupt and oppressive aristocracy." He feared that those desirous of controlling the new government intended to have a "standing army, like Turkish Janissaries," to enforce their despotic laws. The other members of the convention were urged to beware how they sacrificed "their dear-bought rights and privileges."[67]

The above speeches are the only ones given in the records of the convention, but it is stated that "Judge Burke, Mr. Bowman, Dr. Fayssoux and others" spoke against the Constitution, and "Judge Pendleton, Gen. Pinckney, Hon. J. J. Pringle" as well as Charles Pinckney for it.[68] The speeches reported, therefore, cannot do full justice to either side. For several days the opponents of ratification were unwilling to concede defeat. When it appeared that they could not prevent ratification if a vote were taken, General Thomas Sumter on May 21, moved that the convention adjourn till October 20. The request was denied by the vote of eighty-nine to one hundred thirty-five.[69] The way was then open for the ratification two days later. However, the apparently decisive vote of one

[66] *S. C. Debates on Const. for U. S.*, pp. 74-76.
[67] *Ibid.*, pp. 76-78.   [68] *Ibid.*, p. 86.
[69] *Journal of the Convention of South Carolina Which Ratified the Constitution of the United States May 23, 1788* (facsimile), indexed by A. S. Salley (Atlanta: Foote and Davies, 1928), pp. 13-23.

JEFFERSONIAN DEMOCRACY IN S. C.   37

hundred forty-nine to seventy-three[70] is very misleading. If the convention had been representative of the white population of South Carolina, it is doubtful whether ratification would have taken place at all.[71]

Even though a large majority of the delegates was willing to ratify the Constitution, they would not do so without appending their interpretations of certain sections. The state should have complete control of the election of its representatives in the federal Congress. Every power not relinquished to the general government was retained by the state. The federal government should not levy direct taxes until after impost and excise duties had proved inadequate and the states had declined to grant the requisitions, and then they should be levied against only those so declining. Also, the convention thought that the word "other" should be inserted in the third section of the sixth article so that it would read ". . .; but no other religious test shall ever be required as a qualification to any office or public trust under the United States." The future representatives of the state were given "standing instructions" to "exert their utmost abilities and influence to effect an alteration of the Constitution conformably to the foregoing resolutions."[72]

Under such circumstances did South Carolina ratify the federal Constitution and thus did she co-operate with the delegates to the Philadelphia convention who had sought

[70] The vote is given in *ibid.*, pp. 39-49, and in *S. C. Debates on Const. for U. S.*, pp. 85-86.

[71] An analysis of the outcome in the convention shows that the delegates from the lower part of the state voted 88% for and 12% against the Constitution; those from the middle section, 49% for and 51% against; those from the upper, 20% for and 80% against. See O. G. Libby, *Geographical Distribution of the Vote of the Thirteen States on the Federal Constitution, 1787-8*, pp. 42-44.

[72] *Journal of South Carolina Convention*, pp. 50-53. Jefferson wrote Edward Rutledge, July 18, 1788, congratulating him on the ratification of the Constitution by South Carolina; but again he had expressed the desire for a bill of rights. He said, "I own I join those in opinion that a bill of rights is necessary." He was also afraid that an abandonment of the principle of rotation in office of the President and senate would end in abuse. "But my confidence is that there will for a long time be virtue and good sense enough in our countrymen to correct abuses." This letter is reprinted in Paul Leicester Ford, ed., *The Writings of Thomas Jefferson* (New York: G. P. Putnam's Sons, 1892-1899), V, 41-42.

to evolve a constitution which would provide for a strong government, which would give ample protection to property, which would establish public credit, which would curb popular tendencies and enable men of respectability, refinement, education, and wealth to rule, and yet a constitution which would secure liberty.[73]

While many were disposed to give thanks for the ratification of the Constitution, two of South Carolina's representatives in the federal Congress were soon to speak against the resolution asking that the President recommend a day of thanksgiving to the people of the country because of the establishment of the new government.[74] A little later another representative from the same state, this time a "federalist" who was soon to become one of the prominent Federalists, admitted that the "inhabitants of the interior part of South Carolina" were "opposed to the new Government."[75]

So much space has been given to the struggle over the ratification of the Constitution in South Carolina because of the bearing it had on future politics in the state. As will be shown in the next chapter, local questions were often the dominant ones, and the reactions of South Carolinians toward the federal government were generally determined to a very great extent by the probable effect upon their own local interests. At the time of the adoption of the federal Constitution it was to the interest of those then in control of state politics to aid in building up a stronger general government. But those against ratification laid the basis for opposition to this new government. They served notice, as it were, that if those in charge of federal affairs did not show their fears to be groundless, further opposition would develop. The "anti-federalists," not the "federalists," more nearly accorded with the principles later to be called Jeffersonian. Up country South Carolina was to be the

---

[73] This is taken from the keen analysis of the work of the convention in W. W. Pierson, Jr., "The Sovereign State of North Carolina, 1787-1789," *Proceedings of the Seventeenth Annual Session of the State Literary and Historical Association of North Carolina, December 5-6, 1916* (Raleigh: Edwards and Broughton, 1917), p. 61.

[74] Aedanus Burke and Thomas Tudor Tucker. *Annals of Congress*, 1st Cong., 1st Sess. (February 25, 1789), pp. 949-950.

[75] William Loughton Smith. *Ibid.* (April 17, 1789), p. 167.

Republican stronghold. Even Charles Pinckney, who was later to lead the Republicans, in his speeches favoring ratification, voiced his approval of some of the tenets soon to be associated with Jeffersonian democracy. A discussion of the struggle over the federal Constitution is, therefore, an essential part of the study of early party politics in South Carolina.

CHAPTER III

REPUBLICAN BEGINNINGS

1. EARLY DEMOCRATIC STRIVINGS IN SOUTH CAROLINA

When did the democratic influence become strong in South Carolina? Did the Federalists control politics in the state during the 1790's and the most cultivated social groups even later? Or was the spirit of democracy powerful from the earliest days of the colony? To the second question the late Professor U. B. Phillips gave an affirmative answer. On the other hand, Secretary A. S. Salley of the South Carolina Historical Commission would disagree with Professor Phillips and reply affirmatively to the third query.[1] This sketch of the rise of democracy in South Carolina cannot go back to the founding of the colony. In this chapter, evidence dealing with incidents which occurred during the 1780's and the 1790's must be sufficient.

Outside the field of politics, there were democratic tendencies also. The religious groups were leaning toward congregational control. Beginning on the eve of the Revolution and continuing throughout the years with which this study deals there was a noticeable decrease in the influence of the Episcopal Church. If it had not been for the personality of Francis Asbury, the Methodists probably would have developed con-

[1] Phillips, "S. C. Federalists." Salley's opinion may be found in *S. C. Historical and Genealogical Magazine* (of which he was then edtor), III, 118-119. He points out that the legislature voted in 1786 to move the state Capitol in spite of the opposition of those later to be called Federalists. The name "Columbia" was chosen because it was the one favored by the "Democrats." The Federalists wanted to call the new capital city Washington after their leader. A majority of the representatives in Congress was soon, perhaps from the beginning, "Democrats." "There were many Federalists in the Low-Country but they were not in the majority in the State. The Democratic idea obtained root in South Carolina when Albemarle Point was settled in 1670 and has held ground ever since."

JEFFERSONIAN DEMOCRACY IN S. C. 41

gregationalism. Even the Catholics defied one of their bishops. The Baptists with their self-government and the ritualistic appeal of baptism by immersion increased rapidly.[2]

A contemporary, writing years later, thought that the popular doctrines of Jefferson "found nowhere a more genial soil to take root, than in the state of South Carolina. They were cherished here with enthusiasm."[3] In the newspapers of the day were suggestions of such popular devices as the recall.[4]

When the Society of Cincinnati, an organization composed of officers of the army of the Revolution, was suspected of aristocratic tendencies, South Carolinians were among the first to protest. The most effective articles against the succession of the eldest son to membership in the society were the letters of "Cassius" written by Aedanus Burke.[5] This ardent democrat was given credit by Jefferson for first pointing out the aristocratic tendencies of the Society of Cincinnati.[6]

Another illustration of the opposition to exclusive social groups is found in the determination of those outside of the select few not to be outdone in the formation of clubs. Merchants and the followers of other excluded occupations organized under such curious names as the "Free and Easy" and the "Ugly Club," the humor in the latter perhaps not being devoid of sarcasm. At any rate it was the source of much merriment to its members, for the ugliest man was supposed to be chosen

---

[2] David Duncan Wallace, *The Historical Background of Religion in South Carolina*, pp. 25-26, a pamphlet published in 1916, n.p., a copy of which may be found in volume 27 of the pamphlets of the University of South Carolina Library.

[3] Charles Fraser, *Reminiscences of Charleston* (Charleston: 1854), p. 49. These reminiscences cover the years 1785-1854. While this source is subject to the criticisms generally given to reminiscences, it must be said that it is as a whole unusually reliable.

[4] "Amicus," writing in the *Columbian Herald*, August 28, 1788.

[5] Burke, born in Ireland, had come to Bermuda and from there to Charleston. He is said to have served in the Revolution and obtained the rank of major in the militia. He held many civil positions, opposed the ratification of the Constitution and was one of South Carolina's representatives in the first federal Congress. Brief biographical sketches of him may be found in *S. C. Historical and Genealogical Magazine*, XXVI, 183-184, and in John Belton O'Neall, *Biographical Sketches of the Bench and Bar of South Carolina* (Charleston: 1859), I, pp. 35-38.

[6] Ford, *Writings of Jefferson*, IV, 172.

president at each election. The annual ball of the club was always well attended.[7] By the legislative act of incorporation of 1783 Charles Town became Charleston. However, it was still referred to as "town" and to the higher social groups it remained "the town" even after the Capitol was moved to Columbia in 1790.[8]

Persons alarmed at what they consider the present indifferent attitude of public officials and the apathy of the voters might gain comfort from the knowledge that the South Carolina Legislature deemed it necessary in 1787 to place a penalty of twenty shillings upon its members for each day absent.[9] And no doubt some will be shocked by the knowledge that the manager of the polls in St. John's Colleton reported to the legislature in 1788 that during the election of 1787 the inhabitants of the parish had "so much business of their own to do, that they could not spare the time to attend to public business, on which account there was no election."[10] There is a rumor, apparently true, that the first time Charles Pinckney was elected to the legislature the young candidate and the judge of the election, one of Pinckney's overseers, were the only voters who saw fit to go to the polls.[11] But these "rotten boroughs" were low country areas where the electorates were small and the outcome more certain than in the larger and more populous up country dis-

---

[7] Fraser, *Reminiscences*, p. 57. The Ugly Club was formed in 1783. *S. C. Historical and Genealogical Magazine*, XXXII, 77. An example of the announcement of its meeting is given in the *City Gazette*, January 4, 1797. To this particular announcement was appended a rhyme.

>Ugly Mortals hither haste,
>Enjoy our mirth, enjoy our feast;
>Bring rich red noses, noses crooked,
>..................................
>But each bring an honest heart,
>Or hear this sentence—hence! depart!

[8] Mrs. St. Julien Ravenel, *Life and Times of William Lowndes of South Carolina 1782-1822* (Boston: Houghton, Mifflin and Company, 1901), p. 20.

[9] S. C. House Journal, February 6, 12, 16, 17, 1787. *S. C. Statutes at Large*, V, 2-3.

[10] S. C. House Journal, January 8, 1788.

[11] E. S. Thomas, *Reminiscences of the Last Sixty-Five Years* (Hartford: 1840), I, 37-38.

tricts. In the latter section there was more interest in elections even before the reforms in representation and suffrage.

2. THE FIRST TWO STATE CONSTITUTIONS

Before discussing the early participation of South Carolina in federal affairs, let us pause for a brief survey of the internal struggles for a new state constitution. By so doing we shall see the strength of democratic tendencies from still another angle. It will be sufficient here, in regard to the federal government, to say that of the two senators and five representatives sent by South Carolina to the First Congress one of the former and three of the latter soon showed signs of leaning toward some phases of what was later to be called Jeffersonian Republicanism.[12]

The state had had two constitutions, both formed by the legislature, one in 1776 and the other in 1778. The document of 1776 was a very incomplete, unsatisfactory and at best a temporary constitution. Although the provincial congress of South Carolina was to some extent the result of democratic strivings, the constitution it framed was not democratic in nature and would likely have been rejected if it had been submitted to the voters. Only slight representation was granted to the great majority of the people, absolute control of the government being retained by the coast region.

After the colonies began to assert that they were states there was need for more than a temporary constitution. Accordingly, another document was proclaimed by the legislature in 1778. While the new one was more complete than its predecessor it was still inadequate. No supreme court was established. There was the unsatisfactory provision that after seven more years representation would be based on wealth and white population, with reapportionment at the end of each subsequent period of fourteen years. This promised change in representa-

[12] The two senators were Pierce Butler and Ralph Izard, while the representatives were Aedanus Burke, Daniel Huger, William Loughton Smith, Thomas Sumter and Thomas Tudor Tucker. Butler, Burke, Sumter and Tucker were the ones who were later to be identified with the Jeffersonian group. Thus of the seven South Carolinians in both houses of the federal Congress, four had Republican inclinations.

tion was not carried out in 1785. Among the other provisions was the abolition of the veto power of the governor (or the president, according to the language of the document), not to be restored until after the Civil War. The Episcopal Church was no longer to be supported by taxation, but it was allowed to retain its property. Although that particular church was "disestablished" there was not complete disestablishment. "The Christian Protestant religion" was "constituted and declared to be the established religion of this State." In order to be a part of the newly "established" church or religion every congregation must choose its own minister. The governor, lieutenant governor, privy council and all members of the legislature must be of the Protestant faith. No minister could be governor or hold a seat in the legislature. Since several groups were dissatisfied with the constitution, proposals of reform were often made. The attempt of Charles Pinckney to have the convention which was to act on the federal Constitution in 1788 also draw up a new state constitution did not succeed, but so strong were the demands for changes that the meeting of a state convention could be delayed only two more years.[13]

3. THE CONSTITUTION OF 1790

When the question of calling a convention was under consideration, the people of the up country argued that such an action would restore all people of South Carolina to the state of nature and necessitate the election of delegates on the basis of white population. The low country denied this assertion and brought about representation in the convention on the same basis as that in the legislature.[14]

Charles Pinckney, then governor and still only thirty-two years old, though almost a veteran civil official, was chosen

[13] An excellent analysis of the early constitutional history of South Carolina may be found in David Duncan Wallace, "The South Carolina Constitution of 1895," *Bulletin of the University of South Carolina no. 197* (Columbia: 1927). In the appendix of this pamphlet is reprinted the constitution of 1790. It may also be found in vol. I of the *S. C. Statutes at Large*.

[14] *City Gazette*, April 5, 22, 1790. See also Harper, *An Address to the People of S. C.*, pp. 28-29.

president of the convention.[15] Business was transacted smoothly until the question of the permanent seat of government came up.[16] Then the fight became bitter. The up country delegates were determined that the Capitol should be established and permanently located in their section; but they were not unanimous in preferring Columbia, even though the law of 1786 had provided for its removal from Charleston to that point.[17] Some members thought the location of the Capitol was not a constitutional matter; but others felt that the question should be settled. Even though the supporters of Columbia won, the vote of 109 to 105 was so close and the struggle had been so great that the convention was almost broken up. The low country was partly appeased by the establishment of a kind of dual system of government with two treasurers, one at Columbia and one at Charleston and offices maintained by the surveyor-general and the secretary of state in both towns. The high court of appeals must have yearly meetings in each place. The governor was required to reside in Columbia only while the legislature was in session. Sectionalism in South Carolina has never been eliminated but the removal of the capitol to a more central position was an important step in that direction.[18] In accordance with the attitude of the Revolutionary period, the governor was to have no veto power and the legislature continued to

[15] Professor J. H. Easterby of the College of Charleston, who has no doubt studied the career of Charles Pinckney more carefully than any living person, states in the *Dictionary of American Biography,* XIV, 612, that the South Carolina constitution of 1790 was largely evolved from a plan which Pinckney "had apparently modeled as far as possible after the federal instrument."

[16] Letter from Columbia to *City Gazette,* May 31, 1790.

[17] There was really no town worth speaking of at Columbia at that time. The social disadvantages of such a location in comparison with the advantages enjoyed at Charleston no doubt played some part in the opposition of the low country delegates. A letter from Columbia to the *City Gazette,* January 7, 1790, stated that although there were "no sermons, balls or oyster pies" to "amuse and regale the legislature of South Carolina; yet we presume, those to whom racing is a proper amusement, will receive ample gratification in the sports of the turf, which are to commence on Tuesday the 14th instant." It was reported in the same paper on January 22, that races had begun and that a subscription ball had been held in the senate chambers.

[18] Ramsay, *History of S. C.,* II, 435.

elect practically every officer, both state and local, from the governor to the magistrate.

Although democrats and the inhabitants of the up country must have found the constitution of 1790 disappointing, the patient ones knew that something had been gained. Primogeniture was abolished. In line with recent ideas concerning democracy, civil officers replaced church wardens in the control of elections and there was to be no religious qualification for voting. Also the payment of a three-shilling tax might be substituted for a fifty-acre freehold in meeting the requirements for the suffrage. Property qualifications for office were reduced in the case of the governor from the ownership of a £10,000 value to one of £1,500; that of a resident senator from £2,000 to £500; of a non-resident senator from £7,000 to £3,500; of a non-resident representative from £3,500 to £500. The resident representative must be in possession of "a settled freehold estate of five hundred acres of land, and ten Negroes; or a real estate of the value of one hundred and fifty pounds sterling, clear of debt." The provision "clear of debt" was appended to the qualifications for each office. Officials were no longer required to be of the Protestant religion. Freedom of religion was granted with the provision that such liberty of conscience "shall not be construed as to excuse acts of licentiousness or justify practices inconsistent with the peace and safety of this State."

There was disappointment in some quarters because the convention did not include an article providing for the reform of the criminal code. The claim of the up country delegates that representation should be based on population was vehemently denied by those from the low country. Likewise the proposal that population and taxation combined should be the basis was rejected. The fear of the low country that their up country brethren would gain control of the state government and fail to show proper respect for property and the institutions of the existing social order was evident in the convention. The attitude of the leaders in the section then in control of the government may be well expressed by quoting from a letter of Christopher Gadsden, dated May 30, 1790. He was

JEFFERSONIAN DEMOCRACY IN S. C. 47

Apprehensive from a conversation last evening with one of the select committee that a most unreasonable advantage to the back country in regard to representation will be reported to the convention and attempted to be carried. This must throw us back, occasion heats, and takes up no little time and in the meantime the impatience and desertion of our lower members, as it has already given them the first ground, so it will I am afraid completely place us at their mercy in that point.[19]

Every effort to make changes in apportionment was checked by the low country delegates. The number of representatives was reduced to one hundred twenty-four and that of senators increased to thirty-seven. In the house of representatives the low country would have seventy, the up country fifty-four; in the senate, the number was twenty and seventeen, respectively. Thus the low country retained control of both houses of the legislature and by means of legislative elections could indirectly decide the policies of the other departments of the government. Although reform in apportionment was not to take place until after another period of democratic strivings had nearly spent itself, the continued increase in population and the augmentation of property values in the up country caused the struggle to be exceedingly intense in the meantime.

4. The Continuation of Democratic Local Efforts during the 1790's

Again the low country had been the victor in the struggle for the control of the state government. Nevertheless, a person of that section would have been unduly optimistic or unfamiliar with existing conditions if he thought the up country would become permanently resigned to the provisions of the constitution of 1790. It was inevitable that sectionalism should be intensified rather than allayed. The up country could not be content with so much less power than its population and wealth warranted. The fact that its culture and interests were still noticeably different from those of the low country did not make the rule of the latter seem any more justifiable.

[19] Quoted by Fletcher M. Green, *Constitutional Development in the South Atlantic States, 1776-1860. A Study in the Evolution of Democracy* (Chapel Hill: University of North Carolina Press, 1930), p. 121.

Far-sighted men of Charleston had much earlier concluded that some day the up country would become so populous and wealthy that governmental changes favorable to that section could not be prevented any longer. Some tried to postpone the undesirable date as long as possible. Others, being less pessimistic, sought to make the most of the situation by taking steps toward bringing about the unification of outlook. It was thought that a common system of education would go far toward producing a greater like-mindedness. A few men of Charleston with philanthropic inclinations saw that the interests of the low country might be served by the maintenance of colleges in the up country. Organizations were accordingly formed with this in mind; the most important was the Mount Zion Society which was set up as early as 1777 for the purpose of establishing a school one hundred and fifty miles from the coast. One was started in Camden District.[20] Schaper thinks that this is the first time that "the low country joined hands with the up country in any important public concern."[21] As generous as such undertakings were it is easy to detect the element of self-interest and self-preservation. Before the close of the 1790's economic developments came to the aid of the planting interests by bringing about the profitableness of upland cotton, thus insuring the continuation of the institution of slavery in South Carolina. Although there were no outstanding educational institutions in the state in the eighteenth century there were educated people. A careful student has said that "the planter aristocracy that centered at Charleston was perhaps the most cultured and refined bit of America that there was unless it was outstripped by that centering at Richmond."[22] Several governors before 1800, particularly Vanderhorst in 1795 and Charles Pinckney in 1796 and 1798, recommended public education as a means of helping solve the state's problems.[23] The most important result of this movement was the establishment of the South Carolina College in 1801, an act

[20] *S. C. Statutes at Large,* IV, 381; *Charleston Year Book,* for 1887, p. 530.
[21] Schaper, "Sectionalism and Representation in S. C.," p. 402.
[22] *Ibid.,* p. 403.
[23] *Columbian Herald,* December 12, 1797, and December 6, 1798.

JEFFERSONIAN DEMOCRACY IN S. C. 49

which no doubt aided in bringing about a more equitable apportionment of representation a few years later. This latter development, however, will be discussed in a subsequent chapter.

When the first federal census revealed the number of people living in each section, the back country renewed the struggle for reapportionment. A well organized reform association, having a committee in each district, with Robert Goodloe Harper as its leader, took up the fight. The association issued an address to the people of the state, giving the facts and figures which it could muster in support of its case. Other articles and letters set forth additional facts and gave the theoretical basis for their arguments. The statements issued by the association showed that the theories which were talked about during the Revolution had not been entirely forgotten. The reformers declared that the apportionment of representation in South Carolina was arbitrary, lacking in principle and unjust. It was not democratic for one fifth of the population to rule the other four fifths. Aristocracy, not democracy, existed under such circumstances.

The supporters of reform asserted that government had grown out of a compact in which individuals gave up certain rights and became bound by the will of the majority. In the original compact equality of rights was guaranteed to all members. This being the case representation should be equal and in proportion to population. The aristocracy had not injured them so far but they feared that it might do so in the future. The argument that property should be represented was invalid, since society existed long before private property. When public property was changed to private property equal political rights were retained. Wealth would always have influence enough without giving it legal weight in apportioning representatives. Instead of having more votes, the rich man should be given fewer in order to balance the undue power his wealth acquired for him. If property must be represented it should not have representatives in more than one house of the legislature. Certainly the lower house should be reserved to the people.

The argument that the payment of more taxes by the rich

should give them greater influence in the government was unsound, since they also got more benefit from the government. Of what value would be the rich man's wealth if it were not for the protection of the government? Besides, the census figures in regard to property were misleading. In many cases property in the up country owned by men of the low country was listed in such a way as to seem to lie in the latter region. If representation should be based on both population and property it was claimed that the up country would have five representatives to three for the low country.

Furthermore, sectionalism alarmed the reformers. In the up country property was fairly evenly distributed; but in the low country there were some who were very rich and some who were very poor. The nature of the soil and climate in the low country made slaves necessary, thereby giving that section another advantage in regard to property. The reformers were afraid that inequality of wealth would bring about inequality of condition. They feared the rise of the aristocratic spirit with its use of power. It was held that a few hundred wealthy men controlled the low country and thereby the state.

The Capitol had been moved because members from the low country had voted with those from the up country. Such incidents made the situation of the up country seem even more dangerous, for it showed that benefits must go to the more populous section only through the courtesy of the less densely inhabited area. Even though the Capitol had been moved the low country was able to force the establishment of the awkward and expensive dual system.

Finally it was stated that the low country possessed the unlimited power of oppressing the up country in taxation. A poll tax could be substituted for a tax on Negroes, or taxation could be based on area instead of value. Either would make the burden light on the extremely fertile lands of the coast.[24]

While the case was ably presented in the arguments just reviewed its basis was too theoretical. At least it was not practical enough for the leaders in the low country, who feared a

[24] Robert Goodloe Harper, *An Address to the People of S. C.*, already referred to in Chapter I, and the accompanying letters set forth the case for the reformers.

government based on popular theories. Henry William DeSaussure denied that equality was the natural condition of man. If such a theory were put into operation the white people would be forced to "instantly free the unfortunate slaves," and thus bring ruin to both races.[25] The replies of DeSaussure and Timothy Ford to the arguments of the reform association were based more on actual facts concerning the conditions which existed in South Carolina. They did, however, attempt to refute the theory of an original state of nature. Ford held that moral principle and experience were the directing forces of man. According to him "the rights of property, as well as those of life and liberty, are the gifts of nature. The end of civil society is to guard them by stronger sanctions, the moral sense being too weak and too unequal amongst men for that purpose." No compact gave the majority the right to plunder industrious individuals. It was as necessary to respect the rights of certain groups as it was the natural rights of individuals. The equality of groups was not essential. It was all right to have the interests of the planters, for instance, looked after by a majority of the planters but not by a majority of the whole population.

Ford vigorously attacked the so-called "new discovery" of the up country reformers that the constitution of 1790 was defective because of its inequality in representation. The people of the coast region were prior occupants of the state. When others went to the back country there was an understanding amounting to a compact that the newcomers would have the rights of freemen and be permitted to participate in the government but that those already living in the state would never turn their interests over to them to be governed by mere numbers. Thus, according to Timothy Ford, who was himself born outside of the state but then living in the low country, did the people of the up country give their consent to the government already established. He appealed to the middle section to join with the lower in protecting interests common to both.[26]

Although DeSaussure claimed to be non-partisan, his ar-

[25] DeSaussure, *Letters on Alteration of Representation*, pp. 8-9.
[26] Timothy Ford, *The Constitutionalist*.

ticles were clearly designed to refute the arguments of the reformers. Even the latter would not favor the freeing of the slaves, said DeSaussure. Yet their theories would lead to such an outcome. Not one of the Southern states apportioned representatives on the basis of population. That mere numbers did not form the only basis was recognized by the federal convention in giving each state the same number of senators. The differences between the up country and the low country were similar to those between the North and South. According to DeSaussure, the low country had five sixths of the slaves, two ninths of the white population and paid seven ninths of the taxes. The system of taxation then existing was very liberal to the up country. The taxes on slaves and on land were paid mostly by the low country. The carriage and luxury taxes were hardly paid in the up country. Then, too, the poll tax of colonial days had been repealed.[27]

In the autumn of 1794 the house of representatives, by the vote of 58 to 53, declined to change the apportionment in line with the requests of the up country petitioners. The resolution of refusal stated that readjustment was inexpedient since the solution adopted in 1790 had been the result of a compromise which attempted to place the interests of the two sections on an equal basis. A more favorable senate committee recommended that representation be based on white population. But in a sectional vote, except for the support of the up country by a few men from the low country, the senate decided 17 to 16 that it would be unwise to make the changes requested.

In the meantime sixteen senators and fifty-six representatives from the up country decided to draw up a message to the people of the low country. They deeply resented the charges that their constituents sought to gain control of the government in order to lighten their own taxes and plunder the rest of the state. They denied that they had ever been disorderly or had ever encouraged violence of any kind. Instead, they had shown their patience and desire for order by not withdrawing from the legislature and setting up another government as they might have.

[27] DeSaussure, *Letters on the Alteration of Representation.*

In this address the up country leaders were more realistic. They argued that there were three distinct divisions in the state and that these areas were deserving of equal or nearly equal representation. Since there were striking differences between the upper and lower portions the middle section would have the balance of power. According to the statistics cited the low country would still have sixty-eight, the middle country thirty-eight and the up country fifty-nine representatives. This would be fairer for the up country and still give the low country enough votes to prevent an amendment to the constitution. The supposed danger to the institution of slavery was groundless for the members from the back country were already slave owners and those who voted against slavery would be in danger of receiving a coat of tar and feathers upon their return home. Furthermore the middle section would be able to prevent any injuries to the institution if unexpected opposition should develop in the up country. If slavery were abolished the latter section would be forced to pay additional taxes to make up for the revenue that had come from the tax on slaves. Nor would the up country representatives be willing to vote for great increases in taxes because of the difficulty in paying them due largely to scarcity of circulating medium.

The necessity for compromises and sacrifices was recognized but they should be made by both sections. The up country would accept as a boon what it might demand as a right. The wounds would be healed and peace would reign in the state. From the present day standpoint the address signified the admission of the up country that it had no case. All it was arguing for was further compromise, when the government was already based on compromise. If the proposed changes were made the planting aristocracy would still be able to injure the interests of the up country.[28] The chief effect of the address was its arousal of more interest in the reform movement. Petitions continued to greet the members of each succeeding legislature, but often very little consideration was given to them. There was a vote in 1796 but with the same result as in 1794.[29]

[28] *Columbian Herald,* October 29, 1795. The address was printed also in Hartford, Connecticut, October 11, 1795.
[29] *City Gazette,* December 21, 1796.

Another much discussed question in the 1790's was that of plural voting. Although not specifically authorized by the constitution it was considered as implied in the different qualifications for resident and non-resident office holding and in the practice of keeping the polls open two days so as to permit property owners to vote in the various districts in which they had sufficient possessions. Opposition to this practice increased and became particularly heated around the turn of the century.[30] But the solution of this problem, like that of representation, did not come till later. It will not be discussed, therefore, until the story of developments in other fields has been related.[31] Mention must be made now of those other incidents and conditions which brought about the division of the state into political parties. Then the story of the fight for changes in representation will force itself into this study again.

5. Initial Relations between South Carolina and the Federal Government

The South Carolina members of the first Congress under the Constitution very tardily made their appearance at the seat of government. On March 4, 1789, Thomas Tudor Tucker was the only one of the South Carolina group present. Nine days later three more representatives took their places; but Thomas Sumter did not arrive till May 25, too late for the inauguration of Washington. In the meantime Ralph Izard had taken his seat in the senate on April 13, but Pierce Butler did not appear till June 8.[32] Such delays prevented the house of representatives from having a quorum before April 1, and the senate prior to April 6.[33]

---

[30] *Carolina Gazette,* October 30, and December 25, 1800; *The Times* (Charleston), December 19, 1800.

[31] The present writer can hardly exaggerate his indebtedness to Schaper, "Sectionalism and Representation in South Carolina," pp. 400-426, in dealing with the question of representation.

[32] *Annals of Congress,* 1st Cong., 1st Sess. (March 4, 13, May 25, 1789), Senate (April 13, June 8, 1789), pp. 18, 45, 100, 425. Gregorie, *Thomas Sumter,* pp. 224-225.

[33] Before William Loughton Smith could have an absolutely clear title to his seat in the lower house, that body had to decide the contest brought by David Ramsay, a defeated candidate, on the ground that Smith had not been a citizen for seven years. He had been absent

JEFFERSONIAN DEMOCRACY IN S. C.   55

One of the early questions to trouble members of Congress was that of ceremony, particularly in regard to the relations between the executive and legislative departments. Since he had observed the English Parliament, Ralph Izard felt prepared to speak on its customs as possible examples for Congress. John Adams and some of the senators thought that titles should be given to the President and Vice-President. At one time Izard favored the title of "Excellency" for the former but later changed his mind. He was the member of several committees appointed to deal with problems of legislative and executive etiquette. It was, of course, decided that no additional titles should be given to the two chief officers of the executive department.[84] In the house Burke and Tucker expressed disapprobation of bestowing titles. The former even opposed the designation of one of the judges of the Supreme Court as Chief Justice as "a concomitant of royalty" until he was reminded that such a title was specified in the Constitution.[85]

---

from the country from 1770 till November, 1783, according to Ramsay's letter to Madison, April 4, 1789. Madison Papers. The House decided in favor of Smith. *Annals of Congress*, 1st Cong., 1st Sess. (May 22, 1789), pp. 412-425.

[84] *Annals of Congress*, 1st Cong., 1st Sess., Senate (May 7, 14, 1789), pp. 33, 35-36, 41-42; Edward S. Maclay, ed., *Journal of William Maclay, United States Senator from Pennsylvania 1789-1791* (New York: 1890), pp. 7, 24. According to Maclay, Izard abhorred John Adams, the Vice-President. The senator from Pennsylvania reported that Izard, after describing Adams's "air, manner, deportment, and personal figure in the chair, concluded with applying the title of 'Rotundity' to him." Perhaps Maclay was reading too strong an opposition into the actions of Izard because of his own feelings toward Adams. He himself wrote, "God forgive me the vile thought, but I can not help thinking of a monkey just put into breeches when I saw him betray such evidence of self-conceit." *Journal*, p. 30. If there was any really serious hostility between Izard and Adams at this time it must have been removed during the next ten years. In 1799 Adams approved the appointment of Ralph Izard's son as midshipman, with a statement praising his father and speaking of their "long intimacy." When Adams wrote in 1811, of his experiences in Europe as representative of the revolutionary colonies, he spoke of Izard as being exceedingly passionate and violent, but gave him credit for arousing suspicions in his mind concerning Vergennes. Charles Francis Adams, ed., *The Works of John Adams, Second President of the United States with a Life of the Author, Notes and Illustrations by His Grandson* (Boston: 1856), I, 670-671, IX, 37.

[85] *Annals of Congress*, 1st Cong., 1st Sess. (August 24, 1789), pp. 333, 812.

The report of Secretary Hamilton recommending the funding of the nation's debt and the assumption of the obligations contracted by the states in the pursuit of the Revolution caused public securities to rise rapidly in Charleston and the vicinity.[36] With a large amount of unpaid debts, South Carolina was greatly interested in assumption. Ralph Izard decided to support Hamilton's recommendation; but, thinking his colleague, Pierce Butler, would oppose it, he asked Edward Rutledge to inform him as to the attitude of the South Carolina legislature.[37] A resolution passed by that body showed its favorable attitude.[38] Perhaps this approval by the legislature partly accounts for the absence of the opposition expected from other South Carolina members of Congress. Beard found that Burke, Smith and Tucker, all of whom voted for assumption, held state securities.[39] Smith has frequently been listed as one who informed speculators of the proposed plan and co-operated in buying indents before the holders realized that they might rise in value. Just how much he was involved in such practices is still uncertain. Friends gave sworn statements that they had had opportunity to know about his conduct and that they were certain that he had neither speculated himself nor aided others in so doing. In the newspapers of the day, both friendly and hostile letters were printed. It would appear from the tenor of the letters that most of the writers were finally convinced that Smith's guilt was at most not very great. Among those who

[36] *City Gazette*, February 5, 1790.

[37] A copy of this letter written in 1789 is printed in "South Carolina Federalist Correspondence, 1789-1797," *American Historical Review*, XIV, 777-778. Maclay reports in his *Journal*, p. 399, that Izard asserted on February 24, 1791, that no legislature had any more right to instruct a representative than the electors had to instruct a President.

[38] S. C. House Journal, January 19, 1790. Also, a similar resolution favoring still further action was passed on December 20, 1791. S. C. Senate Journal of same date. In Congress, Burke asserted that South Carolina would not have been willing to give up the impost duty through the ratification of the Constitution if it had not been understood that her debt would be assumed. However, he did have some fear of the political consequences to the state governments. *Annals of Congress*, 1st Cong., 2nd Sess. (February 24, 1790), p. 1332.

[39] Charles A. Beard, *Economic Origins of Jeffersonian Democracy* (New York: Macmillan, 1915), p. 192.

JEFFERSONIAN DEMOCRACY IN S. C. 57

came to his defense in no uncertain terms was Christopher Gadsden.[40] Beard was unable to find the names of Sumter and Huger in the records of the security holders; but the former was to be defeated in 1793 largely because of the accusation that he had helped delay the adoption of the funding bill until he and his friends could buy up vast amounts of indents, a charge which was made during his absence in Congress and which he was later able to disprove to the satisfaction of his constituents.[41] Thus most of South Carolina's Congressional delegation were willing to support a measure which would benefit their state financially.

A review of the discussion in Congress on the first impost bill reveals considerable evidence in support of the much ridiculed statement of a later day that the tariff was a "local issue." When the bill was brought up only a few days after a quorum was present, Tucker opposed further consideration on the ground that the Southern states were not adequately represented, he being the only member present from the region south of Virginia. For the time being he thought Congress could safely pass the duties proposed by the Congress of the Confederation in 1783. The imposts then under consideration were declared to be "so novel, and at the same time, so important," that more than a few hours or even a few days would be required for proper discussion. Although he did not care to go into the merits of the tariff bill, he did express his opposition to high tonnage duties. Furthermore, he was ready to oppose special duties on tallow candles and meat. Thereupon, a representative from Pennsylvania accused him of opposing duties on all products that would be imported into his state. Commenting upon the heavy imports into South Carolina, Tucker retorted that she would contribute her portion of duties on any product that might have impost levied upon it. He joined some of the representatives from Virginia in their fight against import taxes on steel on the ground that such a levy would be oppressive to agriculture and unjust since some states could not obtain that metal except from foreign countries. Tucker opposed

[40] *City Gazette,* February 1, 2, 4, 1783.
[41] Gregorie, *Thomas Sumter,* pp. 233-236.

the duty on nails because he thought the manufacturers did not need any assistance.⁴²

The attitudes of other South Carolinians in Congress did not vary greatly from that of Tucker. Thinking that South Carolina and Georgia might begin growing hemp, Burke favored a mildly protective or encouraging duty on it.⁴³ He thought a tax on salt would be especially odious to the people of South Carolina and Georgia. To Tucker the taxing of salt would seem a kind of poll tax, affecting the poor more severely than the rich. According to Smith, such a levy would arouse further opposition to the general government in the interior of South Carolina, a region already unfriendly.⁴⁴

As the discussion continued Tucker thought of other reasons for opposing high duties. They would tend to promote smuggling. Also, some states would profit greatly while others might suffer disastrously.⁴⁵ He frankly admitted that he was voting for excessive rates on articles of interest to other states in an effort to force their representatives to consent to lower duties on goods in which his state was most interested; but he denied that he had made bargains on specific articles.⁴⁶ At the close of one of his speeches, Tucker summarized his attitude toward the whole question.

Mr. Speaker, if gentlemen are content with moderate duties, we are willing to agree to them and give them every reasonable encouragement in our power, but we can not consent to very great oppression. I once more wish that gentlemen will consider great duties as imposing a heavier burden upon the Southern States, as they import more, the others less; and the sum we pay towards revenue must be in proportion to our importation.⁴⁷

⁴² *Annals of Congress,* 1st Cong., 1st Sess. (April 9, 15, 1789), pp. 112-113, 114, 152-153, 154, 155.
⁴³ *Ibid.,* 1st Cong., 1st Sess. (April 16, 1789), pp. 161-162.
⁴⁴ *Ibid.,* 1st Cong., 1st Sess. (April 16, 1789), pp. 165-167.
⁴⁵ *Ibid.,* 1st Cong., 1st Sess. (April 24, May 8, 11, 1789), pp. 206, 303-305.
⁴⁶ *Ibid.,* 1st Cong., 1st Sess. (May 8, 11, 1789), pp. 303-305, 337-339.
⁴⁷ *Ibid.,* 1st Cong., 1st Sess. (May 9, 1789), pp. 307-308.

JEFFERSONIAN DEMOCRACY IN S. C. 59

Both Smith and Tucker vigorously opposed a ten-dollar tax on slaves imported into the country.[48]

In the senate the statements of Butler and Izard in regard to the tariff showed views which were, in general, not radically different from those expressed by the South Carolinians in the house of representatives. According to Maclay, the former gave his opinion in no uncertain terms as soon as possible after his arrival. The senator from Pennsylvania recorded that a "new phenomenon had made its appearance."

Pierce Butler from South Carolina had taken his seat and flamed like a meteor. He arraigned the whole Impost law, and then charged (indirectly) the whole Congress with a design of oppressing South Carolina. He cried out for encouraging the Danes and Swedes and foreigners of every kind to come and take away our produce. In fact, he was for a navigation act reversed.[49]

It is clear that the South Carolinians in the First Congress based their action in regard to the tariff on the probable effect of such legislation on the welfare of their own state. As to tonnage duties on the ships of other nations, they denied that they favored foreign ships, but stated that sufficient vessels were not available yet in this country, and that until the uncertain future date when they were available heavy tonnage duties would be unfair and oppressive to the Southern states.[50]

In discussing the amendments proposed to the new Constitution, the first South Carolina representatives expressed rather pronounced sentiments in regard to the rights and powers of states. In view of the prominence given by debaters in the ratifying conventions to the supposed need for amendments, it is surprising that Congress seemed in no great hurry to take such action. Smith and Burke thought that the new government should be organized before any time should be devoted to modification of the Constitution. Sumter, however, considered the subject of so great importance that action should not be delayed. Burke's opposition to early action was partly due to the

---

[48] *Ibid.*, 1st Cong., 1st Sess. (May 13, 1789), pp. 349-351.
[49] Maclay, *Journal*, p. 72, under date of June 9, 1789.
[50] *Annals of Congress*, 1st Cong., 1st Sess. (April 21, May 5, 8, 1789), pp. 187, 267, 270-274, 301.

fear that unsatisfactory amendments might be proposed in the house and swiftly adopted. He thought that the provisions in some of the state constitutions specifically recognizing the right of the people to instruct their delegates should be remembered and followed. Burke attempted to have one of the proposed amendments declare a "standing army in time of peace" dangerous to the liberties of the people except when necessary for the security of the people and permissable then only upon the favorable vote of two thirds of those present in both houses of Congress.[51] When the proposal that "no State shall infringe the equal rights of conscience, nor the freedom of speech or of the *press,* nor the right of trial by jury in criminal cases" was under discussion, Tucker spoke unfavorably of its provisions on the grounds that it was interference with the rights of states, a practice which some thought had been engaged in too much already. James Madison and others, however, thought this the most important amendment of the list; consequently, the result was defeat for the South Carolinian's motion for rejection.[52] To Burke's suspicious mind there seemed to be need of further safeguards of the rights of states in the holding of elections to choose federal officers. His colleagues joined him in trying to get adopted an amendment forbidding Congress to interfere "in the times, places, or manner of holding elections of Senators, or Representatives, except when any State shall refuse or neglect or be unable, by invasion or rebellion, to make such elections"; but the attempt failed by a close vote.[53]

Undaunted by defeat three of the South Carolina representatives vigorously fought against direct taxation by the federal government. Tucker proposed an amendment providing that Congress should not levy such tax until after revenues from "duties, imposts, and excise" were found insufficient; and even then Congress should first make requisitions of the states, placing direct taxes on only those that refused to pay the requisitions. In his support of this measure, Sumter showed much concern for the future of the states. According to him they

[51] *Ibid.,* 1st Cong., 1st Sess. (August 17, 1789), p. 780.
[52] *Ibid.,* 1st Sess. (August 17, 1789), pp. 783-784.
[53] *Ibid.,* 1st Cong., 1st Sess. (August 21, 1789), pp. 797-802.

faced annihilation if the general government exercised the power of direct taxation. If all sources of revenue were taken from them they could not support their governments or pay their domestic debts. Smith, alone, of the South Carolina group voted against Tucker's proposal; but it was rejected overwhelmingly by the other members of the house of representatives.[54]

In the organization of the federal government Washington and members of his cabinet looked to South Carolina, as well as to other states, for possible appointees. Friendships and acquaintances begun during the period of the Revolution and the Confederation called to the minds of the President and his assistants men who might make efficient officers. Because of their previous activities in the affairs of the nation John and Edward Rutledge and Charles Cotesworth and Thomas Pinckney were the first to be considered. These gentlemen were rather reluctant to accept the positions offered them. Whether this is to be explained by their desire to remain on their plantations, their dissatisfaction with the type of offices tendered them, their early lack of appreciation of the dignity and importance of service under the general government or to a combination of all these, is not quite clear. John Rutledge did serve for a while as Associate-Justice of the Supreme Court but resigned to become chief justice of the supreme court of South Carolina, no doubt considering the latter position a promotion. Thomas Pinckney declined the appointment of a district judgeship but did later serve as the first minister of the United States, under the Constitution, to Great Britain. Having formed a close friendship with Edward Rutledge several years before, Jefferson was keenly disappointed at his steady refusal to enter the service of the general government. On one occasion Jefferson wrote

Would to God yourself, General Pinckney, or Major Pinckney would come forward to aid us with your efforts. You are all known, respected, and wished for, but you refuse yourselves to everything. What is to become of us, my dear friend if the

[54] *Annals of Congress,* 1st Cong., 1st Sess. (August 21, 22, 1789), pp. 797-805.

vine and the fig-tree withdraw, and leave us to the bramble and the thorn?[55]

While Washington was in South Carolina in 1791, he addressed a letter to Edward Rutledge and Charles Cotesworth Pinckney jointly asking one of them to accept the position as Associate-Justice of the Supreme Court, from which John Rutledge had resigned. The President further stated that they would have been offered similar places earlier if he had not been assured by friends of both that they could not be prevailed upon to leave private life. After several days Rutledge and Pinckney jointly declined, basing their nonacceptance on private grounds and on the belief that they could be of more service to both the general and state governments by remaining in the state legislature. They also asserted that in earlier days they had devoted a great part of their time to their country, and if a serious need ever arose again they would respond.[56] More than two years later Jefferson chided Rutledge for remaining at home, observing that even though he may have been happier in so doing he had not proved "that the performance of a *certain* tour of duty in any line which the public calls for, can be rightfully declined."[57] Charles Cotesworth Pinckney did serve the general government at a later date, and John Rutledge accepted the appointment, not to be confirmed, as Chief Justice of the Supreme Court of the United States, but Edward Rutledge continued to put into practice the belief that he could serve best by holding local offices.

After telling of the difficulties that confronted Washington and Jefferson in trying to persuade certain South Carolinians to accept positions of prominence, the recorder of these occurrences would be relating an incomplete story if he failed to mention the disappointment of another outstanding gentleman in not being offered an appointment. Charles Pinckney, the youthful second cousin of Charles Cotesworth and Thomas, who had already held several state offices, had been a member

[55] Quoted in Charles Cotesworth Pinckney, *Life of General Thomas Pinckney* (Boston: 1895), p. 96.
[56] Worthington Chauncey Ford, ed., *The Writings of George Washington* (New York: 1889-1893), XII, 43-44.
[57] Jefferson Papers, December 30, 1793.

JEFFERSONIAN DEMOCRACY IN S. C.   63

of the Congress of the Confederation and had played a prominent part in the framing of the Constitution of the United States, felt that his services should be rewarded. From time to time, he had corresponded with Madison, who he thought was very close to the administration leaders; and it would seem, from the intimacy of the letters, that Pinckney considered Madison a very close friend. In the meantime the young South Carolina leader continued to strengthen his position in local politics. Even before the meeting of the First Congress under the new Constitution, the legislature of his state had chosen him governor, and in January, 1791, he was reelected.

With such a record of political service, and still governor of his state, Charles Pinckney thought his favorable disposition toward federal service would be welcomed. But he did not know Jefferson and was not closely acquainted with Washington. In a long letter in August, 1791, Governor Pinckney asked Madison to recommend to the President and to the Secretary of State his appointment as a minister to some European country, preferably to England. According to information that had come to him, such a position was to be filled soon and likely by a South Carolinian. He reviewed his record, and stated that he liked public office, had tried to fit himself for a diplomatic position, even though he had not yet been to Europe. Mrs. Pinckney, however, had spent much time in England and France and spoke French fluently.[58]

The failure of Washington to appoint him and the choice of Thomas Pinckney instead are sometimes given as among the principal reasons for Charles Pinckney's break with the Federalists. It would possibly be too strong to say that this disappointment had absolutely nothing to do with his future political affiliations; likewise, it might be going too far to assert that the greater success of his two second cousins in dealing with the federal government had no influence at all upon the direction of his political course; but a careful student of his career must admit that earlier, in his opposition to the commercial concessions favored by Eastern leaders, Charles Pinckney had taken a step that started him toward the party which

[58] Madison Papers, August 6, 1791.

was to oppose the Federalists.[59] Certainly one does not need to be an apologist for him to see more consistency in his political career than those do who attribute his championing of the Jeffersonian Republican cause to his inability to lose gracefully or to his fear of being overshadowed by his kinsmen.[60] It is indeed unfortunate that sources of information concerning the activities of Charles Pinckney are so meager.[61] This absence of needed evidence adds to the uncertainties and makes the explanation of his conduct more difficult.

That Charles Pinckney at all times subscribed wholeheartedly to all ideas that were connected with the party of Jefferson, cannot be maintained. The present writer readily admits that, from a social or even a cultural standpoint, he would

[59] See *supra*, p. 20.

[60] Phillips, in his "S. C. Federalists," already referred to, conjectured that Charles Pinckney decided to lead the Republicans partly because of "his dislike for Adams" (when he was President) but more largely as a result of "a desire for a conspicuous career." Professor Phillips, unfortunately, based his estimate of Pinckney too much upon traditions that might be considered by other historians as hardly more than political gossip.

[61] One of his greatest admirers has stated the case rather strongly: "The fate assigned to Pinckney seems to have been oblivion. His house was one of the finest in Charleston, if not the finest, and it was destroyed. He believed his library to be the most valuable library in the South and his great gallery to hold the rarest pictures in this country yet but a few volumes remain of one and but two portraits of the other. His garden was the most beautiful in the State, it was his pride, his delight, and obliteration has been its portion; even the soil which bore flowers and shrubbery and trees laden with all the loveliness of semitropical vegetation is gone; for it was carried away during the Civil War to make military defenses." Nott, *Mystery of the Pinckney Draught*, p. 284.

In 1928 W. E. Bowen of Greenville, S. C., published a pamphlet, *Charles Pinckney, a Forgotten Statesman*, telling of the uncertainty as to where Charles Pinckney was buried, due to the absence of a marker to his grave. After extensive correspondence and conversations on the part of Bowen and those most familiar with the history of South Carolina, it was brought out that the Charleston Board of Health records and the Church records indicated St. Philip's, Charleston, as the probable place of burial. However, the absence of any kind of marker containing such information caused some question to exist still. A copy of Bowen's pamphlet may be found in *Pamphlets, South Carolina Biography*, Vol. 44, University of South Carolina Library.

JEFFERSONIAN DEMOCRACY IN S. C. 65

seem to fit in better with the South Carolina Federalists than with the rank and file of the Republicans. But could not a similar statement be made about Thomas Jefferson and the members of his party in Virginia? It is an easily ascertained fact that, in 1787, Pinckney favored heavy property qualifications for federal officials and a stronger central government than was established. In 1789 he still thought the legislature instead of the electorate should choose the representatives in Congress.[62] Clearly at that time, he did not favor direct popular government. Why then did he join the party that was moving in that direction? Is it not probable that he thought the other party was tending toward policies which would ultimately react against the section, the economic group and the constituents which were most vital to him? The rapid spread of agriculture over a greater portion of South Carolina extended the institutions and practices which at an earlier date had been confined to the area nearer the coast. It should not have required an unusual amount of political acumen to see that the representatives and voters from the upper part of the state were fast becoming less dangerous to the interests of the low country. In fact, many planters from the latter region were acquiring land farther from the coast. A man with practical political sagacity, like Charles Pinckney, could easily perceive the absence of any great danger in joining with the up country planters and farmers. Furthermore, he could readily see the advisability of combining them in the support of the party which he thought could best serve the interests of the state and the South. Such a course was merely the continuation of the policy he had strenuously upheld in the days of the Confederation.

Another act of the federal Congress which soon gave rise to political and economic controversy in South Carolina was the establishment of the Bank of the United States. While the bill was before the house of representatives Smith and Tucker were active in debate. Both were desirous of having the measure recommitted for the purpose of revision. However, when

[62] Madison Papers, March 28, 1789.

the motion failed Smith vigorously supported the passage of the bill as it was.[63] When the constitutionality of the bank was questioned Smith showed such little patience that other representatives accused him of thinking that any act which Congress might consider expedient would be constitutional. In reply he stated that the only guide members of Congress had was their own judgment.

If, in such cases, it appeared to them, on solemn deliberation, that the measure was not prohibited by any part of the constitution, was not a violation of the rights of any State or individual and was peculiarly necessary and proper to carry into operation certain essential powers of the government, it was then not only justifiable on the part of Congress, but it was even their duty to adopt such a measure. That, nevertheless, it was still within the province of the Judiciary to annul the law if it should be by them deemed not to result by fair construction from the powers vested by the constitution.[64]

On the final vote it appears that Smith was the only South Carolina representative to favor the passage of the bill.[65]

Soon after the establishment of the Bank of the United States, citizens of Charleston became interested in obtaining a branch bank for their city.[66] By April, 1792, such an institution had been established in Charleston.[67] Soon after it began business in South Carolina, opposition to its policy or tendencies developed. Some thought that the branch bank was managed from Philadelphia, and that its officers did not take into consideration the particular conditions of their state; consequently, they advocated a local bank which could adopt a policy based on local conditions. The recent order that no note with a life of more than thirty days should be discounted was largely responsible for the calling of a meeting of those interested in

[63] *Annals of Congress,* 1st Cong., 3rd Sess. (February 1, 5, 1791), pp. 1892, 1893, 1928-1930.

[64] *Ibid.,* 1st Cong., 3rd Sess. (February 5, 1791), pp. 1936-1937.

[65] *Ibid.,* 1st Cong., 3rd Sess. (February 8, 1791), p. 1960. Burke and Tucker opposed. The names of the other representatives from South Carolina are not listed. The vote of individual members of the senate on this question is not given. *Ibid.,* p. 1748.

[66] *City Gazette,* May 28, June 1, 1791.

[67] Clark, *History of Banking in S. C.,* p. 40. *City Gazette,* April 9, 1792.

JEFFERSONIAN DEMOCRACY IN S. C. 67

setting up a tontine bank. The enthusiasm for another banking institution may be judged by the fact that subscriptions were taken up in sixty-three minutes. However, a few days later the stockholders voted to change their original plans by calling their organization the Bank of South Carolina and increasing the capitalization from $150,000 to $200,000.[68]

The passage of the excise act heightened the attitude of suspicion and even hostility already held by many of the citizens of the up country. Many of them no doubt agreed with Burke that it was "universally odious."[69] Tucker sought unsuccessfully to limit the duration of the bill. In the end Burke and Tucker voted against and Smith for its passage.[70] When the measure went into operation, Daniel Stevens, supervisor of revenue for the district of South Carolina found considerable discontent, particularly in the back country, over the taxes placed on spirits.[71]

Besides the opposition to measures passed by the federal Congress there was also disapproval of the legislative procedure followed. In 1792 both houses of the South Carolina legislature passed a resolution calling upon the United States senate to open its sessions to the citizens of the nation except when the safety of the country demanded secrecy.[72] However, the policy of holding meetings behind closed doors was continued until the close of the first session of the Third Congress.[73]

Regardless of the party differences which had already developed, the people of South Carolina joined wholeheartedly in welcoming President Washington to their state in 1791.[74]

[68] *City Gazette,* April 9, 11, 27, 1792. See also the files of the same newspaper, May 15, 17, 18, 19, June 9, 12, August 27, October 15, November 19, 1792, for the discussion of a "Redemption Bank" to aid those with mortgages. The Bank of South Carolina was chartered as a state institution in 1801.

[69] *Annals of Congress,* 1st Cong., 3rd Sess. (January 20, 1791), p. 1874.

[70] *Ibid.,* 1st Cong., 3rd Sess. (January 22, 25, 1791), pp. 1850-1851, 1874, 1880, 1884.

[71] An address of Stevens appeared in *City Gazette,* August 5, 1791.

[72] S. C. Senate Journal, December 21, 1792.

[73] See the note of the editor in *Annals of Congress,* I, 16.

[74] The most accurate account of Washington's visit to South Carolina is the pamphlet of A. S. Salley, "President Washington's Tour

Along with the toasts to the visitor whom all delighted to honor were also expressions of confidence in or best wishes for such other persons, organizations or groups as "the King of France our great and noble ally," the National Assembly of France, the United States of America, the federal government and the state of South Carolina.[75] At times other persons or groups were mentioned, as was the case at Charleston when toasts were offered to the Vice-President, the members of the cabinet, "all nations in amity with the United States" and to others.[76] Hope for the future was strongly expressed in some: "may the States be ever united," "may commerce flourish," "may the State of South Carolina be soon the carrier of its own produce," "may merchants and planters understand their own interest, and each agree to assist the other in mutual good offices," "increase our exports and decrease our imports," and "an increase of well established seminaries of learning." These toasts no doubt indicated desires of many South Carolinians and might be considered as showing what subjects the leaders thought interested the citizenry of the state. Regardless of what other expressions were given, there was always a toast to the visitor, such as, "may the circuit of the President round the States be as much admired as that of the earth round the sun."[77]

With the coming of the year 1792 and its poor crops, disappointing economic developments and additional occurrences in Europe, political alignments began to take form.[78] At least two of the Federalist leaders in South Carolina soon incurred the disapproval of Thomas Jefferson. Smith criticized the practice of trial by jury and delivered speeches which Jefferson thought had been written by Hamilton.[79] Both Washington and

---

through South Carolina in 1791," *Bulletins of the Historical Commission of South Carolina.—No. 12* (Columbia, 1932).

[75] Toasts were drunk to these in Georgetown. *City Gazette*, May 3, 1791.   [76] *Ibid.*, May 5, 1791.

[77] *Ibid.*, May 5, 9, 11, June 3, 1791.

[78] A description of the bad economic conditions in a portion of the state, in the form of a petition to the legislature, is reprinted in Gregg, *History of the Old Cheraws*, p. 455.

[79] Albert Ellery Bergh, ed., *The Writings of Thomas Jefferson, Definitive Edition* (Washington: Thomas Jefferson Memorial Association, 1907), I, 295, and Ford, *Works of Jefferson*, VI, 501-502.

Jefferson were displeased because of Izard's loud discussion of state secrets in the presence of the French minister. This was particularly offensive to Jefferson on account of Izard's professed fear that the house of representatives could not keep a secret.[80] As the time for the elections of 1792 approached, Hamilton became alarmed lest Smith should not be a member of the Third Congress. Evidently there had been some doubt as to whether the latter would stand for reelection, for the former wrote Charles Cotesworth Pinckney urging that "means be taken to determine his acquiescence." Hamilton knew of "no man whose loss from the House would be more severely felt by the good cause."[81] In the same letter the Secretary of the Treasury expressed appreciation of Pinckney's "friendly allusion to my unpleasant situation." Jefferson had once been held in high esteem by him, but not so any longer. There were some objections to the Vice-Presidential candidacy of John Adams, but they must break down at the prospect of the alternative election of Jefferson, "a man of sublimated and paradoxical imagination, entertaining and propagating opinions inconsistent with dignified and orderly government."

A few months later Jefferson himself wrote Pinckney's brother, Thomas, who was the minister of the United States to Great Britain, that Adams would be strongly opposed but that "the strength of his personal worth and services will, I think, prevail over the demerit of his political creed." Thomas Pinckney was further informed that the Republicans were gaining in spite of the attempt of the Federalists to identify them with the "anti-federalists" of another day and call them Jacobins.[82] William Loughton Smith was returned to Congress and the Republican Thomas Sumter was replaced by Richard

[80] *Jefferson's Writings, Def. Edit.*, I, 295.
[81] Henry Cabot Lodge, ed., *The Works of Alexander Hamilton* (New York: G. P. Putnam's Sons, n.d.), X, 24.
[82] Ford, *Works of Jefferson*, VI, 143-144. It is extremely interesting to note that, in a letter to Joel Barlow on June 20, Jefferson had referred to Thomas Pinckney as "a good republican" and "an honest, & sensible man." *Ibid.*, VI, 88. The correspondence between the two shows very friendly relations; Pinckney, who was never a very extreme Federalist, had not yet committed himself in regard to the parties then in the process of formation in the United States.

Winn, his former colonel.[83] But the election of Lemuel Benton, the first member to be chosen from the Pedee District, added another to the ranks of the Republicans.[84] When the electoral votes of South Carolina were cast George Washington received eight, John Adams seven and Aaron Burr one.[85]

Although the election of 1792 showed that party lines had not yet been clearly drawn, two distinct political groups were rapidly aligning themselves against each other. The forces and influences already making for party differences were accelerated by the developments next to be discussed.

[83] See *supra*, p. 57.

[84] A brief sketch of Lemuel Benton may be found in Gregg, *History of the Old Cheraws*, pp. 401, 455-456. An indication of Benton's frugal attitude toward the government is seen in his refusal to qualify on June 9, 1794, until he was assured that it would be noted on the journals that he had refused any compensation for the earlier part of the session. He had been delayed because of indisposition of his family and an unduly long journey. *Annals of Congress*, 3rd Cong., 1st Sess., p. 782.

[85] *City Gazette*, December 14, 1792.

CHAPTER IV

THE FRENCH REVOLUTION, THE JAY TREATY AND REPUBLICAN SUCCESSES IN 1796

1. SYMPATHY FOR FRANCE

Closely connected with the development of political parties in South Carolina was the course of events in Europe. The memory of French assistance during the American Revolution and the feeling of sympathy toward a people in midst of civil struggle favorably inclined many in the United States toward France. Nor was it easy to forget the bitterness engendered by the late war against Great Britain. But their education in English schools, their economic interests or a general feeling that they had more in common with the British caused others to be more favorably disposed toward Great Britain. Immediately after the Revolution this latter group was small in South Carolina. However, with the partial renewal of commercial relations, many planters and merchants had economic reasons for desiring closer relations between the United States and Great Britain.[1]

With the outbreak of the French Revolution, the influence of foreign affairs upon American politics became more noticeable. When news of the fall of the Bastille reached Charleston a public demonstration took place.[2] John Rutledge, Jr., then traveling in Europe and later to be an ardent Federalist, wrote Jefferson that the people of France were better behaved than was usually the case during a revolution and "seem only to have been guided by that principle which is constantly operat-

[1] A discussion of the commercial ties between South Carolina and Great Britain may be found in the speech of William Loughton Smith in the house of representatives. *Annals of Congress*, 1st Cong., 1st. Sess. (May 7, 1789), pp. 298-299.
[2] O'Neall, *Bench and Bar in S. C.*, I, 83.

ing in the human breast to bring mankind to a state of equality and enjoyment of all the rights of which they are susceptible in Society."[3] Writing from London nearly a year later he thought the English considered themselves free and did not want any other people to be free. To him, England resembled "an individual, who valuing himself on any one thing becomes jealous of another who shall be thought to possess the same."[4] Edward Rutledge agreed with Jefferson in his "indignation at the trammels imposed on our commerce with Great Britain."[5] The newspapers of the state during the period printed letters of correspondents with similar opinions. Sometime during the year 1792 a French Patriotic Society was organized.[6]

As the year 1793 approached, both the critics and the defenders of the French Revolutionary leaders continued their flood of letters to the newspapers of the state. One, who signed himself "L" and claimed to be a Frenchman, denied that Jacobins favored communism and insisted that the French were liberty loving people, able to defend their liberties, not weak or disorganized.[7] His letter was designed as a reply to recent critical statements that had appeared in the newspapers and in public speeches. Another correspondent protested against the negligence of Charleston clergy in failing to pray for the success of the French nation in the struggle "for the rights of men against the united forces of tyranny."[8] That the leaders of South Carolina still felt closely drawn toward France is clearly shown by the presence of the governor, president of the senate, speaker of the house of representatives and the chief justice of the state at a "feast" on January 9, 1793, in celebration of the adoption of a republican form of government and recent victories by France.[9] In order to arrange for such celebrations an organization had already been formed under the direction of A. B. Mangourit, the French consul at Charleston; and at

[3] *Jefferson Papers,* April 3, 1789.
[4] *Ibid.,* March 25, 1790.   [5] Ford, *Works of Jefferson,* V, 196.
[6] *South Carolina Historical and Genealogical Magazine,* XXXII, 80. This society was soon affiliated with the *Friends of Liberty and Equality* of Bordeaux. *City Gazette,* December 5, 1792.
[7] *City Gazette,* November 17, 1792.
[8] *Ibid.,* November 22, 1792.
[9] *Ibid.,* January 10, 1793. William Moultrie was governor.

JEFFERSONIAN DEMOCRACY IN S. C. 73

least two more similar festivities occurred in January, 1793, at which Christopher Gadsden was awarded liberty trees.[10]

More propitious circumstances could hardly have been prepared for the unexpected arrival of Citizen Genêt, minister plenipotentiary of the French Republic to the United States, on April 8, 1793.[11] In a short while Mangourit and Genêt had conferred with the highest officials of the state, and no doubt the enthusiastic reception of the French minister influenced him in his decision to complete the journey to Philadelphia by land.[12] To what extent Governor Moultrie understood or acquiesced in the machinations of the French consul and minister is not clear, but there is little doubt that they both believed he was in complete sympathy with their plans.[13] Perhaps the governor thought that the regaining of the desired territory by the French would "end Indian border wars."[14] Letters of introduction to leading citizens of Savannah were given readily; and Moultrie is reported to have said that he knew of no law against their project, but "begged that whatever was to be done, might be done without consulting him, that he must know nothing of it."[15] Thinking that he had the governor's approval and believing that the public was ready to give active support, Genêt, with the aid of Mangourit, commissioned privateers and began arrangements for a land expedition against the Spanish possessions. The journey of Genêt through other towns of South Carolina, on the way to Philadelphia, was a triumphal procession.[16]

[10] *Ibid.*, January 4, 7, 15, 17, 1793.   [11] *Ibid.*, April 9, 1793.

[12] More details as well as controversial letters may be found in the *City Gazette,* beginning with Genêt's arrival and continuing until after his departure from Charleston on April 8. An interesting account of his reception and the attitude of Charlestonians is given in *Charleston Year Book,* 1883, pp. 508-509.

[13] Frederick J. Turner, ed., "The Mangourit Correspondence in Respect to Genêt's Projected Attack upon the Floridas, 1793-1794," *Annual Report of the American Historical Association, 1897* (Washington: Government Printing Office, 1898), pp. 569-579.

[14] This view is accepted by Wallace, in his *History of S. C.,* II, 352.

[15] Charles Marion Thomas, *American Neutrality in 1793* (New York: Columbia University Press, 1931), p. 120.

[16] One of the most enthusiastic receptions was given at Camden. Kirkland and Kennedy, *Historic Camden,* I, 314-318. *City Gazette,* May 4, 1793.

During the following months Mangourit continued the organizing activities, apparently fearing that Genêt was overlooking the importance of the services that might be rendered by the group of Carolina frontiersmen under William Tate. In the meantime South Carolinians heatedly discussed the nature and the legal status of the projects being instigated by the French. One correspondent quoted Vattel in his effort to prove that privateering, though possibly disgraceful to Americans, was legal.[17] After the publication of Washington's proclamation of neutrality in the newspapers of the state,[18] the reaction was not uniform. The English also were accused of fitting out privateers in Charleston.[19] Vattel was quoted again to support the practice of aiding a belligerent in time of war; and Locke's statement that the people often suffer more under a good ruler was thought to be true under the existing highly respected executive.[20] Others confessed their sympathy for the French cause and acknowledged the debt to France, but felt obligated to obey their own constitutional authorities when in conflict with the agents of another country.[21]

Early in December, 1793, the legislature began investigating the reported efforts of citizens of the state to organize an army of South Carolinians to be subject to the French officials. The committee, headed by Robert Anderson, reported that several citizens were enlisting men for the purpose of attacking the Spanish on behalf of the French. Resolutions of condemnation were passed; the accused leaders were summoned; and upon the request of the legislature, Governor Moultrie issued a proclamation against the expedition.[22] The undertaking was hin-

[17] *City Gazette,* May 3, 1793.
[18] *Ibid.,* May 10, 1793.
[19] *Ibid.,* August 6, 1783.
[20] *Ibid.,* August 30, 1793.
[21] *Ibid.,* September 4, 17, 1793.
[22] S. C. House Journal, December 2, 5, 11, 17, 18, 1793; May 3, 12, 1794. Alexander Moultrie, *An Appeal to the People on the Conduct of a Certain Public Body in South Carolina Respecting Col. Drayton and Col. Moultrie* (Charleston: 1794); a copy is in the collection of pamphlets of the Charleston Library Society, series 3, vol. 11, no. 2. In the *Appeal* Drayton and Moultrie protested against being compelled to appear before the house of representatives for trial. It was stated that the charges against Stephen Drayton were not violations of the state law. The writer asked if one did not have the right to expatriate himself. Reference was made to the Europeans who aided in the Revolu-

dered further by the rumors that the agents of France had encouraged Negro insurrections in Santo Domingo and were desirous of inciting similar uprisings in the United States.[23] Genêt's successor, Fauchet, according to his instructions, issued a proclamation on March 6, terminating the expedition, but Mangourit was unwilling to give up the project and tried desperately to push the attack on East Florida, professing to believe that the order of the new minister was not genuine. After the movement collapsed, Fauchet himself maintained contacts with the frontier friends of Genêt and "as the French archives show, continued to cherish the hope of using the West to secure territory from Spain."[24] Although many of those willing to join the expedition were motivated by the prospect of personal gain through plundering, still others were actually in sympathy with the French cause. That the movement was allowed to continue for nearly a year and reach such magnitude that an attack on East Florida was barely averted is proof within itself that many who were unwilling to enlist were either sympathizers or silent observers.[25]

Other incidents in 1793 showed the friendly feeling of South Carolinians toward the French. The newspaper articles in defense of France were frequently long and vigorous.[26] The year 1793 also saw the early activities of the Republican and the Democratic societies.[27]

---

tion and settled in this country. Those accused by the committee were, in addition to Drayton, William Tate, John Humbleton, Robert Tate, Jacob Roberts Brown and Richard Speake.

[23] Jefferson heard of such a rumor and though he did not believe it true passed it on to the governor of South Carolina for what it was worth. Jefferson Papers, December 23, 1793.

[24] Turner, "Mangourit Correspondence," p. 574.

[25] The activities in South Carolina were only a part of the general program of the French to gain Spanish territory; but, since this study is primarily concerned with one state, the project has been treated only in so far as it related to the area in question.

[26] See particularly those in the *City Gazette*, July 22 and August 22, 1793, the latter being nearly three columns in length. On August 29, there was an account of the celebration by a group of "respectable citizens" of the victory of the French ship *Ambuscade* over the British ship *Boston*.

[27] In a meeting of the Republican Society on September 5, a resolution was passed stating the fear that, if France were crushed by the

If the expressions of French sympathy were many and vigorous, demonstrations of friendliness toward the British were not entirely lacking. The anniversary of Saint George, "tutelar Saint of England," was commemorated by a dinner at Williams' Coffee House.[28] During the Fourth of July celebration a portion of the Charleston Light Infantry Company refused to eat in a building over which the flags of the United States and France were flying together. Finally the captain took down both to prevent immediate trouble. Under the order of the governor the disaffected portions were later disarmed.[29] On September 20, a Welshman even got permission to print a defense of George III and a justification of the war of Great Britain against France.[30]

With the failure of the plans of Genêt and Mangourit, one might expect a decrease in the enthusiasm of South Carolinians for the French, but the contrary was really true. Indeed the year 1794 has been referred to by a reliable observer as a time

When Sansculottes and their principles had great ascendency in Charleston—when the tri-colored cockade of France was the great badge of honour, and *Ca' ira* and the Marseillaise hymn the most popular airs—and "Vive la republique Francaise!" the universal shout.[31]

In the United States Congress William Loughton Smith was fast becoming one of the most staunch defenders of the British commercial policies and his speeches were placing him among the front ranks of the Federalists. It was he who led the attack upon the proposal of Madison that heavier duties be placed on the goods from nations not giving favorable com-

---

coalition, the United States would be in danger. The members pledged themselves to be as much in favor of liberty for France as for the United States. *City Gazette,* September 7, 1793. See also the files of the same newspaper, November 6, 1793, for the account of the formation of the Democratic Society on September 16, in the Chester Court House in Pinckney District. This organization expressed sympathy for the principles of the American and the French Revolutions and pledged aid to the French in so far as was possible and consistent with the laws of the United States. [28] *City Gazette,* April 26, 1793.
[29] *Ibid.,* July 31, August 1, 6, 1793.
[30] *Ibid.,* September 20, 1793.
[31] Fraser, *Reminiscences,* pp. 35-36.

mercial terms to the United States. It was expected, of course, that the increases would affect primarily the imports from Great Britain. In his discussion, Smith denied that France was making great trade concessions. Furthermore, the proposed increases would operate against his constituents like a "two-edged sword," injuring the sale of their exports and hampering the importation of needed products.[32] If revenue must be raised stamp duties would be preferable to tariff increases. To the latter proposal Alexander Gillon objected.[33] Smith also opposed the non-intercourse bill against Great Britain but three members from South Carolina voted for its final passage.[34] When it was discovered that the existing restrictive measures hurt France as well as England, the friends of the former sought their discontinuance. Although three of South Carolina's six representatives sympathized with this attempt, the vote of only one is recorded in its favor.[35] Meantime the recently announced British commercial rules aroused many South Carolinians. Resolutions of protest were passed at public gatherings. Even David Ramsay sponsored a resolution, which passed, stating that the United States should go to the extent of non-intercourse with Great Britain unless she fulfilled the obligations of the Treaty of Peace and made reparations for American vessels damaged.[36]

[32] *Annals of Congress,* 3rd Cong., 1st Sess. (January 3, 14, 29, 1794), pp. 155-159, 174-209, 401-410. It is worth noting that Senator Butler favored the Madison proposal. The sea ports, he said, might oppose but the landed interests would support. He was in favor of "every measure short of hostility." The time for moderate methods was over. He was willing to join Eastern members of Congress who desired restrictive measures. Madison Papers, February 4, 1794.

[33] *Ibid.,* 3rd Cong., 1st Sess. (May 8, 1794), pp. 659-666.

[34] *Ibid.,* 3rd Cong., 1st Sess. (April 14, 21, 1794). On final passage, the name of Smith is not recorded but the favorable votes of Hunter, Pickens and Winn are found. The names of Benton and Gillon are missing.

[35] Pickens voted with the group, while Gillon and Hunter voted for the continuance because of the desires of their constituents. Smith was personally in favor of continuance. The attitude of Winn can be judged only by his voting with Smith, Gillon and Hunter. The motion for continuation of the restrictions lost. *Annals of Congress,* 3rd Cong., 1st. Sess. (May 12, 1794), p. 683.

[36] *City Gazette,* March 3, 5, 6, 7, 1794.

So popular were the French people and things French that on April 12, 1794, a French theatre was established in Charleston, "with a company of comedians, pantomimists, rope dancers, etc."[37] Now and then the name of Genêt came up again. The Democratic Society of Pinckneyville thought that a minister of a nation had the right to express his opinion in regard to treaty obligations and saw nothing but correct procedure in the conduct of Genêt. It was further declared that the "cause of France is the cause of all nations."[38] A dispatch from Camden stated that on July 14, the anniversary of a great revolution was celebrated while the flags of the United States and France floated together.[39] The people of Great Britain and Ireland were urged to adopt "French fashions in politics." An example of the extent to which prominent people could become excited over statements made concerning the French is the controversy between Jacob Read and the publishers of the *South Carolina State Gazette*. Read had been engaged by a Dutch firm whose ship had been attacked allegedly by the vessel *L'Amie de la Libertie*. A Mr. Carey wrote an article to the newspaper stating that he had called upon Read to prove his assertion that the officers and men of the ship were a lawless band of pirates; the article was treated with contempt, whereupon Carey called Read a liar and a scoundrel. Read then had Carey bound by the court to keep the peace. Two days later a letter of Read was printed, stating that he had evidence as to the piracy of the supposed French ship, denying much of Carey's letter and holding the publishers of the paper as guilty as the writer. The controversy culminated in challenges, withdrawal of challenges, and public fighting between Read, who was then speaker of the South Carolina house of representatives, and both of the publishers of the *South Carolina State Gazette*.[40]

The optimistic editors of the *South Carolina State Gazette* declared the French could not be defeated. As an illustration

[37] Fraser, *Reminiscences*, p. 44.
[38] *S. C. State Gazette*, April 29, 1794.
[39] *Ibid.*, August 15, 1794.
[40] The publishers of the *South Carolina State Gazette* were B. F. Timothy and William Mason, Jr. The story of this sordid affair is printed in their paper July 26-August 9, 1794.

of the contempt France had for her enemies they cited the taking of time during a period of stress to pass a decree ordering the beautification of the national gardens. This was also given as a refutation of the charge that the French had become enemies of art.[41]

2. "Self-Created Societies"

The work of the Republican and Democratic Societies was broadened in 1794 and at least one new organization was formed. Feasts and celebrations continued to be promoted. One of the most colorful of such occasions was the feast of the Republican Society of Charleston on February 13, at which were present the French consul and a few visitors from French ships in the harbor. The members wore the national cockade and hats decorated with "a branch of laurel surmounted with the Cap of Liberty." The flags of France and the United States were displayed over the hotel and in the room. Over the French vessels in the harbor floated the flags of both nations. The merchant vessels, except the British, responded in similar fashion. Among the toasts were, "May the union of the two Republics be co-existent with time"; "Citizen Madison and the Republican part of Congress"; "A speedy revolution in Great Britain and Ireland on Sans-Culotte Principles"; and "The guillotine to all tyrants, plunderers and funding speculators." In the room were two boys—a little Sans-culotte from a French vessel and an American. They stood behind the president's chair for a while. Later each climbed to a chair and wrapped himself in the flag of the other's nation, climaxing their performance by singing in an animated manner the chorus of one of the French Revolutionary songs.[42] The club communicated from time to time with similar groups in other parts of the country.[43] At one meeting the legislature was criticized for departing from its legislative capacity to try Stephen Drayton and Alexander Moultrie.[44] The Republican Society of Pendleton, claiming four hundred members, denounced Great Britain,

[41] *S. C. State Gazette,* November 12, 1794.
[42] *City Gazette,* February 13, 1794.
[43] *Ibid.,* February 20, 1794.   [44] *Ibid.,* June 28, 1794.

praised France and approved "Citizen Madison and the real patriots of the present Congress."[45] In October the Charleston society urged the election of Republican candidates.[46]

As already suggested the member of Congress receiving most attention at the meetings of these societies was James Madison. Being associated with the Washington Administration, Jefferson had not been able to promote Republicanism as actively and as openly as his fellow Virginian. Then, too, while the Secretary of State had many followers in South Carolina, some felt that he had not been as friendly toward Genêt as he might have. However, even when this matter was mentioned great respect was shown for Jefferson in spite of the difference of opinion.[47] For some time, though, Madison continued to receive the more enthusiastic toasts. As an indication of his popularity the Madison Society of Greenville was formed in 1794.[48] In October Edmund Randolph, who had succeeded Jefferson as Secretary of State, wrote Washington of having been informed by Ralph Izard that "a society under the democratic garb has arisen in South Carolina with the name of Madisonian." Randolph expressed the hope that Madison would not become involved with such organizations. He had hitherto favored a policy of silence toward these "self-constituted bodies"; but since "the fruit of their operations was disclosed in the insurrection at Pitsburg" he felt that they could now safely be crushed.[49] A few days later Washington wrote that he did not believe the people would long be deceived by the societies. He, too, hoped that Madison would not become involved in any way. However, in spite of his stated faith in the discernment of the people, Washington was convinced that if these societies were not "discountenanced" they would "destroy the government of this country."[50]

[45] *S. C. State Gazette,* July 1, 1794.
[46] *City Gazette,* October 8, 1794.
[47] See, for example, the letter of "A Citizen" to the *City Gazette,* February 20, 1794.
[48] A notice of the meeting of this society is in the *City Gazette,* July 26, 1794. Among the things favored at this meeting was the distribution of offices. The practice of the legislature of electing members of their own group to positions of "honor, trust or profit" was condemned.
[49] Ford, *Writings of Washington,* pp. 474-475.   [50] *Ibid.,* pp. 475-476.

JEFFERSONIAN DEMOCRACY IN S. C.

That President Washington had become very much aroused by the activities of these organizations was shown in his message to Congress in November. In discussing the recent disturbances in Pennsylvania, he further stated

> As a part of this subject, we cannot withhold our reprobation of the self-created societies which have risen in some parts of the Union, misrepresenting the conduct of the Government, and disturbing the operations of the laws, and which by deceiving and inflaming the ignorant and the weak, may naturally be supposed to have stimulated and urged the insurrection.[51]

In the heated discussion that followed, Smith vigorously upheld the President and strongly urged that the societies be censured. Apparently no other member of the South Carolina delegation spoke on the subject; but the names of Hunter and Pickens, the only other representatives from that state present, opposed any form of censure.[52] Soon a storm of protest arose in South Carolina, as well as in other states where such societies were active. Writers and speakers regretted that the President had descended to the point of using "courtly language of insinuation and innuendo." Objection was made to the use of the term "self-created" in an odious sense. Had not the Society of the Cincinnati and the Society of the Revolution which celebrated Washington's birthday been formed in the same way? In denouncing self-created organizations the President had struck at the rights of free men.[53] Madison is said to have called this denunciation of the "self-created" societies "Perhaps the greatest error" of Washington's political life and Jefferson could not see how they could be condemned without attacking the Cincinnati.[54] The question was kept alive and sometimes brought up when the connection was remote. During the consideration of the naturalization bill, an amendment was proposed to force emigrants with titles to renounce them before becoming citizens, to which Smith was "entirely opposed." He thought it just as sensible to forbid members of such clubs as

[51] *Annals of Congress,* 3rd Cong., 2nd Sess., November 24, 1794.
[52] *Ibid.,* 3rd Cong., 2nd Sess. (November 24, 25, 27, 1794), pp. 901-902, 908, 943-945.
[53] *City Gazette,* December 13, 20, 1794.
[54] Ford, *Writings of Washington,* XII, 476, note.

the Jacobin to wear badges of distinction. His constituents were not afraid of aristocracy.[55]

3. OPPOSITION TO THE JAY TREATY

An even greater outburst of popular indignation than that which followed Washington's denunciation of the "self-created" societies resulted from the mission of John Jay to England and from the treaty he negotiated. Even before it was decided who would be dispatched Jefferson severely criticized the sending of a special envoy. He thought it would show great disrespect for Thomas Pinckney, the regular minister, and that he would be forced to resign "after such a testimony that he is not confided in. I suppose they think he is not thorough fraud enough."[56] Letters in South Carolina newspapers denounced the appointment of Jay as both unconstitutional and unnecessary. Was it because of Pinckney's sympathy for France and republicanism? Or did the executive feel it necessary to test, occasionally, how far he could go against the will of the people? One correspondent was willing to fight for all constitutional agreements but would not consider himself bound by any treaty which John Jay helped form.[57] The editors of the *South Carolina State Gazette* ironically observed that a favorable termination of Jay's negotiations was augured by the speed with which he was getting along. During the month in which he had been

---

[55] Hunter, Benton, Pickens and Winn voted for the amendment. Gillon had died October 6, and his place was not filled by Robert Goodloe Harper until February 9, 1795. *Annals of Congress*, 3rd Cong., 2nd Sess. (December 31, 1794, January 2, 8, 1795), pp. 1030-1032, 1050-1051, 1057-1058, 1064-1066.

Among the few manuscript papers of William Loughton Smith in the Library of Congress is a letter (which the present writer hardly knows whether to consider seriously or not) marked "rec'd in Congress 1794."

"Wm. Smith

"Your aristocratical behaviour in Congress had introduced us to form a conspiracy against you and for that toryism you shall fall by the hands of private murder and nobody shall know who committed it—for all American Sons are crying out against you—you rascal. You shall fall—and so beware of your life—for we are determined to mangle your body at a most—[?] date.

"Fifteen Republicans and boys to extirpate torys."

[56] Ford, *Writings of Jefferson*, VI, 504. Jefferson to Monroe.

[57] *City Gazette*, May 15, and June 14, 1794.

JEFFERSONIAN DEMOCRACY IN S. C.   83

in England he had made his bow to Greenville, had dinner with him and appeared before the king and queen. If it took a month to make two bows and eat one dinner, it would no doubt require a year to state the American claims and a century to adjust them.[58]

No doubt part of the opposition which followed the appointment of Jay and the reception of his treaty resulted from the belief that the President was discriminating against Thomas Pinckney. Apparently Pinckney did have unpleasant feelings when he learned that another man had been commissioned to perform part of what he considered his own duties. However, he loyally gave Jay all the support possible and finally approved the treaty itself.[59]

While the United States senate was considering the Jay Treaty in "strict secrecy," a few copies of it were printed "under the eye of the secretary," not to be given out; but as fast as Pierce Butler could get "sheets of it" he passed them on to James Madison. Butler thought the copy of the treaty would be as safe in the hands of Madison as in those of the ones that then had it. Madison was given permission to send it to Jefferson when he had finished with it, but it should not be communicated to anyone else. Butler believed that the treaty had been unconstitutionally negotiated, since it was made without the advice of the senate and since it provided for the regulation of commerce, the power to do which was invested in Congress.[60] On the vote for ratification the South Carolina senators were divided, Jacob Read favoring and Butler opposing.[61]

When the terms of the treaty became known in Charleston great excitement prevailed. The absence of a satisfactory pro-

[58] *S. C. State Gazette,* September 22, 1794.
[59] Samuel Flagg Bemis, "The London Mission of Thomas Pinckney," *American Historical Review,* XXVIII, p. 244; and by the same author, *Pinckney's Treaty,* pp. 239-240. Pinckney seemed to appreciate the appointment to Spain, though it was not, as often supposed, a direct result of the sending of Jay to England. The Spanish mission and the Pinckney Treaty will be discussed later. See *infra,* pp. 92-95.
[60] Letter to Madison, June 12, 1795, Madison Papers.
[61] *Annals of Congress,* 3rd Cong. Special Senate Session (June 24, 1795), p. 863. The vote on ratification was 20 to 10, a bare two thirds.

vision for the introduction of cotton into England was attributed to the ignorance of the negotiator, "a circumstance which caused both him and the treaty to be spoken of with most marked contempt by the citizens."[62] Public meetings were held at which John Rutledge, Edward Rutledge and other prominent South Carolinians poured forth their wrath. The President was called upon to suspend ratification for at least a short while.[63]

At the early gatherings Charles Pinckney had been absent at his plantation, but on July 22, he again, as he had in 1786, opposed the commercial plans of John Jay. Pinckney held that a treaty negotiated as the one under consideration was reported to have been, was a violation of the "advice and consent" clause of the federal Constitution. Furthermore the terms of the treaty were objectionable in the extreme. The first article permitted the return to this country of people declared obnoxious by state legislatures, a measure he considered repugnant and unnecessary in a treaty. The second article provided for the surrender of posts which should have been surrendered under the Treaty of 1783, but which were now connected with serious concessions on the part of the United States. In article three Jay yielded to the British nearly every possible advantage that could come to this country from trade with the Indians and the western territory. The part dealing with the recovery of debts would place an unnecessary and dishonorable burden upon the government. Most of them had been settled already and a little firmness on the part of Jay would have ended the whole matter. A mode of adjudication was created "unusual and unknown to the laws of this country; and leaves it to be decided by chance, whether the majority of the commissioners to be appointed may be British subjects." The depredations against the commerce with the West Indies was supposed to have been the reason for the sending of Jay. As to how successful he had been in this regard, Pinckney was dubious.

[62] Thomas, *Reminiscences*, I, 35-36.
[63] Henry Tuckniss, ed., *The American Remembrancer or an Impartial Collection of Essays, Resolves, Speeches, &c. Relative, or Having Affinity to the Treaty with Great Britain* (Philadelphia: 1795), pp. 51-52.

As to the 12th Article, which the senate have rejected, there appears but one sentiment throughout the union; there can be but one in the breast of every man of sense, spirit or honesty, in every part of the world; that it is an infamous and degrading surrender of the rights and character of this country, and a mean and ungenerous desertion of the interest of our friends, the French, to whose supplies, at least in the articles they consider as of necessity in their present noble and unexampled struggle for freedom, we are bound by every tie of gratitude and honor to attend.

The United States should never depart from the maxim that "free bottoms make free goods." That was the only way to keep from being involved in all the wars of Europe. Existing conditions confirmed his belief that a larger navy was needed. If Jay could not have obtained better terms he should have refused to sign a treaty at all. Not a single object for which he was sent to England had been accomplished. Had the failure been from ignorance or design? Pinckney hoped that it had not been the latter. The President could not have instructed him to agree to the provision in regard to the exports of the United States. Experience proved that Washington could be trusted. Pinckney wished that the recent treaty showed that the country could trust Mr. Jay.[64]

As information regarding the treaty spread to other parts of the state more meetings were held. The Camden opponents thought that peace should be sought; but that "war, with all its horrors, ought to be preferred to peace upon such disgraceful and dishonorable terms." Pierce Butler and the other minority members of the senate were praised, but Jacob Read and those who favored ratification were deemed unworthy of further public trust.[65] At Laurens, Butler was eulogized as an immigrant who had proved more faithful than Read, a native son.[66] At five different meetings in Washington District the

[64] *American Remembrancer*, pp. 5-20.
[65] *Ibid.*, pp. 54-56.
[66] The meeting, held August 19, was reported in *City Gazette*, October 26, 1795. The same paper on October 6, and 15, had notices of similar meetings in St. Luke's Parish and at Georgetown on August 24, and September 14, respectively.

treaty was denounced in all its parts.[67] At Edgefield effigies of John Jay and Jacob Read were hung, then publicly burned with a copy of the treaty.[68] The members of the Franklin or Republican Society of Pendleton proclaimed their respect and esteem for Washington but felt that he had been misinformed or "wrongly advised." Jay was stigmatized but they rejoiced that he had produced an instrument that would show the real sentiment of the country. They proclaimed their sympathy for France and pledged their aid in bringing Jay to trial by any constitutional means available, as an example to all traitors thereafter of what will happen when they "sport with the interests and feelings of their countrymen."[69]

William Loughton Smith found comfort in the fact that less irritation followed the signing of the treaty by the President than had resulted from the ratification by the senate. In a letter to Oliver Wolcott, he expressed surprise at the earlier outburst of John Rutledge, who, Smith thought, had already repented his action. Edward Rutledge, however, was reported as still giving vent to "a most unconquerable aversion to the British nation." Smith professed to see signs of greater satisfaction with the treaty on the part of the people of the state.[70] Occasionally the newspapers themselves reflected a less violent attitude. In October, a letter signed "Senex," stated that the town of Charleston was sick of the Jay Treaty. The writer believed that correspondents wrote to attract attention and sus-

[67] Meetings held in September, were reported in the *City Gazette*, October 27, 1795.

[68] The demonstrations took place on September 12, and were reported in *City Gazette*, October 20, 1795.

[69] *City Gazette*, October 28, 1795, report of meeting held September 16. Jefferson wrote Edward Rutledge, November 30, 1795, "I join with you in thinking the treaty an execrable thing." Ford, *Writings of Jefferson*, VII, 40.

[70] George Gibbs, *Memoirs of the Administration of Washington and John Adams, Edited from the Papers of Oliver Wolcott, Secretary of the Treasury* (New York: 1846), I, 230-231. Perhaps Smith was less certain of the change in attitude when he learned that he, John Jay, John Adams, Timothy Pickering, Jacob Read and "His Satanic Majesty," all supposedly connected with the despised treaty, were hung in effigy "the whole day, polluted by every mark of indignity, and, in the evening, were carried off to Federal green, where they were burnt." Fraser, *Reminiscences*, p. 45.

JEFFERSONIAN DEMOCRACY IN S. C.   87

pected that some wrote on both sides.[71] Such a view, however, was not held by the state house of representatives, for on December 8, that body passed a resolution declaring that the President and the senate had been mistaken in their right to ratify the treaty.[72] Three days later it was further voted that the document was "Highly injurious to the General Interests of the Said [United] States."[73] The South Carolina senate, by a tie vote, declined to consider a resolution thanking Butler for voting against ratification.[74]

One of the state's representatives in Congress, Robert Goodloe Harper, who was soon to become one of the most prominent Federalists, felt that he should inform his constituents why he favored the treaty.[75] Some parts of his defense

[71] *City Gazette,* October 16, 1795.
[72] *Ibid.,* December 22, 1795.
[73] S. C. House Journal, December 11, 1795.
[74] S. C. Senate Journal, December 18, 1795.
[75] In his earlier public career, Harper had actively supported the reform of the basis of representation in the South Carolina legislature. In fact, he has been accused of belonging to the Jacobin Club of Charleston for a time. Thomas, *Reminiscences,* I, 32-33. The statement of Thomas was written many years later. When fellow congressmen in 1798 charged Harper with conduct inconsistent with his earlier radical inclinations, he insisted that his alleged membership in the Jacobin Club was "one of those falsehoods of party, which, though known to be unfounded is still repeated." He did admit, however, that as a young practitioner in Charleston desirous of making acquaintances and procuring business he had joined an organization called "a Patriotic society." Along with seven or eight other young practitioners he "attended one or two meetings; but finding it composed of persons from whose society much improvement could not be expected, they never went afterwards; and so anti-Jacobin was their conduct considered, that they merited and received expulsion from the society." In the early days of the French Revolution, he had sympathized, but in 1794 and later he came to understand that the principal actors were "A set of worthless scoundrels and mad-headed enthusiasts, who, in endeavoring to reduce their fallacious schemes to practice, have introduced more calamities into the world than ages of good government will be able to cure." *Annals of Congress,* 5th Cong., 2nd Sess. (March 29, 1798), pp. 1354-1355.

When Harper had taken his seat in Congress in 1795, he had a letter of introduction from Pierce Butler to James Madison. Writing directly to Madison, Butler stated that Harper had entreated so earnestly for the introduction that he could not deny him. Moreover, he thought that it might be a means of "keeping him right." Butler admitted only "slender" acquaintance with Harper but thought that from appearance

were daring, for a politician, almost to the point of recklessness. From the beginning, Harper said, he had been led toward the treaty because of the character of John Jay and Thomas Pinckney, who had approved it. Furthermore, Washington had supported it. But before making up his mind he had talked with both friends and opponents of the document. Finally he had decided in its favor. Harper then proceeded to refute the arguments of those in opposition. If the appointment of Jay while he was Chief Justice were unconstitutional, let impeachment proceedings be brought. Harper denied that the treaty was hostile to France. His support had been given with the full knowledge that it was contrary to the views of many of his constituents. If they approved his independent character, his opposition to their desires when he thought he was right, he would appreciate reelection. He added a warning, though, that his course in the future would be the same as it had been in the past.[76] To Harper's communications in support of the treaty, some of his constituents replied in April. At a public meeting at Newberry a committee was chosen by ballot to express the sentiments of the group. The committee reported that they were not in full sympathy with the treaty, that they thought it better to have such a treaty than to go to war, but that they were not certain that armed conflict was the only alternative. Harper was commended, however, for not changing his opinion when he was told that nine tenths of his constituents were opposed to the treaty.[77] "An American,"

---

he seemed to be very ambitious, polite and generous in feelings. He seemed, however, to be a man to whom one would not tell confidences on short association and a person "liable to impressions, and apt to be hurried away by the feelings of the moment." A few months later, Butler apologized to Madison for having made the introduction. Madison Papers, January 23, June 12, 1795.

[76] Robert Goodloe Harper, *Select Works of Robert Goodloe Harper: Consisting of Speeches on Political and Forensic Subjects with the Answer Drawn up by Him to the Articles of Impeachment against Judge Chase, and Sundry Political Tracts from the Original and Carefully Revised* (Baltimore: 1814), I, 1-43. Only one volume of the set was ever published. The defense was originally in the form of an address to his constituents, dated Philadelphia, December 17, 1795.

[77] S. C. *State Gazette*, May 16, 1796. The meeting was held April 2. Harper was reelected in 1796 and 1798.

writing in the *Columbian Herald,* approved the treaty and resented the calling of those favoring it "English, speculators or striped persons." As to the house of the legislature that condemned it, he did not attach much weight to the opinions of about half its members, not more than he would to a decision reached at a coffee house. The statement frequently made that the document was opposed in all states except Connecticut was not justified, for the "American" had talked to a man who had traveled widely and who told him that the majority of the people elsewhere resented the actions that had been taken in South Carolina.[78]

When Congress convened in December, 1795, Butler and Read were again on opposing sides. The former stoutly attacked the provision of the proposed reply to the President's message praising his firmness in preserving the peace of the nation. For his part, Butler could not see any firmness, except in opposition to France or against the will of the people of the United States. The Jay Treaty again came up for discussion. Read regretted that he must differ with his colleagues and many citizens of his state, but he felt that the treaty, by preventing war, had shown itself worthy of support. A majority of the people of South Carolina probably opposed the treaty, but he did not think that to be true elsewhere. Read further stated that in minor matters he would bow to his constituents but on great national issues he considered himself "a Senator for the Union."[79] In the house of representatives, even Harper objected to a very laudatory reply to the President's message.[80]

In the long and heated debate that developed over the question as to whether the house of representatives could constitutionally call upon the President for papers and additional information regarding a treaty, Harper and Smith were among the leading speakers against such a right. The other four South Carolina representatives, while they said little, voted with the

[78] *Columbian Herald,* January 19, 1796.

[79] *Annals of Congress,* 4th Cong., 1st Sess. Senate (December 11, 1795), pp. 17-20. The reply under discussion passed 14 to 8, Read favoring and Butler opposing.

[80] *Ibid.,* House (December 15, 1795), pp. 144-145. The proposed reply was recommitted, to be passed the next day in a modified form.

majority in asking for the additional information. When Washington declined to send the material requested on the ground that the consent of the house of representatives to a treaty was not necessary and that the only use that body could make of such information was for impeachment purposes, which had not been mentioned, all of the South Carolinians in the house except Harper and Smith, voted that it was not necessary for them to state why they desired the President to send information bearing on a subject upon which they as members of Congress were constitutionally empowered to act.[81]

Just before the storm accompanying the Jay Treaty broke upon the country, President Washington asked John Rutledge to become Chief Justice of the United States Supreme Court.[82] When Rutledge's severe denunciation of the treaty became known, the anger of the most extreme Federalists knew no bounds. Wolcott, in a letter to Hamilton, asked

What must the British government think of the United States, when they find the treaty clogged with one condition by the senate, with another by the President, no answer given in a precise form after forty days, no minister in that country to take up negociations proposed by ourselves, the country rising into flames, their minister's house insulted by a mob, their flag dragged through the streets as in Charleston, and burnt before the doors of their consul, a driveller and a fool appointed Chief-Justice? Can they believe that we desire peace? I shall take immediate measures with two of my colleagues this very day. They are firm and honest men, we will if possible, to use a French term, "save our country."[83]

[81] The debate took up much of the time for a month, March 7-April 7, 1796. *Annals of Congress,* 4th Cong., 1st Sess., pp. 426-783, 939-1291; votes on pp. 759, 768-769, 1291. On March 10, Hamilton wrote Smith advising him that the house of representatives did not have powers on the question of treaties. It could not refuse to provide money for carrying a treaty into operation. The members could deliberate only on the "mode of raising and appropriating the money." Lodge, *Works of Hamilton,* X, 147-148.

[82] Washington's letter acknowledging the acceptance is reprinted in Jared Sparks, ed., *The Writings of George Washington* (Boston: 1837), XI, 33-34. The commission was to be dated July 1, 1795, the date upon which Jay's resignation took effect, but it would remain at the seat of government until Rutledge's arrival.

[83] Gibbs, *Memoirs of the Administrations of Washington and Adams,* I, 220.

JEFFERSONIAN DEMOCRACY IN S. C.

In correspondence with Rufus King, Hamilton sought to lay the basis for the rejection of Rutledge on other grounds. For his part, he was willing to forget the South Carolinian's "imprudent sally upon a certain occasion." But the other rumors concerning mental derangement, "sottish" habits and improper conduct in pecuniary transactions should be investigated. The reports that had come to him recently weighed heavily upon his mind against Rutledge.[84] To Jefferson and other Republicans there could be but one reason for the refusal to confirm the nomination.

The rejection of Mr. Rutledge by the Senate is a bold thing, because they cannot pretend any objection to him but his disapprobation of the treaty. It is of course a declaration that they will receive none but tories hereafter into any department of the government.[85]

Whether the United States senate declined to confirm the nomination of John Rutledge as Chief Justice because of his severe criticism of the Jay Treaty or was at least partially in-

[84] John C. Hamilton, ed., *The Works of Alexander Hamilton* (New York: 1851), VI, 76-77. This letter was written December 14, several months after other Federalists had stated their opposition to the confirmation of Rutledge because of his attack on the Jay Treaty. There had not been other rumors then.

[85] Letter of Jefferson to W. B. Giles, December 31, 1795. Ford, *Writings of Jefferson*, VII, 44. The use of this as an issue by the Republicans was feared by Ralph Izard. On November 17, 1795, he wrote Senator Jacob Read urging him to do everything in his power to get Rutledge confirmed. No one had been "more afflicted" than he at the part taken by him in opposing the treaty. It was Izard's opinion that, after the death of his wife, Rutledge's mind was "frequently so much deranged, as to be in a great measure deprived of his senses" and that "he was in that situation when the Treaty was under consideration." Izard had been in his company frequently since then and found him normal again. He felt that "no man in the United States would execute the office of Chief Justice with more ability and integrity than he would." In politics Izard was apparently more alarmed about what the result would be in South Carolina than elsewhere. "The minds of the people in this State begin to be calmed, and I wish that everything may be avoided which will be likely to rekindle the flame which has already given us too much trouble." However, he added, "My regard for Mr. Rutledge and my love for tranquillity would not have induced me to write to you on this subject, if I were not perfectly convinced of the propriety of confirming the appointment." Letter reprinted in *Charleston Year Book*, 1886.

fluenced by the rumors concerning his mental condition, is not entirely clear. It would hardly be an exaggeration, however, to say that the senators, smarting from the painful verbal lashing they had received throughout the country and in South Carolina in particular, were not loath to punish the man who had been among the most cutting in his remarks. The Republicans had an issue which they could use effectively. Indeed many South Carolina Federalists must have come to distrust the leadership of a party, even though they called it their own, that could force upon them a treaty they thought injurious to their interests and in addition refuse to confirm the nomination of a man whom they knew and respected.

4. THE MORE SATISFACTORY TREATY OF THOMAS PINCKNEY

While the people of the United States were excited over the Treaty of 1794 between the United States and Great Britain, Thomas Pinckney negotiated the Treaty of San Lorenzo, or as it is more commonly called, Pinckney's Treaty. Don Manuel de Godoy had intimated that a special envoy to Spain would be welcome. It has been said that the king asked for a gentleman and Washington sent him Thomas Pinckney. Before choosing the latter, however, the President offered the mission to Thomas Jefferson and Patrick Henry, both of whom declined.[86] During the early 1790's the people of what was then the West were extremely restless because of the uncertainties pertaining to the control of the Mississippi River and its valley. Little hope was entertained by Washington that even a special mission to Spain could solve the problem satisfactorily; but, realizing the seriousness of the situation, the President accepted Godoy's invitation.

Fortunately for Pinckney, events in Europe, about which he did not know, had prepared the way for a successful mission. In violation of Spain's treaty of 1793 with England, Godoy had recently made a separate peace with France at Bâle; conse-

[86] Ford, *Writings of Washington*, XII, 459. The offer to Jefferson was made August 24, 1794; his reply is dated September 7. It would be evident from these dates, if there were no other evidence, that the choice of Pinckney as the envoy to Spain was not directly the result of the mission of Jay to England.

JEFFERSONIAN DEMOCRACY IN S. C.

quently, trouble with Great Britain was expected soon. Godoy believed the British would attack Spain in the New World, probably in the vicinity of the Gulf of Mexico, in which event the friendship of the United States would be essential. An alliance was still preferable, but, in any case neutrality, must be assured. In other words, Thomas Pinckney must be satisfied. Thus, it is doubtful if he gained anything that the Spanish minister was not prepared to give already. This fact, however, does not necessarily detract from the firmness or the creditability that characterized Pinckney's conduct. The importance of the treaty finally drafted has been well summarized by Whitaker.

It was a victory not only of the United States over Spain, but also for the expansionists in the United States over the particularists, both Eastern and Western. It appeased frontier discontent, gave a mortal blow to separatism, and secured the Union from a serious menace to its integrity. It completed the work done by Jay's treaty and established the frontiers claimed by the United States at the end of the Revolution; and yet it did more than Jay's treaty, for the rights that it established had hitherto rested on a dubious legal basis. By terminating a dangerous controversy and by securing the American government's terms without the formation of the alliance which Spain had long required as the price of concessions, the treaty carried one step further the government's policy of cutting loose from the European state system; a policy which, in retrospect, seems a kind of stripping for action in the western hemisphere. Finally, by confirming the United States in the possession of virtually the whole of the east bank of the Mississippi and by validating the Americans' claim to the free navigation of that river, the treaty laid a substantial foundation for the further extension of the new republic in North America.[87]

In view of the dissatisfaction in South Carolina over the supplanting of Pinckney in England by Jay and the opportunity for the comparison of the two treaties, it is surprising that greater use was not made as political material of the relative merits of the two documents. Perhaps it was remembered that Pinckney was a Federalist, that he had approved

[87] Arthur Preston Whitaker, *The Spanish-American Frontier: 1783-1795* (New York: Houghton Mifflin, 1927), p. 222. Of interest also is Bemis, *Pinckney's Treaty.*

the Jay Treaty, and that he himself had supplanted the regular American minister in Spain. At any rate, the newspapers of his own state were sparing in the references made to the treaty he had formed.[88] While still in Spain Pinckney wrote Washington asking his recall. In a few months he would have been away four years, as long as he felt that he could give to foreign service at that time. Washington expressed great regret at Pinckney's decision, but stated that under the circumstances he would yield to his desires.[89]

As may be inferred from the space given to it above, the Jay Treaty overshadowed other issues in the development of party politics in South Carolina during the year 1795. There are, however, a few other details that might be mentioned in the story of that year. Close communication was kept between South Carolina party leaders and those of other states. Butler warned Madison of an "underhand game, playing with a view of injuring your unspotted character."[90] The position of Secretary of State was offered to Charles Cotesworth Pinckney, but he declined on the plea that his personal affairs were not yet in such a condition as to permit him to leave South Carolina.[91] While Washington was searching for someone to fill the place offered to Pinckney, he asked the advice of Hamilton concerning certain possibilities. The latter spoke highly of the "abilities, information, and industry, and integrity" of William Loughton Smith; he doubted, however, the advisability of appointing one against whom there were such prejudices because

[88] There were a few letters like that of "An American," who compared the two treaties and contended that a much better treaty would have been made between the United States and Great Britain if Pinckney, instead of Jay, had been the negotiator. He would never have yielded as Jay did in regard to the things his country demanded. *City Gazette*, April 2, 1796.
[89] Ford, *Writings of Washington*, XIV, 169-172.
[90] Madison Papers, August 21, 1795.
[91] Ford, *Writings of Washington*, XIII, 95-97. The previous year, Pinckney had been asked if he would accept the office of Secretary of War in the event of the expected retirement of the man then holding that office. Pinckney had stated his preference for that office above all others, except in case of war when he would rather be in the field. The offer was then made but he was forced to decline on account of personal affairs.

of his "uncomfortable temper" and his very strong inclinations toward the British. Moreover, it was "very important that he should not now be removed from the House of Representatives."[92]

5. REPUBLICAN VICTORIES IN 1796

The political events of 1796 centered around the election of that year, which was to be the first real test of the strength of the parties then in the process of formation. Early in the year the members of both parties began searching for candidates. Even before Thomas Pinckney returned to America, Rufus King and Alexander Hamilton were discussing him as a possible choice for one of the positions. King thought that Pinckney was already popular in the South and that the recent treaty would gain for him the support of the West. Hamilton had been thinking of Patrick Henry as a popular candidate, but hoped that some way would be found to eliminate him so that they would be "at full liberty to take up Pinckney."[93] In a letter to his father-in-law a few days later, William Loughton Smith reported that both parties were unsettled as to Vice-Presidential nominees. Among the Republicans mentioned were Aaron Burr, Pierce Butler and Chancellor Robert Livingston. The only objection to Butler was that both he and Jefferson, who was considered the best choice for President, were from the South. Livingston probably stood highest, having gained popularity because of his articles against the Jay Treaty. Burr was thought to be unsteady in politics and might possibly go over to the other side. Many believed that the two highest in the final election would be Adams and Jefferson and that neither would serve as Vice-President. Thus the question as to whether there would be a Vice-President at all was likely to become an issue.[94]

Jefferson thought the Federalists were playing with Patrick Henry, offering him everything they knew he would not accept.

[92] Hamilton, *Works of Hamilton*, VI, 61-62.
[93] *Ibid.*, VI, 113-114. King's letter was dated May 2, 1796, Hamilton's, May 4.
[94] U. B. Phillips, ed., "South Carolina Federalist Correspondence, 1789-1797," *American Historical Review*, XIV, p. 780. The letter was to Ralph Izard.

They hoped to "produce a schism" in Virginia. Thomas Pinckney was being brought forth, not because of his principles but to get the support of the South. Jefferson told Madison he wished he had been chosen as the candidate instead of himself; but, since he was in the race, he hoped he would come out second or third. Jefferson did not think that the Eastern states would run the risk of having Pinckney elected instead of Adams. They would probably throw their second votes away.[95]

By November, Smith was beginning to fear the outcome of the election. So many tales had been circulated in Pennsylvania that Jefferson would likely get the votes of that state. One or two votes in South Carolina, he thought, might save the election for Adams. But he was frightened by the report that Edward Rutledge would not vote for Adams if he were an elector. There was still the hope that Jefferson's desire for emancipation would ruin him in the South; but Smith wished someone would intimate to Edward Rutledge, who was thought to desire the election of Pinckney, that any votes for Jefferson in South Carolina would cause the latter to receive more votes than his favorite candidate. Rutledge should be brought to support Adams if possible, but by all means he must be kept from voting for Jefferson.[96] Harper found Jefferson popular in both the upper and the lower parts of South Carolina, but he thought Adams might get a few electoral votes. If the latter carried Pennsylvania he would win. Harper was more concerned about Thomas Pinckney than any of the other candidates. Rutledge or others might persuade him that he was being used merely to split the Southern vote, and cause him to withdraw. Such was not the case, for he had learned from "the most certain Knowledge" that Pinckney was being brought out as a Presidential instead of a Vice-Presidential candidate.[97]

[95] *Jefferson's Works,* Def. Ed., IX, 349 and Ford, *Works of Jefferson,* VII, 91.
[96] "S. C. Federalist Correspondence," 781-785.
[97] In his article on Adams in 1800, Hamilton admitted that he had hoped that Adams and Pinckney would have been supported equally in 1796 and that "casual accessions of votes in favor of one or the other" would have brought about the election of Pinckney. The chief object of the Federalists then, he said, had been to defeat Jefferson; and

The main problem was to keep him in the race, for in South Carolina the contest was not between Pinckney and Adams but Pinckney and Jefferson. Only Pinckney or his friends could keep him from being elected.[98]

In the meantime discussions were going on in South Carolina as to the qualifications of the various candidates. Pinckney's record, of course, was well known. Adams and Jefferson had been in public life long enough for many to know a great deal about them, but in the heat of the campaign new stories were circulated about both. The publishers of the *City Gazette* reported that one of their correspondents who was very familiar with conditions in Virginia informed them that if Jefferson had been less qualified for the Presidency he would not have received so much opposition in his own state. He would have been more popular if he had been present at more cock fights, horse races and county courts.[99] A person signing himself "Z" objected to the statement of "Phocian," another correspondent, that Jefferson's philosophical leanings would unfit him for the Presidency. His philosophy had not interfered with his already long and successful public career. Still another writer, under the signature of "A. B.," mentioned Adams's leanings toward monarchy, heredity and wealth and attacked "Phocian" for attempting to lead the people astray by ridiculing Jefferson's philosophical opinions. He hoped that the South Carolina electors would vote for Jefferson and Thomas Pinckney.[100]

The South Carolina legislature felt that the electors should be chosen according to whether they would support Jefferson or Adams, for there were two groups of electors known by the names of these two candidates. It was a question as to who would vote for Jefferson and Pinckney or Adams and Pinckney. It was evident, therefore, that party lines were still not hard and fast when men of opposite parties could be the choice of

---

Pinckney was better fitted for the Presidency than Adams. Lodge, *Works of Hamilton,* VII, 319-320.

[98] Harper to Izard, November 4, 1796. "S. C. Federalists Correspondence," 782-783.

[99] *City Gazette,* November 7, 1796.

[100] *Ibid.,* November 10, 11, 1796.

the same electors. The difference between the votes in the legislature for the "Jefferson ticket" and for the "Adams ticket" did show, however, a rather obvious victory for the Republicans. Pinckney was clearly stronger than the Federalist party. This was largely because he was a native son and was not an extreme partisan.[101]

The contest for governor was confused for a while. The resignation of Pierce Butler from the United States senate led many to suppose that he expected the governorship. John Ewing Colhoun and others had supporters.[102] When it became known that Butler was not a candidate, Charles Pinckney again offered for governor instead of the United States senate and was chosen by the legislature for his third term.[103] Having been out of Congress for a few years, Thomas Sumter was returned by the voters of Camden District in the election of 1796.[104]

[101] S. C. House Journal, December 6, 1796. The Jefferson electors and their vote in the legislature were as follows: Edward Rutledge, 113; Andrew Pickens, 112; John Matthews, 112; Thomas Taylor, 110; Arthur Simkins, 110; John Rutledge, Jr., 109; John Chesnut, 109; and William Thomas, 109. The "Adams ticket" with their votes were Arnold Vanderhorst, 31; H. W. DeSaussure, 29; Robert Barnwell, 28; William A. Washington, 28; David Ramsay, 28; General Barnwell, 28; Nathaniel Russel, 28; and John Bull, 24. *City Gazette*, December 10, 1796.

[102] See sketch of Colhoun by A. S. Salley in *S. C. Historical and Genealogical Magazine*, VII, 153-154. In a letter to Izard November 4, 1796, Harper spoke of the great confusion as to the outcome of the state as well as federal contests in South Carolina. "S. C. Federalist Correspondence," pp. 783-784.

[103] *Columbian Herald*, December 12, 1796. S. C. House Journal, December 8, 1796. The House Journal, December 3, listed Butler as having qualified as a member from the District of Prince William. The same Journal on December 10, recorded the denial by the house of a memorial from Butler requesting the payment in specie of a debt incurred by the public use of indigo belonging to him in 1782. It was stated that he had refused to accept indents offered him on ground that his was a special contract. The house decided to make no discriminations in the settlement of accounts contracted during the war. Butler was to be offered indents only.

[104] In vol. II of the small collection of Sumter papers in the Library of Congress is a broadside used by Sumter in 1796. He deeply resented his defeat in the previous election because of rumors spread while he was away in Congress. Sumter and Lemuel Benton were seasoned Republicans who would be members of the Fifth Congress. William

After the outcome of the election throughout the nation was known, Harper wrote a letter to his constituents. Pinckney, he said, had been his first choice, Adams his second. Jefferson was fitted to be professor in a college, president of a philosophical society or even Secretary of State, but not to be "the first magistrate in a great nation." He deliberated when he ought to act and lacked decision when he did act. It was not proper for a President to favor one nation as Jefferson did France.[105] For a time after the election, John Adams did not know of the attempt to have Pinckney chosen instead of himself. When the news did come to him in a convincing manner, he was extremely bitter. In his opinion Pinckney, whom he referred to as "an unknown being," was out of the question for the Presidency. He had no respect for a people who would be willing, under an elective government, to be ruled by a Pinckney when there was such a large number of superior characters.[106] Edward Rutledge found great satisfaction in Jefferson's decision to serve as Vice-President, even though he were "well fitted and deserving of the first office." Jefferson had acted like himself and put his "calumniators to Silence." Such was the "emanation of a great soul, the recollection of such conduct will be the source of perpetual satisfaction."[107]

Thus in the initial nation-wide test of the first two political parties, South Carolina voted decidedly for the party of Jefferson. Before another election came new political complications developed, the discussion of which must be reserved for the next chapter.

Smith of Pinckney District was a newcomer to the ranks of the Republicans in Congress. John Rutledge, Jr., leaned toward the Republicans in 1796 but later became an extreme Federalist. The latter party retained William Loughton Smith and Robert Goodloe Harper. The two senators from South Carolina were still members of opposite parties—Jacob Read, Federalist; John Hunter, elected in 1796, Republican. Read was not voted upon that year.

[105] Photostat copy in Library of Congress. The letter is dated January 5, 1797.

[106] Adams, *Works of Adams*, VII, 524, 534-536.

[107] Jefferson Papers, May 4, 1797.

CHAPTER V

TEMPORARY FEDERALIST RECOVERY, 1796-1799

1. "The X. Y. Z." Affair and the Struggle over Preparedness

In August, 1796, President Washington had asked Charles Cotesworth Pinckney to become minister plenipotentiary to France. Because of his need for a man "well attached to the government of his own country and not obnoxious to the one to which he is sent," Washington took the liberty of calling upon him again in spite of his past declinations. Pinckney replied that, though his private affairs were not in the proper order, he would accept and proceed to Philadelphia by the first vessel.[1]

Events which had occurred prior to Pinckney's appointment were not such as to insure his friendly reception in France or facilitate the performance of his duties as American minister. His predecessor, James Monroe, having arrived at a time when the French Convention was so preoccupied with a struggle for existence, had not been given an immediate welcome. But Monroe's aggressive nature and fraternal attitude soon secured for him a hearing before the Convention itself. Thereafter his relations with the French government were most friendly. In the meantime, however, developments in the United States and in Great Britain caused the seemingly pro-French activities of Monroe to be disapproved of by his own government. John Jay had been sent to England; Timothy Pickering had succeeded Randolph as Secretary of State; and the more extreme Federalists were gaining greater influence over Washington. Rumors regarding Jay's negotiations in England disturbed Monroe, but, relying on the instructions given him by Ran-

[1] Ford, *Writings of Washington*, XIII, 237-239. The letter of Washington is dated July 8, 1796, that of Pinckney, July 27.

dolph, he assured the French that the treaty being drawn up in London would not in any way conflict with previous agreements between the United States and France. When the publication of the Jay Treaty revealed the inclusion of a clause permitting the seizure of American goods on the way to France, provided the British paid for them, it could hardly be denied that this at least modified the preferential treatment promised by the United States in 1778. Such an apparent discrepancy could not be satisfactorily explained away by citing another provision stating that the new conditions were not to interfere with obligations of preexisting treaties. Failing to defend the Jay Treaty as vigorously as Pickering ordered, Monroe was accused of openly sympathizing with the French and promising a change in policy if the Republicans won in the approaching Presidential election. Considering such conduct unpardonable, the Federalist prevailed upon Washington to recall him in August, 1796. As already indicated, Charles Cotesworth Pinckney was sent to succeed him.[2]

Except for the abnormal conditions in France at the time, Pinckney would have been a highly acceptable minister. Being moderate in his Federalism and of a more considerate attitude toward the French than the Hamilton and Pickering group, he probably would have had a successful mission even during the French Revolution had not the events already related precluded the favorable reception of anyone the United States might send.[3] Indeed, it is doubtful if even a Republican, except

[2] The details of this affair and subsequent events may be followed in general histories of the United States or of the diplomacy of the United States. Channing's treatment in his *History of the United States*, IV, 176-209, is on the whole good. However, his characterization of Charles Cotesworth Pinckney (p. 178) as a "stiff-necked" Federalist, is inaccurate. At least he was not "stiffnecked" enough for Hamilton, who professed the utmost confidence in his integrity but was afraid of his "too much French leaning." This statement of Hamilton was made even after the refusal of the French to receive Pinckney. Hamilton, *Works of Hamilton*, VI, 247.

[3] In regard to Pinckney's moderate Federalism, see also the opinion of Wolcott in Gibbs, *Administrations of Washington and Adams*, I, 487; Hamilton, *Works of Hamilton*, VI, 223. According to Wolcott, Pinckney was so moderate as to be considered a man of "neutral politics."

Jefferson or perhaps a few others, could have gained immediate recognition at that time. In the face of the Directory's failure to recognize him and the cordial farewell to Monroe, Pinckney's conduct was dignified; there is little evidence that he was extremely excited or even greatly surprised. Knowing that changes took place rapidly in French politics, he retired to Amsterdam whence he carried on an active correspondence in an effort to obtain recognition and reception at Paris. After a time, evidence indicated that his labors were to be rewarded; but before going further into this situation, happenings in America must be discussed.[4]

Washington had been succeeded by Adams and party feeling as well as factionalism among the Federalists had become more intense. But the first reaction to the rejection of Pinckney was not extreme on the part of either political group. Some of the Republicans skillfully explained the situation by saying that the "Directory, having suspended their ordinary minister here, could not receive an ordinary minister from the United States." This nation should deal with France as it had with Great Britain and send an "Envoy Extraordinary." In reply to an inquiry from Adams, Wolcott declared that a rupture with France was not unavoidable.[5]

In South Carolina some slight changes in attitude toward France had taken place. The publishers of the *South Carolina State Gazette* had gradually shifted from extreme partisanship toward France to a policy of severe criticism.[6] Thereafter condemnations of the French were frequently printed in their newspaper. The *City Gazette* remained friendly to France and readily published letters from her supporters. In April, French sympathizers in Charleston were greatly offended when applause greeted the singing of a song of the exploits of the British over the French. One of them wrote "An Address to the French and American Patriots," asserting that the British had never won over his countrymen "on an equal footing" and

[4] A satisfactory brief discussion of Pinckney's predicament is given in Louis Martin Sears, *A History of American Foreign Relations* (New York: Thomas Y. Crowell, 1927), pp. 78-79.
[5] Gibbs, *Administrations of Washington and Adams*, I, 505.
[6] *S. C. State Gazette*, April 14, 17, 21, 1797.

JEFFERSONIAN DEMOCRACY IN S. C.   103

warning the Americans to fear the indignant nation that had brought their country into being. Soon there were two replies to this communication, one expressing delight that the French were so treated, the other explaining that the applause was for the way the song had been sung and not for the exploits of the British.[7] In the election of 1796 the voters of South Carolina had chosen to represent them in the federal house of representatives two Federalists, two Republicans and two who were temporarily non-partisan but who, the voters thought, had Republican leanings. Before long, each party had gained one of the two last mentioned, thereby evenly dividing the representatives between the two parties.[8] The senators were also divided—John Hunter, a Republican, and Jacob Read, a Federalist. Thus, when all were present, an evenly divided vote might be expected from South Carolina's representatives in both houses of Congress on political questions.[9] From the standpoint of aggressiveness in debate, William Loughton Smith, Harper and Rutledge excelled their three Republican opponents. William Loughton Smith had been a member of all Congresses under

[7] *Ibid.,* April 15, 16, 1797.
[8] The Federalists were Harper and William Loughton Smith; the Republicans were Sumter and Benton; the supposedly non-partisans were John Rutledge, Jr., and William Smith of Pinckney District. The two Smiths have been confused in American history. Up until about this time the first one mentioned had also been known as William Smith but he began adding his mother's name Loughton possibly to distinguish himself from others with the same name. In this study, the full name has been given from the first to avoid confusion. Rutledge had been enough Republican a few months before to serve on the "Jefferson ticket" of Presidential electors, but on account of the rejection of Charles Cotesworth Pinckney and other developments early in 1797 he joined the Federalists and became one of their most ardent members. Both parties made a bid for William Smith. William Loughton Smith and Rutledge attempted to enlist him but Sumter got him a seat between himself and other Republicans thereby keeping him from joining the Federalists. In May W. L. Smith was writing Izard that his attempts had failed and referring to his "namesake" as a "thin puritanical Methodist," a "great simpleton," and "composed of materials very unpromising." "S. C. Federalist Correspondence," p. 787.
[9] Lemuel Benton seemed to have the habit of appearing late. This gave the South Carolina Federalists a voting advantage before his arrival. For example, in the special session called by Adams to meet May 15, Benton did not get to Philadelphia till June 26. *Annals of Congress,* 5th Cong., 1st Sess. (June 26, 1797), p. 386.

the Constitution and must be listed as one of the two principal leaders of his party in the house. Robert Goodloe Harper had become perhaps the ablest debater and pamphleteer in that body. The latter's address to his constituents in May, 1797, on the relations between the United States and France was widely reprinted in this country and in Europe.[10]

The special session of the Fifth Congress called by President Adams as the result of the attitude of France toward Charles Cotesworth Pinckney convened on May 15, 1797. On the following day the President delivered an address in which he called upon Congress to join him in upholding the honor of the nation. A "permanent system of Naval Defense" and the general protection of American commerce at home and abroad were recommended. The house was urged to give careful consideration to the means of providing funds that would be necessary to make the nation secure. Although Adams did not think the United States should support, in a commercial way, either of the warring sides, he did believe it "an indispensible duty" of Congress to assert a positive tone in repelling "insinuations so derogatory to the honor, and aggressions so dangerous to the constitution, union and even independence of the nation." An inquiry into the cause of the French action was not necessary. The conduct of the United States had been "just and impartial to foreign nations." He pledged himself never to do anything that would "impair the national engagements" or surrender "in any manner the rights of the Government." God, the national legislature and the patriotism of the American people were called upon to sustain him in this declaration.[11]

Desiring to go into the causes of the French actions, the Republicans strongly opposed a firm reply to the President's message. William Loughton Smith upheld the Administration and opposed the discussion of causes. He severely criticized Nicholas of Virginia for referring to the Jay Treaty. Rutledge,

---

[10] This pamphlet is reported to have gone through at least seven American editions, fourteen British, one French and one Portuguese edition. Samuel Eliot Morrison, *The Life and Letters of Harrison Gray Otis, Federalist, 1765-1848* (Boston: Houghton Mifflin, 1913), I, 61, 67.

[11] *Annals of Congress*, 5th Cong., 1st Sess. (May 16, 1797), pp. 54-59.

who had been a sort of "silent member" of the committee that drew up the proposed reply, would not oppose amendments that did not change the substance.[12] Harper was uncompromising and extreme in his denunciation of the French, insisting that he desired firmness not because he wanted war but because he thought such a tone was necessary in order to preserve peace.[13] A moderate reply, he said, was not needed, for the President would do everything proper to conciliate the French. Smith spoke several times, still demanding firmness but asserting his desire for peace. Gallatin flatly said he did not believe that Smith wanted peace. Smith countered with the statement that even though Gallatin had expressed willingness to go to war in case France could not be satisfied through a moderate stand on the part of the United States, he did not believe him.[14] As the debate wore on Harper grew more intolerant of opposition. Following Samuel Smith of Maryland in the debate, he characterized the latter's speech as of the type he had learned to expect from him. A part of Samuel Smith's speech, which was in support of a moderate reply to the President's message, Harper declared, was indicative of his "want of sense and good manners."[15] Although they refrained from speaking, Sumter and William Smith supported all efforts to modify the tone toward France. Then on final passage, they voted against the whole reply itself. Benton had not yet arrived. Harper, Rutledge and William Loughton Smith, of course, favored the reply in its final form, which was still rather firm toward France.[16] In the senate Hunter opposed and Read favored approving the past conduct of the government in regard to foreign affairs and promising strong support in the future.[17]

The story of the voting and speaking on the question of preparedness is similar to that just recorded in regard to the reply to the President's message. For more than a month a vigorous fight was waged to increase the naval and military

[12] *Ibid.*, 5th Cong. (May 16, 22, 23, 1797), pp. 78-80, 98-99, 109-110.
[13] *Ibid.* (May 29, 1797), pp. 169-191.
[14] *Ibid.* (May 31, 1797), pp. 207-209.
[15] *Ibid.* (June 2, 1797), p. 223.
[16] *Ibid.* (June 2, 1797), pp. 233-234.
[17] *Ibid.*, Senate, May 23, 1797.

strength of the United States. William Loughton Smith and Harper led in the debate but were ably supported at times by Rutledge and representatives from other states. Again no speeches of Sumter or William Smith are recorded, but in every case where there is a record of votes, their names are found among those opposing the Federalists in their defense program. However, in spite of their hostile votes such measures as the completion of the three frigates—*the United States, Constitution* and *Constellation;* the authorization of the President to call out 80,000 militia; and the provision for the strengthening of fortifications were passed.[18] In the senate Read and Hunter again voted on opposite sides. In nearly every case the former supported and the latter opposed the program of preparedness.[19] On tax measures to finance the program the story of the conduct of the South Carolina representatives in both houses was the same, except that Benton had arrived to support his Republican colleagues, Sumter and William Smith.[20]

During the discussions in Congress the newspaper correspondents kept up the controversy, with the friends of France being more aggressive. Edward Rutledge wrote Jefferson that little foreign news had yet reached South Carolina.[21] The latter wrote Thomas Pinckney a very friendly letter, stating that his brother's conduct in France had met with "universal approbation." The French had been mistaken in their attitude toward him.[22] The letters in the South Carolina newspapers became heated indeed. Pierre Fran. Des Verneys boldly signed his name to a communication accusing the English of sending paid writers to America to bring about war against France by means of "their pens, impoisoned with obscenities and impostures." Articles which had recently appeared in the *South Carolina State*

[18] The more than a month long struggle over preparedness is recorded in *Annals of Congress*, 5th Cong., 1st Sess., beginning June 5, 1797, p. 239.

[19] *Annals of Congress*, 5th Cong., 1st Sess., Senate (June 8-27, 1797), pp. 18-30.

[20] *Ibid.* (July 5); and House (June 27-July 3, 1797), pp. 391, 430, 433, 443, 446-447.

[21] Jefferson Papers, May 19, 1797.

[22] Ford, *Writings of Jefferson*, VII, 127-130.

JEFFERSONIAN DEMOCRACY IN S. C. 107

Gazette under the signature of "Leonidas" and "Friend to Truth" were cited as examples of the type of contributions which might be expected from British propagandists. He received regularly the Paris papers, but he had not yet seen an article that contained "an insult on America."[23] "Americanus" severely denounced Harper for his alleged advocacy of alliance with Great Britain. Both the United States and England were commercial nations. The latter would be our rival and under no circumstances would she protect our commerce when in competition with hers even though there were an alliance. Great Britain was at the time merely interested in doing injury to the French by breaking up our friendly relations with that nation.[24] "A Farmer" wrote that there was a strong group in the United States desirous of stamping out republicanism. Those who cried the loudest in defense of the Constitution were really its worst enemies. If the United States went to war against France it meant an alliance with Great Britain which was really worse than the war, since it would be a step toward monarchy. The French were hated because they were republicans. He closed with the final stab that "Atheists and Jews have been converted to Christianity; but there are no instances of tories being converted to whigs."[25] Indicative of the interest of the people of the "back country" in the nation's affairs was the letter of "Repubesco" requesting the publishers of the *City Gazette* to include the "acts of the federal government" in the new weekly they were planning to begin.[26] Toward the close of the year there were some signs of decrease in party strife.[27]

But in the meantime what steps had been taken to restore diplomatic relations with France? No one could accuse John Adams of being a lover of France; but he did not want war, as did Pickering and other extreme Federalists. Realizing that war would be unwise at the time, Hamilton exerted his influ-

[23] *City Gazette*, June 1, 1797.   [24] *Ibid.*, June 24, 1797.
[25] *Ibid.*, July 29, 1797.   [26] *Ibid.*, November 21, 1797.
[27] An example of such an attitude is the unsigned article in the *City Gazette*, December 20, 1797, in which the writer said that it had not yet been proved that Jefferson or Madison were "very ignorant or supremely vicious"; nor had it been shown that there were no good aristocrats.

ence for peace. Strange as it may seem, independently, both Adams and Hamilton had been toying with the idea of sending to France a Republican leader like Jefferson or Madison;[28] to this the extreme Federalists in the cabinet would not agree. Likewise Madison and Jefferson were unwilling to undertake the mission. After much discussion a commission of three, finally composed of Pinckney, John Marshall and Elbridge Gerry, was chosen. Gerry was a close friend of Adams but a man with Republican inclinations.

Whatever may have been the chances of Pinckney's favorable reception a few weeks earlier, the moment at which the commissioners arrived in Paris was certainly not propitious. The recent elimination of moderates from the Directory, French naval reverses having been made up for by land victories, and the memories of the Jay Treaty and the Monroe episode, combined to make the government indifferent to the American representatives. After an initial meeting with Talleyrand the three commissioners discovered that further relations with the government must be through such secret agents as Hottenguer, Bellamy and Hauteval, who were later designated in communications to the United States senate as X, Y and Z. Before the American side of the issues would be discussed, Pinckney, Marshall and Gerry must apologize for President Adams's remarks concerning France in his message to Congress, make arrangements for a loan to France and present a "gift" to the Directory. Apparently the three gentlemen from the United States were not shocked by the terms proposed. They were familiar with the ways of diplomacy and knew what type of intrigue to expect in Paris at the time. There is little evidence that they were agitated by moral questions. Instead of shouting in a thunderous tone, "millions for defence, but not one cent for tribute," they considered the matter from a business and

---

[28] Hamilton favored a commission of three to go to France after the rejection of Pinckney. This group should be composed of Pinckney, Jefferson or Madison and a third Federalist to hold Pinckney in line and keep him from being too much influenced by the Republican member. Hamilton, *Works of Hamilton*, VI, 247. Adams' idea of sending Jefferson had already been mentioned to members of his cabinet and it seems that both they and Jefferson opposed it. Adams, *Works of Adams*, VIII, 538.

JEFFERSONIAN DEMOCRACY IN S. C. 109

legal view. The main obstacle from their standpoint was the breach of neutrality involved in the loaning of money to France. But even in that case, obviating possibilities were discussed unsuccessfully. After dilly-dallying proceedings for some time the commissioners were asked again whether they proposed to make the gift of money. Apparently their previous answers had not been definite enough to satisfy the agents of Talleyrand. If not, Pinckney's reply, "No, no; not a sixpence," should have been sufficiently categorical.[29]

By this time the American Commissioners had decided that they might as well force the issue. Whereupon Talleyrand admitted that the Directory was unwilling to treat with two of them, but that further negotiations might be carried on with the third member of their group, "whose opinions, presumed to be more impartial, promise in the course of the explanation more of that reciprocal confidence which is indispensable." Marshall prepared to return to the United States. Pinckney, after some difficulty, secured permission to carry his daughter, who was ill, to the southern part of France. Thinking that he might prevent war and possibly negotiate a treaty, Gerry indiscreetly decided to continue the discussion with the French government.[30]

In the meantime, the government of the United States was marking time. When Adams learned that the ministers were still being ignored officially, he informed Congress without waiting to learn the full details contained in the remainder of the despatches. Pickering was ready to declare war immedi-

[29] The phrase "Millions for defence, but not one cent for tribute" seems to have been coined by Robert Goodloe Harper at a public meeting in America. It was attributed to Pinckney, however, and became a Federalist slogan. *S. C. Historical and Genealogical Magazine*, I, 100-103. Wallace, *History of S. C.*, II, 354. *American State Papers, Foreign Relations* (Washington: 1833), II, 161.

[30] Documents relating to this affair are reprinted in *American State Papers, Foreign Relations*, II, 169-182. Satisfactory general treatments may be found in Sears, *American Foreign Relations*, 79-82; John Spencer Bassett, "The Federalist System 1789-1801," *The American Nation: A History*, Vol. XI (New York: Harper & Brothers, 1906), pp. 230-234; and Channing, *History of the U. S.*, IV, 181-189. These works may be referred to for further details in this chapter on the relations with France.

ately, but again he and the other extremists were restrained by Adams and Hamilton. John Rutledge, Jr., and Harrison Gray Otis took war for granted and began to plan the most effective means of framing legislation so as to get the support of both the South and the East.[31] Rutledge argued in Congress that there was no need to wait for additional communications from the President before taking defensive measures; on the other hand, the Republicans contended that nothing should be done until the complete details were known. Thomas Pinckney, who had succeeded William Loughton Smith in the house following the appointment of the latter as minister to Portugal,[32] thought that the country should be put in a state of defense but was unwilling to impeach the motives of those who desired further information. He believed that all desired peace. Giles differed with Pinckney in regard to peace, for he was convinced that

[31] Jefferson wrote in the *Anas,* under date of March 11, 1798, an account of such a discussion between Rutledge and Otis, reported to him by Senator John Hunter, who lodged with Rutledge.

[32] William Loughton Smith had gone to Portugal the previous summer. In 1800 he was transferred to Spain but returned to America in 1801. Some of his letters to Pickering are reprinted in *S. C. Historical and Genealogical Magazine,* XXV, 57-76, 113-132, 159-172; and XXVI, 1-20. In regard to Gerry's remaining in France, Smith wrote, "This melancholy catastrophe evinces how difficult it is for men of a certain age to change bad habits and proves that it is scarcely in the nature of an Anti-fed or a Jacobin ever to become a very sound politician. Can we be much astonished if the *inconsistent* character, who in '88 declared he wo'd not sign the Constitution 'because it did not secure our Liberties,' and in '89, 'that that same Constitution was our Salvation,' sho'd in '98 swerve suddenly from principles which were deemed to have taken root?" XXV, 59. Smith tried to send the news as he gathered it from newspapers or reports from individuals, but frequently what he sent was very much out of date when it reached America. It also was often based so much on hearsay or opinion that corrections had to be inserted in the next letter. He remained as strong a Federalist of the Hamilton school as ever. Smith wanted to go to as many European Capitals as possible. At one time he was discussing a trip to Constantinople. On another occasion he urged Pickering to secure the President's permission for him to go to London on a visit. The latter replied that Adams considered such a visit inexpedient. "He remarked that the appointments of yourself to Lisbon and his son to Berlin, (the latter in consequence of the former) had created more clamour than any act of his administration; and that at this time in particular, while negotiations with France are pending, it would be impolitic." *Ibid.,* XXVI, p. 17.

not only a part of the house but also a "part of the government" were determined to go to war. It was his opinion that two recent acts of the British Parliament were more alarming than the decrees of the French Directory. To this, Harper retorted that it was not unusual for the gentleman from Virginia to display his ignorance of facts. Giles replied that he "did not suppose that the gentleman from South Carolina would get much from his *polite* method of expressing himself. He knew it was usual for him to suppose he had a monopoly of knowledge; but he did not suppose his telling an enlightened assembly like this, could produce any effect in his favor." Finally Harper agreed to wait for further information. He defended the President for not sending copies of the acts of Parliament on the grounds that the merchants had been fully informed. In answer to Giles's statement that he did not believe that Harper desired peace, the latter declared that "if peace meant submitting to the insults of a foreign power he did not favor peace." But he was willing to wait for further communications from the President.[33]

Several days elapsed before the President was formally requested to send the instructions given to the three commissioners and the despatches he had received from them. During this time the argument continued between those desiring and those opposing immediate measures of preparedness. Harper and Giles became even more personal in their remarks about each other. Giles accused Harper of action entirely inconsistent with his course when he had been interested in the "rights of man" in 1791 and 1792. The latter denied that he had ever been interested in the "rights of man" as the gentleman from Virginia understood the term. He had attended a meeting or two of a patriotic organization in Charleston but had never in any way been connected with the Jacobin Club. At first he had considered the leaders in the French Revolution high-minded men but had since learned of his mistake and now looked upon the whole movement as tragic to the extreme. Charges concerning his earlier affiliation with radical groups were merely

[33] *Annals of Congress,* 5th Cong., 2nd Sess. (March 13, 1798), pp. 1252-1260.

political propaganda which were known to be false but were repeated for party purposes.[34] When the President was asked to send the additional information concerning the relations with France, he promptly complied.[35]

The reaction that followed the communication of the despatches of the American commissioners to Congress was an outburst from the Federalists that was no doubt stronger than that which came from the Republicans when the terms of the Jay Treaty were first known. For a time the Republicans themselves seemed to be at a loss as to what course they should pursue. Every effort was made to prevent war and all energy was directed toward preventing the passage of measures hostile to France. In most of these endeavors the South Carolina Republicans joined wholeheartedly. On the question of the suspension of commercial relations, William Smith did break away, but Sumter and Benton opposed that also.[36] All three supported the resolution of Livingston of New York requesting the President to proceed with the negotiation of a treaty with France.[37] Furthermore the Republicans from South Carolina opposed the termination of the treaty of 1778.[38]

In the meantime the fight for preparedness continued in both houses of Congress. Harper became more and more supercilious. Pinckney was much more moderate and considerate than William Loughton Smith, whom he had succeeded, and the South Carolina Federalists were, as a whole, not quite as extreme as they had been in the previous session. But as time passed the increased impetuosity and the contemptuous manner of Harper, along with the display of similar characteristics by Rutledge, partly offset the moderation brought by Pinckney.

[34] See *supra*, pp. 87-88 and note.
[35] *Annals of Congress,* 5th Cong., 2nd Sess. (April 2, 3, 1798), pp. 1371-1376.
[36] *Ibid.* (June 1, 1798), pp. 1865-1866.
[37] The resolution was lost 30 to 51. Harper opposed; the votes of Pinckney and Rutledge are not listed. *Ibid.* (July 2, 1798), pp. 2086-2087.
[38] Harper and Rutledge favored, Smith and Sumter opposed, Pinckney and Benton are not listed. The vote was 47 to 37. *Annals of Congress,* 5th Cong., 2nd Sess. (July 6, 1789), pp. 2127-2128. The measure passed, however, 47 to 37.

JEFFERSONIAN DEMOCRACY IN S. C.

Harper's attitude in a debate with Edward Livingston may be given as an example of his tone throughout the session. When the motion to build twelve convoys instead of sixteen was under discussion, Livingston favored the larger number, not because he wanted any at all, but on the ground that they would get the United States into war, in which case twelve would not be enough. Harper was glad the gentleman from New York was trying to get on the side of the majority but he thought that Livingston "had made a silly speech." As for his part he was not supporting measures that would bring about an offensive war; and he believed that "what the gentleman had said on this subject was one of those puffs which were introduced for no other purpose than to round off a period; and he was astonished that any gentleman could get his own consent thus to impose upon himself."[39]

In the heated debate over increasing the military forces, Thomas Sumter made one of the few speeches recorded under his name in the records of Congress. Sumter opposed the principle of the bill, the objects it was expected to effect, and above all, "transferring the Constitutional Legislative power of Congress to the President or Executive branch of Government." No information had been presented to show that any nation even intended to invade the United States. The belligerents would be engaged with each other for so long a time that the bill would be unnecessary. Sumter was greatly surprised that some members wanted to change the number of men from 10,000 to 20,000. He became extremely sarcastic in his refutation of Harper's description of the dangers that threatened the South. The latter had

> by his nice and minute delineations of the conditions of the Southern States, shown to the House a terrifying picture of Southern imbecility, and had also published to his cruel, malicious, and insidious enemy (as he terms them), an enemy sufficiently penetrating without his aid, every point, every avenue, every position, most advantageous for them to take in attack; he has exposed our most vulnerable part to their inveteracy, and our wealthiest part to their rapacity.

[39] *Annals of Congress*, 5th Cong., 2nd Sess. (April 20, 1798), pp. 1519-1520.

Sumter particularly resented the comparison Harper had made between the regular army and the militia. Harper might know something about the geography of his state, but he knew nothing about the ability of the Southern people to defend themselves. Sumter had seen the corps to which Harper said he had once belonged and must admit that it seemed disorganized. However, Sumter remarked that he had not seen Harper among its officers when he visited it and intimated that he did not believe that the latter knew much about its condition. There might be some reason to protect the seacoast and make provision for the militia, but there was no need whatever for "that worst of all expedients, a standing army." The whole question of increasing the military forces should be put off for consideration at future sessions of Congress.[40] Harper did not attempt an elaborate answer to Sumter, but did reply that if he had been as anxious to "degrade" the militia as his colleague had said, he would have given details which he had refrained from mentioning. He was willing to grant that the militia was the material out of which a defense might be built, but at least 10,000 men of the regular army would be needed as an aid.[41] On the vote to insert 10,000 instead of 20,000 even Rutledge sided with Sumter, Benton and William Smith in favor of the smaller number.[42]

Sumter opposed giving the President any control over the militia as "a flagrant breach of the rights of the individual States"; but his motion to strike out the provision giving the chief executive the authority to commission officers of voluntary groups and accept their services provided they were not sent outside the state in which they were organized, was defeated.[43] On the final passage of the bill to raise the 10,000 additional men Harper and Rutledge gave their support while Sumter, Benton and William Smith opposed.[44]

In the debate on the bill to arm the merchant vessels Harper asserted that the nation was already at war whether members

[40] *Annals of Congress,* 5th Cong., 2nd Sess. (May 10, 1798), pp. 1665-1671.   [41] *Ibid.* (May 11, 1798), p. 1692.
[42] *Ibid.* (May 17, 1798), pp. 1769-1770.
[43] *Ibid.* (May 16, 1798), p. 1758.
[44] *Ibid.* (May 17, 1798), p. 1772.

of Congress were willing to recognize it or not. If the bill did not pass the country would still be at war, "a war of the most calamitous kind—a war in which we are unable to defend ourselves."[45] Along with his legislative activities, Harper had found time to interest himself in the reorganization of the War Department. He wrote Alexander Hamilton urging him to express his willingness to replace Secretary McHenry, asserting that the size of the army and voluntary groups to be brought into existence would be large. "This, under proper direction, will give us the flower of the country; and every thing will depend on the *name* of the general and the *talents* of the minister." Harper stated that he had no authority to offer Hamilton the place, but recent conversations with the President led him to believe that arrangements could be made. All that was needed was his expression of willingness.[46]

A provisional army having been provided for, it was necessary for the President to recommend officers to the senate. It was generally agreed that the first general of the army should be George Washington; but there was much difference of opinion as to who should be second in command. On account of Washington's age and health, the second position was expected to be the more important one. Hamilton at first did not seem particularly anxious for the place, but soon he and his satellites in the cabinet were using every means imaginable to get Washington to request his appointment. Thinking that some consideration ought to be given to the rank of the officers in the Revolution and to the section of the country that might be invaded, Washington at first favored Charles Cotesworth Pinckney. Adams preferred going according to the Revolutionary rank and appointing Henry Knox, Pinckney and Hamilton in that order. But Hamilton persisted and intrigued until he won Washington over. When the latter requested Hamilton as his assistant, Adams was forced to acquiesce. Knox refused to serve under a person who had held a subordinate rank during the Revolution; but Pinckney good-naturedly accepted the third position stating that if Knox also had been placed above him

[45] *Ibid.* (July 2, 1798), p. 2072.
[46] Hamilton, *Works of Hamilton*, VI, 282. The letter was dated April 27, 1798.

it would not have embarrassed him.[47] With Hamilton next to Washington, Harper felt that he should have no difficulty in securing an appointment for himself. Hamilton accordingly recommended him, extolling his virtues, pointing out that the "only shade to his useful qualities" was vanity, and concluding that "the good much out-weighs the ill." Washington replied that he had no immediate need for an official family; but that when its members were chosen they should be men of experience. However, he did add that sometimes such matters as political and geographical factors had to be considered.[48]

2. The Passage of the Alien and Sedition Acts

The augmentation of the military and naval forces and the passage of commercial regulations were not sufficient for the members of the second session of the Fifth Congress. Were not the internal enemies of the government just as dangerous as the external? Two groups in particular were thought to be undermining the political structure of the country—the foreign born residents of the United States and the citizens with foreign sympathies, especially if their sympathies were toward France. Extremely noticeable to the Federalists was the fact that a very large proportion of the foreign born residents joined the Republicans and began criticizing the administration. Of course the extremists favored restrictive measures of a rigid type even in peace; but they could not get the support of the moderates until war seemed imminent.

Opposition to the foreign born became almost an obsession with Robert Goodloe Harper. If the formation of policy were left to him, no person should thereafter be granted the suffrage or "the rights of citizens of the United States except by birth." The only concessions he would make were the privileges of holding and transferring property. When he was accused of displaying ignorance of the Constitution in the ad-

[47] Many of the letters that passed between Hamilton and Washington, Pickering, Wolcott and others in regard to the appointment of the person to be second in command of the army, are printed in vol. VI of Hamilton, *Works of Hamilton*, some of the most interesting ones being on pp. 331, 342, 369. See also Gibbs, *Administrations of Washington and Adams*, II, 102-104.

[48] Hamilton, *Works of Hamilton*, VI, 334-338.

JEFFERSONIAN DEMOCRACY IN S. C.   117

vocacy of his motions, Harper withdrew them until he could study that document further.[49] Rutledge argued that if Americans in France should start spreading propaganda or soliciting aid, they would be placed in prison or sent out of the country. This was one of the policies of the French with which he agreed. The President of the United States should have the authority to banish "such intriguing agents and spies as are now spread all over the country."[50] Harper could not treat the constitutional objections to the deportation of aliens as serious. He was reminded of the "saying of a witty writer upon a book still more sacred than the Constitution, viz.: 'that it was a rich field into which all parties sent their troops to forage.'" The conduct of those offering constitutional objections was curious. When an objectionable measure was clearly expedient and even necessary it was called unconstitutional. If there were no doubt about its constitutionality it was then said to be unnecessary. Harper was not much impressed by Gallatin's argument that the general welfare provision was not a separate power within itself. Congress must look out for the general welfare of the United States and in so doing might find it necessary to deport certain aliens whom the states had seen fit to admit. Even this pretended restriction on the power of Congress would pass out of existence in 1808 and then Gallatin's "fine-spun arguments" on such a basis "would fall to the ground." There then ensued a lengthy encounter between Harper and Gallatin into which passion entered rather strongly.[51] On the final passage of the Alien Bill, Sumter, Benton and William Smith opposed as usual.[52]

In supporting a sedition bill Harper asserted that the tone of the press had become alarming.[53] He thought the amend-

[49] *Annals of Congress*, 5th Cong., 2nd Sess. (May 2, 1798), pp. 1567-1569.
[50] *Ibid.* (May 3, 1798), pp. 1573-1575.
[51] *Ibid.* (June 19, 1798), pp. 1989-1997.
[52] *Ibid.* (June 21, 1798), pp. 2028-2029. Harper and Rutledge favored, of course. Pinckney is not listed. The vote was 46 to 40. Individual votes on the Alien Enemy Bill, which also passed, are not given. *Ibid.* (June 26, July 3, 1798), pp. 2049, 2088.
[53] *Ibid.* (July 5, 1798), p. 2103.

ment to make the juries in such cases judges of the law as well as the fact unnecessary, since such was the practice already in libel cases, but he voted for it. Rutledge, however, opposed even this amendment. Pinckney is not listed.[54] In his debate on the passage of the bill, Harper argued that its provisions would not be abused in their enforcement. Edward Livingston had quoted John Adams's *Defence of the American Constitutions,* in support of the argument that the government was advancing rapidly toward a despotism. The gentleman had, Harper said, forgotten one part of the passage. The author was describing a government in which all power was in one branch and whose whole power was in one popular body. Adams also had told of how leaders in wealthy families got into the assembly and seized control. Harper then accused Livingston of trying to get all power for the house "by demolishing, piece by piece, the checks established in the Senate and Executive power." Harper insinuated that it might be the purpose of the New York representative and his friends to bring about the conditions which Adams warned against. He, the son of a cabinet maker, could have no such ambition. It was just as natural for him to struggle for the retention of the constitutional structure as it was for "the gentleman from New York to aim at its destruction, which would be the first step toward his own greatness." The Sedition Bill, Harper argued, would be a means of preventing the critics of the government from destroying the constitutional structure and thus bringing about the conditions described in the book of the President. On final passage, Sumter, Benton and William Smith again voted negatively. Harper and Rutledge supported the bill, while Pinckney is again not listed.[55]

In the senate Jacob Read continued his support of the measures of the Federalist party. Hunter voted for bills to protect the commerce and the coasts of the United States.[56]

[54] *Ibid.* (July 9, 1798), pp. 2137-2138.
[55] The vote was 44 to 41. *Ibid.* (July 9, 1798), pp. 2164-2171.
[56] *Ibid.,* Senate section (April 9, and May 23, 1798), pp. 537-538, 546, 563.

JEFFERSONIAN DEMOCRACY IN S. C.   119

The latter seems to have been absent when most of the other measures were passed and later on in the year he resigned.[57]

During the second session of the Fifth Congress, the house of representatives found time also to act upon the request of Thomas Pinckney to permit his acceptance of the gifts offered him when he left the Spanish Capital. Both Harper and Rutledge spoke in favor of granting the requested permission; but the house declined by the vote of 49 to 37, Sumter, Benton and William Smith joining with the majority. A resolution was adopted unanimously stating that the members of the house were "induced to such refusal solely by motives of general policy and not by any view personal to the said Thomas Pinckney."[58]

3. Preparedness Measures in South Carolina

During the spring and summer of 1798 the people of South Carolina were even more interested than usual in the relations between the United States and France. Late in March, Robert Simons accused Adams and his cabinet of bringing on the strained relations and stated that they should resign.[59] Most of the people of the state, however, were not so bitter toward the administration. This was especially true after the publication of the despatches from the American commissioners in France.

Beginning early in May public meetings were held in various parts of South Carolina. After several days of agitation the people of Charleston got together on May 5. Resolutions were passed expressing regret at the strained relations with France and sorrow because of the occurrences in Paris. At such a time the government of the nation must be upheld. A committee was appointed to address the three branches of the federal government in support of measures necessary for the protection of commerce and the defense of the country. It was also decided to raise contributions and in a few minutes thirty persons had promised $2,250. The meeting was harmonious and without

---

[57] Hunter's letter signifying his resignation was called to the attention of the senate on December 31, 1798. See *ibid.*, 3rd Sess., p. 2199.

[58] *Annals of Congress*, 5th Cong., 2nd Sess. (May 4, 21, 1798), pp. 1582-1592, 1775-1776.

[59] Letter to publisher of *S. C. State Gazette*, March 29, 1798.

much difference of opinion. A few felt that France should not be mentioned by name in the address to the Federal government, but the majority decided otherwise.[60] The people of Georgetown "regardless of political views" expressed confidence in Congress and pledged support in time of danger. In St. Luke's Parish France was severely criticized but those present desired peace. The citizens of Pendleton counseled moderation in the attitude toward France but called for complete adherence to the United States against any foreign nation.[61] At a dinner in honor of Wade Hampton, the attendants were reported to have had but "one sentiment"—that the French conduct must be held "in the utmost abhorrence and detestation." They pledged their support of the government "against all foreign interference, intrigues and attacks whatsoever."[62]

In July, Christopher Gadsden wrote Senator Read, reiterating a statement he had made several years before, that "a better and finer piece of live oak was not to be found in the United States" than John Adams. He wished that Gerry had not remained, for he felt that the French were trying to "gain time to repair their shattered perfidious dividing scheme against us." Gadsden hoped that the treaty with France would be terminated and that a "proper alien bill" would be passed. Unless the United States adopted the European attitude of not permitting citizens to renounce their allegiance, in an emergency the country would find itself "in a precarious situation, with numbers we can place little or no dependence on." Great Britain was also criticized for her interference with the direct trade between Charleston and Germany in the sale of rice. "I am, dear Read, for no see-saw work, now this favorite, now that; for risking no operations or tendencies to preferential

---

[60] *City Gazette,* May 3, 4, 5, 6, 7, 1798. Beginning May 18, and appearing day after day for weeks were articles of a somewhat controversial nature under such signatures as "A True Republican," "A Federalist," and "A Democrat."

[61] For accounts of these meetings and others see *City Gazette,* May 22, 28, 30, June 9, 12, 21, 1798.

[62] *S. C. State Gazette,* May 11, 1798. Letter from Columbia concerning dinner held May 3.

jealousies, but in our open corner shop to give a kindly welcome Sir to every friendly pop-in customer."[63]

During the period of highest feeling about fifty of the young men of Charleston formed a military organization known as the "Federalist Club."[64] Regular meetings were held and apparently some form of military training was engaged in for several months. Early the next year Miss Mary Legare, daughter of Thomas Legare of Charleston, presented the club with a standard, in the presentation of which she denounced the designs of France against the United States and referred to the former as a "nation of atheists." She spoke as if the outbreak of war was expected any moment.[65]

The high point of concerted effort of South Carolinians in the support of the general government was the financing and building of the sloop-of-war *John Adams*. In accordance with the act of Congress authorizing the President to accept volunteer ships as loans, the citizens of Charleston between July 3, and August 11, 1798, raised $100,000 for the building of a ship to be offered the government of the United States. It was built at the shipyard on Cooper River, named after the President and launched on June 5, 1799.[66]

4. SLIGHT FEDERALIST GAINS IN 1798

In 1798 the South Carolina Federalists expected the voters to choose their candidates instead of those of the party that had been more friendly to France. The conduct of the French Directory, however, could not be made as great an issue as the Federalists wished; for, at the time of the crisis, the Republicans had been as loyal as they. Some had opposed mentioning the name of France in resolutions of censure; but they had loudly asserted that, if the choice were between the United States and France, they would support their own nation without the slightest hesitation. At the risk of legislative censure

[63] MS. letter dated July 16, 1798, owned by Mrs. Helen Kohn Hennig, Columbia, S. C., quoted by Wallace in *History of S. C.*, II, 355.
[64] *City Gazette*, July 9 and (corrected account) July 10, 1798.
[65] *Ibid.*, January 5, 1799.
[66] *Ibid.*, August 4, 11, 14, 1798; April 29, June 4, 6, November 15, 1799. *S. C. State Gazette*, July 17, 1799; *Charleston Year Book*, 1883, pp. 510-511.

Governor Charles Pinckney, upon the advice of certain members of the legislature, paid out of state funds through the treasurer at Charleston, seven thousand and eighty pounds sterling for the purchase of arms.[67] Edward Rutledge, a devoted friend of Jefferson and a man of Republican inclinations in 1796, was chairman of the committee to raise the funds for the building of the subscription ship, *John Adams*.[68] The Republicans refused to repudiate their friendship for the French or Republicanism, insisting that neither France nor the republican form of government should be blamed for the misdeeds of a small number of persons temporarily in power. The voters were called upon to support only those candidates "with republican principles."[69]

It was natural that the Federalists should condemn the three Republicans in the federal house of representatives who had voted against the administration's program. A wag remarked that the three Jacobins, Thomas Sumter, Lemuel Benton and William Smith were being paid $4,200 to utter the monosyllable "No—No—No—." At first Sumter had two opponents, Richard Winn and John Chesnut, but before the election the latter withdrew. A Stateburg writer charged that Sumter was heavily in debt to the state and used the privileges of membership in Congress to evade final settlement. The candidate issued a very forceful broadside on September 27, flatly denying the charges. The accusations against him and his colleagues in Congress, he said, were merely part of a party program to defeat those who opposed certain measures at the last session. He had tried to vote as he thought his constituents desired. If they had changed their views he no longer represented them, and he realized that they had the right to bestow their suffrage on their choice.[70] On election day Sumter was overwhelmingly approved of by his constituents, who gave him

[67] S. C. House Journal, December 15, 1798. A Camden grand jury declared Pinckney's act a violation of the state constitution in that money was appropriated without legislative authorization. *Georgetown Gazette*, December 18, 1798.
[68] *City Gazette*, August 14, 1798.
[69] *Georgetown Gazette*, September 18, 21, 1798.
[70] Broadside in Sumter Papers, L. C. See also Gregorie, *Thomas Sumter*, p. 240, for other details concerning the election.

JEFFERSONIAN DEMOCRACY IN S. C. 123

nearly twice as many votes as his opponent. His two Republican colleagues, however, were not as fortunate. William Smith was succeeded by Abraham Nott and Benjamin Huger defeated Lemuel Benton.[71]

Since the governor and a United States senator were to be chosen by the legislature, brief attention must be given to local elections. Greatly mortified by the results in Charleston, the Federalist publishers of the *South Carolina State Gazette* enclosed the election news with a heavy black bar, as if in mourning. The editor, B. F. Timothy, bewailed the removal of "the best citizens of our country, those in whom are combined talents, integrity and patriotism, and who, in this juncture of our political affairs, are best calculated to serve us." He almost despaired of the ability of the people to choose capable representatives. Lest the reader join the mourning editor in his despair, it will be added that among those elected in the "unpromising" delegation from Charleston, were such future leaders as Thomas Lowndes, John Blake, Thomas Lehre, William Johnson and John Drayton.[72] Although the party affiliation of each member elected in 1798 cannot be determined from the records available today, the tone of the legislature may be judged by its action in selecting William Johnson, a Republican, as speaker of the house of representatives.[73] The Republicans in both the upper and lower parts of the state joined in changing the practice of choosing the two United States senators from different sections of South Carolina and elected Charles Pinckney. In view of the fact that he and Jacob Read were both from the lower part of the state and since many of the Republicans were in the up country, Pinckney promised to "look out for the Republican interests."[74] For governor, the moderate Edward Rutledge, who had voted for Jefferson in

---

[71] Interesting information concerning Benton may be found in Gregg, *History of the Old Cheraws*, p. 401.

[72] *S. C. State Gazette*, October 12, 15, 1798.

[73] Johnson had been elected in 1794, 1796, and was known to be a Republican. See the sketch of him in O'Neal, *Bench and Bar in S. C.*, I, 73.

[74] See letter of Charles Pinckney to Jefferson in 1800, in which he described the election of 1798. *American Historical Review*, IV, 121. S. C. Senate Journal, December 6, 1798.

1796 and who remained one of his close friends, was chosen.[75] In the face of these Republican victories, the elections of 1798 cannot be cited as proof that South Carolina was strongly Federalist. The state's delegation in Congress would have, however, fewer Republicans than the previous one. To that extent only could the Federalists point to gains.

5. THE CONTINUANCE OF THE FEDERALIST PROGRAM IN THE FACE OF RISING REPUBLICAN OPPOSITION

While the people of the United States were uncertain as to whether there would actually be war with France, one of the most curious episodes in American diplomacy occurred. Dr. George Logan, an anti-Federalist Quaker of Philadelphia and one of the earliest of American pacifists, made an unofficial attempt to improve the relations with France. Carrying a letter of identification from Jefferson, also unofficial, he assured the leading members of the Directory of the good will of the American people. Apparently he hoped to get the French government to do something that would indicate a desire for peace; the Federalists charged that he had gone to give treasonable information which would be of value to the enemy in case of war. Logan was well received, succeeded in getting some American prisoners released who had been taken by privateers, and returned to America with the belief that his mission had been successful. When the third session of the Fifth Congress convened, much was made of this unauthorized attempt of Logan to carry on diplomatic activities. Harper, Pinckney and Rutledge strongly favored the enactment of a law making such conduct illegal.[76]

The leaders in the passage of the Alien and Sedition Acts during the previous session were quite aware of the reception being given those measures. Harper thought that such a small

---

[75] S. C. House Journal, December 6, 1798.

[76] *Annals of Congress*, 5th Cong., 3rd Sess. (December 26, 1798; January 9, 10, 17, 1799), pp. 2495, 2500-2502, 2502-2512, 2535-2545, 2583-2586, 2608-2648, 2703-2704. William Smith voted against the bill on final passage. Benton and Sumter are not listed. In the course of the debate Harper and Gallatin again engaged in a heated argument, this time over Harper's attempt to identify Logan as the representative of "the French party" in the United States.

JEFFERSONIAN DEMOCRACY IN S. C. 125

number of newspapers printed the complete acts that few people knew their actual provisions. The senate bill which had not been passed was read at public meetings as if it were the law. Believing that most of the discontent grew out of ignorance, he proposed that the federal government print and distribute free copies of the Alien and Sedition Acts. Nicholas of Virginia denied that all the opposition was due to lack of knowledge, but was not surprised that Harper thought so since he habitually attributed all opposition to himself to ignorance. Whereupon the latter replied that if he should ascribe all his opposition to ignorance, he would have to consider Nicholas "the most ignorant of mankind"; instead of having such an opinion of his Virginia opponent he freely recognized his "superior talents." Dawson, also of Virginia, desired to amend the measure so as to provide for the publication of all clauses of the Constitution which seemed to authorize or forbid the passage of such legislation. Rutledge suspected that the motive of this amendment was to persuade the people that the laws were unconstitutional. He was opposed to asking the people to rule on their constitutionality after the members of both houses of Congress and the judges that executed them had sanctioned them. According to Harper the idea of printing a few sections of the Constitution was deserving of laughter rather than argument; but he would vote to print 500,000 copies of the whole document. Dawson accepted the suggestion and changed his amendment to include the whole Constitution but it failed to pass. The next proposal was to print the amendments to the Constitution instead of the whole document; it too was voted down. Then Harper's resolution itself was rejected.[77] When the house voted on the report of a committee that the repeal of the Alien and Sedition Laws was inexpedient, Harper, Pinckney and Rutledge, agreed, while Sumter and William Smith dissented.[78] In the voting on further measures of preparedness during the last session of the Fifth Congress, Sumter

[77] *Annals of Congress,* 5th Cong., 3rd Sess. (December 11, 12, 14, 1798), pp. 2426-2427, 2429-2433, 2445-2454.
[78] *Ibid.* (February 25, 1799), pp. 3016-3017. Benton is not listed.

and William Smith continued their opposition.[79] Benton was apparently absent.

Upon his return from France in February in 1799, Charles Cotesworth Pinckney was enthusiastically welcomed. For several days he was entertained at meetings sponsored by the local military organizations and others. At a gathering held at the city hall the governor, lieutenant-governor, president of the senate, speaker of the house of representatives, several judges and the foreign consuls were present. Toasts were offered to the guest of honor, the President of the United States, the commander of the army, and others. Also, these sentiments were expressed: "Agriculture and commerce: may the toil of the husbandman, aided by the active enterprize of the merchant, be ever productive of union and wealth in our country"; "The cause of Republicanism: may those enjoy its blessings who know how to appreciate them"; and "Millions for defence, but not one cent for tribute."[80]

In March considerable commotion resulted from the news that four French conspirators were on their way to Charleston. When the suspected persons arrived, they were promptly arrested and confined for a short while. Wild rumors were circulated as to what might be the intentions of the alleged conspirators, the one repeated most often being that they planned to stir up race troubles. The incident was immediately seized upon by writers as ample proof of the absolute necessity of the Alien Law. But the opponents of that measure soon pointed out that there was little if any evidence as to the guilt of the persons arrested; and that, after they had been permitted to depart for the West Indies, information had been received indicating their innocence.[81]

During most of the remainder of the year 1799 there was a period of comparative quiet. Of course the friends of Great Britain and France retained their interest in foreign affairs and occasionally there was an attack or ironical thrust at one nation or the other. Local politics too attracted some interest.

[79] *Ibid.* (January 25, February 11, March 1, 1799), pp. 2791-2792, 3044.
[80] *City Gazette,* February 6, 7, 9, 1799.
[81] *Ibid.,* March 23, 25, 1799.

JEFFERSONIAN DEMOCRACY IN S. C.   127

When the news came that new republics would probably be founded in Europe, the health of George III was drunk with the toast, "His Britannic Majesty—the founder of the American *free* Republic, and continued fomentor of new ones—may his invaluable life be preserved, until his glorious achievements encompass the universe entire."[82] Following the description of this incident in the *City Gazette,* "Vindicator" called the dispatcher of the news a French sympathizer and an enemy of the general government. The British king was defended. The system of taxation had caused the American Revolution, not the king himself, except in a very remote sense. Whereupon "A Federal Republican" charged "Vindicator" with being pro-British and sorry that the United States was independent. Then "Moderator" criticized the publishers for printing either of the articles. According to him all that had been proved was that one was hostile to republicanism and the other opposed to monarchy. The newspaper, though, continued printing letters from both.[83] The supporters of John Rutledge, Jr., in Orangeburg toasted him as "Our representative in Congress—may he long continue to wear the odium of the Jacobins, the most distinguished and incontestable proof of merit and true patriotism."[84]

In the summer and fall no little agitation was caused by the discussion of the Jonathan Robbins case. Early in the year a man claiming to be Jonathan Robbins of Danbury, Connecticut, but accused of being Thomas Nash, a British subject wanted on charge of mutiny, had been arrested in Charleston at the request of the British consul. After a trial in the federal district court, Judge Bee, without a jury, turned him over to the British authorities to be tried and hanged. The Jay Treaty came up for criticism again, for it was under the twenty-seventh article of that document that the prisoner had been delivered to the British. The Republicans made much of the surrendering, by a federal court without a jury, of a person who had affidavits of citizenship and who swore that he had

[82] *Ibid.,* May 3, 1799.
[83] *Ibid.,* May 3, 8, 9, 10, 1799.
[84] *Ibid.,* July 12, 1799.

not changed allegiance. Little was said of his possible guilt of the charge of mutiny, but much was said of the failure of the federal courts to protect persons who seemed to be American citizens. Charles Pinckney gained considerable notice through his letters and pamphlets on the subject.[85] In the same series of letters Pinckney stated that France could not be excused any more than Great Britain for seizing American ships; that the government was justified in its firm attitude toward that nation; but that an equally firm tone should be taken toward Great Britain. The English had gone beyond the provisions of the Jay Treaty. He was very confident, however, that the American people would ever rise to defend the honor of their country. No such corruption as that which marred the European republics would tarnish the United States.[86]

The reaction to the Alien and Sedition Laws in South Carolina during 1799 seems to have been rather negative. Perhaps it was a period of "watchful waiting." No doubt some were influenced by the frequent rumors of the coming of French conspirators from the West Indies to believe that the Alien Act was needed. That there was interest in these two measures, however, is evident from the close vote of the South Carolina senate in declining to consider the Kentucky Resolutions.[87]

With the replacement of Lemuel Benton and William Smith by Benjamin Huger and Abraham Nott, two Federal-

---

[85] Letters of "A South Carolina Planter" published in newspapers in August and later in pamphlet form. A copy of the pamphlet together with various affidavits is in pamphlet series 3, vol. 12, Charleston Library Society.

McMaster says that, "At the last moment of his life Nash followed the custom of the criminals of his time, made a confession, and owned that Ireland was his native soil." *History of the People of the U. S.*, II, 447.

[86] Letters II and III of "A South Carolina Planter."

[87] By the vote of 14 to 11, the South Carolina senate passed the following resolution, "Resolved, That the Governor of the state, be required to signify to the Executive of the State of Kentucky, that the pressure of the business of this State, prevents the Legislature from taking into consideration the Resolves of the Legislature of Kentucky of the 16th day of November, 1798, and to bestow on them that attention which the importance of the subjects demands." S. C. Senate Journal, December 20, 1799.

JEFFERSONIAN DEMOCRACY IN S. C.   129

ists, the even balance of parties in the South Carolina delegation to the federal house of representatives was changed to a five-to-one count in favor of the Federalists. In the senate the situation remained the same as to numbers; but the election of Charles Pinckney, the most vigorous and influential Republican of the state, added force to the Jeffersonian group. Before the meeting of the first session of the Sixth Congress Pinckney was corresponding with the national leaders of his party concerning its political program. To Jefferson and others he sent copies of his articles on the Jonathan Robbins case. Jefferson thanked him with the prophecy that the "piece" he had sent would likely "run through all the republican papers and carry the question home to every man's mind." In referring to the defeat of two of the Republican members of the previous Congress, Jefferson expressed the hope that South Carolina was "recovering from the delusion which affected their last election."[88] That South Carolina was "recovering" may be indirectly evidenced by the removal of the leading South Carolina Federalist representative to another state. No doubt Robert Goodloe Harper had personal reasons for changing his residence to Maryland in 1799; but the knowledge that he no longer represented his constituents certainly did not delay his departure. Although he did not return to the state, he continued to represent his district in Congress for the remainder of the term and wrote letters to his constituents as late as 1801.[89] In one of his early speeches in the senate, Pinckney attempted to present the desires of the Southern planter in regard to foreign affairs. According to him the planter would suffer most in the event of the cessation of commercial relations with France. Particular emphasis was given to the probable damage to the tobacco trade.[90]

To the attempts of the Republicans in 1799 and 1800 to reduce the army or modify the Federalist program of defense, Harper, Pinckney, Rutledge, Huger and Nott gave their consistent opposition. Only Sumter was left to give his support.

[88] Jefferson Papers, October 29, 1799.
[89] Morrison, *Life and Letters of Otis*, I, 192.
[90] *Annals of Congress*, 6th Cong., 1st Sess., Senate, December 26, 1799.

Harper insisted that any serious modifications would be unwise so long as the outcome of the pending negotiations was uncertain. Ministers had again been sent to France and it was necessary to remain firm. Huger thought that such improvement as had come in foreign relations had resulted from the defensive measures recently adopted. President Adams's willingness to negotiate with France had his hearty approval. He was willing to show an amicable disposition by refraining from increasing the military forces further, but he was opposed to reductions.[91] A matter related to the attempt to reduce the defense facilities of the nation, not of any great importance within itself but which caused considerable excitement and discussion, was the alleged insult of John Randolph of Virginia by two naval officers. This fiery Republican virtually demanded that the President have the officers disciplined. Instead of acting himself, Adams transmitted Randolph's letter to the house. After taking the testimonies of the parties concerned the committee appointed to study the problem submitted a report which amounted to a censure of the Virginian. Whereupon the question of adopting the report became a party matter, for Randolph insisted that he actually had been insulted and that it had been because of his opposition to the military and naval bills. The Federalists made much of the President's refraining from mentioning the tone of the Virginia representative's letter. "No, sir," said Harper, "his mind moves in a sphere too exalted; his character is grounded on a basis too broad, for him to feel what in itself was extremely insignificant." Of the South Carolina group, only the Republican Sumter opposed the censure of Randolph.[92]

In the senate Charles Pinckney proposed the reformation of the method of selecting federal juries. He was astonished that Congress in setting up the judiciary system had not provided that the juries throughout the country should be chosen by lot. In many instances the territories from which the jurors were to be selected were not fixed but left to the clerk or the

[91] *Ibid.* (January 10, 22, 23, 24, 1800; and 2nd Sess., December 17, 1800), pp. 325-350, 369, 389-393, 402-404, 405, 825-836.
[92] *Ibid.* (January 14, 20, 24, 29, 1800), pp. 372-373, 377-388, 426-507.

marshal. The greatest of all defects, said Pinckney, was leaving the choice of the juries to the marshal, a political officer, appointed by the President and holding office at his pleasure. So much importance did he attach to the matter that he would consider it one of the most fortunate moments of his life that permitted him to make the first motion "in a question on which the true freedom and happiness of our country so much depends." If he could only promote the alteration of the "present unjust and oppressive system," he would receive ample compensation for "all the remarks and odium which the mover in so important a reform must naturally expect." The existing plan of allowing each state to prescribe its own method did not insure impartial juries. The general government should establish the uniform impartial system of choosing all federal juries by lot. Not until then could a citizen be assured of a fair trial or a counsel feel at perfect liberty to serve his client.[98]

Another practice of which Pinckney greatly disapproved was the appointment of the Chief Justice or any federal judge to another position, or office under the federal government or the states so long as he retained his judgeship. First he proposed that such an appointment, if accepted, should be declared by constitutional amendment to terminate the term of the judge concerned. Later, however, Pinckney decided that his purpose could be attained by an act of Congress. He, therefore, proposed an amendment to the judiciary act to that effect. A judge, said Pinckney, should not help form a treaty he might be called upon to interpret. The President might use the promise of a mission to a foreign country to influence his conduct as a judge. The number of judges did not make it advisable for one to be out of the country. If a President feared impeachment, could he not send the Chief Justice as an envoy

[98] *Annals of Congress,* 6th Cong., 1st Sess. (January 23, 31, 1800), pp. 28, 35-41. All that Pinckney was able to obtain was an "alteration." On April 30, the following was passed: "That jurors to serve in the courts of the United States shall be designated by lot, or otherwise, in each State or district respectively, according to the mode of forming juries to serve in the highest courts of law therein now practiced, so far as the same shall render such designation practicable by the courts and marshals of the United States." Appendix, p. 1526.

to prevent his being present to preside over the trial? Personally he did not think the judges should be appointed by the President; but since the Constitution had so fixed it all safeguards possible ought to be set up to remove them from the influence of the executive. He was not, Pinckney declared, taking this step as a way of censuring any President, but for the purpose of bringing about a needed reform.[94]

Under the direction of Edward Livingston, the Jonathan Robbins case was reviewed before the house. Upon the request of that body Adams sent the documents connected with the case. The letter of the British consul telling of the prisoner's confession was ignored by the Republicans. Livingston argued that the Constitution extended the power of the judiciary to cases arising under treaties, that cases on the high seas should be heard in regions where the offender was apprehended or into which he was first brought, and that the decision as to what should be done was exclusively a judiciary question. Furthermore, trial for all crimes, except in the case of impeachment, was to be by jury. The President, therefore, in authorizing and the judge in permitting, had brought about "a sacrifice of the constitutional independence of the Judicial power" when they delivered Jonathan Robbins over to the British officials without a trial by jury, thereby exposing the administration of the case to "suspicion and reproach." After Livingston's resolutions had been discussed for a whole day and nothing had been accomplished, a motion was made that no further consideration be given them. To this Harper and Rutledge were vigorously opposed. The President had been accused of unconstitutional acts. Were impeachment proceedings to be brought? The President's name must be cleared. During the further discussion of the question, Republicans asked that the chief executive be requested to send information concerning several other cases. This was opposed by Harper and Rutledge on the ground that they had no connection with the case under consideration. As in other instances, Sumter alone of the South Carolina delegation supported the Republi-

[94] *Annals of Congress*, 6th Cong., 1st Sess. (February 3, March 5, April 3, 1800), pp. 41-42, 96-102, 150. The measure failed to pass— 12 to 14. Read opposed it.

JEFFERSONIAN DEMOCRACY IN S. C.   133

can program throughout the whole procedure. The resolutions of Livingston were finally rejected.[95]

In February, 1800, the *Aurora* published a copy of a bill dealing with the method of deciding the election of the President and Vice-President in case of a dispute and stated that Charles Pinckney, a member of the committee that drew it up, had not been consulted before its being reported to the senate. Senator Tracy of Connecticut introduced a resolution calling upon the committee on privileges to ascertain the name of the editor of the newspaper, how he obtained the information, and under what authority he printed it. Pinckney was opposed to the resolution. He knew that there were many abuses of the freedom of the press and speech, but he thought it was dangerous for a legislative body to interfere in such matters. His comments were rather impersonal, without any mention of his own connection with the case. Read supported the resolution. An amendment to investigate in a similar manner the *United States Gazette* was rejected. William Duane, editor of the *Aurora,* was finally summoned. When he was denied the privilege of being heard by counsel, he refused to appear again. Whereupon the President was requested to initiate the prosecution of Duane "for certain false, defamatory, scandalous, and malicious publications" for the purpose of defaming the senate of the United States, and bringing them "into disrepute," and exciting "against them the hatred of the good people of the United States."[96]

The conduct of the Federalists in such instances as the investigation of the *Aurora* showed clearly that they were on the defensive. The brief period of popularity following the rash acts of the French Directory had been too much for the party in power. Rashness on the part of the Federalists themselves and division within their own ranks weakened their position

[95] *Annals of Congress,* 6th Cong., 1st Sess. (February 4, 7, 17, 20, 27, March 4, 5, 6, 10, 1800), pp. 511-518, 526, 532-533, 541-577, 584-595, 619-621.

[96] *Ibid.,* Senate (February 26, March 5, 8, 20, 24, 26, 27, May 14, 1800), pp. 63, 68-84, 93-96, 105, 113, 117-124, 184. Read supported the investigation and the prosecution. Pinckney opposed the investigation, but was absent when the question of prosecution came up for vote.

in the face of rising Republican sentiment. The Federalists hoped that the American people would remember their whole record since 1789 instead of their weaknesses during recent months. But the Republicans were determined that the abuses of power during the latter period should be kept uppermost in the public mind. If the Federalists could persuade the people that the opposition of the Republicans was aimed at the government itself instead of their party, they could continue in power. On the other hand, if the Republicans could convince the voters that they did not desire to bring the government "into disrepute," but wished, instead, to eliminate abuses in governmental administration, they would be entrusted with the political control of the nation. The election of 1800, which will now be discussed at length, was to register the decision of the electorate as to which party was more deserving of public trust.

CHAPTER VI

THE JEFFERSONIAN TRIUMPH IN 1800

1. THE NOMINATION OF CANDIDATES

Although the election of 1800 was one of the bitterest in the history of the nation, the opening day of that year was marked by quietude and solemnity in South Carolina. According to Francis Asbury, politics receded for the moment. The news of the death of George Washington had just reached Charleston.

A universal cloud sat upon the faces of the citizens of Charleston; the pulpits cloathed in black—the bells muffled—the paraded soldiery—a public oration decreed to be delivered on the 14th of this month—a marble statue to be placed in some proper situation. These were the expressions of sorrow and these the marks of respect paid by his fellow-citizens to the memory of this great man.[1]

On January 23, occurred the death of Governor Edward Rutledge, who had long been a moderating influence in South Carolina politics.[2] Trusted by Washington and a devoted friend of Jefferson, who might really be called both a Federalist and a Republican, he was perhaps the most influential man in South Carolina during the last few years of his life. Claimed by the Republicans, feared by the Federalists, but courted by both, in what political party he would have been found had he lived another twelve months, one cannot be certain. That he was stirred by the "X. Y. Z." affair is evident. Whether this and other political complications would have turned him away from the Republicans is a matter of speculation. Edward Rut-

---

[1] Asbury, *Journal*, II, 365-366. See also, *City Gazette*, January 4, 11, 17, 1800.
[2] There is a notice of Rutledge's death on January 23, in the *City Gazette*, January 25, 1800.

ledge was neither a radical nor a reactionary. In spite of the sneers of the Federalists in 1796, he had voted for Jefferson. Regardless of what position he might have taken if he had lived, it is very easy to imagine his writing Jefferson a complimentary letter as soon as he read the latter's first inaugural address.

In nominating their candidates for the Presidency and Vice-Presidency in the election of 1800 the Republicans presented a more nearly united front. Jefferson had long been recognized as the choice for the first position; and after being promised equal support, Aaron Burr became the candidate for the second.[3] Among the Federalists the situation was different. At times the independence of Adams infuriated Hamilton. The animosities resulting from the latter's appointment as second in command of the army and then the sudden restoration of diplomatic relations with France by the President had widened the breach between the two men. Hamilton's efforts in favor of Thomas Pinckney in 1796 were not forgotten. Many Federalists wished to substitute another for Adams in 1800, but the party was unable to agree upon anyone with as good a chance of election. It was finally decided to renominate the President but that Charles Cotesworth Pinckney should receive equal support. Nevertheless, neither faction was satisfied; and each distrusted the other. Apparently Adams had some years before come to suspect the whole Pinckney family; and his estimate of Charles Cotesworth Pinckney had not been raised by his willingness to serve under Hamilton in the existing army after having outranked him during the Revolution.[4] The Hamilton supporters, on the other hand, took no great pains to conceal their desire for the election of Pinckney over the President. Believing that South Carolina and some of the districts in North Carolina would vote for Jefferson and

[3] Burr feared a repetition of 1796, in which year he had not received the support he had expected in some of the Southern States. In South Carolina, for instance, he had been ignored while the electoral votes went to Jefferson and Pinckney. In North Carolina he had received only six to Jefferson's eleven. No doubt he preferred the governorship of New York to the risk of defeat for the Vice-Presidency.

[4] Adams, *Works of Adams*, I, 565-566.

Pinckney and hoping that New England and other Federalist areas would equally support Adams and Pinckney, they trusted that their desire would be fulfilled. There was some fear, though, that Massachusetts might in part "omit Gen. Pinckney; unless the train of information between this time and the election of President should convince them of the impossibility of continuing Mr. Adams."[5] The reorganization of the cabinet, with the elimination of Hamilton's friends, Adams's alleged accusation that Hamilton had worked against him in New York and his identification of the latter with the British party threw the contest into greater confusion. Then in the course of the campaign, Hamilton put himself into the ridiculous position of being the author of a pamphlet that attempted to prove Adams's unworthiness but at the same time called upon the electors to vote for him.[6]

2. CAMPAIGN METHODS AND PRACTICES

Early in 1800 the political atmosphere of South Carolina began ringing with charges and countercharges. Rumors regarding the Mazzei letter were passed around, but Jefferson's friends promptly answered that his statements in the letter were similar to those drawn up by the leading citizens of South Carolina during the excitement over the Jay Treaty.[7] When Jefferson was accused of supporting the Revolution because of his desire to be free from his British debts, his friends replied that by 1787 he had so satisfied his creditors that his agreement had since been used by those favoring the payment

[5] Letter of Pickering to W. L. Smith, May 7, 1800. William Loughton Smith Papers, Library of Congress.

[6] A copy of Hamilton's pamphlet on Adams is in Lodge, *Works of Hamilton*, VII, 309-365. The charge that Adams accused Hamilton of working against him in New York was made by McHenry. It was supposed to have been done at the time of or on the day previous to the dismissal of McHenry. The latter further stated that Adams spoke of Jefferson in a much more favorable way than of Hamilton even to the point of saying that the former if elected President would "act wisely." Pickering retold that story to Timothy Williams and William Loughton Smith, and further charged that Adams would work against Pinckney in favor of Jefferson in Massachusetts. These letters, dated May 19, and 28, are quoted in Channing, *History of the U. S.*, IV, 240 and notes.

[7] *City Gazette*, April 5, 7, 8, 1800.

of the British debts.[8] The matter was not put at rest, however; for, when writers praised Jefferson in July for the Declaration of Independence, "Truth" replied that the story of his noble purpose was "for the cloven footed Americans." It should be remembered that "it was not the public weal, that brought forth that manly, energetic and noble declaration—no, no, it was Jefferson's own private weal; that he might be free from his British debts."[9]

In a campaign as heated as that of 1800 it was to be expected that the Republicans would attempt to offset the popularity of the two Federalist Pinckneys, Thomas and Charles Cotesworth, by playing up the virtues of the third, Charles Pinckney, a member of their own party. On March 27, the *Aurora,* in an article reprinted in Charleston, had presented a comparison of the three prominent South Carolinians. The public records of the two Federalists were reviewed. The partiality of Hamilton toward them and the coolness of Adams were pointed out. Then without any grave criticism of either, the attention was directed to the Republican Pinckney, at that time a senator from South Carolina. He had, according to the article, never been in Europe, but had been "educated in a republican seminary, the influence of which is seen now." At sixteen he had drawn his sword "for the rights of man." At the siege of Savannah he had distinguished himself along with Pulaski and Laurens. After this military experience Charles Pinckney had left the army and become a leader in the South Carolina legislature. He had also held, since then, such offices as member of Congress under the Confederation, delegate to the federal convention of 1787, governor of his state, president of the state constitutional convention and United States senator. Pinckney had been uniformly "the honest and independent republican." His public life had ever been "fair, honorable and praiseworthy" and his private life "a mirror of virtue." Tories sickened at his attack and tried to defame him. His three celebrated letters calling attention to the Robbins case had aroused the hatred of the merchants and the British party.

[8] *Ibid.,* May 19, 1800. The letter of Jefferson on January 5, 1787, was reprinted in this issue.
[9] *S. C. State Gazette,* July 9, 1800.

The aristocracy had become so terrified by him that they resorted to calumny and slander. But all this had no effect upon him, for "his principles are too solid to be shaken by the feeble assaults of the public enemies, and his character is too fair and too white to be shaded by the foul aspersions of office seekers." The enemies of Charles Pinckney seized upon this extreme eulogy with bitter glee. The editor of the *South Carolina State Gazette* declared that if there is any sensibility in the grave "what must Laurens and Pulaski feel at having associated with their names that of Lieut. Charles Pinckney!" "An old soldier" took the author of the article in the *Aurora* to task for comparing the three Pinckneys so as to show the advantages of Charles. If such articles continued he might have to write the biography of Charles Pinckney himself. Then he proceeded to give a sample of the type that would be written.

Mr. Charles Pinckney, you say, was distinguished by his valor at Savannah, and in the discharge of his duties, as a husband, he was the mirror of virtue! Lieutenant Pinckney was at the siege of Savannah, and he has had a wife—but whether I shall give his private memoirs, will, Sir, depend upon yourself.[10]

As the summer came on more rumors were spread and greater confusion prevailed in the Federalist party. Some of the stories reached Charles Cotesworth Pinckney in South Carolina. In a letter to McHenry he expressed confidence that their party would still triumph in spite of the defeat in New York and "the tergiversation of Mr. A——." Could Adams really be "endeavoring to coalesce" with Jefferson and had he actually

[10] *S. C. State Gazette*, April 18, 1800. Rumors and charges continued to be made concerning Charles Pinckney throughout his life. Some of them have been repeated as if they were considered true by Professor U. B. Phillips. Of the whole matter Dr. D. D. Wallace has aptly said, "I would be very careful regarding ugly stories about a man who stirred such hatred as did Charles Pinckney. I cannot agree with Prof. Phillips' view of him as of 'no principles in particular'—a rather strange view of a man of positive and aggressive turn from his activity for a stronger Federal government in the 1780's to his unyielding position on the constitutional rights of slavery before most southern men realized the significance of the issue in 1820. The rumor of his having acted dishonorably in money matters has never been supported by a word of proof. His challenge of proof when this was rumored in the campaign of 1818 brought none." *History of S. C.*, III, 358 note.

tried to stigmatize the Federalists "with the odius appellation of a British party?" Pinckney felt that the Federalists must be bound by the agreement reached at Philadelphia and thought that everyone would unless the Eastern states were convinced that Adams had abandoned "federal principles," had attempted to form a new party with Jefferson, and that he was unfitted for the Presidency. If this should happen, some would be willing to substitute another candidate, an event which Pinckney did "not think impossible and his conduct may require it"; the whole tone of the South Carolina candidate's letter was uncompromising toward what he called "the Jacobinical party" of Jefferson.[11] From Annapolis, Harper wrote Otis that his friends in South Carolina had informed him that the Federalists there were supporting Adams solidly. Pinckney was not being brought forward for the Presidency. The "mass of opinion" was divided between Adams and Jefferson; but Pinckney would be supported "on the general ground of giving the friends of the gov't two strings to their bow instead of one."[12]

Soon Jefferson and Adams were being compared in the newspapers of the state. "Constitutionalist" heaped reproach on the President because of his statement that a republic "may mean anything." The editors, however, pointed out that the writer had hardly been fair. Adams, they said, had been writing as a political scientist and had said that a republic had never been defined.[13] On July 4, "Americans" called upon the readers to remember on that day the principles of the Declaration of Independence and "the virtues and services of the long-tried Jefferson."[14] Most of the patriotic organizations gave toasts to "the Vice-president" along with others. There was one notable exception—the Charleston Ancient Battalion offered instead "The cause of Republicanism—may only those enjoy its blessings who know how to appreciate them."[15] *The South Carolina State Gazette* printed for a Federalist correspondent an account of a meeting at which John Adams, "our worthy

[11] This letter is quoted in Beard, *Economic Origins of Jeffersonian Democracy*, pp. 57-58.
[12] Morrison, *Life and Letters of Otis*, 1, 192.
[13] *City Gazette*, July 27, 1800. [14] *Ibid.*, July 4, 1800.
[15] *Ibid.*, July 7, 11, August 7, 1800.

JEFFERSONIAN DEMOCRACY IN S. C.   141

president, was dwelt on with emphatic praise and gratitude" for having been responsible for the Declaration of Independence. Jefferson was grudgingly credited with its "elegance of language." Except for that, the communication continued, "the American people are unacquainted with any act which can exalt him or benefit them."[16] On July 14, Bastille Day "and possibly his birthday," Sumter was given an elaborate dinner by his admirers. He was toasted as "Our representative in Congress—the man who hath persevered in well doing." To which he replied, "The yeomanry, mechanics, and manufacturers of the United States, whose intelligence and patriotism support our Constitution, as their labors do our lives."[17]

In spite of the political controversy and the heat of an unusually hot summer some citizens remained calm and unworried about the possible results of the Presidential election. "Moderator" defended both Adams and Jefferson, stated that he would be satisfied with the election of either, and greatly regretted the vilifications of the partisans.[18] "C. G." disapproved of electioneering and wished that each state should be permitted to choose its own electors without meddling from others.[19]

One of the cleverest types of political propaganda used was that of the imaginary dialogue. In August a correspondent sent to the *City Gazette* a fancied conversation between a Federalist and a Republican. Upon being asked who would be chosen President the former said that he had heard that Adams would continue in office and that the Democrats would be driven out. The Republican observed that such might be the outcome but that he hoped the opposition would be given a chance to show that they could manage the government. If one group remained in power too long its members might come to believe that the government itself belonged to them. The Republican asked for a definition of Federalism. The interlocutor thought that everyone understood the term, but would explain it. Federalism was adherence to the government

[16] *S. C. State Gazette*, July 7, 1800.
[17] Gregorie, *Thomas Sumter*, pp. 243-244.
[18] *City Gazette*, July 14, 1800.
[19] *S. C. State Gazette*, July 15, 1800.

of the Union and its officers, devotion to the commercial interests of the country and to the nation that could aid in this most, antagonism to everything French and opposition to all democracy as an "overbearing influence of the people." The Republican then proceeded to tell the Federalist that his party misused the term. The true Federalist was one who desired a government according to the Constitution regardless of the wishes of the officers. In defining a Democrat, the Federalist characterizes him as a person who insisted that the government "be subordinate to the people instead of the people being subordinate to the government." The Republican thought that a glorious definition. According to him, democracy was the most honorable form of government, "one founded by the power of the people and for the preservation of their happiness." The government of the United States was democratic in origin but mixed in operation. The Federalist replied that he was ingenious but not convincing. In speaking of the coming election the Federalist remarked that Jefferson's chief fault was his liberal religious beliefs; the Republican countered that one should be judged by conduct and not by beliefs. Moreover, Jefferson was primarily interested in religious freedom and the cessation of persecution. Both praised the part of Adams in the Revolution, but the Republican did not like his discussion of the Constitution or his hostility to the French. The Federalist mentioned Jefferson's dislike of the British. In discussing the Sedition Act, the Republican argued for the freedom of the press subject to suits for libel. When the Federalist expressed shock at his willingness to grant such privileges to all, he admitted that he thought "Porcupine" should have been punished for his excessive British zeal. The Federalist approved the Sedition Act and thought the President should be elected or approved by the senate. Then he professed surprise that Congress could not prescribe such a method of election without a Constitutional amendment. Could Congress not change the Constitution? The Republican replied that the possession of such a power by Congress would be absurd. If Congress could change the Constitution the inferior would control the superior. As to the commercial situation,

JEFFERSONIAN DEMOCRACY IN S. C. 143

the Federalist admitted that the British were violating our commerce but asked his opponent if he wanted war. To which the latter replied negatively but if there must be war, he would prefer to fight the British rather than the French. Economic pressure in the form of an embargo would no doubt be better than armed conflict in either case. In his opinion, the act of the British of sending a commission to negotiate on the spoliation claims and continuing the depredations was as insulting as the "X. Y. Z." affair. The Republican did not favor Pinckney for President, because he was high in the command of the army. Civil authority should not be turned over to a military official. The same objection applied to Hamilton. The Federalist hoped that Pinckney would be elected and thought that he would even though he heard that Adams would be the choice. People were betting on Pinckney and must have some private knowledge to that effect.[20]

Another favorite method of pointing out the defects of the opposite party was by defining its principles. A correspondent of the *City Gazette,* after reading "a Receipt for a Jacobin" in another newspaper, decided to offer a "Receipt for forming a Federal Jacobin." Apparently his formula was to apply to "Federal Jacobins" as distinguished from "Republican Jacobins."

Begin by asserting preeminence in *abilities, virtues and patriotism:* consequently the right of judging for others, as well as yourselves; and the exclusive right of governing. Attribute the *worst* motifs to every man who does not adopt *your* political creed. Advocate standing armies, sedition acts, *efficient* governments, not stopping at monarchies. Call the liberty of the press licentiusness; redicule the sovereignty of the people; cry down all republics and republicans, as the word *republic*

[20] The first dialogue between the Federalist and the Republican appeared in the *City Gazette,* August 11, 1800. A second was printed on August 16. At that time the Federalist argued that the last objection to Pinckney had been eliminated with the disbanding of the army. A change in tone of government was denounced as "Jacobin." The Republican replied that the states did not oppose change for many made the governor ineligible for immediate reelection. His preference for the Presidency was a man of moderation, philosophical mind, who had not been insulted by any foreign government against which he might be influenced as President.

"may mean anything." Pretend to be a warm advocate of the Christian religion; but it is very immaterial whether you add example to precept. "Do as I say not as I do." But all this will not do unless you are unqualified in your abuse of Mr. Jefferson's character. Never mind whether what you say against him be true or not; it will have the desired effect with many. Leave "no stone upturned"—hesitate not to utter the most abominable falsehoods: for, as the nation will be ruined, should that *infidel* be elected our president, the *"end"* answered of keeping him out must justify the means; his advocates of course must be *all villains.* Use, on all occasions the words *Jacobinic, democratic,* &c. apply them indiscriminately to anything that does not accord with your own opinions; abominate everything that is *French,*—and extol everything that is *English.* Practice all these things, and in a very short time you will become as *high toned* a Federalist, alas, a *Federal Jacobin* as ever patronized Porcupine.[21]

One writer recommended abandoning all the leading candidates and substituting Elbridge Gerry. Since Adams and Jefferson had both held high offices another might be tried. Besides, Jefferson was said to be an infidel and it was unwise to raise such a man to the Presidency.[22]

Not to be outdone by the Republicans, the Federalists contributed dialogues. One of these was an imaginary conversation between a Republican and a mechanic. The former attempted to show the latter how the Federalists were depriving him of his liberties. The mechanic paid little attention, telling the Republican that a gentleman's word is always taken above his and that the only time he received attention was just before elections. Then he was flattered by those like the Republican who desired his vote. The mechanic had heard the Republican criticize the officers but had not seen him punished for it. Malicious lies should not be permitted. For that purpose sedition laws were necessary. As for the Alien Law it merely gave the President the power to send out of the country those who were dangerous. The mechanic said that he did not have

[21] *City Gazette,* August 23, 1800.
[22] As to be expected both sides argued on the religious question. *City Gazette,* September 20, 1800. See also in the same paper, July 21, the articles of "Back Countryman" and "Fair Play." It had then been stated that nothing was found in Jefferson's *Notes on Virginia* to keep one from thinking that he believed in the "Christian Dispensation."

as much education as the Republican but he had some sense. The Republican was advised to attend to his business, and give up gaming and office hunting. A clever person could make more money in business than in office. If the Republicans would start working and get to the point at which they could enjoy the fruits of their "own labours," they would see that it had been they and not the country that had been going to ruin.[23]

3. DIVISION AMONG THE FEDERALISTS

Late in August Harper became alarmed at the rumors he had been hearing in regard to the working of Adams's friends against Pinckney in New England. Writing to Otis, who was thought to have influence with the President, he declared that Adams was in desperate need of votes. If the stories concerning the discrimination against Pinckney were believed by the latter's friends they might stop work in disgust and there was no way of telling how far they might go. Harper said that he personally thought Pinckney was better fitted for the Presidency. This preference was not because of private friendship, for he and Pinckney had always been "on ill terms." On the other hand, his relations with Adams had been all that he could have expected; but the latter's qualifications did not equal those of his running mate. However, at that time, it was his firm conviction that the public good demanded the reelection of the President. His labors toward that end had been unceasing and would continue to be. The Federalists in South Carolina likewise were keeping up the fight. It was looking doubtful for Adams there, though, because of the method of choosing the electors. If they were chosen directly by the voters, according to letters from his South Carolina correspondents of a late date, the Federalists would get four fifths of the electors. But the choice by the legislature enabled "a few artful Jacobins" to defeat the will of the electorate by misleading "the uninformed though well-meaning men of whom it is composed." The rumors regarding Adams's alleged conduct were making it hard for his friends. He could not believe that the President was willing to be on the same ticket with Jefferson as it had

[23] *S. C. State Gazette,* September 26, 1800.

been reported.[24] About a month later Hamilton wrote Wolcott, asking his advice concerning the sending of a letter dealing with Adams's conduct to certain influential individuals in New England. Two purposes might be facilitated by that procedure —"the promoting of Mr. Pinckney's election, and the vindication of ourselves." Since most of the information had come from his three friends in the cabinet, he wished Wolcott's approval. The latter was undecided. If vindication alone were the motive, its publication might be deferred until after election; however, he felt that something must be done to counteract the expected voting for Adams but not Pinckney in Maryland. Wolcott thought that steps should be taken to encourage a few Federalists to vote for Pinckney but not Adams. Such an act would not contribute to the election of Jefferson. Instead, it would probably "be the means of referring the choice of a President to the House of Representatives."[25]

Soon Hamilton's pamphlet appeared in print, thereby placing him in the embarrassing position of asking electors to vote for a man whom he unmercifully criticized.[26] One act of Adams which Hamilton referred to was his charge that the Pinckneys had been instrumental in getting his mission to England fixed to a definite period so that Thomas Pinckney could go there later as the American minister.[27]

[24] Harper to Otis, from Baltimore, August 28, 1800. Morrison, *Life and Letters of Otis,* I, 192-196.

[25] Gibbs, *Administrations of Washington and Adams,* II, 421-422, 430-432. The letters were dated September 26, and October 2, 1800, respectively.

[26] Other details in regard to his reasons for writing the article on Adams have been given *supra,* pp. 136-137.

[27] Adams had been confused regarding the Pinckneys. It was Charles Pinckney who had been in Congress at that time and he certainly should not have been accused of trying to further the interests of Thomas Pinckney. It seems that the suspicion of the father was communicated to his son. At any rate John Quincy Adams while in Berlin in 1798 wrote in a disparaging way concerning the political stability of Thomas Pinckney. Worthington Chauncey Ford, ed., *The Writings of John Quincy Adams* (New York: Macmillan Co., 1913-1917), II, 243-244. On October 27, 1800, John Adams wrote Thomas Pinckney to apologize for the letter he had written Tench Coxe in 1792 concerning the British mission. It was too late then, however, to obtain any political advantage from it in the election of that year. Adams stated in the letter that he had not known any of the Pinckneys in 1792. He had heard

JEFFERSONIAN DEMOCRACY IN S. C.   147

Hamilton also referred to Adams's assertion that British influence had contributed to the appointment of Thomas Pinckney.[28] Hamilton pointed out that the charges of friendliness toward the British was apparently based on the fact that the two brothers had been educated in England and had known the Duke of Leeds and others well while they were all boys; but such friendships "in their juvenile years" had not prevented their fighting against the British during the Revolution. The appointment, said Hamilton, had originated with Washington and had satisfied even Jefferson. In the remainder of the article Hamilton took up his own attitude toward Adams and Thomas Pinckney in 1796 and other matters of controversy. Finally he said that in spite of his disapproval of the President he recommended that John Adams and Charles Cotesworth Pinckney be given equal support in the coming election. Thus did Alexander Hamilton seek to vindicate himself and prevent the electors in certain states from voting against Pinckney.[29]

In the meantime Harper had been trying to convince Adams's friends, through Otis, that Pinckney was not a competitor for the Presidency. It greatly vexed him that he was still referred to as such. On October 10, Harper wrote in a more hopeful mood about South Carolina. His latest correspondence indicated that that state's votes would go to both Adams and Pinckney. Charles Cotesworth Pinckney and his brother were doing all they could, in spite of the Tench Coxe letter, to bring victory for the two Federalist candidates. Harper hoped for the best but had forebodings unless Otis and others were convinced that Pinckney was not competing

---

rumors and had formed a mistaken opinion. He now admitted he was wrong. "And I will add, in the sincerity of my heart, that I know of no two gentlemen whose characters and conduct are more deserving of confidence." Gibbs, *Administrations of Washington and Adams*, II, 425-426; Adams, *Works of Adams*, II, 587, note.

[28] Such a rumor had reached Washington in 1799. Perhaps he did not know who started it. At any rate he wrote McHenry, November 17, of that year, asking him the source. The ex-President thought that his fighting against the British should have freed him from charges of being influenced by them. He considered it an indignity for one to make such an insinuation and strongly urged McHenry to explain. Ford, *Writings of Washington*, XIV, 216-217.

[29] Lodge, *Works of Hamilton*, VII, 309-365.

with Adams for the first place. He insisted that he himself had never heard of Pinckney's being spoken of as such "by those who proposed the policy of bringing him forward."[30]

4. THE CONTINUED VIGOR OF THE CAMPAIGN

Unquestionably the most tireless worker for the Republican cause in South Carolina, perhaps in the Southern states, was Charles Pinckney. Few men kept in closer touch with both state and federal political affairs. Still in his early forties, he had held more important positions than most public men do in a lifetime. Having been extremely influential in the formation of the constitutions of the United States and of South Carolina, and having been well schooled in the practical phases of government in his own state, he was now emerging on the national scene. Aware of the fast hardening of party lines and the capriciousness of local governmental machinery, he early realized the supreme difficulties that would face the Republicans in 1800. More than a year before the election, Pinckney wrote Madison suggesting the passing of a law in Virginia providing for the choice of Presidential and Vice-Presidential electors by a joint vote of both houses of the legislature. If it turned out, as it then seemed likely, that the party strength should be close, such a change might mean victory instead of defeat for the Republicans.[31]

In no previous election had the voters been confronted with such a flood of campaign literature. In a letter to Jefferson, Charles Pinckney wrote, "We have Literally sprinkled Georgia and North Carolina *from the mountains to the Ocean.*"[32] That

[30] Morrison, *Life and Letters of Otis*, I, 197-198. Morrison, in note, p. 197, says in regard to Harper's professed ignorance of any plan to secure the election of Pinckney as President, "This statement is hard to believe. Harper was in communication with Cabot and McHenry, both of whom considered Pinckney very much the competitor of Adams, and he must have talked with other Hamiltonians in Philadelphia who held similar views." McHenry had written Wolcott, July 22, "Mr. Harper is now clearly of the opinion that General Pinckney ought to be preferred. Whether this will produce any effect I know not." Gibbs, *Administration of Washington and Adams*, II, 385.

[31] September 30, 1799, Madison Papers. In the arrangement of the letters, this one was misplaced with those dated, 1789.

[32] Several letters in regard to the election of 1800 in South Carolina are printed in the *American Historical Review*, IV, 111-129. The letter

both parties resorted to this practice is indicated by the statement of a correspondent from St. Bartholomew that he had never before been so "pestered with politics" and that he was being overwhelmed by pamphlets from Federalists and Republicans alike.[33] "A Republican Federalist" regretted the tendency of the leaders to try to dictate as to how one should vote. The electorate should be left to its own choice. He was not convinced that the country would be ruined if Adams were reelected; nor did he fear dangerous policies in the event of Jefferson's victory.[34] Two pamphlets indicative of the line of reasoning of the leaders in each party, will be discussed here. The articles of Henry William DeSaussure are chosen for the presentation of Federalist views, while the writings of Charles Pinckney are selected to represent the Republicans.

DeSaussure stated that the United States had been in a very serious condition after the Revolution but that the Federalists had saved the day. Under the most trying circumstances the country under Washington and Adams "had pursued a steady course," repelling the aggressions of both Great Britain and France, yet maintaining peace. In the course of the European war American commerce had grown and agriculture had been encouraged by the demand for our productions. The nation had become prosperous and happy. All along the Federalists had been opposed, DeSaussure continued, by the "antifederals," who would have sided with France and whose policy would have culminated in such dire consequences as war with Great Britain, the interruption of prosperity, the decrease in revenues and the necessity for new taxes. The sponsors of such a course were now the supporters of Jefferson.

Next DeSaussure compared the candidates. Jefferson was admittedly "distinguished by shewy talents, for theoretic learning, and for elegance of his *written* style." He described Jef-

---

quoted above was written October 12, 1800, and the particular page references are 113-114. Pinckney made accurate prediction as to the outcome in the Southern states. According to him Tennessee and Georgia would be unanimous for the Republicans and in North Carolina they would get eight or nine electoral votes. In the final count, in the last state the party got eight; in the other cases the vote was unanimous.

[33] *City Gazette*, October 3, 1800. [34] *Ibid.*, October 13, 1800.

ferson as having been an inefficient governor of Virginia, thus being responsible for her very feeble defense when invaded in 1781. His record as minister in France lacked distinction. It was during his absence that the Constitution was formed and the movements leading to prosperity had been begun without Jefferson's aid. He had even advised that some of the states refuse to ratify the Constitution until it was amended. It had taken all of Madison's ability to overcome his influence in Virginia. The Republican candidate was accused of making insinuations against Washington in the Mazzei letter. DeSaussure charged that Jefferson would seize any opportunity to overthrow the Constitution. The *National Gazette* had been fostered by Jefferson's patronage and he had no doubt encouraged Genêt in his appeal to the American public. The people should not choose as President a man who had favored and been favored by France, a nation that had heaped injuries upon the United States. In addition to all this Jefferson had, in his *Notes on Virginia,* London edition of 1787, advocated the emancipation of the slaves. He had even gone so far as to draw up an amendment looking to that end to be submitted to the Virginia legislature. In another portion of his book Jefferson had expressed the belief that the time was approaching when total emancipation would take place. In view of what had happened in Santo Domingo, such doctrines were dangerous.

On the other hand, according to DeSaussure, a study of Adams's life was more pleasing. No such defects were connected with the Federalist candidate. In spite of all the criticism of the Alien and Sedition Laws the voters had shown in the election of 1798 that they approved their passage. Besides, the Alien Act had expired and the Sedition Law would cease to be effective in 1801. A person was at liberty to express his opinions as freely as ever; it was left to a jury to decide whether he had intended to "defame the government." Such a proposition, he thought, was fair. The association of Charles Cotesworth Pinckney with Adams added strength to the Federalist ticket. The former's military career had been distinguished; but none of his experiences with the army would interfere with his admirable fitness for civil office. Of such a temperament was he that not even the insults of France would cause him to be vindictive. The election of Adams and Pinckney would inspire confidence at home and respect abroad. It would be a sign that the past firm tone in foreign affairs would be continued. Due to the almost balanced state of parties in the country it was of great importance that South Carolina vote for Adams and Pinckney. In fact, her electoral votes might be sufficient to decide the election.[35]

In a series of articles in the *City Gazette* between August 28, and October 14, Charles Pinckney attempted to show why South Carolina and the Southern states should give their electoral votes to Jefferson and Burr. The Alien and Sedition Laws were declared to be oppressive and destructive of liberties; the judiciary system was said to lack uniformity and not to guarantee an impartial trial; the system of taxation was condemned as discriminative in favor of the commercial group; and Jefferson was held up as most eminently qualified for the Presidency. Being a close student of politics, Pinckney concluded that those primarily interested in commerce could hardly be won over by the Republicans in any great numbers. He therefore concentrated his energies on trying to show that it was to the interest of agrarian and planting groups to support Jefferson. First, Pinckney asserted that in spite of all the taxes contrived by the Federalists the public debt had increased $10,000,000. The direct tax was declared to be particularly odious because it attempted to shift so great a burden to agriculture. Why had such a tax not been levied on other products as well as slaves and the possessions of the planter and landholder? Were the planters and landholders obnoxious to the government? What had they done to be so punished? Whenever one group of citizens was singled out to be taxed and all others exempt, "it operates both in the nature of a punishment and a stigma." It showed that the government was "least in-

[35] A copy of DeSaussure's pamphlet, signed "A Federal Republican," is in the Charleston Library Society's pamphlets, series 5, vol. I, no. 6. It was in the form of "An Address to the Citizens of South-Carolina on the Approaching Election of President and Vice-President of the United States."

clined to favor them, or even to protect their equal rights;" and proved that when heavy burdens were to be meted out the landed interests would be called upon to bear them.

Our government by this invidious distinction, has placed the landholder and the planter in an oppressive and degrading predicament. And what is this done for? Why, clearly, to exempt all the monied interest, which is by far the largest in the Northern States and the greatest favorite of the federal party, from bearing any share of the public burdens, and throwing all direct taxes entirely upon the landed and planting interests; that if any man in a Northern State is worth half a million of stock or money at interest he shall not pay a shilling to a direct tax, while a poor Virginia or Carolina planter, who owns a little land and a few negroes, and perhaps owes for part of them, is obliged to contribute his share.

To make the issue more pointed, Pinckney stated that Adams, who probably owned a good deal of stock, was free from a direct tax, while Jefferson

Whose whole estate is exactly like that of your own planters, who owns two hundred negroes himself, and who, in order to remove all doubts upon the subject has authorized his friends to declare as his assertion: "That the Constitution has not empowered the federal legislature to touch in the remotest degree the question respecting the condition or property of slaves in any of the States, and that any attempt of that sort would be unconstitutional and a usurpation of rights Congress do not possess."

The record of the Federalist party was before them. Its policies were injurious to agriculture, while on the other hand Jefferson was a planter himself and vitally interested in the welfare of the landed group. If in the face of such evidence they chose to favor a member of the Federalist party they would be "content to be more oppressed and degraded and to bear heavier and more unequal burdens" than he believed they were.[36]

[36] The article emphasized above appeared in the *City Gazette*, October 3, 1800, signed "A Republican." The quoted portions are taken from the partial reproduction in Beard, *Economic Origins of Jeffersonian Democracy*, pp. 373-375. The twenty-four "numbers" of the "Republican" were reprinted from the newspaper and spread widely for campaign purposes. Copies of them and others by Pinckney were sent to Jefferson. *American Historical Review*, IV, 113.

JEFFERSONIAN DEMOCRACY IN S. C.   153

As the election date approached, party lines became more closely defined than ever. It was commonly believed by both sides that the outcome in South Carolina could elect or defeat a Presidential aspirant, so nearly divided were the parties elsewhere. From the first, the Federalists had counted strongly on the state's votes for one if not for both of their candidates. Jefferson and Monroe thought that the result in South Carolina would be decisive.[37] With the narrow coast section in possession of a representation in the legislature out of proportion to its population, the Republicans knew that it would take all their energies to bring about the choice of enough members of their party to insure victory for their electoral ticket. The commercial interests, the friends of the United States Bank, the recent complications in regard to foreign affairs, and the popularity of Charles Cotesworth Pinckney were all against the Republicans. In addition to his candidacy for the Vice-Presidency, in order to strengthen the party at the polls and in the legislature, the Federalists were running Pinckney for the state senate. So bitter did the campaign become that, according to the report of Charles Pinckney, his kinsman would not speak to him when they met.[38] It was charged that Jeffer-

---

[37] In a letter to Jefferson, November 22, Charles Pinckney referred to a recent communication from Monroe stating that he believed the vote of South Carolina would decide the Presidency. *American Historical Review*, IV, 118. On December 5, Jefferson wrote Thomas Mann Randolph that, the results in the other states being as they seemed to be, South Carolina would decide whether he or Adams would be President. *Writings of Jefferson*, Def. Edition, XVIII, 226-227. In the same letter Jefferson stated his belief that Charles Cotesworth Pinckney would be one of the two to get the electoral votes of the state, but would not venture an opinion as to who would be the second. Thus it is seen that he considered it a very doubtful state so far as he was concerned. His news from South Carolina was rather scant at about the time the electors were to be chosen. Distrusting the mail he wrote few letters himself and then generally without the franking privilege. Charles Pinckney complained of his mail being opened and frequently found that letters he had written to Jefferson, Madison and others had not gotten to them. *American Historical Review*, IV, 113, 116, 118. Samuel Flagg Bemis, ed., *The American Secretaries of State and Their Diplomacy* (New York: Alfred A. Knopf, 1927-1929), III, 6.

[38] Charles Pinckney to Jefferson, November 22, 1800, *American Historical Review*, IV, 118. The former stated that in order to gain Republican members in the legislature he had had to oppose Charles Cotes-

son had promised Charles Pinckney the place as minister in Paris or some other European country if he could deliver the electoral votes of the state to the Republicans, an accusation which Pinckney promptly denied.[39] Some thought that Charles Cotesworth Pinckney should not be candidate for the state senate and the Vice-Presidency of the United States at the same time.[40] Others answered that those who considered it indelicate for him to serve in the legislature while he was being voted on for the Vice-Presidency did not know or understand his character. The possibility of his being chosen for the latter position would not influence his conduct in the slightest degree.[41]

Just before the legislative elections, the statements that Charles Cotesworth Pinckney was really a candidate for the Presidency instead of the Vice-Presidency became more frequent; but there is evidence that some of these assertions were made by Republicans instead of Federalists. For instance, "Rice Planter" gives himself away by arguing that, since Adams and Pinckney were both candidates for the first place, the risk of a tie should be avoided by voting for Jefferson and Burr.[42] Christopher Gadsden desired the election of Adams

worth Pinckney in Charleston, the first time it had ever been done. Because of resentment at this opposition his kinsman no longer spoke to him.

[39] In the *South Carolina State Gazette,* October 4, 1800, "One who likes fair play" reported that Charles Pinckney's creditors were becoming alarmed lest he be sent to Europe before he made suitable arrangements in regard to his debts. He was pleased to read in the *City Gazette,* the editors of which were close friends to Pinckney, that the latter was making plans to pay his creditors and was not a candidate for a foreign appointment. The writer of the letter continued, however, as if he did not believe the statement. It had been his understanding that such a post had been promised by Jefferson. Pinckney had preferred England but had thought it popular to denounce the British. However, the appointment to France would be satisfactory, "as it is understood Paris now has more *polite girls,* and Italian pictures, and as it is known his *chaste taste,* is particularly interested in such subjects." The writer of the letter, claiming to be one of Pinckney's creditors, requested that the recent correspondent to the *City Gazette* inform him personally as to the plans to be made concerning the debts.

[40] *City Gazette,* October 7, 1800.   [41] *Ibid.,* October 8, 1800.

[42] *Ibid.,* November 19, 1800. Also in the same paper, October 3, 7.

JEFFERSONIAN DEMOCRACY IN S. C.   155

and Pinckney as President and Vice-President respectively; but if that could not be brought about there were others who could carry on the government well. He deplored the attitude that Adams and Jefferson were the only persons that should be considered for the Presidency.[43] The bitterness of the campaign, however, had so divided the electorate into Federalists or Republicans that each group felt compelled to stand by the candidates of its own party to the end. It had been comparatively easy for the same person to vote for a Federalist and a Republican both in 1796, but the closeness of party lines in 1800 made such an act almost out of the question. Certainly some of them might differ as to whether Pinckney or Adams should be President; but they were both Federalists. The linking of Pinckney and Jefferson in 1800 was an entirely different matter. As shown above, in his letter to McHenry months before, Charles Cotesworth Pinckney considered the very idea of the Federalists having any connection with the "Jacobinic" party of Jefferson as obnoxious to the extreme.[44]

5. REPUBLICAN VICTORIES IN SOUTH CAROLINA

The election for members of the state legislature was held on October 15. The Republicans did not expect to get more than one third of the fifteen members from Charleston, but they hoped to make up for their losses there by victories where the commercial and British influence was not so strong. On the day after the election Charles Pinckney wrote Jefferson that only four Republicans had been declared elected by the managers at Charleston. He had never before known the extent of the federal interest, he said.

Connected with the British & the aid of the Bank & of the federal treasury and their officers—they have endeavoured to shake *Republicanism in South Carolina* to its foundations—but we have resisted it firmly and I trust successfully—Our country interest out of the reach of Banks & Custom House & federal officers is I think as powerful as ever—I rejoice our Legislature meets 130 or 140 miles from the Sea,—As much as I have

---

[43] *S. C. State Gazette,* October 8, 1800.
[44] *Supra* pp. 139-140. Pinckney's idea was that if any substitutions should be made, it would be another Federalist for Adams, but not a joining with Republicans under any circumstances.

been accustomed to politics & to study mankind this Election in Charleston has opened my eyes to a new View of things. Never certainly was such an election in America. We mean to contest it for 8 or 9 of the 15—it is said several Hundred more voted than paid taxes—the Lame, crippled, diseased and blind were either led, lifted or brought in carriages to the Poll.—the sacred right to Ballots was struck at (for at a late hour when too late to counteract it) in order to know how men, who were supposed to be under the influence of Bank & federal officers & English merchants, voted, & that they might be watched to know whether they voted as they were directed the novel & unwarranted measure was used of voting with tickets printed on *Green & blue & red & yellow paper* & men stationed to watch the voters.

He himself, Pinckney continued, had been singled out for special persecution. The Federalists had blamed him for their reverses, and "so much abuse & private slander, I believe no man has ever yet sustained." Some "false private charges" he had been "obliged to come forward and deny."[45] In later communications to Jefferson and Madison, Pinckney informed them that daily he was receiving news of Republican victories in other counties. So small, however, was the differences in strength between the two parties that he felt his influence would be needed in Columbia while the legislature was choosing the Presidential electors. This would make it impossible for him to attend the early meetings of the Congress soon to assemble.[46]

In the Congressional elections in South Carolina, Pinckney told Jefferson that the Republicans had won in three districts and had lost in a fourth by "a narrow Squeeze."[47] Having moved to Maryland and not having stood for reelection, Robert Goodloe Harper was to be succeeded by William Butler, a Republican. Likewise the seat of the Federalist Abraham Nott was to be taken by the Republican Thomas Moore. The third

[45] Charles Pinckney to Jefferson, October 16, on same sheet as letter of October 12, 1800, the latter letter not having been mailed before the former was written. Jefferson Papers. Also in *American Historical Review*, IV, 114-116.

[46] Charles Pinckney to Madison, October 26, and to Jefferson, November 22, 1800. *American Historical Review*, IV, 116-119.

[47] *Ibid.*, IV, p. 119.

JEFFERSONIAN DEMOCRACY IN S. C. 157

Republican, Thomas Sumter, apparently the most popular representative of his part in the state in so far as the electorate was concerned, easily defeated two opponents, one of whom was the former Congressman Richard Winn.[48] On the Federalist side, Benjamin Huger and John Rutledge were reelected and Thomas Lowndes succeeded Thomas Pinckney, who had also been a Federalist.[49] Thus in the Seventh Congress the South Carolina representatives were evenly divided for a time between the two parties. In the senate, however, both were to be Republicans, due to the election of John Ewing Colhoun over Jacob Read by the state legislature.[50]

When the South Carolina legislature assembled on the fourth Monday in November, 1800, both the Federalists and the Republicans hoped to secure the choice of Presidential and Vice-Presidential electors favorable to their candidates.[51] On Wednesday evening, the third day of the session, the Republican caucus met for the purpose of deciding upon a list of electors. Robert Anderson was called to the chair; a nominating committee was appointed; and in a short while it submitted its report. The committee was instructed to ask the nominees if they favored Jefferson and Burr. About fifty-five of those present pledged in writing to support the list of electors chosen by the caucus. On the following evening the Republicans again met, at which time the committee reported that the proposed electors had signified their loyalty to Jefferson and Burr, and

[48] The vote was Sumter, 1,259; Winn, 649; and Williams Bracey, 82. Gregorie, *Thomas Sumter*, p. 246.

[49] John Rutledge of the Seventh Congress was the John Rutledge, Jr., of the previous Congress. His father John Rutledge, Sr., had died in the meantime.

[50] *S. C. Historical and Genealogical Magazine*, VII, 153-154. The vote was close, 75 to 73.

[51] During the course of the controversy which developed later as to whether a compromise was offered, John Bee Holmes, a leading member of the Federalist group stated that it was his opinion that both sides were opposed to compromise and had so stated it in the presence of the leaders of both parties two days before the election by the legislature. He did think, however, at a later date, that Charles Cotesworth Pinckney could have gotten the votes of South Carolina if the Federalists had been willing to relinquish Adams earlier. He did not say, though, how early such an action would have been necessary. *City Gazette,* July 27, 1802.

the enrollment of those pledged to the Republican electors was increased to seventy or seventy-five. A few present, evidently not having made up their minds fully, did not sign. On Friday evening the Federalists held their meeting at the home of the president of the senate to choose their list of electors. After the adjournment of the legislature on the following Monday Robert Anderson, John Taylor and John Hunter, all leading Republicans, were informed by a person whose name has not been divulged that a group of Federalists were going to attend the Republican caucus that evening for the purpose of offering a compromise. After some discussion, Anderson, the Republican chairman, instructed Taylor to place a note on the door of the meeting hall stating that no caucus would be held that night. The next day the legislature chose the electors pledged to Jefferson and Burr over those in favor of Adams and Pinckney by an average majority of about nineteen.[52] The Re-

[52] The above details of the caucus meetings and other events in Columbia prior to the choosing of the electors are based largely on the letter of John Hunter to Madison, April 16, 1801 (Madison Papers), and the communication by Hunter to the *City Gazette*, July 21, 1802, the accuracy of which has not been contradicted. Statements of a similar nature may be found in the letter of Charles Pinckney to Jefferson, January 24, 1801, *American Historical Review*, IV, 127-128. The Republican list of electors and their votes were, John Hunter, 87; Paul Hamilton, 87; Robert Anderson, 85; Theodore Gaillard, 85; Arthur Simkins, 84; Wade Hampton, 82; Andrew Love, 82; and Joseph Blyth, 82. The Federalist group and their votes were, William Washington, 69; John Ward, 69; Thomas Roper, 67; James Postell, 66; John Blosingame, 66; William McPherson, 64; William Falconer, 64; and Henry Dana Ward, 63. Peter Freneau to Jefferson, December 2, 1800, *American Historical Review*, IV, 120.

A tradition has persisted till today that Charles Cotesworth Pinckney was offered the votes of the South Carolina electors if he would permit his name to be linked with that of Jefferson. The chief sources are the statements of Henry William DeSaussure and the assertions of John Rutledge and others largely based on DeSaussure's communications. A letter alleged to have been written by DeSaussure, December 2, 1800, to Rutledge was quoted in an anonymous correspondence from Washington (really written by Senator Theodore Foster to Nicholas Brown) to the *Providence Journal* and appeared December 24, 1800. In it DeSaussure is reported to have said, "We could easily have formed a ticket of Mr. Jefferson and Gen. Pinckney. But on the most mature deliberation, we deemed it wisest and most honorable to adhere to the federal arrangements for the equal support of Mr. Adams." *American*

JEFFERSONIAN DEMOCRACY IN S. C. 159

publicans thus selected to cast the votes of South Carolina for

Historical Review, IV, 112. Other references in regard to DeSaussure's remarks as to a possible compromise may be found in Reverend C. C. Pinckney's *Life of General Thomas Pinckney* (Boston: 1895), pp. 255-257, based on statements made by DeSaussure twenty-five years later, a rather long time for one's memory to remain entirely accurate. It will be noticed that the words of DeSaussure do not contain the names or the party affiliations of the persons who were supposed to have been supporters of compromise. The inference, however, which he seems to have desired one to draw is that the Federalists were the ones that opposed. When John Rutledge gave such an interpretation to the failure of South Carolina to vote for Charles Cotesworth Pinckney, John Hunter promptly charged that he was merely trying to keep alive a party that had failed. Likewise, Robert Anderson denied that the Republicans had shown any inclination toward compromise. He said that Rutledge had not been in Columbia at that time and nobody who was would believe his statement. John Bee Holmes, a Federalist, corroborated Hunter's statement that the Republican leaders agreed with his own remark that both parties were opposed to compromise. Present at the time Holmes gave this opinion were Robert Anderson, John Hunter, Holmes and DeSaussure himself. *City Gazette*, July 21, 22, 27, 1802.

So the question remains—who were these members of the legislature who wanted a Jefferson and Pinckney ticket? Eliminating the seventy to seventy-five Republicans who pledged themselves to Jefferson and Burr, one finds left only twelve to seventeen Republicans and the Federalists. In order to have obtained a majority for a so-called compromise ticket at least ten Republicans and the entire Federalist membership would have been necessary. Furthermore, it would have required a virtually unanimous willingness of the Federalists to relinquish Adams and support Jefferson. To have accomplished this would, no doubt, have necessitated the open support of Charles Cotesworth Pinckney himself. This, he obviously could not give, after the stand he had taken against Jefferson and his "Jacobinical" party and the extreme criticism he had meted out when the rumor came to him that Adams was inclined to join with the Republican candidate. (*Supra*, pp. 139-140). The next question a curious investigator might like to ask is—how could DeSaussure himself, in view of the picture he had painted of Jefferson as such a dangerous and unstable person even seriously consider giving his own partial support to him? One might well wonder if the young representative was not speculating about what could have been accomplished if other things had not been thus and so. Perhaps to a young politician as well as to a poet, the saddest of words are, "it might have been."

It seems to the present writer that the strongest case for the Federalists was presented by a correspondent to the *City Gazette*, July 23, 1802, under the signature "Pyrrhus." He said that no one maintained that there was an actual, organized meeting in which the Republicans offered to compromise with the Federalists and vote for General Pinckney along with Jefferson. "Pyrrhus" held that if twelve of those who voted for the Republicans had cast their ballots with the Federalists Pinckney could have been substituted for Burr. It was his opinion that there were that many who were willing to change. He further believed that the Republican leaders called off the meeting on the evening before the choosing of the electors because they were afraid to have a compromise proposal submitted at their caucus. "Pyrrhus" supported his analysis by a copy of a letter of John Ward, one of the electors proposed by the Federalists and who along with William Washington apparently received the votes of every Federalist in the legislature. In this letter which Ward was reported to have written to John Rutledge, it was said that enough Republicans stated their preference for Pinckney over Burr to have effected the compromise. Ward said that they so stated to him but that he was opposed to changing the ticket decided upon by the Federalists. It will be noted by the admission of these two Federalists, one of them a proposed elector receiving all the votes of his party, that a compromise would have required virtually the unanimous support of their members in the legislature. Ward stated that he opposed the compromise when the matter was discussed with individual Republicans. The strongest point against the Republicans is the calling off of the meeting. This may have shown some fear on the part of the leaders, but it by no means even indicates that a compromise would have been accepted by the Republicans if it had been proposed. There is no evidence that anyone who might have appeared before the caucus could have pledged the support of any group of Federalists. There might have been some confusion, a few speeches by the visiting Federalists and the Republicans who had not pledged themselves to stand by Jefferson and Burr. It would hardly be reasonable to suppose that a majority of the Republicans would have changed suddenly on the night before the election. On the other hand to have had a compromise proposed and then openly voted down would have meant the unnecessary public rejection of Charles Cotesworth Pinckney, who was a member of the legislature itself, who was highly respected by all and against whom they would have to vote the next day when they chose the electors. The public discussion and wrangling would have merely intensified party strife, the prevention of which within itself would have justified the calling off of the meeting. Besides, the Federalists could have seen and no doubt did see the sign on the door that no meeting would be held. If there were so many of their number ardently desirous of bringing about a compromise, the individual Republicans could have been interviewed that night. If that had failed and there had been any great number still determined to effect the compromise they could have brought about a postponement of the choosing of the electors by the legislature until the groups could get together and discuss the matter. This they did not attempt to do.

Thus it seems that the sum total of evidence in the case points to only this—a few people thought that a compromise could have been brought about, but no person was willing to say openly that he was in

JEFFERSONIAN DEMOCRACY IN S. C.   161

withhold one of the votes from Burr, but when the voting time came they supported him equally with Jefferson.[53]

The choice of electors over, Charles Pinckney began making preparation to go to Washington to attend the last session of the Sixth Congress, which had begun a few weeks before. He had gone to Columbia to be present during the early part of the legislative session, on the theory that the election of a President was of more importance than any business Congress might have to transact in his absence. Before leaving South Carolina, Pinckney wrote Jefferson requesting that no appointments for his state be made until after his arrival in Washington. According to the South Carolina senator there was a good deal of information concerning the local situation which the President-elect should have at hand before making his decisions. However, before Pinckney finally saw Jefferson, he asked him to ignore the request, since on further consideration he had decided it an improper one. In reply Jefferson stated that it was far from improper, that he counted upon him for advice and that he would be glad to see him soon, suggesting that Pinckney come the next day for dinner.[54] A few days later Jefferson offered the position of minister to Spain to Charles Pinckney, who promptly accepted.[55]

6. JEFFERSON FINALLY CHOSEN PRESIDENT

Before the votes of the electors were formally announced to the joint session of the two houses of Congress, it was known that Jefferson and Burr had been supported equally and that the house of representatives would be called upon to decide between them.[56] Thinking that Burr might be more favorable

---

favor of it. Not even DeSaussure went that far. In his statements concerning the matter he was always speaking for a group of unnamed persons, whose party affiliations were not mentioned.

[53] Peter Freneau to Jefferson, December 2, 1800. *American Historical Review*, IV, 120.

[54] Pinckney to Jefferson, January 24, February 9; Jefferson to Pinckney, March 6, 1801. Jefferson Papers.

[55] On March 17, 1801, Jefferson wrote Pinckney a letter in which he mentioned receiving his acceptance of the post as minister to Spain. Jefferson Papers.

[56] The official vote may be found in *Annals of Congress*, 6th Cong., 2nd Sess. (February 11, 1801), p. 744. Jefferson and Burr received 73

to them than Jefferson, many of the Federalists decided to support him. In December Hamilton had written John Rutledge urging him to have no part in such a plan.[57] Again on January 4, Hamilton wrote Rutledge stating that Burr's private, public and business habits and record showed him unfit for the Presidency.[58] To the second communication Rutledge replied that his determination to support Burr had been shaken and that he would discuss the matter further with his friends. The Federalists were of the opinion, he added, that Burr was less dangerous than Jefferson. He would at least break up the Virginia faction. Rutledge further stated that he was afraid Jefferson would try to change the Constitution so as to give the government to the people and "end by throwing everything into their hands."[59] On February 11, Rutledge was still unconvinced, for on the first ballot, the votes of the five South Carolina representatives present were cast for Burr.[60] On the following ballots Benjamin Huger separated from his Federalist colleagues and voted for Jefferson.[61] Soon Nott went home and the other Federalists having decided to refrain from voting, Huger also absented himself, thereby enabling South Carolina to present a blank vote on the thirty-sixth ballot. Delaware likewise presented a blank ballot. Whereupon Jefferson was declared elected.[62]

The part that many South Carolinians believed their state

---

each; John Adams, 65; Charles Cotesworth Pinckney, 64; and John Jay, 1 (from Rhode Island).

[57] Lodge, *Works of Hamilton*, X, 404-405. Hamilton had written Wolcott a letter equally as strong against Burr, but which contained this statement "yet it may be well enough to throw out a line for him, in order to tempt him to start for the plate, and thus lay the foundation of dissension between the two chiefs." *Gibbs, Administrations of Washington and Adams*, II, 458.

[58] Quoted in Channing, *History of U. S.*, IV, 242.

[59] Hamilton, *Works of Hamilton*, VI, 509-511.

[60] *Annals of Congress*, 6th Cong., 2nd Sess., February 11, 1801, reprinted from the *National Intelligencer* for February 13. Sumter was too ill to be present, but would have come if necessary (pp. 1027-1030).

[61] This was believed at the time and admitted later in a speech in Congress. *Annals of Congress*, 8th Cong., 1st Sess. (October 28, 1803), p. 532.

[62] *Ibid.*, 6th Cong., 2nd Sess. (February 17, 1801, reprint from *National Intelligencer*, February 18), pp. 1032-1033, note.

JEFFERSONIAN DEMOCRACY IN S. C.   163

had played in the recent election and the strong desire they had to see the influence of Jefferson increased were well expressed in a toast offered at a public celebration in Charleston—"The State of South Carolina, whose voice secured to the United States their present Chief Magistrate:—he should not have been a blank at the city of Washington." The first toast of the evening had been to the Constitution, followed by one to the new President, "Thomas Jefferson, President of the United States—Peace and happiness to his administration. The man who drafted our glorious declaration of independence will continue to exert his admirable talents for the happiness of his country."

Over the chair was suspended an elegant transparent portrait of Mr. Jefferson, as large as life, which, on drinking the second toast, was immediately lighted, and produced a spontaneous burst of applause—above the head was painted the American eagle, with the olive branch in his beak; around the head, in large characters, "The man of the People," and underneath the following quotation from his Notes on Virginia—"*It should be our duty to cultivate peace and friendship with all nations.*"[63]

At Columbia shortly after Jefferson's inauguration a group of citizens had already expressed their attitude in an even more explicit tone.

> We rejoice in common, with the rest of our republican fellow citizens, that the Clouds which lately overshadowed our Country are happily dispelled, and our political horizon again exhibits a serene aspect in consequence of your accession to the Presidential Chair—It is with difficulty that we can refrain from expressing our indignation, at the nefarious efforts, which have been made, to defeat your election and destroy the ardent hopes of a free and enlightened people.
> . . . .
> Relying, Sir, on the wisdom, virtue and disinterestedness, which have invariably characterized your public conduct, we now look forward, with the pleasing expectation that the national constitution, that boast of our country, will be preserved inviolate—that the malignant Spirit of faction, which has long convulsed the United States will be completely extinguished and that peace, safety and concord will revive our native Land,

[63] *City Gazette,* March 14, 1801. The meeting had been held March 12.

and be long enjoyed by people zealously engaged in the pursuit of blessings so essential to the happiness of mankind.[64]

For weeks the Federalists had known that their party would soon go out of power. They were not ready, however, to relinquish control. John Rutledge wrote, "We shall profit by our short-lived majority, and do as much good as we can before the end of this session.[65] One of the chief ways in which the Federalists felt that "good" could be done for the country and their own party was the reorganization of the federal judiciary. In this attempt the South Carolina Federalists gave unanimous support, while Sumter continued his opposition to the Adams administration. Nott argued that Congress was bound by the Constitution to set up inferior courts. There was nothing in that document which authorized the delegation of jurisdiction in federal cases to state courts. Harper thought that there was great need not only for more courts but also for higher salaries for the judges.[66] Under the new judiciary act, Read, who had recently been defeated for reelection as senator, was given appointment by President Adams.[67]

As a kind of valedictory to the voters of the district which he had represented for over six years, Robert Goodloe Harper wrote another letter to his constituents. This time the subject was the accomplishments of Federalists since the formation of the government under the Constitution. His party had prepared the way for the happy condition which the nation had attained. Jefferson's inaugural address was commended. The new administration should be successful if it conducted the government "on rational principles, and with steadiness, vigor and prudence." The course of the Republicans would be easy

[64] Jefferson Papers, March 5, 1801.
[65] Morrison, *Life and Letters of Otis,* 1, 199.
[66] *Annals of Congress,* 6th Cong., 2nd Sess. (January 7, 9, 20, 1801; and Senate section, February 7), pp. 892-896, 901-903, 915; 742. Charles Pinckney was absent on final passage of the bill. Read supported it.
[67] Read was to take the place of Judge Thomas Bee, who was in turn to be advanced to chief judge of the new circuit. Since Judge Bee declined the new appointment and the judiciary act was repealed in 1802, Read never served. He retained the commission sent him and as late as 1809 was still trying to secure a judgeship on the basis of it. Jacob Read to Madison, May 8, 1809, *Madison Papers*

if they would but follow the well-beaten path of their predecessors; but if they departed therefrom a happy journey for the nation could not be predicted. Harper begged that his party be judged by what it had done. After an expression of appreciation for the confidence his constituents had bestowed upon him, he bade them "a last and affectionate adieu."[68]

In South Carolina the aged Christopher Gadsden, who had been a prominent actor in the initiation of the Revolution against Great Britain, thought that political and social changes had long since gone too far. In a letter of consolation to John Adams, he bewailed the "reversement" in South Carolina brought on by "new-comers cajoled and imposed upon by emissaries from without, and egged on by a numerous or rather innumerable tribe of young law-followers amongst ourselves."

Long have I been led to think our planet a mere bedlam, and the uncommonly extravagant ravings of our times, especially for a few years past, and still in the highest rant, have greatly increased and confirmed that opinion. Look around our whirling globe, my friend, where you will, east, west, north, or south, where is the spot in which there are not many thousands of these lunatics?

But in spite of his disappointment at the defeat of Adams, even Christopher Gadsden was willing to wish a successful administration for Jefferson. He hoped that the new President would have the "constitutional assistance and countenance of every citizen of the Union; and that his public actions may be judged with candor and generosity without any captious hole-picking." Above all he hoped that harmony would be restored.[69]

Thus one party had given way to another. Would the government be turned over to the people, as Rutledge feared? How far would the Republicans depart from the course of the Federalists? Would Gadsden's desire for harmony be realized? Since, as Harper insisted, a party must be judged by its accomplishments, the answers must await the examination of the new administration.

[68] Harper, *Select Works*, I, 324-350.
[69] Christopher Gadsden to John Adams, March 11, 1801. Adams, *Works of Adams*, IX, 578-580.

CHAPTER VII

THE ESTABLISHMENT OF JEFFERSONIAN DEMOCRACY, 1801-1805

1. THE PRINCIPLES OF JEFFERSONIAN DEMOCRACY

What were the chief ideas and practices of Jeffersonian democracy? How nearly did the government and society of South Carolina conform to its tenets? These questions directly concern the would-be narrator of the history of South Carolina during the last century and a half. When they shall have been answered adequately our story will be told.

In brief, what can one say of Jefferson's political, economic, and social philosophy? If one thinks of philosophy as the theory of an idle dreamer, then Jefferson was no philosopher. But if one has in mind practical wisdom, then Jefferson was a philosopher *par excellence*. His philosophy might be said to be a combination of Lockian principles and Jeffersonian ideas interpreted in terms of the frontier. From it was born that theory of government and life known today as Jeffersonian Democracy, the essence of which was a belief in the perfectibility of man.

Essential contributions of Jeffersonian Democracy to political life comprise confidence in majority rule, the theory of natural rights, and a system of governmental units. Of these three, belief in majority rule was perhaps the most important. But the theory of natural rights included the right of revolution and the rights to periodic revision of the constitution and fundamental laws, both stressed by Jefferson. Of the governmental units, emphasis was particularly laid on local government as the heart of true republicanism.

Contributions of Jeffersonian Democracy in the fields of economic and social philosophy perhaps were as great. The core of his economic policy was an agrarian America, with every man a landowner. The chief aim of his social reforms was the well being of the individual. He disliked all things that smacked of oppression. His was a liberalizing influence; that Jefferson set the stamp of liberty on American life can not

JEFFERSONIAN DEMOCRACY IN S. C.

be denied. Among other things, he advocated free schools, free press, and freedom of religion.[1]

Another summary of Jefferson's views, this one largely dealing with his ideas concerning the nature and mission of the American Union, will fittingly complete our general description of what constituted Jeffersonian democracy.

. . . Champion of State's rights he has been consistently painted, but Jefferson was in practice and largely in theory a consistent federalist, a supporter of the adoption of the Articles of Confederation, a critic of its defects, an advocate of the adoption of the Constitution, and one of its ardent defenders to the end of his days.

The close of the Revolution found him confirmed in the belief, which was presently strengthened by his residence abroad, that America offered a unique opportunity for the establishment of the most perfect system of government the world had seen, if only the dangers of the European system could be kept out. Entangling alliances must be avoided at any cost. He was even distrustful of a developing commerce because of its international implications. Manufacturing was also dangerous to American ideals. He would have preferred the United States to resemble in its self-sufficiency his plantation at Monticello. Let America be an agricultural nation. "Those who labor in the earth are the chosen people of God . . . whose breasts he has made his peculiar deposit for substantial and genuine virtue. It is the focus in which he keeps alive that sacred fire which otherwise might escape from the face of the earth. . . . While we have land to labor then, let us never wish to see our citizens occupied at a work-bench, or twirling a distaff. Carpenters, masons, smiths, are wanting in husbandry; but, for the general operations of manufacture, let our workshops remain in Europe. It is better to carry provisions and materials to workmen there than to bring them to the provisions and materials, and with them their manners and principles." But progressive and ever ready to admit error, Jefferson was presently to favor the development of industry as a necessity in a self-sufficient nation.

Peace was an essential part of his system, war being one of the chief burdens of the human race, but he advocated a reasonable preparedness.

Individual liberty was the foundation stone of the Jeffersonian structure and since free government in his thinking

[1] Carrie Isobel French, "The Early Political, Economic and Social Philosophy of Thomas Jefferson," M.A. thesis, University of Chicago, 1932 (manuscript), pp. 43-44.

could not exist without widely diffused knowledge, he advocated public education as a necessity. Common schools and a free press would prepare the mass of the people for civic duties and universities would train experts and leaders.

America, applying to the business of government the wisdom of all time, as adapted to its needs, would be an example and a hope to the world.

Deeply convinced as he was that America had a world mission, Jefferson was no missionary. Nowhere in him was there any fire of desire to reform the world or anybody in it other than by example. He was unsympathetic with the offer of revolutionary France to free the rest of the world, for his liberalism in addition to being tolerant, was of a sort that made him believe men fit to be free only when they were determined to be. He was as averse to forcing men's political beliefs as he was to forcing their ideas on religion and morals. Freedom in these was among the inalienable rights of sovereign men.[2]

2. Early Appointments under Jefferson

Thomas Jefferson's inaugural statement that all were Republicans and all were Federalists, together with its possible practical implications, evoked varied responses in South Carolina. Apparently few in either party expected the appointments to office to be made on a nonpolitical basis.[3] Soon Jefferson's followers in the state were volunteering their advice. The request of Charles Pinckney made soon after the election in Columbia, the conference with the President in Washington, and his early appointment as minister to Spain have already been mentioned.

In a contest as bitter as that of 1800 in South Carolina, it was natural that some of the victors should have no confidence in their opponents and seek to replace them as early and completely as constitutionally possible. From Charleston Jefferson received a graphic explanation of why at least one leader thought Federalism should be disestablished.

I have no confidence in federalists, every day exposes their cloven feet, and if our government does not act with a firm

[2] J. G. de Roulhac Hamilton, "Jefferson's Americanism," a review of Gilbert Chinard, *Thomas Jefferson: the Apostle of Americanism*, in *Virginia Quarterly Review* (January, 1930), pp. 120-121.

[3] An analysis of public opinion in regard to appointments and Jefferson's reaction may be found in Gaillard Hunt, "Office-Seeking during Jefferson's Administration," *American Historical Review*, III, 270-291.

hand, and make an example of all those who have trodden down the liberties of the people, and who ruled with a Robespeirian sway in 98 and 99, they will rise into power again, and all the trouble the republicans have been at to bring things back to first principles have been exerted in vain. The Banks ought to be purified, the branch bank here has 12 federalists to 1 republican. The monied interest I fear is hostile to the present administration, without this engine is turned about, or in some measure bridled, it will overset the vessel, and I am sure it could not be done if due precautions are taken, for as a party, the federalists are not formidable, they are composed of trifling lawyers, men swoln with family pride, ignorance and impudence; fellows thirsting for gain; others filled with an itch for dipping their hands in the public purse, under cover of appointments; and all the old tories and their descendants. The Judiciary is also inimical, but I fear, the only purifier of the engine will be time; as the judges die off, the government must be careful to replace honest men in the room of the present set of flexible gentry; until these desirable events take place they must be watched well.[4]

A second letter from Charleston, however, one from the vigorous democrat of many years, Aedanus Burke, requested that Edward Weyman, "Surveyor for this port," be retained.[5] To the President's letter asking his opinion in regard to removals, Pierce Butler advised that they should be made sparingly. According to him, Washington, during the latter part of his administration, and Adams, during all of his, had been partial

[4] Hunt, "Office-Seeking during Jefferson's Administration," pp. 278-279. A copy of this letter, without its signature, was found by Hunt in the files of the State Department. It was dated, Charleston, July 24, 1801; the original went to Jefferson, a copy being sent to the Secretary of State. The name of the writer is unknown; but, from its tone, one might judge that he was prominent in state politics. At least such is the conclusion of Hunt.

[5] *Ibid.,* p. 280. September 13, 1801. Burke did not know Gallatin well. He, therefore, wrote to Madison to speak to the Secretary of the Treasury in Weyman's behalf. The latter was praised for his conduct during the trying times of 1798-1799. It is interesting to note also that Burke, in the same letter, told of the financial difficulties of Phillip Freneau and expressed the hope that he would be given an appointment. Burke reminded Madison that it was upon his request several years ago that the latter had spoken to Jefferson and secured a place for Freneau in the State Department. Freneau was again in difficulties and Burke was making a second request. According to Hunt he was not given an appointment by the Jefferson administration.

in their appointments. Jefferson should not follow in their footsteps. A person who would not be loyal without the gift of a position was not worth gaining. The aim of the Republicans should be to prove to "the great body of the landed interests, the true support of good government, that the present administration are the friends of an equal, mild, economical and just government."[6]

Any action Jefferson might take would be compared with his statements upon taking the oath of office. Some of the same criticisms that had been employed against the former administration were soon to be directed at him. The President was accused of using removals as a means of destroying Federalism in spite of his inaugural statement that he would be the chief executive of the whole country. Jefferson was charged with taking the first step toward despotism and was warned that the American people would not stand for it.[7]

In the face of the dire forebodings of Federalists, the recently organized daily newspaper, the *Times*, declared that the state was experiencing unexampled prosperity. As evidence of the increased commercial activities, the editor cited the demand for the organization of another bank and the expected increase in the capital of one already organized.[8]

In July, 1801, Charles Pinckney left for Spain, thereby temporarily relinquishing his leadership of the South Carolina Republicans to others.[9] A few months later the legislature showed its approval of his long fight for the Republican cause against Federalist opposition and majorities in Congress by elevating Thomas Sumter to the United States senate to fill the vacancy resulting from the resignation of Pinckney.[10] The

[6] Jefferson Papers, August 26; September 19, 1801. Jefferson's letter of inquiry is in Ford, *Writings of Jefferson*, VIII, 82-83.

[7] "Americanus" in *S. C. State Gazette*, August 1, 1801.

[8] May 11, 1801. *The Times and Political and Evening Gazette* began publication October 6, 1800. The name was changed twice, finally becoming the *Times*, early in 1801.

[9] A notice of the departure of "his excellency Charles Pinckney esq., minister plenipotentiary to the Court of Madrid," from the port of Charleston on the previous Saturday was published in the *Carolina Gazette* (Thursday), July 30, 1801.

[10] S. C. Senate Journal, December 3, 1801. The election of Sumter was apparently without his solicitation or even his knowledge of its

previous year John Drayton had been chosen governor and Theodore Gaillard speaker of the house of representatives, both being strong Republicans.[11] To these and others whose names will be mentioned in the course of this study fell the leadership of South Carolina Republicanism.

3. SOUTH CAROLINA EDUCATION UNDER JEFFERSONIAN DEMOCRACY

The most important act of the state legislature in 1801, indeed one of the most important enactments in its history, was the establishment of the South Carolina College, later to become the University of South Carolina. Public schools had been recommended by several governors before 1800.[12] Pamphlet writers also called attention to the need for better educational facilities. It was argued that public schools and colleges were the only certain means of improving the electorate to any great degree. The low country said that the back country was not educated enough to share equally in the government. The upper part of the state then asked the more wealthy section to provide free schools. Knowing that their political and economic status might be endangered, the low country aristocracy refused. Thus reasoned a writer in 1797. After telling of calamities that might result from the absence of adequate opportunities, he said

Let us conclude these speculations with impressing on our minds, in a few words, a most momentous truth. To establish the blessings, and avert the curses, we have had in contemplation, there is one, and but one means: Let every citizen of the republick, from the wealthiest planter to the needy peasant, and all in all in equal and most ample measure be furnished at the publick expense with opportunities of instruction, by the multiplication of schools and colleges; then will the poor, who must

---

likelihood. However, he stated his pleasure at being sent to the senate because of greater need for Republicans there than in the house. Gregorie, *Thomas Sumter,* pp. 249-250.

[11] S. C. House Journal, December 4, 1800; O'Neall, *Bench and Bar in S. C.,* I, 253-269.

[12] Especially notable were the suggestions of Vanderhorst and Charles Pinckney in 1795, 1796 and 1798. *Columbian Herald,* December 4, 1795; *City Gazette,* December 8, 1796; December 12, 1797; December 6, 1798.

ever be the largest body, merit the rod they shall feel, if, with the accomplishments of scholars, they maintain not the dignity of freeman.[13]

The fight for public education was taken up by John Drayton, as acting chief executive of the state following the death of Edward Rutledge. In his message to the legislature in 1800, he recommended schools and colleges as the most effective means of merging the many population elements of South Carolina into one citizenship. Thus would the stability of the government be insured by the patriotism and intelligence of the people. Returning to the subject in 1801, after his election as governor, Drayton pointed out that the five colleges already incorporated had made little progress. Cambridge and Winnsborough colleges had soon been discontinued because of lack of funds. Even though the latter had been recently revived by the Mount Zion Society, it was still nothing more than an elementary school which could not develop into a college from its present support. Beaufort and Alexandria colleges were hardly known outside their immediate vicinity, while Charleston College could not be considered higher than a respectable academy or grammar school. The governor thought that the legislature should concentrate the higher education of the state at Columbia or some other central and healthful site. By so doing the citizens of South Carolina would be able to educate their children at home instead of sending them abroad or to another state. An institution amply supported by public funds could secure "learned and respectable Professors in the various branches of science," and the needed library and laboratory facilities. These would lead "the pursuits of our youth from theory to practice. The friendships of young men would thence be promoted and strengthened throughout the State, and our political union much advanced thereby."[14] Acting upon Dray-

[13] Richard Beresford, *Aristocracy the Bane of Liberty; Learning the Antidote Designed to Recommend the General Establishment of Free Schools and Colleges in Republicks* (Charleston: 1797). A copy is in the pamphlets of the Charleston Library Society, series 1, vol. 12, no. 7½.

[14] Governor Drayton's message is quoted in M. La Borde, *History of South Carolina College from its Incorporation December 19, 1801, to*

ton's suggestion, the legislature, thinking that the proper education of youth contributed greatly "to the prosperity of society and ought always to be an object of legislative attention," and that the establishment of a college near the central part of the state offering opportunities to all young men would "highly promote the instruction, the good order and the harmony of the whole community," voted to set up a college at Columbia. Fifty thousand dollars was appropriated for building purposes and $6,000 to pay the faculty.[15]

On January 10, 1805, the South Carolina College began its instruction in a modest way. Two teachers having declined the positions offered them, the faculty for a short while was composed of only two members. A few months later the number was increased to four. Although the degree of Bachelor of Arts had been voted to Anderson Crenshaw late in the previous year, the first commencement was held in 1807. On this occasion all of the seniors and at least twelve of the juniors displayed their forensic abilities. According to La Borde the trustees "used pretty freely the authority to confer degrees."[16] The commencements, we are informed by the same authority, were affairs of dignity with the governor, judges, members of the legislature, students and visitors in attendance.

For that day the legislative appropriations must have seemed liberal. In comparison with the aid given the University of North Carolina, the South Carolina College was considered to

---

Nov. 25, 1857, Including sketches of its Presidents and Professors (Columbia: 1859), pp. 19-20.

[15] *S. C. Statutes at Large,* V, 403-405. Wallace, *History of S. C.,* II, 372 and note, citing O. F. Crow's manuscript history of the government of the University of South Carolina, states that "the up country heartily cooperated in the founding of the college." The long repeated error in regard to the attitude of the up country grew out of "the inaccuracy of the memory" of Henry William DeSaussure. The present writer might add here that it was upon the same gentleman's memory that the still repeated story of the possibility of a compromise in the election of 1800 was largely based.

[16] La Borde, *History of S. C. College,* pp. 33-44. A.B.'s, LL.D.'s, D.D.'s, were distributed at the first commencement on the third Monday in December, 1807. Former Governor John Drayton was the recipient of the LL.D. degree. Those to receive the D.D. degree were William Percy, Richard Furman, Joseph Alexander and Moses Waddel.

be receiving "munificent support."[17] Before the formal opening of the college the trustees decided that the president's salary should be $2,500, that of the professors of mathematics and natural philosophy $1,500 and that of all other professors $1,000.[18] About the time of the first commencement the legislature appropriated $8,000 for the building of a president's home, provided for a teacher of French and authorized the trustees to employ tutors at the salary of $600 a year. Two years later $8,000 was voted for the building of a house or houses for the accommodation of the professors.[19]

Thus had the Republican legislature of South Carolina in 1801 begun, in a liberal way for the time, the appropriations for a state-supported institution of higher learning. Its location near the center of the state and within sight of the legislative assembly halls caused the college to have a statewide appeal instead of an exclusive one as would have been the case had it been established in Charleston. Because of its nearness to the Capitol, the connection between the government and the South Carolina College or the University of South Carolina students and graduates has always been extremely close. From the standpoint of advantages to be received and the location of the institution, the establishment of the South Carolina College should be considered a victory for Republicanism and the up country.[20]

[17] Delbert Harold Gilpatrick, *Jeffersonian Democracy in North Carolina, 1787-1816* (New York: Columbia University Press, 1931), p. 143, citing quotation from *National Intelligencer*, in *Raleigh Register*, December 31, 1804.

[18] La Borde, *History of S. C. College*, p. 28.

[19] *Ibid.*, pp. 40, 50, 69, 106. In order to equalize the salaries of the professors the trustees voted from funds available an additional amount to those receiving only $1,000. In 1819, there were, in addition to the president, four professors and two tutors. In its first ten commencements (1807-1816) the college graduated 282 students. *Ibid.*, pp. 438-441.

[20] So close were the relations between the legislature and the college that for several years the annual balls were held in the legislative halls. Schaper thinks that the voting of the up country members against granting the privilege of the use of the halls and the voting of the low country members for the permission "probably indicates the difference in attitude taken by the Episcopal as compared with other churches. The Episcopal Church being very strong in the low country, we should expect the members from that section in the legis-

In 1811 the legislature established what has been referred to by some as "the free school system." Hitherto, societies such as the Fellowship, the German Friendly, the Mount Zion, the Catholic Societies of Charleston, the St. David Society of St. David's Parish, the Winyah Indigo Society of Georgetown, the St. Andrew's Society and others had aided the poorer children who were unable to attend private schools.[21] Following the policy of Charles Pinckney and other governors, Henry Middleton in his message to the legislature in 1811 recommended free schools. Strangely enough the chairman of the committee that brought in the bill was not an ardent Republican but the Charleston intellectual, notable botanist and later prominent banker, Stephen Elliott, a Federalist. Whatever may have been the purpose of the majority of the members, the Elliott group favored a real public school system for all the people of the state. However, the small amount of appropriation—$37,200 for the establishment of one elementary free school for each member of the lower house of the state legislature, or one hundred and twenty-four in all—and the preference given to the poor and orphans almost inevitably resulted in the setting up of "pauper" rather than free schools. In spite of the later recommendations of governors and friends of education little improvement occurred before the Civil War, except the doubling of the appropriation in 1852. Some were even opposed to voting any funds to districts until they furnished an equal sum themselves. The *Charleston Courier* thought that the legislature had acted wisely in passing measures for the promotion of the interests of the wealthy but urged that that body not neglect the schools in which the poor were largely concerned.

This miserable makeshift, sometimes even officially called "pauper schools," pleased neither the rich nor poor, the one refusing to associate with "paupers" and the latter largely scorning to class their children as such.

---

lature to be liberal on such questions." "Sectionalism and Representation in S. C.," p. 406.

[21] J. H. Easterby, *History of the St. Andrew's Society of Charleston, South Carolina, 1729-1929* (Charleston: Walker Evans & Cogswell, 1929), pp. 66-69. After the passage of the "free school act" the St. Andrew's school and perhaps those of some of the other societies were discontinued.

In large towns there were free schools for the poor only. But generally the fund for the district (i.e. the later county) was used to pay the tuition of poor children applying at private schools. It was the saying in many up country districts in 1856, "We have no free schools." For three years, 1812-14, the system fought against attempts at its abolition. Despite the obvious benefit of educating 4,659 poor children in 1814, the Senate had to save the schools from the House. William Crafts and Philip Moser, true to their careers of beneficence, and other Charleston members were the chief bulwarks against attacks mainly from the up country, perhaps due to the absence of massed poor there as well as to lack of appreciation of education.[22]

Thus the education act of 1811, which in theory thoroughly accorded with Jeffersonian principles, in practice did not measure up to democratic tenets.

4. The Repeal of Federalist Legislation

Judging from the tone of the first session of the Seventh Congress one might conclude that its members were in a repealing mood. The internal taxes and the recent Federalist legislation that had not expired were particular objects of attack. In nearly every case the South Carolina Republicans supported the repeal activities. One of the very few exceptions was the attitude of Senator John Ewing Colhoun toward the Judiciary Act of 1801. Thinking that the judges could not, in any constitutional way, be deprived of their positions, he spoke and voted against the measure. Sumter, however, voted with the majority in repealing the act.[23] In the house of representatives Rutledge became very much irritated by the demand of Republicans for an immediate vote. Huger declared that repeal would be "unconstitutional and mischievous." According to him there was need for the new judges, for the Constitution had not intended that the Supreme Court Justices should preside over inferior courts. Congress should respect the inde-

---

[22] Wallace, *History of S. C.*, III, 29-30.
[23] *Annals of Congress,* 7th Cong., 1st Sess. (January 19, 27, February 2, 3, 1802), pp. 138-145, 150, 160, 183. The vote in the senate was close, 16 to 15.

JEFFERSONIAN DEMOCRACY IN S. C. 177

pendence of the judiciary. On the final vote Moore and William Butler supported the repeal measure, while the Federalists Huger, Lowndes and Rutledge opposed.[24]

In the contest over the repeal of the internal taxes the Federalists resorted to several devices. Acting on the charge of Republicans that they cost too much to collect, the Federalists proposed a resolution calling on the Secretary of the Treasury to submit information in regard to the collecting expenses. Huger and Rutledge spoke in favor of the resolution. After taking little part in the discussion, the Republicans voted it down, a practice Rutledge could not understand. He would not call such action disrespectful to the minority but ventured the opinion that the people would not approve such silent voting. Another Federalist device was the proposal that the repeal be postponed until it was known whether the revenue derived therefrom would be needed; this failed also. In the end the South Carolinians voted according to their party affiliations, except Huger, who joined the Republicans. In the senate both Colhoun and Sumter favored the repeal of the taxes.[25]

Another enactment of the Federalists to incur the opposition of the Republican Congress was the Naturalization Act. Moore, William Butler and both Colhoun and Sumter joined the other

[24] *Ibid.*, House (February 15, 23, 24, 25, 1802), pp. 510-511, 518, 665-693, 734-746. The seat left vacant by the going of Sumter to the senate had not been filled. The following year the petitions of the judges appointed under the act of 1801 were denied. By that time Richard Winn, who had several times opposed Sumter for Congress, had been chosen to succeed him. Winn, Moore and William Butler opposed the petitions. Huger, Lowndes and Rutledge favored them. *Ibid.*, 2nd Sess. (January 27, 1803), pp. 427-428, 440-441. In the senate Sumter voted to deny the petitions. The place left vacant by the death of Colhoun had not been filled. *Ibid.*, Senate (February 3, 1803), p. 178.

[25] *Annals of Congress*, 7th Cong., 1st Sess. (January 25, March 15, 17, 1802; Senate, March 31, 1802), pp. 447, 451-456, 1003-1004, 1009-1010, 1021; 250. In discussing another measure Rutledge stated that he had learned that the only question being asked in that body was whether a proposal was introduced by a Federalist or a Republican. He had respect for the President but objected to the frequent remarks that the President had not asked for such a measure or that the chief executive must be consulted first. *Ibid.*, House (January 22, 25, 1802), pp. 434-446, 458-461. The South Carolina representatives voted according to party lines on Rutledge's resolution.

members of their party in modifying the process of naturalization. Again Huger, Lowndes and Rutledge opposed.[26] In the vote on the reduction of the peace-time army, both Federalists and Republicans approved.[27] The former, however, opposed the decrease in the naval appropriation.[28]

Ever watchful for possible mistakes of the Republicans which might be turned into popular political issues, the Federalists seized upon the repeal of the Judiciary Act. Alexander Hamilton wrote Charles Cotesworth Pinckney that he would take it for granted that he would also "view this measure as a vital blow to the constitution." In order to present a unified opposition, Hamilton suggested that leading Federalists from various states assemble in Washington at the same time as the meeting of the Cincinnati. He had taken the liberty to invite William R. Davie of North Carolina and asked Pinckney to second the invitation.[29]

In the so-called "attack" of the administration on the federal courts, the Republicans as a whole, when present, supported the impeachments and trials of John Pickering and Samuel Chase. The Federalists from South Carolina, when present, opposed. Huger had spoken against the resolution to impeach Pickering late in the second session of the Seventh Congress. It had, however, been considered and passed by the vote of 45 to 8.[30] In the senate, Sumter, the only South Carolina senator at the time, voted for conviction.[31] Both Huger and Lowndes opposed the appointment of a committee to investigate the conduct of Judge Chase, but the five Republicans

---

[26] *Ibid.* (March 10, 1802; Senate, April 3), pp. 293; 252.

[27] *Ibid.* (House, January 21, 1802), p. 431. On the question of agreeing to senate amendments the party members divided, Moore and William Butler opposing, Huger, Lowndes and Rutledge favoring. *Ibid.* (March 10, 1802), pp. 994-995.

[28] *Ibid.* (April 17, 19, 1802), pp. 1198-1203.

[29] Hamilton to C. C. Pinckney, March 15, 1802. Lodge, *Works of Hamilton*, X, 428-429.

[30] *Annals of Congress*, 7th Cong., 2nd Sess. (March 2, 1803), p. 642. William Butler, the only South Carolina representative present on the final passage of the resolution, voted for impeachment.

[31] *Ibid.*, 8th Cong., 1st Sess., March 12, 1804. Pierce Butler's place had not been filled. The vote was 20 to 6 for removing Pickering.

present voted affirmatively.[32] Being on the committee of investigation, Huger vigorously opposed the report which, he said, had been prepared without the consultation of himself and Roger Griswold, the two Federalist members. Randolph stated that they had been sent for but the messengers were unable to find them. Whereupon the committee had unanimously adopted the report submitted. Huger said that if he had been present he would have insisted that more evidence be examined before recommendations should be made to the house; but after he had discovered what had been done he thought it useless to object in the committee. By the vote of 73 to 32 the house impeached Samuel Chase.[33] The South Carolina senators, though both Republicans, divided on the conviction of Chase. On nearly all the counts Sumter voted that the judge was guilty; but John Gaillard, recently elected to succeed Pierce Butler, consistently favored acquittal. Since the necessary two-thirds were lacking, Chase escaped removal.[34]

5. The "Geffroy Letters" and the Retirement of John Rutledge

The climax of political scheming with which South Carolinians were accused of being connected in 1802 was reached in the so-called "Geffroy letters." In August, 1801, two letters had been sent from Newport, Rhode Island, to President Jefferson. In the first one high tribute was paid to Jefferson. It was stated that during the Adams administration, Fort Adams had been begun largely so that General Knox might sell mate-

[32] *Ibid.*, House (January 6, 7, 1804), pp. 825-826, 875-876. Hampton was absent.

[33] *Ibid.* (March 12, 1804), pp. 1171, 1178-1181. William Butler, Casey, John B. Earle and Winn voted affirmatively, Huger and Lowndes negatively. Moore and Hampton are not listed. The articles of impeachment themselves passed December 4, by different votes, Moore supporting in addition to the above. 2nd Sess., pp. 748-762. Huger was absent. After giving Chase an opportunity to answer the charges, the house on February 6, 1805, voted that his reply was unsatisfactory and that it was ready to "prove charges" against him. Butler, Casey, Moore, and Winn supported the majority, while Lowndes opposed. Huger, Hampton, and Earle were not present, pp. 1181-1183.

[34] *Ibid.*, 8th Cong., 2nd Sess. (Record of Trial of Chase, March 1, 1805), pp. 665-669. The highest count mustered was 19 to 15.

rials at a high price. Also land had been bought from Mrs. Adams's sister at an enormous sum. The community was gratified that the new President had stopped the building of the fortifications. Jefferson was said to have improved matters in Rhode Island by removals and appointments, but he had only made a beginning. A general substitution of "Whigs" for all the "Tories" was recommended. Such, the writer of the letter said, was expected by the people. In the second letter it was stated that since the writing of the first, news had come that the fortifications were to be completed after all. To do so would be a mistake. The people were opposed and did not want soldiers around them. Again it was recommended that the "Tories" be deprived of their positions. Their continuance in office was causing people to say that the President could not find enough persons in his own party to fill the places. In both letters possible appointees were suggested.

After receiving a reply from Jefferson to the letters bearing his name as signature, Nicholas Geffroy denied having written them. Thereupon an attempt was made to identify the writer by his handwriting. Some suspected that a Federalist had written them with the expectation of using their contents later as political propaganda. It happened that John Rutledge frequently spent the summer or part of it at Newport and had been there at the time the letters were supposed to have been written. Upon comparison of the handwriting of Rutledge with that of the letters, several prominent persons in Rhode Island, including one of the United States senators, the lieutenant governor, the secretary of state, and other civil officials as well as military officers made affidavits that the handwritings were the same. On the other side Rutledge swore that he had not written either of the letters and secured affidavits from persons of prominence, including the cashier of the Bank of Rhode Island, others in that state and Jacob Read, Thomas Lowndes, Cleland Kinlock and several more of South Carolina stating that the handwritings were not the same. The longer the controversy continued the more confusing it became. The South Carolina Republicans vigorously asserted that there was no doubt about Rutledge's having devised such a scheme to

JEFFERSONIAN DEMOCRACY IN S. C.   181

injure their party, while the Federalists strongly vouched for his innocence.[35] The postmaster in Newport and his assistant swore that the letters were brought to the postoffice by a girl who said she lived at the Rutledge home. The assistant later modified his statement slightly and the girls who were said to have worked for the Rutledges at the time stated that they had not carried the letters to the postoffice. Rutledge wrote Jefferson denying the authorship and asserting that he could not believe the President thought he had written them even though he had permitted their publication. So great was the party feeling, he said, that the fact he was a Federalist made many think he would be guilty of anything infamous.[36]

The "Geffroy letters," Rutledge's uncompromising attitude in Congress, the growing strength of the Republicans and other factors caused him to announce that he would not be a candidate for reelection to Congress. In his statement he gave a description of the ruin which he thought had come to the country and professed pessimism for the future.[37]

6. THE ELECTIONS OF 1802 AND THE ESTABLISHMENT OF THE *Charleston Courier*

In the Congressional elections of 1802, two Federalists—Thomas Lowndes and Benjamin Huger—were reelected. Richard Winn who had defeated Sumter in 1792 and had since been unsuccessful in his attempts to return to Congress, had already succeeded the latter following his elevation to the senate. Winn had never been a strong Federalist if indeed he had deserved that name at all. However, in his contests with Sumter he had received Federalist support. By 1802 he had become a highly acceptable Republican. The other five representatives likewise belonged to the party of Jefferson.[38] The legislature chose a

[35] The details of the controversy may be found in the *City Gazette*, November 24, 26, 27, 29, 30, 1802.
[36] Rutledge to Jefferson, October 20, 1802. Jefferson Papers.
[37] *Charleston Courier*, February 2, 1803.
[38] The reapportionment after the census of 1800 gave South Carolina eight representatives instead of six. The Republican members of the eighth Congress were William Butler, Wade Hampton, Thomas Moore, Richard Winn, John B. Earle and Levi Casey in the house. In the senate Sumter continued, and the place of the deceased Colhoun was filled in 1803 by Pierce Butler, also a Republican.

Republican governor, James B. Richardson, who seems to have been the first person elected governor of South Carolina who was not a Charlestonian.[39]

A few months after the elections of 1802 a keen Republican analyst surveyed the political situation and announced that South Carolina was Republican as a whole but that there were a few areas in which the Federalists were strong. The presence of so many Scotch and English in the Charleston District caused the Republicans to be at a serious disadvantage. Also in the town of Beaufort, but not in the district, the Federalists outnumbered their opponents. There was "a little knot of Federalists" at Orangeburg but not enough to carry the election. The Republicans had a majority in Georgetown and Cheraw but did not send a member of their party to Congress because of the failure of "a decent man" to oppose Huger. The Federalists were beginning to feel that their situation was desperate. Charles Cotesworth Pinckney had been deeply mortified by his defeat in 1800, consequently he and his brother kept aloof and were seldom seen on the streets.[40]

The most important act of the South Carolina Federalists in 1803 was the founding of the *Charleston Courier,* a most vigorous party newspaper. For a time the Republicans were taken aback. Hoping that the new paper would soon fail for want of support, the publishers of the *City Gazette* attempted to ignore its sharp and bitter attacks; but the new Federalist organ did not die.[41] Under the direction of two energetic young men a South Carolina newspaper for the first time began the presentation of regular and pronounced editorial expressions of opinion.[42]

[39] S. C. House Journal, December 8, 1802. Thomas Petigru Lesesne, *History of Charleston County South Carolina* (Charleston: A. H. Cawston, 1931), p. 78.

[40] Peter Freneau to Jefferson, June 17, 1803. Jefferson Papers.

[41] Peter Freneau to Jefferson, June 17, 1803. Jefferson Papers. Peter Freneau and David R. Williams were the publishers of the Republican *City Gazette* at the time.

[42] The first issue of the *Charleston Courier* appeared on January 10, 1803. A. S. Salley, "A Century of the Courier," *Centennial Edition of the News and Courier,* is an excellent brief sketch of this paper and others in South Carolina. Loring Andrews was said to be the editor and A. S. Willington the publisher. Both were natives of Massachusetts;

JEFFERSONIAN DEMOCRACY IN S. C. 183

The editor of the recently organized Federalist newspaper got unusual pleasure from pointing out what he thought were inconsistencies between early statements of Jefferson and present practices. Particular emphasis was laid on the attitude of the Republicans toward the judiciary. A letter of Jefferson to Judge Wythe in 1776 advocating independent courts was cited. As to the general practices of the party in power, the editor remarked that

It would take a long and laborious life to collect into one mass, and display in their true colours, the endless inconsistencies and contradictions of the anti-federal politicians and advocates. Here they are found parading in fine robes, borrowed from the federal party when in office—there we see them strutting in their own dowlas and tinsel. Here contradicting evident matters of fact, there contradicting themselves. Yesterday asserting that black is white, today that white is black. Now denying to the late administration the smallest particle of merit—again, in the eagerness and impetuosity of self-applause, confessing what they so denied.[43]

Andrews was about thirty-six and Willington about twenty-two in 1803. In 1805 Andrews severed his connections with the paper preparatory to returning to his former home in the North, but suddenly became sick and died while still in Charleston. Willington remained in Charleston till his death in 1862, when he was still connected with the *Charleston Courier*. Many others were also connected with it in the meantime.

The Republicans believed that the real writer of the editorials and the moving spirit behind the newspaper was Stephen Cullen Carpenter, who, they said, had been sent to Charleston by Alexander Hamilton. (Peter Freneau to Jefferson, June 17, 1803, Jefferson Papers.) Carpenter was connected with the paper, perhaps from the first, though his name did not appear except as "and Co.," beginning about 1805. He was born in Ireland, had been a writer for a London newspaper and had reported the trial that followed the impeachment of Warren Hastings. He had come to Charleston about the same time as Andrews. Seeing that the town could hardly support two newspapers of somewhat the same type they had joined together, with Carpenter remaining in the background. In the latter part of 1806 he left Charleston. He was later connected with newspapers and magazines in New York and Philadelphia. His writings, of a miscellaneous nature, were published in London in six volumes in 1811. In 1818 Carpenter went to Washington and, having changed his politics from Federalist to Republican or Democratic, was given a clerkship in the Quartermaster's Department. He died in 1820. Salley, "A Century of the Courier."

[43] *Charleston Courier*, April 6, 1803.

The *Charleston Courier* had not been in operation long before the editor stated that there was a conspiracy among the democrats to "crush the freedom of political discussion."[44] The exuberantly patriotic language used by him at times may be illustrated by his statement in regard to the Fourth of July.

> Never since the moment when the earth first sprung from its Chaotick rudiments into shape did that luminary ordained by Omnipotence to give light and heat to all created things rise upon a day so auspicious to the human race, as that which the grateful people of America are this day to commemorate. . . . The consequences of that day, which are yet in the womb of time, who shall be daring enough to predict? To America, prepared by nurture in the lap of liberty, and trained by early knowledge to possess all its benefits, the consequences must be great, happy, and (without gross mismanagement, wickedness and impolicy), permanent.

Thus even in such an outburst of patriotism animadversions to the Republicans could not be omitted. The editor greatly regretted their subservience to the French. However, the spirit of the day kept him from believing that such a policy would be persisted in until ruin befell the nation.[45]

7. THE PURCHASE OF LOUISIANA AND THE INTEREST IN FLORIDA

An eminent American historian has said that the "most significant achievement of Jefferson's first administration was the procurement of Louisiana."[46] Be that as it may, the new Federalist newspaper soon began a fierce tirade against the dilatoriness of the Republicans in gaining possession of that territory. Immediate and forceful action was called for. In the second issue of the paper, the editor remarked that it cost nothing to believe that the President was as capable of inspiring courage in armies and navies, if America had any, as he was of infusing spirit in his cabinet. But he would rather see evidence of it than hope to see it. What was needed was an army on the banks and a navy in the mouth of the Mississippi River. A few days later he proclaimed that the "day the French get

[44] *Ibid.*, April 20, 1803. [45] *Ibid.*, July 4, 1803.
[46] Channing, *History of U. S.*, IV, 275.

JEFFERSONIAN DEMOCRACY IN S. C. 185

a firm, immovable possession of Louisiana, the Sun of America may set never to rise again." The western states "may then be considered as not much longer to be a part of the union." If France took possession it would mark the rise of the French and the decline of English language in the world.[47]

When Jefferson informed Congress that Louisiana had been ceded to France and that some action on its part would be in order, the Federalist members wished to call upon the President for information he had concerning the nature of the cession. Thomas Lowndes wanted to know whether the closing of the port was connected with the change in ownership of Louisiana. He questioned Spain's right to give the United States a new neighbor under circumstances different from those under which she herself had held the province. All resolutions calling for the information were defeated, but the Federalists continued to introduce them. They also continued to oppose legislative expressions of confidence in the administration's conduct of foreign affairs. They professed great concern over the situation at the mouth of the Mississippi, asserted their desire for action, denied that they would refrain from support of a vigorous policy even under Jefferson, but stated their regret that there was not a Washington in charge of the government.[48]

In the meantime the *Charleston Courier* kept up its criticism of Jefferson for delaying the settlement of the Louisiana question. Passage through the mouth of the Mississippi should be forced, if necessary, for the benefit of the merchants and planters.[49] When time passed and no news of definite action had come, the editor stated that it was evident that the party in power expected to meet France and Spain in negotiations, compromise the whole matter, and accuse the Federalists of desiring war. Such an accusation would be unfair; but it should be understood that even war for so great a purpose would not be an evil.[50] The idea of negotiating with Bonaparte, who had

[47] *Charleston Courier*, January 11, 14, 15, 1803.
[48] *Annals of Congress,* 7th Cong., 2nd Sess. (January 4, 6, 7, 11, 12, 1803), pp. 312, 326-327, 337-338, 352-354, 339-343, 353-358, 363-368, 370-374.
[49] *Charleston Courier*, February 14, 1803.
[50] *Ibid.,* March 11, 1803.

broken the treaties he had made, was ludicrous.[51] The United States had the right of deposit and the right to force the recognition of it. The acquisition of a mere depot at the mouth of the river was not sufficient.[52] Late in June the procurement of all of Louisiana was supported as a means of insuring the independence of the United States "of all the rest of the world in war or in peace." Furthermore, the possession of the territory would unite "the hitherto disjointed and sometimes discordant branches of the union."[53] When it seemed evident that the territory would be purchased, it was hailed as the most fortunate incident since independence. The editor regretted, however, that Florida was not being obtained also. The greatest advantage of the purchase of Louisiana would be the freedom from contact with the French. For the great event, though, no credit should be given to Jefferson whose policy had been "timid and irresolute." The President was criticized for not attempting to remove from the country's honor the stain placed there by the act of Spain in closing the river to commerce and transferring the territory to France.[54]

Still bitter, but slightly more hopeful concerning the downfall of the Republicans, John Rutledge gave a somewhat different estimate of the results that might follow the acquisition of Louisiana. Not being a member of the Congress soon to meet, he expressed his views in a letter to Otis.

I really believe the fever of democracy has had its crisis here and that things will now be growing better. . . . Our master (Jefferson) will have mighty fine tales to amuse his *Mountain* & their mob with—we shall have the prosperous condition of the Republic eulogized, & hear much of the great advantages which will obtain to us by the purchase of a trackless world. A country which when worth the holding will I have no doubt rival & oppose the Atlantic States. I do not mean New Orleans which was absolutely necessary for us to get—and which in *substance* is all we have got for our fifteen millions. This seems to me a miserably calamitous business—indeed I think it must result in the disunion of these States—and yet such is the force

[51] *Ibid.*, March 31, 1803.
[52] *Ibid.*, May 14, 1803.
[53] *Ibid.*, June 23, 1803.
[54] *Ibid.*, July 14, 18, 1803.

of prejudice & popular delusion that the measure cannot yet be even brought to the bar of argument.[55]

Sumter was absent when the senate ratified the treaty of purchase, but Pierce Butler's vote was on the side of the majority.[56] At last the *Charleston Courier* had found something done by a part of the federal government worthy of praise. The senate was to be commended for its speed in ratifying the treaty. But the editor still called for Florida, the cession of which would no more than atone for the dishonor done to the United States by Spain.[57] The failure to acquire Florida, however, did not decrease the newspaper's emphasis on the purchase of Louisiana. The editor doubted if there was ever an act peaceably brought about of such importance as the addition of this new territory to the nation. It would be but the beginning of American expansion. By cultivating British habits and manners, another Britain would be built. Already wagers were being placed that within five years after the United States took possession of Louisiana an American port would be opened on the Pacific Ocean.[58]

By more than a two-thirds majority the South Carolina house of representatives declared its "high sense of the happy situation of the United States when contrasted with that of European powers," and its belief that the "wise measures adopted and pursued by the Executive" in obtaining Louisiana could be taken as "a Sure pledge that every exertion Consistent with National Honor will be made by him to continue and secure to us the Blessings of Peace."[59]

In line with the attitude of the house was the toast given at the anniversary of the Ancient Battalion of Artillery—"The President of the United States—By whose wisdom our terri-

[55] John Rutledge to Otis, October 1, 1803, Morrison, *Life and Letters of Otis*, I, 279.

[56] *Annals of Congress*, 8th Cong., 1st Sess., Executive Journal (October 20, 1803), p. 308. On the passage of the bill by the house to carry the treaty into effect, all South Carolina representatives, except Lowndes, who is not listed, voted affirmatively. *Ibid.*, House (October 29, 1803), pp. 548-549.

[57] *Charleston Courier*, November 12, 1803.

[58] *Ibid.*, December 2, 1803.

[59] S. C. House Journal, December 1, 1803. The vote was 69 to 31.

tories have been beneficially extended without blood shed, and our peace preserved without humility."[60] On May 12, 1804, a general meeting was held in Charleston, as was done throughout the country, to celebrate the acquisition of Louisiana, at which the opening address was made by Dr. David Ramsay, a mild Federalist. Ramsay attempted to refute the arguments of those who opposed the purchase. During the afternoon other gatherings took place in smaller groups, at which toasts were offered, of which the following is an example: "Louisiana—The Acquisition of this extensive and luxuriant Country by *honest* means, and without bloodshed, is a cause of joy to every virtuous citizen—Its inhabitants are no longer our enemies or rivals, they have become our brothers—Hail Liberty, celestial name."[61]

After he had learned of the policy of Federalists in the North the editor of the *Charleston Courier* modified his attitude toward Louisiana but still insisted that Florida must be obtained. The proposal that Louisiana, except New Orleans, should be given to Spain for Florida, he thought a good way of adjusting the question. Spain would never be able to settle the region beyond the Mississippi. She would make a treaty promising not to sell to any other European country or permit other Europeans to settle there. Ultimately the United States could regain the region.[62]

8. The Reopening of the Slave Trade

In 1803 the South Carolina legislature took a significant step in regard to slavery. Sixteen years before an act had been

[60] *City Gazette,* December 16, 1803.

[61] *Ibid.,* and *Times,* May 14, 1803. A similar attitude was expressed at a meeting at Pendleton, but in a more vigorous and political tone, "Thomas Jefferson, President of the United States—the father of our political, economic and moral improvement, the framer of our independence and the friend of man." "Our affectionate Western Brethren—when necessary Republicans will be one body, one mind, one arm to assert their rights—Perish the wretch who would dissever the union, or enfeeble the tie that now link together the various parts." "Peace to the Great Family of the Universe—'Peace' is the motto of our national government." These were toasts at the Fourth of July celebration. Robert Anderson presided. *City Gazette,* August 9, 1803.

[62] *Charleston Courier,* October 31, 1804.

JEFFERSONIAN DEMOCRACY IN S. C. 189

passed which, renewed and modified at intervals, prohibited both foreign and domestic slave trade.[63] Heavy penalties were specified for violating the measure, but by 1803 many had come to consider its enforcement impossible.[64] In his annual message in 1803 Governor James B. Richardson expressed the opinion that the trade could not be stopped. Following this message which "betrays the trace of the desire that the restrictions be removed," the legislature repealed all laws against the slave traffic, but made illegal the importation of male slaves over fifteen years of age from other states.[65] Soon after this action had been taken, a movement was begun in Congress to lay a tax of ten dollars on each slave imported into the United States. The South Carolina representatives resented this as a measure directed at their state. Most of them were opposed to the repeal and hoped that the action would be reconsidered by the legislature. Largely because of the expectation that South Carolina would renew her prohibitions, the consideration of the tax was postponed.[66] Further attempts to pass such a measure in 1805 failed.

[63] *S. C. Statutes at Large,* V, 38, 91, 204, 248, 284, 330, 433. It was possible for a person who intended to become a citizen to carry his slaves into the state with him and any slaves acquired through marriage to a person in another state might be brought in.

[64] A letter of John Drayton to Jefferson, September 12, 1802, shows that there was always great fear of Negro trouble in South Carolina. Rumors were frequently spread that French ships were bringing unruly Negroes or whites that might incite uprisings. Jefferson Papers. In Jefferson's papers there is another letter from Governor Drayton to Thomas Tudor Tucker, November 9, 1802, which gives some light on the slave trade. It seems that Tucker had written at the President's request to ask if the South Carolina laws would prohibit the latter's son-in-law from carrying slaves through the state to Georgia. The governor replied that it was feared that slaves had been smuggled into the state under the pretext of carrying them through it. Permission had been forbidden to Wade Hampton. It was likely that the legislature would soon take some action in regard to the slave trade. Drayton advised a delay. If no action were taken he "may then act in such manner as he shall think most to his advantage and safety."

[65] H. M. Henry, *The Police Control of the Slave in South Carolina* (Emory, Virginia: 1914), p. 103. *S. C. Statutes at Large,* V, 463.

[66] The governor did recommend the placing of restrictions on the traffic in 1805 and 1806. A bill passed the house in 1805 but was defeated in the senate 15 to 16. The following year a similar bill passed the house but was lost on second reading in the senate by the vote of 16 to 16.

The statements of South Carolina members of Congress during the course of the debate of the tax bill are worthy of notice here. Lowndes opposed the tax, because he thought it was aimed at South Carolina. He regretted that the restrictions had been removed, but thought the trade could not be prohibited without the assistance of the federal government. It was probably better to repeal the law than to have it openly violated. He was very much opposed to the importation of slaves and should he be a member of Congress in 1808 he would favor a federal prohibition law. Moore argued that since the proposed tax would not keep slaves out, the purpose of the measure must be to raise revenue. If that be true, it was surprising that gentlemen thought the traffic "horrid and infamous" but still were willing to derive revenue from it. He was likewise opposed to the trade and if he believed the ten-dollar tax would stop it he would support the bill. Huger also was opposed to importing slaves but wanted it clearly understood that South Carolina had the full right to repeal her restrictions at any time she saw fit. It was hardly fair for Congress to permit the Eastern states to import German redemptioners but attempt to prevent the South from bringing in slaves. Huger strongly resented any interference with the activities of the South in regard to slavery.[67]

When the debate was brought up in the next Congress, Robert Marion and David R. Williams, two newcomers, opposed an import duty on slaves. Marion stated that he had never bought a slave and did not intend to. He had evidently obtained some by other means, however, for he said that a tax would increase the value of the ones he possessed. He was as much in favor of stopping the importation as anyone, but did not think the tax of ten dollars would accomplish the purpose. That being the case it was not fair to pass a revenue measure that would affect only one state. Williams strongly defended South Carolina against the disparaging remarks made during the debate. No state in the Union "had appropriated so much

---

Charleston Courier, December 9, 10, 18, 1805; December 17, 24, 1806. There had been only two negative votes in the house of representatives.

[67] *Annals of Congress,* 8th Cong., 1st Sess. (February 14, 15, 17, 1804), pp. 991-993, 1004-1008, 1016, 1024-1027, 1035.

money for objects of munificence and improvement, for encouragement of literature, for the maintenance of the poor." South Carolina's part in the Revolution was recalled. In the house was a descendant of one of her leaders in that conflict. In the senate sat one of her citizens "who may be called the hero of liberty; a man who in the worst of times did not despair of the Republic." Furthermore, some thought that the nation was faced with a war. At a time like that domestic harmony should not be disrupted by such a measure as the bill to place a duty on slaves.[68]

When the bill to prohibit, after 1808, the importation of slaves into the United States was before the house in 1807, Williams opposed it. According to him, the trade could not be stopped by penalties. Those who would break the law were the shipowners of Rhode Island. Williams would not directly charge that such was the motive of the Northern representatives, "but their conduct certainly justifies a suspicion that their object is to pass such a law as will connive at the continuance of the trade for their constituents."[69]

The motives of the members of the legislature in reopening the slave trade were varied. Many agreed with the governor that the law could not be enforced. The editor of the *Charleston Courier* thought that more laborers were needed. Some no

[68] *Annals of Congress*, 9th Cong., 1st Sess. (December 11, 1805; January 22, February 4, 5, 6, 1806), pp. 374, 434-439, 444. The slavery question was not a party matter in South Carolina, for the *Charleston Courier* resented the statements made in the North concerning the renewal of the slave trade even more than did Marion and Williams, Republican members of Congress. A great deal was made of the fact that a Philadelphia paper had in the same issue a severe criticism of South Carolina and a notice, "A German Boy, to be sold at private sale, who is about 14 years of age." *Charleston Courier*, July 10, 1806.

[69] *Annals of Congress*, 9th Cong., 2nd Sess. (December 17, 1806), p. 183. On the passage of the first bill of prohibition Elias Earle, Marion, Moore, Winn, voted affirmatively. Williams opposed. William Butler and O'Brien Smith were apparently absent. One place was vacant. After further amendment by the senate and the conference committee that forbade "the transportation of slaves coastwise, in vessels under forty tons, with a view to sale," William Butler, Marion, Moore, Williams and Winn opposed. Earle and Smith are not listed. *Ibid.* (February 13, 26, 1808), pp. 486-487, 626-627. The bill passed the house, though, 63 to 49.

doubt hoped to obtain profit from selling slaves in the regions farther westward.[70]

A curious comment upon the results of the renewal of the slave trade is that of a Charleston bookdealer. E. S. Thomas records that in 1803 he imported 50,000 volumes of books; but after the planters began investing their money in slaves again, they had so much less for such luxuries as reading materials that he found it extremely difficult to dispose of his stock.[71] The extent of the traffic has been summed up by a recent historian.

Of the 39,075 Africans imported 1805-07, 21,027 came in British and French vessels, and 18,048 in American. 2,006 were imported by native South Carolinians in Charleston vessels, but most came from Rhode Island and British merchants. This was quite natural, as many old and New Englanders were engaged in shipping, and few Carolinians. The attempt of later generations to throw the blame on outsiders is ridiculous; for South Carolinians alone authorized the trade. In the debate after which the House in 1805 voted to stop the trade and the Senate by one vote dissented, economic considerations, the danger from more blacks, and moral reasons were stressed, though denouncing the trade as immoral and unchristian gave some offense.[72]

[70] Henry, *Control of Slaves in S. C.*, p. 104.
[71] Thomas, *Reminiscences*, II, 36.
[72] Wallace, *History of S. C.*, II, 384. The figures as to the importations 1804-1807 are from a speech of Senator William Smith of South Carolina during the discussion of the Missouri controversy, 1820-21. It has been reprinted in the *Charleston Year Book* for 1880 and elsewhere. It seems that only about one thousand of those attributed to the British and French above were brought by the latter.

At the close of the period covered by this study a law was passed by the South Carolina legislature to prohibit the bringing of slaves from the sister states. This was done to stop the inflow of bad Negroes and to free the people from the obnoxious practices of the speculators who bought and sold slaves. Act of 1816, *S. C. Statutes at Large,* VII, 451. The disregard of the law and the practice of passing special acts by the legislature caused the problem to remain unsolved. *City Gazette,* December 4, 1817. After 1818, with a few restrictions, the trade was completely open again. "Thus it will be seen that South Carolina assumed for the benefit of the large planters the responsibility for making the state an open market for the surplus slaves." Henry, *Control of Slaves in S. C.*, p. 108.

JEFFERSONIAN DEMOCRACY IN S. C. 193

The number of people who left South Carolina because of slavery was apparently not large. Some twelve hundred Quakers are said to have gone to the Middle West during the first two decades of the nineteenth century. These and a few others were probably influenced to some extent by the laws favoring the slavery interests.[73]

The number of free Negroes in South Carolina was relatively small.[74] But the increase resulting from birth, purchase of freedom, and the granting of liberty for meritorious services, along with the growing fear of insurrection led the legislature in 1820 to prohibit further emancipation. In the same act were provisions to prevent the coming of free Negroes into the state.[75]

In South Carolina there seems to have been more unity of feeling toward the Negroes than in others of the old slave states. The early spreading of similar agricultural interests and the fairly rapid introduction of slaves into the upper portions of the state brought about a feeling of similar interests as to this one question at least. The planters had great financial sums invested in Negroes and wanted them controlled. The masses of the whites desired that they be well regulated in order to obtain security for themselves and families. There is, therefore, no evidence of a widespread movement for the abolition of slavery in South Carolina.

Apparently no anti-slavery leaders like those in Virginia or North Carolina flourished in South Carolina. The Quakers who were opposed to slavery, left the state in the early part of the nineteenth century, or gave up their scruples about it. The German settlers in Orangeburg and Lexington districts sought to abstain from slavery but drifted with the current and became slaveholders. Some doubtless deprecated slavery in an academic way, and some even maintained in practice their belief that slavery was wrong. Whether there was no tendency toward agitation or public sentiment suppressed it, it would be hard

[73] Henry, *Control of Slaves in S. C.*, p. 104.

[74] 1790--1, 801; 1800--3, 185, 1820--6, 826; and 1860--9, 914. In 1850, Charleston district had forty-three per cent of the total in the state. Henry, *Control of Slaves in S. C.*, p. 177; Wallace, *History of S. C.*, II, 507, drawing from *Charleston Free Negro Books (MS)*, DeBow, December, 1848, and Robert Gourdin, *News and Courier*, July-August, 1904.

[75] *S. C. Statutes at Large*, VII, 415.

to say. There is little reason to believe that such discussion would have received an intelligent hearing.[76]

9. The Ratification of the Twelfth Amendment and Political Developments in 1804

Let us return to the discussion of the political developments during the early years of the nineteenth century. After the tie in the electoral votes in 1800 there had been much discussion of possible ways of preventing its recurrence. During the debate of the proposed twelfth amendment Huger and Lowndes, the two Federalists in the house and Pierce Butler, one of the two Republicans in the senate from South Carolina, spoke against such a change. The other members, on one vote or another, voted affirmatively.[77] Even after the passage of the amendment by both houses of Congress, Senator Butler was not ready to give up his fight. In letters to the governor of South Carolina he urged that the state refuse to ratify it. Under such a plan the smaller states could never hope to have one of their citizens chosen as either President or Vice-President. There would hardly ever be a repetition of the situation of 1800. If both candidates continued to be voted upon without designation as to office the smaller states would have better chances. Whereas if one were listed as Vice-President, the office would be filled by intrigue and its nominee unworthy of succeeding the President in case of the latter's death.[78] In spite of the objections offered by Butler and others the South Carolina legislature ratified the twelfth amendment.[79]

By the beginning of the last year of Jefferson's first admin-

[76] Henry, *Control of Slaves in S. C.*, pp. 190-191. Since slavery ceased to be an issue between the parties in South Carolina, if it ever was a really great one, and came to be a question concerning which there was relative agreement, further mention of the problem will be only incidental in this study of party politics.

[77] *Annals of Congress*, 8th Cong., 1st Sess. (October 28, December 6, 8, 1803; Senate, November 23, December 2, 1803), pp. 515-535, 544-545, 646-649, 662-663, 707-711, 775-776; 85-87, 207-209. The vote was 22 to 10 in the senate and 83 to 41 in the house.

[78] Pierce Butler to the governor of South Carolina, December 6, 1803, and April 3, 1804, quoted by Channing, *History of the U. S.*, IV, 295.

[79] S. C. House Journal, May 14, 1804. The vote in the house was 65 to 25.

JEFFERSONIAN DEMOCRACY IN S. C.   195

istration political passion seems to have subsided greatly in South Carolina. Such is indicated by the toast of the Society of the Cincinnati, many of whose members had been extremely anti-Jefferson—"Party Spirit: may it be kept within due bounds—we are all Republicans—all Federalists." Next, after one to Washington, had come a toast to the President.[80] Another sign of the return to calmness was the devotion of much more space in the newspapers to literature and art.[81] Being under more moderate management and perhaps finding less support for its violent criticism of the administration of the federal government, the *Charleston Courier* toned down considerably. It occasionally found space to print a witticism against its own party, one of which is reproduced here because of its reference to a man later to be president of South Carolina College and prominent in the politics of the state—"Tom Cooper, (a democrat) now of Northumberland, Pennsylvania, formerly of Birmingham, England, says, 'the federalists read little and know less.' "[82] This Federalist newspaper was not ready, though, to endorse the policies of the Republicans. It did aim blows at what seemed to be the most vulnerable part of their program from the standpoint of the Charleston readers. The editor contended that the miserable economies of the Jefferson administration had stripped the coast of the proper defense. He declared that every mail brought news of "American vessels captured, or, if not detained, robbed, plundered, and insulted." The country's flag had been stained because of "the supineness of the government." "The device of abusing the public credulity with the tale of economy is too stale for further use."[83] However, the toasts on the Fourth of July were as a whole unusually friendly to Jefferson.[84]

[80] *The Times*, February 24, 1804.
[81] See especially the many articles on poetry and painting in the *Times* during January, 1804.
[82] *Charleston Courier*, June 18, 1804.
[83] *Ibid.*, March 28, August 3, 1804.
[84] The sentiments of the American Revolutionary Society were "Thomas Jefferson—the Great political luminary of America." A toast of the Charleston Ancient Battalion of Artillery was "The President of the United States—may his exertions to serve his country, procure him the gratitude of his fellow citizens." *City Gazette*, July 6, 1804.

After the resignation of Associate Justice Alfred Moore of North Carolina, Jefferson decided to fill the vacancy on the Supreme Court by the appointment of a South Carolina lawyer. Briefs for those best fitted were drawn up upon information supplied largely by Wade Hampton and Thomas Sumter. At least five attorneys were given serious consideration. The "two principal of those called Republicans" were John Julius Pringle and Thomas Waties, both "of oldstanding, and of highest repute." Pringle had gone over to the Federalists for a while but had returned. Both were moderate, voted Republican, but "never meddle otherwise." Pringle was very rich, confined his practice to Charleston, and was not likely to leave that town for a commission requiring much traveling from court to court. Waties was too sickly to ride a great deal and also might not have the confidence of the Republicans. A third, William Johnson, was a state judge, an excellent lawyer, "prompt, eloquent, and irreproachable character, republican connections, and of good nerves in his political principles, about 35 years old, was speaker some years." "Trisvan" (no doubt Judge Lewis C. Trezevant) was a state judge also and of equal qualifications and respectability as Johnson. His age was about the same as that of Johnson but his body was so feeble that he would hardly be physically fit for the position. Gilliard (Theodore Gaillard) was speaker of the South Carolina house of representatives, had talents equal to those of Johnson and was also a young man. His family having been tories during the Revolution, their estate had been confiscated; but his father had regained part of it. The son was educated in England. When he returned to America he was "soured ag^t those in power for what his family had suffered." Having nothing to hope from them, he joined the Republicans. His conduct had been firm, "almost vindictive," in the assembly; but "in an instance or two, from family influence or interest he has swerved a little from sound principles. Upon the whole, his standing is not quite as respectable as that of Johnson." After mature consideration of these and no doubt other factors, Jefferson appointed Johnson, sending the nomination to the senate, March 23, 1804.[85]

[85] The "briefs" are given in Hunt, "Office-Seeking during Jefferson's Administration," p. 282. Pringle had served as district attorney for

10. SOUTH CAROLINA'S VOTE OF CONFIDENCE IN JEFFERSONIAN DEMOCRACY

The elections of 1804 resulted in almost complete victories for the Republicans in South Carolina. Except for a small number in the legislature, few Federalists remained in office. In the Ninth Congress both senators and all the representatives from South Carolina were Republicans. The easy choice of electors favoring Jefferson and George Clinton was a contrast to the struggle of 1800. For the first time the Federalists were defeated in the Charleston Congressional District. Robert Marion, the Republican candidate, received nearly twice the number of votes of his Federalist opponent, Robert Smith. In the other districts what opposition existed was largely confined to the candidacies of other Republicans.[86] For governor, the legislature chose Paul Hamilton, also a Republican.[87]

Even though the victories of the Republicans in 1804 had seemed all but complete, there were still enough Federalists in South Carolina to continue the fight. A battle of words began in the two leading newspapers soon after the second inauguration of Jefferson. The *Charleston Courier* as usual catered to those hostile to the administration, while the *City Gazette* printed letters on both sides but unquestionably leaned toward the Republicans. In April the writer of "We also" in the latter paper joined "We" of the Federalist organ of expression in deploring the reelection of Jefferson by the almost unanimous vote of his

---

upper South Carolina during Washington's first administration, had been offered other positions but declined. In 1805 Jefferson offered him the position of Attorney General but he declined again. He was attorney general of South Carolina 1792-1808. He died in 1843, being almost ninety at the time. O'Neall, *Bench and Bar in S. C.*, II, 3-10.

[86] Peter Freneau to Jefferson, October 14, 1804, Jefferson Papers. *Annals of Congress*, 8th Cong., 2nd Sess. (February 3, 1805), p. 56. There were no alleged compromise possibilities to argue about in 1804. Charles Cotesworth Pinckney was the Federalist candidate for President but his fourteen votes came from Connecticut, Delaware and Maryland.

The two senators who would represent the state in the federal Congress were Thomas Sumter and John Gaillard. The representatives were William Butler, Levi Casey, Elias Earle, Robert Marion, Thomas Moore, O'Brien Smith, David R. Williams and Richard Winn.

[87] S. C. House Journal, December 8, 1804.

"*deluded* countrymen." The administration had reduced taxes, deprived needy collectors of their places and had degraded the public character and the courts by "so penurious an economy." Warlike achievements and the glory of arms had been avoided. "A howling wilderness" had been added to the territory of the country. Democracy, mob rule, something akin to anarchy, was gaining force. The President was again attacked for saying in 1801 that he was the chief executive of the whole people and then appointing only Republicans. Jefferson was accused of attacking the courts and aiding the Congressional onset upon "the honorable Judge Chase."[88] Soon the editor of the *Charleston Courier* was said to be the writer of the "We" letters. "Sly Boots" called upon him to prove that men had been turned out of office recklessly. The editor was also asked to explain why equally capable Republicans should not be appointed to vacancies.[89] The reply not having been satisfactory "Sly Boots" continued to discuss appointments. The President had the authority to fill places unless the Constitution specified other methods. Had he violated that document? Why did "We" not compare the present administration's policy with that of the previous ones? Soon the foreign birth of S. C. Carpenter of the *Charleston Courier* was pointed out. "Sly Boots" did not want to discount the rights of aliens in this country but thought that they ought to respect the government that protected them. Had not the party of Jefferson fought for the aliens?[90] "Columbianus," a Republican but not a rabid one, living some distance from Charleston, welcomed the statement of opposing views in the newspapers. He had sometime earlier noticed the liberality of the Federalist press in approving the purchase of Louisiana and the act to restrain the arming of merchant vessels sailing to some parts of the West Indies and had thought of subscribing to the *Charleston Courier;* but the recent uncompromising attitude of the editor had caused him to change his mind. "Columbianus" now thought that the misrepresentations of the Federalist editor showed him to be a hired partisan who must please his employers.[91] "Sydney" called upon Carpenter to forbear "those *infamous libels* upon a people who have received

[88] *City Gazette,* April 10, 12, 13, 1805.
[89] *Ibid.,* April 27, 1805.
[90] *Ibid.,* May 1, 7, 1805.   [91] *Ibid.,* May 11, 1805.

you into their bosom, and on a government which has given you that protection you acknowledge to have been denied you in your own country."[92] "Ulysses" did not hope to silence the Federalists but did wish to refute their arguments. The Jefferson administration did not lack energy but had a different kind as seen in the humbling of the Barbary pirates. As to dignity, the Republicans treated all alike, disliking fuss, commotion or pretense of form. In regard to courage, he did not think the attitude of the Federalists in acting the part of a "bully" while France was in so much trouble showed that they were courageous. The Republicans felt national indignity as strongly as their opponents but used commercial methods of resistance. As to Jefferson, "Ulysses" thought that "the laurels with which history will adorn his name, will keep their verdure fresher, for having never been watered with blood!"[93] In October "An injured Merchant" who recalled the great commotion caused in Charleston when a French privateer had captured the ship *Two Friends* stated that he had been waiting in vain for one of the anti-French group to denounce with equal vehemence the conduct of the British in seizing ships "prosecuting lawful voyages with cargoes of West-Indies produce."[94]

A notice in the *City Gazette* in the fall of 1805 indicated the approaching return to the state of Charles Pinckney. Suggestive of his political power after an absence of over four years is his election to the South Carolina house of representatives from Christ's Church Parish even before he actually arrived.[95] Thus did the most vigorous leader of South Carolina Republicanism return to this country at a time when international developments were fast forcing the United States into a situation perhaps more serious and difficult than that of the late 1790's. It was to be expected that one who had spent such a large portion of his life in public office would resume immediately his activity in governmental affairs.[96]

[92] *Ibid.*, May 16, 1805.
[93] *Ibid.*, May 27, 1805.   [94] *Ibid.*, October 1, 1805.
[95] *Ibid.*, October 24, 1805. On January 10, 1806, the editor of the *Times* had the following notice in his paper: "Charles Pinckney, Esq. late Minister Plenipotentiary from the United States to the Court of Madrid, came passenger in the Henricus IV, from Lisbon."
[96] Because of its extremely controversial nature the mission of Charles Pinckney to Spain has been omitted as a topic of discussion

Jefferson's second administration was beset with even more perplexing problems than those of his first. During the years,

for the body of this study. Historians have been extremely unfriendly to Pinckney, particularly to his activities in Spain. Such an estimate is partly supported by Jefferson's letter to Monroe, January 8, 1804. Jefferson Papers. The President wrote: "There is here a great sense of the inadequacy of C. Pinckney to the office he is in. His continuance is made a subject of standing reproach to myself personally, by whom appointment was made before I had collected the administration. He declared at the time that nothing would induce him to continue so as not to be here at the ensuing Presidential election. I am persuaded he expected to be proposed at it as V. P. After he got to Europe his letters asked only a continuance of two years. But he now does not drop the least hint of a voluntary return. Pray, my dear sir, avail yourself of his vanity, his expectations, his fears, and whatever will weigh with him to induce him to ask leave to return, and obtain from him to be the bearer of the letter yourself. You will render us in this the most acceptable service possible. His enemies here are perpetually dragging his character in the dirt, and charging it on the administration. He does, or ought to know this, and to feel the necessity of coming home to vindicate himself, if he looks to anything further in the career of honor." Without citing any source Channing says, "Jefferson somewhat grudgingly appointed Charles Pinckney minister to Spain, where he blundered as he had at home." *History of U. S.,* IV, 234. Sears, *American Foreign Relations,* p. 102, states that "Charles Pinckney, brought not only himself but his government into discredit at Madrid. Pinckney was an overzealous diplomat not guided or curbed by adequate instructions." Then after taking up the issues between the United States and Spain he states further (p. 103), "Far from recalling Pinckney, the administration left him to the *embarrassments of his own creation,* and decided once more to seek its own ends by a special mission of Monroe to Paris." (The italics are the present writer's.) A more detached and fairer view is given by Charles E. Hill in his account of James Madison as Secretary of State, Bemis, ed., *American Secretaries of State,* III, 9-56. In the last, Pinckney's conduct is presented in broader perspective. It is incidentally of interest that more sources are cited by Hill.

After a careful study the present writer is ready to accept the general treatment of the Spanish mission of Charles Pinckney written by Professor J. H. Easterby for the *Dictionary of American Biography,* XIV, 613-614. Because of its acceptability and because of the importance of these more than four years in the life of South Carolina's most prominent Republican, a rather lengthy quotation is given. After discussing the activity of Pinckney in the election of 1800, the author takes up the mission to Spain.

"Pinckney's reward was the appointment (March, 1801) as minister to Spain. After a leisurely journey through the Netherlands and France he addressed himself in Madrid to the original object of his mission and was able to send home on August 11, 1802, a convention providing

1801-1805, when Jeffersonian Democracy was being established as an operative program, South Carolina had not only remained

for a joint tribunal to settle claims arising from spoliations committed in recent years upon American shipping by Spanish cruisers, and leaving open for future negotiations similar claims for French depredations carried out within Spain's jurisdiction (American State Papers. Foreign Relations, Vol. II, 1832, pp. 475-76, 482-483). Unfortunately, the administration permitted delays in ratification which allowed the agreement to become entangled with larger difficulties which were even then developing between the two countries. One cause of ill feeling he successfully removed by securing, with the aid of the Spanish minister to the United States, the restoration of the right of deposit at New Orleans which had been withdrawn by the intendant. When Pinckney was on the point of renewing his efforts to have the French spoliations included in the claims convention, Bonaparte reached the momentous decision to sell Louisiana to the United States. To Pinckney's cares was now added the task of inducing Spain to acquiesce in this transaction (*Ibid.*, II, 570-71). Having been met with an even more stubborn resistance than hitherto in the claims matter and having good reason to believe that the time was ripe to press for the cession of the Floridas to the United States, a subject which had long been included in his instructions but which of late he had been ordered not to urge without the concurrence of Monroe who was at this time in London, Pinckney combined these three points in a positive note to the Spanish government on January 11, 1804 (*ibid.*, II, 616-17). A month later, Spain, acting under French compulsion, acceded to the sale of Louisiana, but the unexpected decision of the United States to accept the claims agreement in its original form and the passage of the Mobile Act authorizing the erection of a part of West Florida into a United States customs district left Pinckney no ground to stand upon in the other two matters. His request for Spain's renewal of the ratification of the convention being met with refusal unless the United States abandon altogether the French spoliations and repeal the Mobile Act he now threatened to ask for his passports, believing that his government was prepared to defend its actions (*ibid.*, II, 618-24); Ford Transcripts [of letters to Jefferson, Madison and Monroe from Pinckney], July 30, 1804. Thus matters stood until the arrival of Monroe. Together the two ministers renewed the negotiations but accomplished nothing. In October, 1805, Pinckney sailed for home. His mission had not been successful. In the Florida matter he had exceeded his instructions, but the main cause of failure lay with the administration."

In concluding his summary, Easterby writes:

"Handsome, vain, and doubtless, something of a roue, though capable of the tenderest devotion to his three young children after the death of their mother (1794), Pinckney possessed that iridescent genius which offends some and dazzles others. To his Federalist contemporaries he was 'Blackguard Charlie,' a demogogue, a spoilsman, and a corruptionist; to his followers he was a demigod fit for the presidency. His

Republican but had become more strongly so. The misunderstanding on the part of Jefferson of the work of Charles Pinckney in Spain was the only notable development of an untoward nature. Even this was temporary, for Pinckney soon became again one of the prominent South Carolina leaders and convinced Jefferson of his staunch Republicanism. With the coming of new complications South Carolina continued to furnish leaders and support for the Jefferson program.

---

great egoism induced in him a habit of seeing his own deeds in heroic dimensions. He honestly believed that he had virtually written the Federal Constitution, and this, together with other extravagant claims that he made for himself, has raised doubts in the minds of historians which have obscured his real achievements."

CHAPTER VIII

REPUBLICAN EFFORTS TO PRESERVE PEACE, 1806-1810

1. THE INDEPENDENCE OF WILLIAMS AND SUMTER AND THE PASSAGE OF THE NON-INTERCOURSE ACT

Never having ceased to be an issue, foreign affairs, by 1806, again had become a very important factor in South Carolina politics. Although the state's representatives in Congress wanted to stay out of war, not all of them agreed with the methods proposed by the Republican leaders. Of the South Carolina members of the Ninth Congress, David R. Williams, a new member, probably went to Washington with the highest recommendations.[1] He was, however, a man of independent nature, one who was unwilling to accept a policy merely because it met the approval of party leaders. So independent was he that he declined to dine with the President because he felt that to do so might in some way interfere with his freedom of action.[2]

[1] Having been connected with him in the management of the *City Gazette* for a time and having known him and his record, Peter Freneau, who had been corresponding with Jefferson for several years, wrote the President about the admirable characteristics of the new representative. Freneau wrote, "I have had the satisfaction of being connected with him in business for a considerable time, some years ago; from the knowledge I then gained of him, and from the universal report of his neighbors, I am fully authorized to say, that he is a gentleman of the strictest integrity, of the most unblemished reputation, in the most easy and affluent circumstances, and of the soundest political principles. With such qualifications I know he will receive the attention which is due to him.

"I consider him well informed of the domestic affairs of this State and able to make any explanations thereon you may be desirous of receiving." Jefferson Papers, November 4, 1805.

[2] Jefferson Papers, January 31, 1806. Jefferson wrote in reply: "The independence of the mind is one of its best qualities, & if you suppose it could have been lessened by that kind of intercourse, you are right in declining it, and no one has a right to complain. be assured that

Early in his Congressional experience Williams acquired an aversion for the term "contingent expenses." During the consideration of the naval appropriation bill in 1806, he urged the house to ask for an itemized list of the uses to which the requested amount would be put. His purpose was to abolish appropriations in such lump sums, not to reduce the total grant. But when his resolution failed to pass he expressed willingness to risk unpopularity by working for smaller appropriations until the navy department specified particular items. He told of his early experiences in Washington. Being interested in the navy, he had gone to the navy yard. When he had asked under what appropriations "an elegant building" was being constructed, he was told that it was the contingent fund. The expenditures in this case and in others he had investigated might all be proper; but the voters should have a more definite report of how their money was spent. In his attempts Williams got only divided support from his colleagues. On the final passage of the bill itself in the house, he voted negatively.[3]

On the passage of the appropriations to aid in the acquisition of Florida it was Thomas Sumter, the Republican of long standing, who displayed most independence. He argued that the United States would be better off without that region. Already having seacoast of nearly five hundred miles the country had enough for trading purposes and too much for her means of defense. Florida was near Cuba, making it favorable to smuggling. As it was, the region furnished a barrier for the

---

understanding the motive I take not the least umbrage at it, and shall always be glad to associate with you in any other way more agreeable to you." The President stated that he cultivated intercourse with members of the legislative branch of the government so that they might understand each other and in order that they might advise him in regard to local situations. "I pray you however to be assured that with respect to yourself I yield with frankness to your particular way of thinking and shall be glad to receive any communications from you in whatever way you shall prefer & at whatever times; tendering you my salutations & assurance of great respect and esteem."

[3] *Annals of Congress,* 9th Cong., 1st Sess., April 10, 18, 1806, pp. 998-1005, 1078. The bill passed the house 58 to 28. The votes of the other South Carolina representatives are not listed. An interesting statement of Williams's independence may be found in Harvey Toliver Cook, *The Life and Legacy of David Rogerson Williams* (New York: the Country Life Press, 1916), pp. 70-71.

JEFFERSONIAN DEMOCRACY IN S. C. 205

United States. Furthermore, there was nothing to fear from Florida. No recent development made the purchase advisable. If the object of the proposed appropriation was to settle the boundary, the sum requested was too large. Sumter was opposed to the secrecy around the matter. It had always been his policy to refrain from voting in the dark. Neither the message from the President nor the communications from the American ministers had asked for such a sum. It was unusual to grant an amount of that extent to ambassadors. Neither justice nor policy requiring the passage of the bill, he felt compelled to vote against it.[4]

In 1806 Williams strongly opposed the complete prohibition of the importation of goods from Great Britain. Such an act would mean injury to his constituents and deprive the nation of revenue at a time when it needed money for protection. Then, too, he was unwilling to go that far in the defense of merchants. In his opinion the differences with Great Britain could be settled by diplomacy. The cessation of importation was not a good means for the promotion of a settlement. Furthermore, the merchants were not without blame. Had some of them not concealed enemy goods? "The carrying merchants, and their friends have dished up their own injuries. For one, I am determined not to work out their salvation at the expense of everything dear to the nation." Williams, however, joined four of his colleagues in favoring the stoppage of the importation of certain goods from Great Britain, apparently thinking that the modified measure would be less injurious to his constituents and not as likely to lead to war.[5] On the final passage

[4] William Plumer, *Memorandum of the Proceedings in the United States Senate 1803-1807*, edited by Everette Somerville Brown (New York: Macmillan, 1923), pp. 421-422. The measure, however, passed both houses. Gaillard in the senate and Earle, Marion and O'Brien Smith in the house voted for it, while Sumter in the senate and Butler, Casey, Moore and D. R. Williams opposed it. Winn is not listed. *Annals of Congress*, 9th Cong., 1st Sess., House and Senate (February 7, 1806), p. 88, 1120-1127. The house on January 14 had passed a measure stating that it was of the opinion that the problem of Florida could best be settled by the exchange of territory between the United States and Spain. Winn was absent. All others except Earle voted "aye."

[5] *Annals of Congress*, 9th Cong., 1st Sess. (March 7, 17, 1806), pp. 643-650, 823. Casey and Elias Earle opposed. O'Brien Smith was absent.

of the Non-importation Act of 1806 the six South Carolina representatives present voted affirmatively. The two senators divided, Gaillard favoring and Sumter opposing.[6] At the next session of Congress all the representatives from South Carolina present opposed the suspension of the measure until December 31, 1807.[7] Again all present favored the substitution of July 1, as the termination of the suspension; but on the final passage of the bill to suspend till July 1, Williams voted negatively.[8] On the question of agreeing to the senate amendment to allow the President to suspend operation till the first Monday in December, 1807, if he thought public good demanded, Williams again opposed.[9]

2. THE *Phocian* LETTERS—THE STRONGEST CASE FOR THE FEDERALISTS

The discussion of foreign affairs brought back into prominence Federalist leaders of the 1790's. The strongest presentation of the case against the policy of the Jefferson administration was the celebrated letters of *Phocian* really written by William Loughton Smith, formerly leader of his party in the federal house of representatives and American minister to Portugal. These letters, first printed in the *Charleston Courier,* beginning early in 1806, were later published in pamphlet form in both the United States and Great Britain.[10]

[6] *Ibid.* (March 26; Senate, April 15, 1806), pp. 877-878, 240. Casey and O'Brien Smith are not listed. The vote in the house was 93 to 32 for passage, in the senate, 19 to 9. The non-importation of the enumerated articles was to go into effect November 15, 1806.
[7] *Ibid.,* 2nd Sess., House (December 5, 1806), p. 115. Winn, Moore and O'Brien Smith were absent.
[8] *Ibid.,* 2nd Sess. (December 6, 1806), pp. 125-127. The vote for passage was 97 to 12. Moore was present on this vote. Winn and O'Brien Smith, however, were absent.
[9] *Ibid.* (December 15, 1806), pp. 153-158. The others, except Winn and O'Brien Smith not listed, voted for the measure.
[10] [William Loughton Smith], *The Numbers of Phocian, Which Were Originally Published in the Charleston Courier, in 1806 on the Subject of Neutral Rights* (Charleston: 1806). The pamphlet edition began with number five. The previous ones were printed in the newspaper February 18, 21, 25 and March 1, 1806. The pamphlet may be found in the pamphlets of the Charleston Library Society, series three, vol. XII, no. 17. The preface of the British edition stated that the

JEFFERSONIAN DEMOCRACY IN S. C.   207

In the *Phocian* letters Smith pointed out the difference between actual armed conflict and a "paper war." He did not doubt that the people of the country would be patriotic during actual military warfare, but during a "paper war" they would consider the nation at peace and continue to trade with Great Britain.[11] The administration's practice of having Congress pass measures, suspend them during negotiations and then put them into effect if diplomacy failed, was denounced as a poor method of dealing with a foreign country. It was unwise to present the ultimatum first. Besides, greater demands were made of Great Britain than were warranted. The United States had never claimed the right of direct trade between the colonies and the parent nation as Jefferson and his colleagues were then doing. All that the commercial interests had ever asked was the right to carry goods to the United States, land them, enter them at the customs houses and re-ship them. In his opinion the only purpose of the administration was that of "embroiling us with England."[12]

According to Smith, Great Britain had not violated the laws of nations. The opinion of Arthur Browne, who relied on Grotius, Hernecius, Valin, Vattel and others, was quoted to prove that the demands of the neutrals in the existing war were unjustified. Moreover, he asserted, the advocates of the neutrals had already admitted the legality of the Rule of 1756. The supposed concessions of France were not made because of her desire to trade with the United States but on account of her need for goods at the particular time. Jefferson's claim that the British conduct was "an interpolation of the laws of nations" would not stand.[13] If the United States and Great Britain were at war and the trade of the English colonies were opened to the Danes, Swedes and other neutrals it would mean disaster for this country. The British could then turn her merchantmen into war ships and leave commerce to neutrals. Rather than see these neutral nations carry on the British trade with her colonies, Jefferson would attack them, thus violating the rule

---

numbers had been widely circulated in the United States. Citations are to Charleston edition.

[11] [W. L. Smith], *Phocian Numbers*, no. 5.
[12] *Ibid.*, no. 6.   [13] *Ibid.*, no. 7.

they were then so strongly advocating.[14] In the tenth number Smith held that even Madison in 1794 had stood for principles quite inconsistent with his policy as Secretary of State. The change was attributed to the influence of Jefferson and his French sympathy. Much was made of the pro-French attitude of Monroe during the Washington administration. Yet this same man had been sent by Jefferson and entrusted with "in spite of his *economies, three missions* at once, with *three outfits* amounting to twenty-seven thousand dollars, exclusive of his annual salary of nine thousand dollars!—" Not only were unwarranted demands made, but hostile representatives were sent.[15] Smith severely criticized Jefferson for not negotiating directly instead of asking the advice of the senate. If foreign nations knew the instructions of the minister they would be less inclined to yield.[16] In the fourteenth and fifteenth numbers the author denounced Congress for its inability to protect the country during a crisis. The ports were unfortified, yet the legislative body was willing to reduce governmental revenues from import duties during non-importation without voting other taxes.

On vital points, Smith claimed that he and John Randolph were in agreement, "*First,* that we have no business with the *direct carrying trade.—Secondly,* That if we had, it would not be polite to urge our claims.—*Thirdly,* That the means selected for enforcing it are not those which ought to be resorted to." Moreover, Great Britain would not interfere with our commerce unless compelled by practices "striking at her very existence."[17] In numbers twenty-two, twenty-three and twenty-four Smith discussed the question of what constituted a break in the continuity of voyage. Intention was the only criterion. The act of Congress in 1805 tending to do away with the bond in case of reexportation showed the intention of the government to encourage a continuous voyage. The *Essex* Case was not inconsistent with that of the *Polly,* he argued. Madison was accused of quoting only part of the latter case and Monroe of misinterpreting it. In the *Polly* decision it had been stated that the duty must be paid, the goods landed and warehoused for

[14] *Ibid.,* no. 8.
[15] *Ibid.,* no. 11.
[16] *Ibid.,* no. 13.
[17] *Ibid.,* no. 17.

"a considerable time." Then if this were done it would devolve upon the captors to prove that the original intention had been to send the goods to the parent nation.

Finally, Smith declared that his attitude had been impartial and that he had been actuated only by interest in his own country. He had, however, been made very angry by the partiality of the administration in its adoption of a policy that could lead only to a calamitous war.[18]

Protection of the seacoast and of commerce became the cry of the Federalists. The blockading of the harbors by the British squadron and French privateers was declared to be insulting to the nation's honor and destructive of her commercial interests. Any other administration would have protected at least the harbors.[19] Some Federalists expected relief through the opening of new commercial fields in Spanish America. The editor of the *Charleston Courier* predicted the success of the Miranda expedition and hoped that the most brilliant success would "attend the standards of those who fight for the cause of rational liberty, and for the dignity of the human species."[20] John Rutledge continued to paint a gloomy picture of the future under a party that neither knew nor cared anything about commerce or the protection of the country; but he hoped still that fortune would soon play the "wonderfully fools a trick, & make their fall in proportion to their elevation." Curious indeed was the act of the "bungling politicians" in affronting all the powers of Europe at once. The New World would be greatly affected by the outcome of the conflict in the old. England, he believed, would "forever hold out" because of her ability to raise money.

I have long considered england as but the advance guard of our country, & it is to be lamented, that the conduct of that government should be such toward a portion of our countrymen, as to prevent any one american from wishing that their resistance may be successful. If they fall we do—Bonaparte neither loves nor values any thing, but the aggrandizement of the nation, & the extension of his own military fame.[21]

[18] *Phocian Numbers*, no. 27.
[19] *Charleston Courier*, May 13, 1806.   [20] *Ibid.*, May 15, 1806.
[21] Rutledge to Otis, July 29, 1806. Morrison, *Life and Letters of Otis*, I, 281-282.

3. THE ELECTION OF 1806

On the eve of the election of 1806 the Federalists centered their attack on the administration's foreign policy. Less effort, however, was made to defend the British. In the face of great dangers, they declared, the proceedings of the last Congress "consisted of so many imbecile acts, as to make their best friends blush."[22] The same writer two days later bewailed the contrast between the South Carolina leadership then in Congress and that of the days when Federalists controlled. In former times the people understood the problems, but now nobody in Congress seemed to understand the issues facing the country. Marion was called an excellent gentleman but no statesman. Possibly with the view of sounding out the attitude of the voters toward William Loughton Smith, the writer stated that he would be glad to support him if it were not for his political affiliations.[23] Since the President had "shrunk from leadership" and called for instruction from Congress, the *Charleston Courier* thought particular attention should be given to choosing the next representatives.[24] The editor asked whether Charleston was to be represented by an able Federal Republican familiar with its needs or by a stranger to their city, ignorant of the commercial interests and indifferent to their welfare. William Loughton Smith was suggested as the competent Federal Republican.[25]

The outcome of the elections of 1806 showed that South Carolina was still overwhelmingly Republican. The composition of the Congressional delegation remained unchanged in political affiliation. The vacancy caused by the death of Levi Casey had been filled by Joseph Calhoun, who had served for a time in the Ninth Congress. Elias Earle and O'Brien Smith were succeeded by Lemuel J. Alston and John Taylor, both Republicans. The time had come when serious contests were among Republicans themselves instead of between two distinct parties. In the heat of the campaign they would sometimes call each other Federalists. Lemuel J. Alston, for example, was accused

[22] The *Times*, October 4, 1806, letter signed "A Republican," but probably written by a Federalist.   [23] *Ibid.*, October 6, 7, 1806.
[24] *Charleston Courier*, October 11, 1806.
[25] *Ibid.*, October 13, 1806.

JEFFERSONIAN DEMOCRACY IN S. C. 211

of being a Federalist by his opponents.[26] The other five representatives and the two senators retained their seats. The political strength of Charles Pinckney was again demonstrated when the legislature elected him governor of South Carolina for the fourth time.[27]

In 1806 the South Carolina house of representatives chose as speaker Joseph Alston, whom Hooker described as a "beauish young man of about 28."[28] In 1801 Alston had married Theo-

[26] Edward Hooker, a young teacher little more than twenty years of age, a graduate of Yale, who had been teaching at Cambridge, S. C., was surprised at the great interest of the voters in the Congressional campaign of 1806. "A stranger would be led to think the fate of the United States depended on the choice which these people are about to make of Captain Elias Earle, or Col. Alston, or Dr. Hunter for a Congressman, neither of whom, nor the people who vote for them, are probably *valued a straw* at the seat of government." Hunter was said to be too valuable a physician to send to Congress. It was stated that Earle cared little for religion and that instead of going inside the church would stay out under the shade with anyone who would remain and drink with him. Whereas Alston was pictured as a Federalist, too rich, and even in favor of a stamp tax. Especially interesting was the "treating" of the voters to drinks. Dr. Hunter was more reserved than his opponents. Alston carried the constituents to the bar for their drinks, but Earle had his in the open serving as bartender himself. Edward Hooker, "Diary, 1805-1806," *Report of the American Historical Association*, 1896, I, 893, 898, 900-901. Two years later after seeing Alston in Washington, Hooker wrote, "Col. Alston is full of polite airs and polite talk;— not a great man but a pretty man. I once saw him in S. C. but did not now recognize him till I heard his name and he seems not to recollect me." *Ibid.*, p. 926. Hooker taught also at the South Carolina College for a short while before returning to New England.

[27] On the first ballot no one was given a majority, but on the second, Pinckney received 73 votes to 66 for Henry Middleton, his nearest rival. S. C. House Journal, December 9, 1806. A few days earlier Governor Paul Hamilton had resigned. The matter is not quite clear but his action seems to have been connected with the political trouble he had been having in regard to appointments and promotions of military officials. Hamilton had declined to promote William Rouse in spite of his being next in order. In this the governor had apparently gone counter to the will of the legislature. Already a movement had been started to impeach him. After his resignation the house voted that Hamilton had erred in judgment in withholding Rouse's commission but that he had done so on conscientious grounds. In the opinion of the house, therefore, no grounds existed for his impeachment. *Ibid.*, December 3, 15, 20, 1806.

[28] Hooker, "Diary," p. 864. Since Alston was born in 1779 he was evidently twenty-seven. He had been trained by tutors at home suffi-

dosia Burr, the brilliant daughter of the Vice-President-Elect. Because of the great influence which Aaron Burr seemed to exert over his son-in-law and on account of his presence along with Theodosia at the supposed discussion of the alleged conspiracy, Alston has been thought by some to have been implicated in the schemes of his father-in-law. It can hardly be denied that he knew that some kind of plans were being made and there is some indication of his possible connection with them but evidence is lacking to prove that he knew their extent.[29]

---

ciently to permit him to enter the junior class at Princeton in 1795. He left the following year without graduating. After studying law in the office of Edward Rutledge he was admitted to the bar. However, he had no sooner won the privilege of practicing than he abandoned the profession of law for planting and an active career in politics. Except for the 1804 session Alston seems to have been a member of the legislature till 1812 when he was elected governor. His administration as chief executive of the state will be taken up in connection with the War of 1812. See the sketch of Alston by J. H. Easterby in the *Dictionary of American Biography*, I, 229-230.

[29] Easterby, in the *Dictionary of American Biography*, I, 229-230, says that if Burr "actually entertained thoughts of dismembering the Union, it is improbable that Alston was cognizant of them. It is true that in his haste to deny that he had been a party to treasonable designs, he was led into a somewhat unbecoming repudiation of Burr (W. H. Safford, Blennerhassett Papers, 1864, pp. 227-30); but at the moment he had good grounds to suspect the latter of double-dealing, and he later made amends by zealously aiding the Colonel to establish his innocence. According to Harman Blennerhassett, whose fortune was swept away by the failure of Burr's schemes, Alston had guaranteed him against losses to the extent of $50,000 but later refused to reimburse him beyond the amount of $12,000 (*ibid.*, pp. 533-38). Blennerhasset, however, never produced convincing proof of his claim, though he several times threatened a public exposure."

Jefferson was clearly of the opinion that Alston was deeply implicated. Jefferson to Governor Charles Pinckney, January 20, 1807, Jefferson Papers. Alston's letter of denial did not convince the President as may be seen from the following quotation from his letter to Gallatin, February 22, 1807: "He thinks to get over this matter by putting a bold face on it. I have the names of three persons whose evidence, *taken together*, can fix on him the actual endeavor to engage men in Burr's enterprise." Ford, *Writings of Jefferson*, IX, 13. Alston's enemies or persons whom he offended continued to believe in his guilt. Apparently his personality did not make him a very popular person. For later references to the matter, see Thomas, *Reminiscences*, II, 69-82; and *Corre-*

JEFFERSONIAN DEMOCRACY IN S. C. 213

4. BRITISH-FRENCH DEPREDATIONS IN 1807 AND THE PASSAGE OF THE EMBARGO

As the relations between the United States and Great Britain and France became more strained David R. Williams seemed to lay greater stress on the conduct of those interested in the carrying trade. According to him, they were at the foundation of the difficulties with foreign powers.[30] Little unity of feeling was manifest in the votes of the South Carolina representatives in regard to the fortification of harbors and the building of gunboats.[31] All of the state's delegation present joined with the overwhelming majority of the house in refusing to consider in secret the senate bill suspending the writ of habeas corpus in cases of persons "charged on oath with treason, misprison of treason, or other high crime or misdemeanor, endangering the peace, safety, or neutrality of the United States." The arrests were to come by order of the President or the governor or persons acting for them. Then all of the group except Elias Earle aided in bringing about the unusual house action of rejecting the bill itself on the first reading.[32]

In the face of the depredations of both the leading belligerents their symphathizers continued their attempts to explain or defend the conduct of their favorite nation. One pro-French enthusiast contended that for every dollar of damage done by the French the British injured the United States to the amount of one hundred thousand dollars.[33]

spondence of Aaron Burr and His Daughter Theodosia, edited by Mark Van Doren (New York: Covivi-Friede, 1929), pp. 327-328.

[30] *Annals of Congress*, 9th Cong., 2nd Sess. (February 3, 1807), p. 432.

[31] Williams was very much opposed to vesting the President with power to increase the naval strength at will. The attempt of Eastern representatives to get the support of South Carolinians for the fortification of other ports by including Charleston failed. *Ibid.*, 9th Cong., 2nd Sess. (February 4, 5, 7, 13, 23, 1807), pp. 437, 469-470, 473-475, 487-495, 616-618. Bills to appropriate $150,000 for fortifying harbors and the same amount for building gunboats passed the house. For the former, Marion cast his vote, while Butler, Moore, and Williams opposed. On the latter Butler and Marion voted affirmatively and Moore and Williams negatively. The others were apparently absent.

[32] *Ibid.*, 9th Cong., 2nd Sess. (January 26, 1807), pp. 403, 424-425. Possibly it was the unusual procedure to which Earle objected.

[33] *City Gazette*, April 10, 1807.

The revival of the Beaumarchais claims was the signal for a bitter attack on the Jefferson administration by the *Charleston Courier*. The editor held that sufficient payment had been made twenty years before for "the muskets, which were useless, the rotten clothing for our troops, shipped to America in the times of her distress, and charged at enormous prices." He remarked sarcastically that he did not know which to admire more, the "modesty of the French government in preferring Beaumarchais's long exploded claim or the amiableness of the President in readily laying it before Congress." The ultimate payment of "a few more millions" was predicted.[34] The controversy was enlivened by the hostility between the editors of the two leading newspapers. The editors of the *City Gazette* claimed that they had an article in the handwriting of their rival asking in 1800 that Jefferson be elected as the only man who could cause the United States to be respected at home and abroad. He had also condemned the Sedition Act as an effort of Federalists to protect themselves against the people and the growing strength of the Republicans. Others thought that the editor of the *Charleston Courier* should be ignored as one who had so practiced attributing bad motives that he had come to enjoy it.[35]

The coming of another anniversary of the Declaration of Independence afforded the *Charleston Courier* an opportunity for a vehement outburst in the name of patriotism. The swords of Washington and Hamilton slept "with them in their graves." "The Heroes and Patriots, whose souls swell indignant at the violation which our constitution has suffered" had once been consulted on the affairs of the nation, but they were now neglected and forgotten. The sovereignty and independence of the country had been violated by Great Britain, France and Spain. The flag was being insulted and the rights of citizens were ignored. The principles for which the Revolution had been fought no longer influenced the leaders of the nation. The people were urged to rise from their lethargy and place in high political positions "those who achieved our independence." Then the British would no longer patrol New York harbor and

[34] *Charleston Courier*, March 3, 1807.
[35] *City Gazette*, April 15, 17, 20, 1807.

JEFFERSONIAN DEMOCRACY IN S. C.   215

the French would cease to use the Chesapeake as a place of rendezvous to blockade our ports.[86]

Both Federalists and Republicans were aroused by the attack of the British ship *Leopard* upon the *Chesapeake* late in June, 1807. At a public meeting in Charleston resolutions were drawn up denouncing the outrage. Until the constitutional authorities ruled otherwise, they would consider anyone an enemy who aided a British vessel of war. The pilots of the port were called upon to refrain from rendering professional services to them. As testimony of regret and respect for the men killed on the *Chesapeake* the people were asked to wear crape on their left arms for ten days. A nonpartisan committee was chosen to put the resolutions into effect.[87] During the following weeks, military societies and civilian groups gathered in public meetings in nearly every part of South Carolina, pledged their support to the general government in protecting American citizens and ships.[88] The captains of the *Leopard* and the *Leander* were burned in effigy in front of the Charleston Courthouse.[89] The masters of the port offered their services to the President in any way useful to the country. Jefferson replied that if a similar outrage should occur near Charleston they would have an opportunity to render that port secure.[40]

Although editorial comment was becoming less frequent in the *Charleston Courier,* statements were noticeably few during the weeks following the *Chesapeake-Leopard* incident. Late in August the editor defended his Federalist colleagues against the charge that they were aiding the British by not supporting the President. He himself deplored as much as anyone that

[86] *Charleston Courier,* July 4, 1807.

[87] *City Gazette,* July 9, 1807. The meeting had been held on the previous day. Those on the committee were John Ward, Charles Cotesworth Pinckney, Langdon Cheves, John Blake, Major Rouse, Thomas Pinckney, Major Robertson, David Ramsay, Colonel Roper, Thomas Lee, Peter Freneau, Thomas Somarsall, John Johnson, Jr., John Dawson, Jr., General Washington, John Rutledge, Richard Howard, K. L. Simons, John Stoney, Simon Magwood.

[88] *City Gazette,* July 16, 18, 29, August 12, 13, 14, 18, 22, 29, September 2, 3, 11, 18, 21, October 26, 1807. An Irishman wanted to organize "a Company of Pikemen," *ibid.,* September 18, 21, 1807.

[89] *Charleston Courier,* July 13, 1807.

[40] *Writings of Jefferson,* Def. Edit., XI, 302.

the nation had been permitted to get into a condition in which other countries could insult it, but he thought that criticism might better be reserved for the future. Regardless of who was President, he deserved support in resenting the conduct of the British.[41] "One of the People" denounced the "British editors" for their criticism of public meetings of protest against the *Chesapeake* incident. These editors, the writer said, could not understand that in the United States "mobocracy" did not prevail and that the best people attended the meetings. He believed that the editors were hirelings.[42]

John Rutledge, who certainly was not a British hater in 1807 thought an armed conflict even with Great Britain "would prove more honorable prosperous & safe, & less costly than a state of Peace in which a foreign nation is to exercise the right of searching our National Ships." Rutledge, however, did not think the question of impressment worth discussing. According to him, for every American on British ships there were twenty British on American merchantmen. This fact, he said, had been recognized in New England. The moanings were now coming from Virginia where there were neither sailors nor ships. Although he had nothing but the most severe censure for the administration, Rutledge felt that it must be supported in time of attack from another nation.[43]

In spite of his bombastic patriotism, the editor of the Federalist news organ did not advocate war at the time of the convening of the special session of Congress, but he did insist that the national honor be preserved.[44] During the Congressional session most of the South Carolina representatives supported the program to strengthen the navy. Williams, though, stated that he would vote "on all occasions, against any measure, under any circumstances, which shall have for its object an increase

[41] *Charleston Courier,* July 13, 1807.

[42] *The Times,* September 29, 1807. An example of a pamphlet of the period is "A Native of South Carolina," *The Tocsin: or the Call to Arms! An Essay; Being an Enquiry into the Late Proceedings of Great Britain in Her Unjustifiable Attack upon the Liberty and Independence of the United States of America* (Charleston: 1807). A copy is in series 3, vol. 12, no. 19, Charleston Library Society Pamphlets.

[43] Morrison, *Life and Letters of Otis,* I, 284.

[44] *Charleston Courier,* October 26, 1807.

JEFFERSONIAN DEMOCRACY IN S. C.   217

of the Navy." But he resented the implication of Willis Alston, Jr., of North Carolina that everyone opposing the bill was an enemy of the administration. On the final passage, Williams and a representative from Pennsylvania were the only ones to oppose.[45] Likewise was he against the Embargo but was absent when it passed the house. All other South Carolina members voted for it.[46]

After the passage of the embargo measures the Republican leaders in Congress felt that the position of the country should be strengthened by the augmentation of the military peace establishment. To this administrative measure, all the South Carolina representatives except Williams gave their support. Taylor thought the proposed increase insufficient but was willing to vote for even that much. He thought that there was some danger in building fortifications and not adequately manning them. The enemy might get control and use them against their builders. Taylor thought that the United States needed to be prepared, for "nowadays, a formal declaration of war is dispensed with, and a *coup de main* is the order of the day." Williams feared the building up of an army in peace time as a possible wedge for the establishment of a large standing army.[47] Even after the transmission of the President's message, on February 26, recommending the increase of the regular army

[45] *Annals of Congress,* 10th Cong., 1st Sess. (November 10, 1807), pp. 843-845, 852-853.

[46] *Ibid.* (December 18, 21, 1807), pp. 1216, 1221-1222. On February 20, 1808, Williams stated that if he had been present he would have voted against the measure, but that since it had been passed he was in favor of supporting it. He did, however, think that provision ought to be made for the exemption of smaller vessels from putting up bonds. On March 18, Williams joined the other representatives from South Carolina except Moore, who was absent, in opposing the resolution to appoint a committee to bring in a bill repealing the embargo. Then on April 12, Williams expressed the opinion that the measure was working toward the accomplishment of the purpose for which it had been passed. He did not agree with Randolph that it was unconstitutional. When the house voted on the measure from the senate authorizing the President to suspend the Embargo, Williams and Taylor opposed its passage; but the other members from their state except Moore, who was absent, supported it. The bill passed 60 to 36. *Ibid.* (April 19, 1808), p. 2198.

[47] *Ibid.* (February 17, 1808), pp. 1620, 1622-1624, 1632.

and the militia, Williams continued his opposition. According to him the addition of a force of 6,000 men would be worthless. If hostile actions were to be taken, let the United States go to war and talk in terms of 50,000, not 6,000 men. Taylor stated that even though he was supporting the measure he felt somewhat as Williams did. When they had come to Congress they had believed that war should be declared against Great Britain. But in the face of what amounted to an order from the French emperor that they go to war with the British, he and Williams decided that the nation should not take such a step at that time. Taylor thought that the Embargo should be permitted to work as effectively as possible and that the military forces should be increased. The arguments of the danger of a standard army and the need for economy were weak when used against protective measures. Williams stated in his next speech that he had been misunderstood. His contention was that armed hostility was inconsistent with the Embargo. "I am opposed to half-way measures; I am no 'quid.' Whatever system I pursue, I wish to go up to the hub with it. If it be peace, let us have it; if war, let us go directly to the object." Williams thought that if the merchants had been as honest as the planters, the West Indies would have been starved. On final passage of the measure to increase the military forces by 6,000, all the South Carolina representatives except Williams voted affirmatively.[48]

5. Reform in the Basis of Representation in the State Legislature

At the time when the Embargo was threatening to divide the people of the United States along sectional and economic lines, South Carolinians showed that at last they realized that there was little basis for a lasting state sectionalism. By 1808 the interests of the lower and the upper parts of South Carolina were much more nearly the same than had been the case in 1790. Joseph Alston, one of the leaders in the movement for reform in the basis of representation in the legislature, stated that, with the exception of the towns in each area, the interests of the people were predominantly agricultural. Indeed, the

[48] *Annals of Congress,* 10th Cong., 1st Sess. (March 21, 1808).

JEFFERSONIAN DEMOCRACY IN S. C.   219

same crops were produced in both sections, except for rice. Furthermore, slavery was no longer an issue. While there might be some difference in the size of the holdings, slaves were possessed by people in both the low and the up country. Alston thought that the time had come for the establishment of a uniform basis of representation. The important thing, he said, was the adoption of some principle as a basis in order to prevent so important a question as representation from being dependent upon an arbitrary decree of the legislature itself. The question should no longer be a party issue.[49]

In December, 1807, both houses of the legislature passed a resolution providing for a special session the following month to consider the reform of the basis of representation.[50] That there was little opposition to such reform is seen from the fact that the plan decided upon was opposed by only two in each house. According to the new basis, each district should have one representative in the house of representatives for each sixty-second part of the white population it possessed and one for each sixty-second part of state's taxes it paid. The total number in the lower house was to be 124. No district was to be unrepresented. In order to make up the total number specified those districts having the largest fractions left over would be awarded additional representatives. A census should be taken in 1809 and at ten-year intervals thereafter. After a few slight changes in district boundaries, all except Charleston district, which was to have two, should elect one senator to represent it in the state legislature.[51]

According to the new arrangement the low country retained control of the senate but thereafter the up country had a majority in the house of representatives. This might seem, to a

[49] Alston's speech, printed in Georgetown, S. C., in 1807, is drawn upon at length by Schaper in his "Sectionalism and Representation in S. C.," pp. 431-433.

[50] *Charleston Courier,* December 19, 1807. The house passed the resolution on December 16 and the senate two days later.

[51] *S. C. Statutes at Large,* VI, 638-640. The measure was added to the state constitution as an amendment. The process of amendment then was by passage in both houses by two thirds vote, the publication of the proposal three months before the next election and the repassage by the members then elected by the same majority.

casual observer, a generous compromise on the part of the former region; but sectional names meant much less in 1808 than they had in the 1790's. The whole state was becoming more and more a sort of low country "writ large." Thus, after the population and the interests of South Carolina approached assimilation and in the seventh year of the operation of Jeffersonian democracy, the representation system was sufficiently reformed to remove much of the sectional animosity. The physical nature of South Carolina, the spread of the agricultural system, changes in the constitution, the later issue of the power of the state against that of the national government and perhaps other influences brought about more harmony and less sectionalism in South Carolina than in her sister states.[52]

6. The Embargo in Operation

Soon after the passage of the Embargo the *Charleston Courier* declared its opposition to the measure. At first the editor professed ignorance as to whether it had grown out of the confused relations between the United States and Great Britain or had been passed at the demand of France. In either case it was expected to benefit Bonaparte. Those who knew the value of the commerce of the United States would appreciate the "effects of this act."[53] The editor further displayed his hostility by his "definition" of the Embargo and other terms from the viewpoint of the commercial group.[54] Shortly thereafter the paper published in the editorial section a communication stating that although it was impossible to say what the effect would be abroad there was little uncertainty as to the results at home. Rice had had a brisk sale some weeks before at $3.50; but it was now *"nominally"* worth only $1.75. Black seed cotton had fallen from thirty-four cents to "22a 25 and no sale." Corn was down to fifty-six cents. What would the

[52] This problem is ably discussed in Green, *Constitutional Development in the South Atlantic States*, pp. 162-164.

[53] *Charleston Courier*, January 6, 1808.

[54] "*Embargo*—a restraint on the liberty of a mercantile nation. *War*—a reference to arms for the possession of power. *Executive*—men assuming to dictate the inclinations of a nation. *Nation*—the body of the people compelled to submit to the will of an assumed power or opinion." *Charleston Courier*, January 12, 1808.

JEFFERSONIAN DEMOCRACY IN S. C. 221

end be, asked the writer, if this was the beginning?[55] To the Federalist editor and his contributors, the term "liberty of the sea" had little meaning. Why was such a doctrine advocated? Was it to permit an enemy to ship its goods in neutral ships? If this were true there was no need to fight for it in time of peace and no nation would permit it in time of war.[56]

Governor Charles Pinckney, as was characteristic of his policy, used his influence and power in the support of the administration's program. Since the South Carolina legislature had adjourned before the Embargo had been passed, Pinckney asked the advice of Jefferson as to whether a special session should be called and requested suggestions as to how the state might co-operate.[57] The President sent a confidential note to Pinckney and other governors describing the foreign situation. There was no immediate danger of war with France and armed hostilities with Great Britain had been postponed for that year by the passage of the Embargo. The future of the Embargo itself would have to be decided by the next session of Congress. There was some evidence of an approaching peace in Europe. If the nations at war formed themselves "into an armed neutrality to enforce their principles" the United States might then have something to fear. In order to be prepared the militia should be kept in the best condition possible and the seaports should be placed in "that state of defence which Congress has thought proportioned to our circumstances and situation." The federal government would send sufficient gunboats by midsummer. The militia must furnish the remainder of the defense.[58]

---

[55] *Charleston Courier*, January 20, 1808. In the same newspaper on March 26, "a Planter" stated that while the Embargo was being considered only as news in Great Britain people in the United States were suffering grievously. Citizens were forced to sacrifice their property and grand juries were asking the governor to call the legislature to "stop the course of justice." Jefferson with a salary of $25,000, Madison receiving $5,000, and members of Congress getting $6 a day might not dislike the Embargo, but the "cries of an oppressed people must be heard by them." Since it was having no effect in England it ought to be repealed.

[56] *Ibid.*, February 1, 1808.

[57] Pinckney to Jefferson, March 8, 1808, Jefferson Papers.

[58] Jefferson to Pinckney, March 30, 1808, Jefferson Papers.

No doubt the early attitude of South Carolina Republicans toward the Embargo was well expressed by Wade Hampton in a letter to Thomas Sumter.

It is difficult to imagine the pecuniary effect and the individual distress, occasioned by the embargo. It pervades all classes, and extends to every corner of the state. The peculiar stage of the African trade had stripped the planting interests, pretty generally, of their resources, and involved many of them in debt. The crop was just coming to their aid, but being cut off from this, there remains nothing between the hammer of the sheriff's auctioneer and their property—and indeed sales of this description have multiplied to an astonishing degree, in every part of the state. Yet, notwithstanding this distress, and the gloomy prospect afforded by the latter mails from Washington, there is everywhere an acquiescence in the measure proceeding from a confidence in the government that really exceeds anything that could be expected. For myself, I viewed it, at the first, as a substitute for war, and although more distressing in a pecuniary view, at least to individuals, yet I hoped it might turn out less so to the country, if the end could be answered by it. Under this impression, I had no idea of its being soon removed, and indeed if it had, I should have been the more inclined to deprecate it as having been uselessly oppressive but if the measure had been adopted as a *defensive* one, is preserved in, and answers the end, it can but be preferred to war. After all the imperial and royal decrees of the governments of England and France, have turned out the most powerful advocates for the wisdom of the embargo, and have contributed very much to reconcile the people of all classes to it.

Be that as it may, we must face it, with all its consequences, you and I, shall, at least, have this consolation, that we cannot expect worse times than we have passed through.[59]

In the enforcement of the Embargo Jefferson decided to depend to a great extent upon the governors and the collectors of the ports. In letters to the governors of the commercial states, the President stated that the shipment of flour to most harbors was suspicious. Charleston was listed as one of the few that must receive this product but the governor was asked to prevent abuse.[60] Governor Pinckney readily co-operated with Jef-

[59] Hampton's letter, dated March 15, 1808, was published in the *City Gazette*, April 15, 1808.
[60] Jefferson to the governors of New Orleans, Georgia, South Carolina, Massachusetts and New Hampshire, May 6, 1808. *Writings of Jef-*

JEFFERSONIAN DEMOCRACY IN S. C. 223

ferson in an effort to prevent violations of the Embargo. His wholehearted support was needed in view of the none-too-friendly attitude of the federal circuit court. Pinckney sent the President copies of the court proceedings and asked for further instructions. He expressed sorrow that there were in the state people who were willing to work for the defeat of the Embargo in order to make private gains. Great concern was expressed by the President over the "proceedings of the court on the mandamus to the collector of Charleston." Because of the place from which the action came he felt that it could not be ascribed to "any political waywardness." Jefferson thought that the collector of Charleston erred in trying to judge shippers instead of considering the whole trade in flour suspicious. Such a practice had been begun in another state but had been stopped immediately. He thought the matter had "too many important bearings on the constitutional organization of our government to let it go off so carelessly." But Jefferson had nothing but praise for the way Pinckney had acted as governor during such a period. The President further stated that he owed the same approbation to the governors of some of the other states but not to all.[61]

During the next session of the South Carolina legislature

---

ferson, Definitive Edit., XII, 51-52. When Jefferson informed Gallatin of sending circulars to the governors, giving them permission to ask for supplies which their states needed, the Secretary of Treasury protested against changing from the system of licenses issued by agents of the treasury subject to the federal government to the issuance by state officials. He feared that the governors would be likely to submit to popular clamor. "Knowing Governors Sullivan and Charles Pinckney as we do, we can have no confidence in the last, and must rest assured that the others will refuse no certificates." Henry Adams, ed., *The Writings of Albert Gallatin* (Philadelphia: 1879), I, 389-391. The reasons for Gallatin's lack of confidence in Pinckney are not given. In the case of the Embargo, at least, his judgment was faulty, for Charles Pinckney, as will appear below, loyally supported the administration in the enforcement of the measure.

[61] Pinckney to Jefferson, May 28; and Jefferson to Pinckney, June 18, 1808. Jefferson Papers. Even some of the Federalists advocated the enforcement of the Embargo so long as it was law. If the sentiment of the people opposed the measure, let the voters choose men that would change the law. Such an opinion was expressed by "Z" in the *Charleston Courier*, June 10, 1808.

many petitions were presented asking for some kind of relief from the distresses alleged to have been caused by the Embargo. Finally a report of a house and senate committee stating that "the exigencies of the Country do not require any Legislative interference" was adopted.[62] The willingness of the members of the house of representatives to aid in the enforcement of the Embargo was expressed in a series of resolutions passed on the last day of the session. It was voted that the President in recommending and Congress in passing the Embargo had "deserved well of their country," that citizens of South Carolina should aid in the execution of "this important national measure," and that "this state will to the utmost of its power, and at all hazards support the General Government in all measures calculated to maintain the rights and support the Independence of the United States.[63] Another interesting action taken at this session of the legislature was the passage of a resolution by both houses calling upon their members to appear at the next session clothed in garments manufactured in the United States.[64]

[62] S. C. House Journal, June 24, 27, 1808.

[63] *Ibid.*, June 29, 1808. Joseph Alston, as speaker of the house, transmitted the resolutions to Jefferson. In his letter Alston stated that they had been passed unanimously by both houses. He told the President that they were not to be taken as evidence of the "perfect unanimity of political opinion" in South Carolina or of the view that the state had not felt the Embargo. Instead, the resolutions showed that though there were both Federalists and Republicans in South Carolina their patriotism was stronger than their party affiliation. Alston to Jefferson, July 6, 1808. Jefferson Papers. In his reply the President said that he was very sensible of the resolutions because of the effect of the Embargo on South Carolina. *Ibid.*, August 4, 1808.

[64] S. C. Senate Journal, June 29, 1808. For a time it seemed possible that manufacturing might develop in South Carolina. On March 10, 1808, the *Charleston Courier* printed an advertisement of the local Orphan House stating that wool was wanted for manufacturing purpose. A Homespun Company was organized in Charleston. *Ibid.*, August 10, 11, 1808. Great plans were made but the developments did not meet the expectations of the promoters. In the *Times,* September 10, 1808, "A Jeffersonian" expressed great surprise that some of the influential men of Charleston opposed the introduction of manufacturing. Such opposition, he said, might arouse suspicion of their motives and intentions. Besides they would be unable to prevent industrial development. Manufacturing would be established in Charleston, the writer contended. For the general effects of the Embargo see Louis Martin Sears, "The South and the Embargo," *South Atlantic Quarterly,* XX, 254-255, and by the same

In most of the toasts given on July 4, 1808, the Embargo seems to have been mentioned. The Washington Light Infantry drank to the sentiment. "Agriculture and Commerce—a temporary *separation* to prevent an eternal divorce."[65] In Edgefield District the Embargo was described as "a wise, just, provident and the *only measure*—Union and energy to enforce it until we can traverse the ocean like a free nation."[66] In nearly every part of the state and by many of the military organizations, the records show that similar views were expressed.[67]

During the remainder of the summer the attitude toward the Embargo continued to be substantially the same in South Carolina. The Republicans defended it as preferable to war. There was, to be sure, a gradual increase in the opposition of the Federalists, who insisted that the administration was taking orders from the French. On the first day of August "Musty" stated that the sum of the arguments against the Embargo was that their produce was rotting in their houses and that the merchants' goods were spoiling in their stores. The complaints of the Federalists, he said, were effective with only those incapable of putting public good for a short time above private avarice. The writer had hoped that the enthusiasm for liberty exhibited by the Federalists after the *Chesapeake* affair would be strong enough to enable them to place public above private interest for a while, but evidently it was too much to expect them to withstand economic loss.[68] The Republicans attacked the depredations of Great Britain more than those of France. "Freemen" held that those who defended the British became party to their guilt. Where was the consistency "of that man who would call upon his government to protect his trade, and yet unite with the principles of its destroyers?"[69] "M. C. D." thought that the most effective method of dealing with both France and Great Britain would be the building up of domestic

---

author, *Jefferson and the Embargo* (Durham: Duke University Press, 1927), pp. 228-252. Still another work of value is Walter Wilson Jennings, *The American Embargo 1807-1809* (Iowa City: the University of Iowa, 1921), especially pp. 108-109, 122-123, 214, 231.

[65] *City Gazette*, July 7, 1808.   [66] *Ibid.*, July 28, 1808.
[67] *Ibid.*, July 6, 7, 12, 14, 19, 28, 1808.
[68] *Ibid.*, August 1, 1808.   [69] *Ibid.*, August 6, 1808.

industries.[70] "Sydney" accused "Native Federalist" of lack of patriotism in claiming that the acts of the British were legal and neutral. It was absurd, he argued, to say that the Embargo had been passed because of French influence. If the French had injured the United States as much as the British had, war would have already been declared.[71] The Federalists found it easy to criticize the policies of the Republicans, but they were embarrassed when asked what course they would recommend.[72] A feeling of sympathy seemed to bind the *Charleston Courier* and the citizens of New England who protested against the policies of the federal administration. The attitude of "Mr. Jefferson's *Moniteur* at Washington" toward the Boston petitioners was severely criticized. Perhaps, said the editor, the administration did not relish petitions so cutting in irony as those coming from Boston. He rejoiced that news from Spain indicated that that nation was being emancipated from the "shackles of the 'Imperial Jacobin' and that she has asserted her ancient dignity and independence."[73]

In early September some of the most ardent Republicans announced that the Federalist party had passed away except for revilers, disappointed demagogues and a few others. "Aristides" stated that the former Federalists had become "Republican-Federalists."[74] A few weeks later "Independence" asserted that the British hoped to bring about a revolution in the United States through the opposition to the Embargo. Such might be the result in some states but he believed that South Carolina would remain firm.[75] This confidence in his state was shown to be well founded by the conduct of Governor Pinckney and the members of the legislature. Throughout his term Pinckney continued his loyal assistance in the enforcement of the Embargo. The President's advice was frequently asked and the governor sent information concerning violations in South Carolina and nearby regions. Jefferson was told that

[70] *Ibid.*, August 9, 1808.   [71] *Ibid.*, August 13, 1808.
[72] See, for example, the letter of "Querist" in reply to "Brutus," *City Gazette*, August 29, 1808.
[73] *Charleston Courier*, August 29, 1808.
[74] *City Gazette*, September 3, 1808.
[75] *Ibid.*, October 7, 1808.

JEFFERSONIAN DEMOCRACY IN S. C. 227

the state still preferred commercial restrictions to war but that South Carolina would be ready to fight in case of armed hostilities. The President seemed to appreciate the loyalty of South Carolina because of his knowledge of how greatly a portion of her people was interested in commerce.[76] Pinckney's annual message to the legislature, filled with praise of the Jefferson administration and its measures, was given an enthusiastic reception by that body.[77]

7. The Election of 1808

The election of 1808 in South Carolina was greatly influenced by the developments in regard to the Embargo. For that reason it will be discussed before the commercial policies of the federal administration are considered further.

Several months earlier, some of the South Carolina Republicans had asserted that the next President should not come from Virginia;[78] but by the early summer of 1808 it was taken for granted that Madison would be the candidate of the party in power. Wherever toasts were offered on July 4, his name was generally mentioned.[79] The Republicans early began to defend Madison against the charge of the Federalists that he had not had sufficient practical training.[80] Only two others, Monroe and George Clinton, were seriously mentioned. It was stated that the country had not come to look upon Monroe as the probable successor to Jefferson. Clinton was pictured as a patriotic citizen who had an excellent record during the Revolution but who had not displayed himself in civil life as the statesman needed in the present crisis.[81] "Aristides" cited Madison's opposition to Hamilton's financial program as evidence of his political firmness and as justification of his claim for the gratitude of his countrymen. The writer further main-

[76] Charles Pinckney to Jefferson, September 10, October 23, November 30, December 8, 1808; and Jefferson to Pinckney, November 8, 1808. Jefferson Papers.
[77] Thomas Lehre to Jefferson, November 29, 1808. Jefferson Papers.
[78] *City Gazette*, May 9, 1807. The legislature had endorsed Jefferson for a third term. S. C. House Journal, December 10, 1807.
[79] *City Gazette*, July 6, 14, 22, 1808.
[80] *Ibid.*, August 16, 20, 1808.
[81] *Ibid.*, September 9, 13, 1808.

tained that, next to Jefferson, Madison was the most popular man in the country.[82] Few indeed were the letters in the newspapers favoring a Republican other than Madison.[83]

Secrecy and uncertainty characterized the Federalist conduct in 1808, in so far as national politics was concerned. In August delegates from eight states met in New York to make plans for the party. John Rutledge was one of the thirty-five delegates to this "convention." The Federalists tried to keep the meeting a secret, but the Republican newspapers would not let the gathering of so many notables pass without comment. Little is known about the "convention" except that the members refused to join a Clinton coalition and nominated Charles Cotesworth Pinckney and Rufus King for President and Vice-President.[84] The seemingly growing unpopularity of the Embargo and the results of the early state elections in New York and New England gave the Federalists renewed confidence. Writing to Otis on September 10, Rutledge stated that "a real & great change" was taking place and expressed the belief that the nation was "about to return to the golden days when the government of the country, placed in the ablest and best hands, will administer our affairs on manly and correct Principles."[85]

In striking contrast to the tone and the predictions of Rutledge were the reassuring words of Peter Freneau in his letter to Jefferson.

Eight years are now nearly ended since 69 members of our Legislature voted that you, Sir, ought not to be the President of the United States, fortunately for America 87 said otherwise; one year ago when the Legislature resolved that you had deserved well of the country, there were to be found only six members in the negative, and in June last, when a resolution was brought forward approving of the reasons you gave for

[82] *Ibid.*, September 19, 21, 1808.

[83] One of the few exceptions was the letter from Barnwell District, under the date of August 25, signed "Thousands." The writer called for the election of Clinton and Monroe as President and Vice-President respectively. Madison was described as an amiable man who would be lost in the Presidency.

[84] Morrison, *Life and Letters of Otis*, I, 306, 314-315. Reprinted here is the "Official Notification" of the nominations made by the "convention."

[85] *Ibid.*, I, 332-333.

recommending the Embargo, not one arose in opposition. This change in the minds of our Legislature, so honorable to your administration, is, in my opinion, a complete refutation of all the abuse the federal papers have abounded with, and if the authors of it could possibly have the feelings of honest men would drive them to despair.—

The vote of this State for President will certainly be given to Mr. Madison, some weak attempts are making in favor of General Pinckney but they will be of no avail.

The Embargo bears heavy on us, but there are no people, generally speaking, who bear it more cheerfully, they are convinced that it was the only prudent measure that could be pursued at the time.[86]

The *Charleston Courier* was as receptive as ever to communications, but the Federalist letters to that paper were outnumbered by those of the Republicans sent to the *City Gazette*. The argument most often used by the former was that Charles Cotesworth Pinckney was a native son. If the state voted for Madison it would be laughed at by his supporters elsewhere and be held in contempt by those who supported Pinckney.[87] In an effort to refute the argument that the Federalist candidate had no chance of election, the editor stated that he was authorized to say that Pinckney would receive the votes of the Federalists in other parts of the country.[88] Before the day of the election arrived the friends of both candidates became very personal in regard to the opposing aspirants for the Presidency. Implied reflections were made upon Madison by such a statement as that of a Federalist writer that Pinckney was a friend of religion; but the friends of the Republican candidate were always ready to reply.[89] "Junius" addressed an open letter to General Pinckney asking him if he knew that he was being used as a tool by vicious men who had no intentions of electing him President.[90] Another advanced the view that the British were using the Federalists and their opposition to the Embargo to cause dissensions in the hope that a revolution would take place.[91] "An American" argued that in spite of all the talk

[86] Peter Freneau to Jefferson, September 18, 1808. Jefferson Papers.
[87] *Charleston Courier*, September 21, 22, 1808.
[88] *Ibid.*, October 3, 1808.
[89] *City Gazette*, October 1, 3, 1808.
[90] *Ibid.*, October 4, 1808.   [91] *Ibid.*, October 7, 1808.

about Pinckney's military record he had not risen above the rank of colonel during the Revolution. All the Federalists could promise was a little more profit and that at such a great cost—the surrender of the country's liberty.[92]

The campaign was particularly bitter in Charleston. For a time it seemed possible that the Federalists would elect their candidate for the federal house of representatives; but division and bitterness within their own ranks aided the Republicans. Robert Marion, the Republican incumbent, was said not to be the proper representative of a district so much interested in commerce. His friends, however, denied the charge that he had never visited the town of Charleston and insisted that there was no reason why a planter should not also be well informed about commerce.[93] William Loughton Smith, who had toned down considerably since the days when he had been the Federalist leader in Congress, expected to be the candidate of his party against Marion. He, however, was considered too mild. Indeed, Smith had sharply denounced the British conduct in the *Leopard-Chesapeake* affair, had approved some of the administration policies and on July 4, 1808, had even worn a homespun coat. Such acts on the part of one whom the party had so highly honored were considered unpardonable by the extreme Federalists. They, consequently, brought forward Thomas Lowndes in opposition to him.[94] So wide did the breach in the party become that Smith withdrew in favor of Marion.[95] The campaign continued to be extremely bitter, with both parties fighting till the last.[96] On October 12, the Republican candidates were overwhelmingly elected in Charleston District.[97] In other parts of the state the results were similar.

[92] *Ibid.*, October 8, 1808. This paper on October 10, was amost filled with letters in support of Madison and the local Republican candidates.
[93] *Ibid.*, September 20, 22, 1808.
[94] Peter Freneau to Jefferson, September 18, 1808. Jefferson Papers.
[95] *City Gazette,* September 29, 1808.
[96] Thomas Lehre to Jefferson, October 14, 1808; and Charles Pinckney to Jefferson, October 23, 1808, Jefferson Papers. Charles Pinckney wrote that because of the unheard-of vehemence of the Federalists the Republicans had been compelled to attack Charles Cotesworth Pinckney himself.
[97] Marion received 775 votes to the 391 for Lowndes. In the contests for the representatives in the state legislature the votes of the Republi-

Very few Federalists would be members of the next South Carolina legislature.[98]

After the election of the members of the legislature there was no doubt as to the outcome of the Presidential election in South Carolina. At the meeting of the Republican caucus, Madison was unanimously approved; but there was strong opposition to George Clinton for Vice-President on the ground that he had not supported the Jefferson administration, and particularly because of his attitude toward the Embargo. Although it was finally decided to support him along with Madison, the decision in the caucus was not unanimous.[99] The weakness of the Federalists was demonstrated by their decision not to present a list of electors to the legislature.[100] The Madison and Clinton electors, therefore, were chosen unanimously.[101] The only change in composition of the South Carolina delegation in the next Congress resulted from the declination of David R. Williams to be a candidate in 1808. Robert Witherspoon was chosen in his place. Further changes did occur later as the result of resignations, but these did not alter the political composition. John Drayton was chosen governor.[102] Thus the elections of 1808 showed South Carolina to be still predominantly Republican. In December the legislature passed resolutions highly praising Jefferson without a dissenting vote.[103] The *Charleston Courier,* however, was pessimistic about the future after the results of the elections throughout the country indicated the continuation of the Republicans in power. In an editorial, "The Embargo Tells," the editor gave his analysis of that measure.

It tells That after nine months experience, we are left ruinous, and dreadful as the consequences are, to deplore a continuation of it, without any prospect of its being repealed.

---

can nominees ranged from 702 to 802, those of the Federalists varied from 357 to 440. John Drayton was elected state senator over Thomas Roper by the vote of 770 to 389. *City Gazette,* October 13, 14, 1808.

[98] Thomas Lehre to Jefferson, November 1, 1808, Jefferson Papers.
[99] *Ibid.,* December 1, 1808.   [100] *Ibid.,* December 2, 1808.
[101] *Ibid.,* December 7, 1808. S. C. Senate Journal, December 6, 1808.
[102] S. C. House Journal, December 7, 1808.
[103] Thomas Lehre to Jefferson, December 18, 1808. Jefferson Papers.

It tells That the Farmer with all his prudency and industry, is unable to meet the demands against him; when under the Federal administration, his produce commanded a high price, a ready sale, and he waxed fat.

It tells That the Mechanick and Merchant are grievously afflicted; and that the day laborer who lives by the sweat of his brow, finds his scanty profit diminished by the operation of this wretched policy.

It tells That you are getting poorer daily; that taxes become more and more serious; and that every month finds a still greater difficulty in getting money than it did the month before.

It tells That a standing army is raised; that troops are daily marching in various directions; and that the din of arms resounds throughout our country.

It tells That our seamen are banished from American bottoms and American flags, to the British fleet.

It tells That national impartiality and neutrality consists in an eternal hatred to one nation and a blind submission to another.

It tells That the relinquishment of our rightful commerce is a virtual surrender of our independence.

It tells That if a little Gun-Powder had burnt fifteen months ago, no occasion would have existed to burn Gin now.

It tells That the Embargo is the best commentary on Democratick legislation.[104]

8. FURTHER EFFORTS TO ENFORCE THE EMBARGO; THE SUBSTITUTION OF OTHER MEASURES OF ECONOMIC COERCION

Early in 1809 many citizens of Charleston felt that there was a large number of Embargo violations that could be prevented. The grand jury of the country recommended that those disobeying the measure be considered in contempt of court.[105] Determined that as many violations as possible should cease, the more active citizens held a public meeting to discuss possible methods of procedure. A committee of forty-five was chosen to aid the collector of Charleston in the enforcement of the Embargo. The resolutions adopted stated that at no time since the Revolution had their patriotism been put to such a test.

[104] *Charleston Courier,* December 1, 1808.

[105] Thomas Lehre to Jefferson, January 18, 21, 1809. Jefferson Papers. Lehre referred to the existence of a small group of Federalists in the state, who he said, were actuated by the same motives as those of the Essex Junto and who would go any lengths to destroy the Republican form of government.

JEFFERSONIAN DEMOCRACY IN S. C. 233

The committee was to choose five of its members as a select committee to direct the activities. They were to co-operate with the collector of the port in preventing further violations, patrol the regions where the offenders were likely to make their entrance into the state and report all suspicious persons.[106]

The opposition in New England to the commercial measures of the Jefferson administration continued to attract a great deal of interest in South Carolina. The leaders in the state were just as ardent in support of the Embargo as those of Massachusetts were in opposition to it. Considerable discussion and agitation resulted from the publication in February of a letter sent from Charleston by a native of Massachusetts to his friends in Salem. The writer showed no little contempt for South Carolinians.

I am quite tired of this Jacobinical place. They talk a great deal about hanging and driving (poor devils! fit only for slave drivers) the people of Massachusetts into Nova Scotia. They talk big of patriotism, the rights of man, &c. in this region of slavery! There has not been a night this week, without alarms of fires and murders; and the panic has become so great, they were last night obliged to order three detachments of Infantry, and part of the horse from several companies, to guard the city; and should the embargo continue another year, I believe that the poor will stir up such commotions, that they will find the whole militia, instead of detachments, necessary for that purpose. I can only say, God of his infinite mercy grant, that my dear native Massachusetts may always be as unlike as possible this country of Jacobinism and slavery.

The publishers of the *City Gazette* printed the letter with evident contempt, stating that they did not know the writer's name but that he was no doubt an outcast from Massachusetts whose wretched existence was being prolonged by the courtesy of those whom he sought to revile.[107] Massachusetts was said to be threatening to dissolve the Union.[108] The South Carolina Marine Society drank to the toast, "Timothy Pickering—may

[106] *City Gazette*, January 17, 24, 26, 1808. The select committee was composed of John Blake, Thomas Lee, John Johnson, Jr., Simon Magwood and John H. Silliman. See also Thomas Lehre to Jefferson, January 18, 1808. Jefferson Papers.
[107] *Ibid.*, February 17, 1809.
[108] *Ibid.*, February 20, 1809.

the production of a Rope-Walk be the neck-cloth of him who attempts to untwist the political cable of our union."[109] Throughout all this agitation the *Charleston Courier* insisted that the Embargo had failed, that the conduct of France and Great Britain was unchanged and that the commercial rivals of the United States were reaping the benefits.[110]

A recent student of the Embargo has the following statement in regard to the losses which South Carolina and the South underwent in remaining loyal to the policies of the Jefferson administration:

Generally speaking, the agricultural South suffered less immediate, but greater permanent loss from the commercial restrictions of 1808 than a region so wholly given over to commerce as New England. In comparison with the Middle States, moreover, her opportunities to recuperate by manufactures was slight, although this was not at first realized. The South, then, suffered absolutely as much as her neighbors, and relatively more.[111]

Although the Republican leaders in South Carolina believed in supporting the Embargo so long as it was used as an alternative to war, some were coming to believe that the nation should no longer delay armed hostility. Early in 1809 John Taylor expressed the belief that the time had arrived when it would be dangerous to postpone defense measures. He thought the United States could redress her grievances by going to war and taking Canada. The coast of Halifax, Taylor said, was necessary for the security and sovereignty of the nation. The region was as necessary to the United States as Gibraltar was to Great Britain. It was described as "a point from which we could at any time sweep the whole commerce of Europe in these seas." Once taken, Taylor thought, the area would be easy to hold.[112] In discussing the resolution stating that the Embargo should be repealed, David R. Williams cast rather thinly veiled reflections upon the loyalty of the people in the Northeast but expressed opposition to enforcing commercial

[109] *Ibid.*, February 25, 1812.
[110] *Charleston Courier*, February 6, 1808.
[111] Sears, "The South and the Embargo," p. 254.
[112] *Annals of Congress*, 10th Cong., 2nd Sess. (January 28, 1809), pp. 1208-1214.

JEFFERSONIAN DEMOCRACY IN S. C. 235

restrictions there with the bayonet. If the Embargo was to be removed, he favored war. But Williams admitted that he was embarrassed.[113] Both Williams and Taylor opposed the Non-intercourse bill as a substitute for the Embargo. The former was "decidedly in favor of issuing letters of marque and reprisal at once." He did not think that the mere interdiction of the commerce would solve the problem. Instead, he proposed that the ports of the United States be interdicted to all armed or unarmed ships of the belligerents and that a duty of fifty per cent be placed on their manufactured goods. Such a measure, Williams thought, would force them to declare war or treat. He believed they would prefer to do the latter.[114] "I am for war," Williams declared, "the people south of the Delaware are for war; but you have been humbled into an acknowledgement of the truth of the declaration, that you cannot be kicked into a war, because the Eastern people will not follow you." His proposal, however, was rejected.[115] Taylor attacked the Non-intercourse bill as a sign of submission. He supported Williams in his attempt to amend the measure so as to place heavy duties on goods from Great Britain and France; but again they were unsuccessful.[116] When the Non-intercourse bill itself was passed, four South Carolina representatives voted affirmatively, two negatively and two were absent.[117] In the senate Gaillard voted for the measure, while Sumter opposed it.[118]

That South Carolina was not being completely ruined by the commercial restrictions and that there was still money left in the state are attested by the amounts offered as prizes to the winners in the lottery drawings. In March the prize was

[113] *Ibid.*, 10th Cong., 2nd Sess. (January 30, 1809), pp. 1236-1238.
[114] *Ibid.* (February 15, 1809), pp. 1439-1441.
[115] *Ibid.* (February 17, 1809), pp. 1449-1451.
[116] *Ibid.* (February 23, 1809), pp. 1511, 1513, 1516. The motion was rejected by the close vote of 51 to 50. Individual votes are not given.
[117] *Ibid.* (February 27, 1809), p. 1541. Alston, Butler, Marion and Moore favored the measure, Joseph Calhoun and Taylor voted against it, while Williams and Winn were absent. Williams would have voted negatively if he had been present. The vote was 81 to 40.
[118] *Ibid.* (Senate, February 21, 1809), p. 436.

$15,000, and in June there was another for $12,000. There were, of course, several others throughout the year.[119]

On July 4, 1809, the *Charleston Courier* again placed the responsibility for all the nation's troubles on the Republican administration. The United States was on that day, the editor said, one of the most interesting objects the world had ever beheld—the only republic in existence. The country had an expansive territory and a noble people with animated courage. Nothing was needed to carry the nation to its proper height except "a wise, impartial administration of the powers of our government." "The system pursued by the late administration, of a preference of party-men to patriotick characters; of theoretical speculation as opposed to practical assurance; a system of weak, inefficient and time-serving measures, could have but one result, and could be followed by but one effect—internal weakness, attended with foreign contempt and aggression." The editor hoped that Madison would return to the policies of Washington, who had not favored one foreign nation above another.[120]

In spite of the Non-intercourse Act, British and French goods continued to be brought into South Carolina. To help prevent this an organization was formed known as the "'Seventy-Six Association." Its members pledged themselves not to purchase for use any French or British articles that could be procured of domestic growth, production or manufacture at a price up to fifteen per cent higher than the European price. Further, they promised to wear homespun at certain specified times.[121] Other meetings were held during the summer at which resolutions were passed approving the Madison administration for its conduct of foreign affairs and condemning the British for not endorsing the negotiations conducted by her minister in Washington. At one of these meetings in Charleston some of the Federalists tried to bring about immediate adjournment but other members of their party joined with the Republicans in continuing the assembly until resolutions were adopted. That it was not entirely a Republican affair is seen

[119] *Charleston Courier*, March 18, June 19, 22, 1809. See also, August 9, 1810.
[120] *Ibid.*, July 4, 1809.   [121] *Times*, August 18, 1809.

by the election of David Ramsay, a moderate Federalist, as chairman. Charles Pinckney was chairman of the committee that drew up the resolutions approving the Madison administration.[122] All the vigilance of the friends of the administration, however, did not prevent European goods from flowing into the state. In November, Charles Pinckney wrote Madison that British goods were smuggled in at Amelia in Florida and that Southern products were sold there. The Non-intercourse law, he said, was being broken down. British articles were easy to buy and were sold at very low prices. Pinckney thought that the British were sending enough of their manufactured products into the country through Florida to supply the whole nation. He was writing, he said, at the behest of friends who considered the problem a very serious one.[123] Francis Asbury, arriving in Charleston toward the close of the year, asked himself, "Where does the cotton go, that arrives in such quantities?—to England and France, in spite of the non-intercourse. I am mainly ignorant of these things, and have no wish to be wiser."[124]

In 1810 John Taylor continued his criticism of the Non-intercourse Act in speeches before fellow members of Congress. The measure had produced the results expected. "We are, as the country now stands, the enemies of the commercial interests, for we are giving foreign nations the entire benefit of our commerce, and depriving our honest citizens of the advantages which this bill will offer them." Besides, goods were brought into this country regardless of the laws and without the payment of duties. He had been informed, Taylor said, that at that moment there were one hundred British merchant vessels at Amelia Island. It was possible, he continued, that among those one hundred were many who were once American but now changed to British so that they could carry on commerce. He favored modification of the restrictions so that Americans could carry on trade in a legitimate way. Furthermore, the

[122] Pinckney to Madison, September 6, 1809, Ramsay to Madison, September 5. Madison Papers. Pinckney to Jefferson, letter marked as received September 30, 1809. Jefferson Papers. *City Gazette,* August 30, September 6, 1809.
[123] Pinckney to Madison, November 18, 1809, Madison Papers.
[124] Asbury, *Journal,* III, 280, under date of December 10, 1809.

coasts and harbors should be protected from pirates and plunderers.[125] Apparently Taylor was willing to accept almost any change that would help stop smuggling and bring relief to the American commercial interests. Of course, in so doing, he expected also to aid the planting group.[126] He thought the Non-intercourse Act not only useless but also injurious, especially to the Southern tobacco and cotton growers. The measure had failed to have the desired effect upon Great Britain and France. It encouraged violations and had demoralized American citizens. The Non-intercourse Act, Taylor argued, should be repealed immediately.[127] While the other South Carolina representatives did little talking not more than half of them were so insistent as Taylor that almost any modification would be preferable to the Non-intercourse Act.[128] Macon's Bill No. 2, Taylor thought, was not very coercive but an improvement over the Non-intercourse Act. No time should be lost in aiding American producers and carriers. On the passage of the measure, all the South Carolina representatives present except Thomas Moore voted affirmatively.[129]

While the members of Congress were discussing the relative merits of Embargo, the Non-intercourse Act, Macon's Bill No. 2 and other measures, correspondents to South Carolina newspapers were also showing interest in foreign affairs. When the *Charleston Courier* attacked France, "Plato" reviewed the relations between the United States and the two leading European nations. The readers were asked to remember the British disregard of portions of the Treaty of 1783, and the unpleasantnesses associated with the Jay Treaty and the *Chesapeake* affair.[130] The Federalist newspaper protested against the alleged apathy of people of Charleston in regard to the conduct of the French privateers. They preyed upon American ships when they felt like it, said the editor. When they needed supplies they came into our ports and if anyone interfered they did not hesi-

[125] *Annals of Congress,* 11th Cong., 2nd Sess. (January 8, 1810), pp. 1164-1165.
[126] *Ibid.* (March 27, 1810).
[127] *Ibid.* (April 2, 1809), pp. 1714-1718.
[128] *Ibid.* (March 31, 1810), p. 1701.
[129] Alston and Marion were absent. *Ibid.* (April 19, 1810), p. 1931.
[130] *City Gazette,* April 5, 1810.

tate to shoot him even in the mouth of the harbor. Where, he asked, were the town meetings, the men-of-war, the gunboats, the cutters and the 100,000 militia that were marshalled in the *Chesapeake* incident?[131] "Philo-Patris" insisted that the United States had nothing to expect from either France or Great Britain. She must look to herself alone and she had no time to waste.[132] The editor of the *Charleston Courier* enjoyed the embarrassment of the Republicans in regard to commercial restrictions.

We have seen the benefits of the embargo throughly—we see them say democratick demogogues, by the effect of its removal. France is plundering us and Great Britain is not. See what a situation we are in and Federalists have brought us to it.

One word about this business. Who voted for the Embargo? Democrats.—Who applauded the Embargo? Democrats. Who cut it up, destroyed it and utterly annihilated it? Democrats. They were the fathers, nurses, and executioners of this political monster. The federalists did nothing but cry out "monster" all the time; but its own parents destroyed it. They made it and unmade it. Congress, Senate and President took off the Embargo. The embargo died by other than federal hands as you may see by the journals of Congress.

These remarks of the editor were by way of preface to his statement that it was time to drive out of office those who had deceived and misled the people of the nation.[133]

Despite all the tumult connected with foreign affairs the South Carolina legislature found time in 1810 to establish another bank and alter the suffrage requirements. The former grew out of the needs of certain groups, as signified by its name, Planters' and Mechanics' Bank, and the refusal of an existing bank to lend Editor E. S. Thomas of the *City Gazette* as much money as he needed. That the new bank was intended to serve the agricultural interests of the whole state is seen by the provision in its act of establishment that branches might be set up in Columbia, Camden or in any other town in South Carolina upon the vote of a majority of the stockholders.[134]

[131] *Charleston Courier*, May 5, 1810.
[132] *City Gazette*, June 29, 1810.
[133] *Charleston Courier*, July 19, 1810.
[134] Clark, *History of Banking in S. C.*, pp. 70-73. Thomas, *Reminiscences*, II, 48-50.

9. THE EXTENSION OF THE SUFFRAGE AND THE ELECTION OF 1810

One of the most important political changes in the history of South Carolina was the modification of the voting qualifications. Many of the staunch Republicans withstood manhood suffrage as long as possible and continued to doubt the wisdom of it in practice.[135] Nevertheless, the state constitution was amended in 1810 to provide that every white man of the age of twenty-one years, except paupers, non-commissioned officers and private soldiers of the army of the United States, was given the right to vote if he were a citizen of the state and had lived in the election district for six months.[136] Thus, in that year South Carolina took her stand along with Maryland as the first of the original thirteen states to establish manhood suffrage. With the exception of five other comparatively unimportant amendments, the Constitution of 1790 withstood the fierce onslaughts of the up countrymen for the popular election of governor and presidential electors and their dissatisfaction with the position of power assigned to wealth in the apportionment of representatives. So bitter was the conflict that some even feared that in the plainly approaching war between North and South the up country would stand aloof; but so groundless was such an idea that a convention set up "the Constitution of 1861" by merely making such verbal changes as separation from the United States made proper.[137]

Unfortunately not a great deal of detailed knowledge has come down to us concerning the election of 1810. No doubt for that reason many confusing and inaccurate statements have been made regarding the contests of that year. E. S. Thomas thought he remembered that eight of the nine representatives in Congress from South Carolina were defeated in that year and that the weekly edition of his newspaper, known as the *Carolina Gazette,* had been influential in bringing about their

---

[135] O'Neall, in *Bench and Bar in S. C.,* II, 254, tells of the doubts of himself, John Joel Chappell and others as to the wisdom of the change made in 1810.

[136] *S. C. Statutes at Large,* VI, 640. The act did not do away with voting in other districts if one had the proper amount of property there, but this practice "came by custom to be confined to a man's voting only for local officers in more than one district." Wallace, *History of S. C.,* II, 375.

[137] Wallace, *The S. C. Constitution of 1895,* p. 15.

JEFFERSONIAN DEMOCRACY IN S. C.   241

defeat.[138] As a matter of fact the state had only eight representatives and three of those who had been in the previous Congress remained in office. A fourth, John Taylor, was soon sent to the United States senate following the resignation of Thomas Sumter. A fifth, Robert Witherspoon, declined to be a candidate but supported David R. Williams, who was elected in his place. Langdon Cheves succeeded Robert Marion, who had resigned. John C. Calhoun and William Lowndes filled the places of Joseph Calhoun and John Taylor. Perhaps the only real case of defeat was that of Lemuel J. Alston by Elias Earle. The contest between Earle and Alston was an old one, in which much bitterness had entered and in which the latter had been accused of being a Federalist. Since there seems to have been only one actual defeat in the South Carolina Congressional elections of 1810 it is hardly accurate to say that the people were dissatisfied with their representatives.[139] In the case of the United States senators the results were similar. The term of John Gaillard had not expired and Thomas Sumter was reelected. The latter, however, was forced to resign less than a month later because of his advanced age and illness resulting from the abscessing of a wound which he had received during the Revolution.[140] The choice of the legislature for governor was Henry Middleton.[141]

In the first decade of the operation of Jeffersonian democracy, South Carolina had kept pace with the other states. She had become almost thoroughly Republican; she had in 1808 established a fairer basis of representation; and in 1810 she had amended her constitution so as to permit manhood suffrage. Here, however, her democratic movement of a constitutional nature ceased until after the Civil War. The second decade of Jeffersonian democracy was tremendously influenced by the activities of the group of young and vigorous Republicans sent by South Carolina to the Twelfth Congress. A description of them and their work will constitute an important part of the final chapter of this study.

[138] Thomas, *Reminiscences*, II, 50-53.
[139] The errors in the statement of Thomas were first called to the attention of the present writer by the reading of Cook's discussion of the election of 1810 in his *Life and Legacy of Williams*, p. 84.
[140] Gregorie, *Thomas Sumter*, p. 263.
[141] S. C. House Journal, December 8, 1810.

CHAPTER IX

YOUNG REPUBLICANS AND THE WAR OF 1812

1. New Vigor in Republican Leadership

During the entire first decade of Jeffersonian control, 1801-1810, both of South Carolina's United States senators and a majority of her representatives had been Republicans. Indeed, during the second half of the decade she did not send a Federalist to either house of Congress. Though suffering tremendously from their effect, South Carolina had supported commercial restrictions as an alternative to war; and with few exceptions the men who represented her in Congress were regular in their advocacy of administration measures. In local politics the situation had been similar, with a Republican majority in the legislature choosing governors and most of the other officers from their party. However, the Federalists continued vigorous and numerous enough in Charleston and in a few other sections to elect local officers at times. Though small in number the Federalist group in the legislature generally included some of the most influential men of the state. Rapidly changing conditions and the entrance of younger men into politics temporarily revived South Carolina Federalists and gave rise to more vigor, independence and self-assertion on the part of the Republicans.

Although they may not have expressed their opinions with the same degree of frankness, by the summer of 1811 most South Carolina Federalists and not a few Republicans agreed with the views of "Phocian" in his "letter" to President Madison.

You stand, Sir, in the way of men who are more able to serve the country than you are. You are losing reputation from hour to hour. The prosperity of your country falls with the declining honours of your name. You must retire from publick

JEFFERSONIAN DEMOCRACY IN S. C. 243

life; your own quiet calls for this retirement—your country demands it.[1]

Certainly at least half of the state's representatives in the Twelfth Congress possessed the spirit of a different generation from that of the President. If they were not ready to call for his retirement, they were prepared to demand action. With the impatience of youth they soon became self-assertive.

The independence of David R. Williams and his advocacy of war in the Tenth Congress have been discussed in the preceding chapter. Elected to represent South Carolina in the Twelfth Congress, along with Williams, were three young men who became even more vigorous in their insistence upon war. The oldest of the three, Langdon Cheves, was only thirty-five; the other two were each twenty-nine.[2] William Lowndes was the son of Rawlins Lowndes, the leading opponent of the ratification of the federal Constitution.[3] John Caldwell Calhoun

[1] *Charleston Courier*, August 20, 1811.

[2] Born in the Abbeville District, Cheves had lived a greater part of his life in Charleston, where he had gained business experience and studied law. Although he had never received much formal education, he was one of the most prominent lawyers of the state. Before going to Congress, Cheves had held local offices in Charleston, had served in the state legislature, 1802-1809, and had been elected attorney-general of South Carolina in the latter year. Louisa P. Haskell, "Langdon Cheves and the United States Bank: a study from Neglected Sources," *Annual Report of the American Historical Association*, 1896, I, 361-371; sketch by James Elliot Walmsley in the *Dictionary of American Biography*, IV, 62-65.

[3] Lowndes was sent to school in England for a short time during his boyhood, but his poor health prevented him from pursuing his education very far in Europe or America, except in private schools of his native state for a few years. He was admitted to the bar in 1804 but soon gave up the profession for the life of the planter. In 1806 he was elected to the South Carolina legislature. James Elliot Walmsley in *Dictionary of American Biography*, XI, 473-474; Mrs. St. Julien Ravenel, *Life and Times of William Lowndes of South Carolina, 1782-1822* (Boston: Houghton, Mifflin, 1901), pp. 37, 38, 50, 53, 62.

The Lowndes family was sharply divided in politics. Thomas Lowndes, a Federalist brother, had served in Congress; William's wife, a daughter of Thomas Pinckney, had been urged by her father not to marry him because of his poor health and his Republicanism. She did marry Lowndes but remained a Federalist. Ravenel, *Life of Lowndes*, pp. 58-60.

was also the son of an opponent of the federal Constitution.[4] Though without experience in national politics, Cheves, Lowndes and Calhoun soon took their places among the leaders in Congress. Along with David R. Williams, they formed a group of "insurgents seldom surpassed in ability and vigor."[5] Shortly after taking his seat in Congress, Calhoun expressed the views of himself and several other young Republicans in regard to the nation. In discussing the question of Congressional reapportionment, he asserted that he did not represent his own state alone. "I renounce the idea, and I will show, by my vote, that I contend for the interests of the whole people of the community."[6]

[4] Although Calhoun's father would hardly have been considered wealthy, he seems to have been independent economically. Young Calhoun's preparation for college came largely from the training he received from his brother-in-law, Moses Waddel. Having entered Yale College in 1802 as a junior, he graduated two years later. His legal training was obtained in Tapping Reeve's School at Litchfield, Connecticut, and in the law office of Henry W. DeSaussure at Charleston. He was admitted to the bar in 1807; but not particularly liking the profession, he resolved to leave it as soon as possible. Calhoun's election to office and his marriage in 1811 to a wealthy cousin, Floride Colhoun, made the practice of law less necessary. He had already served in the South Carolina legislature before going to the federal Congress in 1811. A. S. Salley in *S. C. Historical and Genealogical Magazine*, VII, 158-159; U. B. Phillips in *Dictionary of American Biography*, III, 411-419.

[5] D. R. Anderson, "The Insurgents of 1811," *Annual Report of the American Historical Association*, 1911, I, 167-176, p. 72. This author further states that South Carolina, "having wrested the economic supremacy of the South from the Old Dominion, was now threatening her political control." As evidence he cites the exports of South Carolina in 1810 as $5,290,614 and those of Virginia as $4,822,611.

[6] *Annals of Congress*, 12th Cong., 1st Sess., December 5, 1811, pp. 404-406. An interesting interpretation of Calhoun and his friends and colleagues, with which the present writer cannot wholly agree, is that of N. W. Stephenson in "Calhoun 1812, and After," *American Historical Review*, XXXI, 701-707. According to Stephenson the "War Hawks" thought seriously about neither nationalism nor sectionalism. They were, he says, merely young, self-willed, determined, practical politicians, who were tired of the rule of elderly gentlemen and wanted to govern themselves. They were not interested in theories or particularly concerned with the Constitution one way or another. Seeing an opportunity to align the South with the West against the Northeast, they seized it. They expected to be praised by posterity as a group that knew what they wanted and how to get it. Instead they were to be known, ac-

JEFFERSONIAN DEMOCRACY IN S. C. 245

2. The Struggle for National Preparedness

Soon after the Twelfth Congress assembled, the members were discussing the probability and the desirability of war. Calhoun agreed with John Randolph that the United States was unprepared, but insisted that she should not long remain so. He denied that it would cost too much and that the people would not pay the taxes. The only principle upon which the nation could be made great and a real spirit of union built was to be found in the protection of every citizen "in the lawful pursuit of his business." Independence and national affection could not be measured in terms of money. War was dangerous but South Carolina did not fear war. The patriotism of the youth and the bounties offered would cause enlistment. The militia also would be of great service. Calhoun attempted to refute Randolph's statement that the representatives from the West wanted war because they thought that it would make the price of hemp rise. Patriotism, not material gain, moved them. The South had suffered greatly because of the disruption of foreign commerce; but she knew that the nations at war in Europe were to blame. She was not ready to be reduced to a colony again. There were grievances against France, but she had recently professed respect for American rights. Great Britain would not provoke war for fear of uniting all parties in America; and, besides, she thought that the policy of patience and submission would be continued. The United States must show that she was a power to be reckoned with. In order to do this she must be prepared.[7] Although not many of the South Carolina representatives made lengthy speeches, they showed by their votes that they favored preparation for a possible war.[8]

---

cording to Stephenson, as those who brought sectionalism to the front and were unable to control it.

[7] *Annals of Congress*, 12th Cong., 1st Sess. (December 12, 1811), pp. 476-483.

[8] All voted for the resolution stating that an additional force of 10,000 regular troops should be raised for a period of three years. All except Elias Earle, who was absent, favored the resolution authorizing the President to accept the services of volunteers up to the number of 50,000, to be trained, organized and kept in readiness to serve in any way needed. All except Moore, who was absent, voted that the President

The agreement of the South Carolina house of representatives with the views of Calhoun is shown by the "address" it sent to President Madison, stating that the time had come when definite action should be taken to protect the commerce and the honor of the nation. France had withdrawn her obnoxious decrees and steps should be taken to bring Great Britain to follow her example. The members of Congress were called upon "to recollect the solemn pledge they have made to vindicate promptly and at every hazard, our national Honor." War, however, would probably not be necessary. The determined stand of a prepared nation would be sufficient. A firm foreign policy from the beginning would have prevented much of the loss to agriculture. If the general government felt that the time had come for a declaration of and an insistence upon the commercial rights of the country, South Carolina would "with unanimity and ardor, hazard everything in support of their acts."[9]

Letters to the *City Gazette* early in 1812 expressed views similar to those of the "address" of the house of representa-

---

should be authorized to order out such detachments of the militia as he thought public service demanded. Williams was the only South Carolina member to oppose the resolution stating that all ships worthy of repair should be made fit and put into commission. *Annals of Congress*, 12th Cong., 1st Sess. (December 16, 1811), pp. 545-548. Butler, Cheves, Calhoun and Moore supported while Lowndes and Williams opposed the resolution asserting that it was expedient to permit merchant vessels owned, controlled, commanded and navigated by citizens of the United States to arm, according to prescribed regulations, as a protection against unlawful proceedings on the high seas. Earle and Winn were absent. *Ibid.* (December 19, 1811), pp. 865-866. Senators Gaillard and Taylor also supported the preparedness program. *Ibid.* (Senate, December 16, 20, 1811), pp. 33, 85.

[9] South Carolina House Journal, December 11, 1811. Charles Pinckney wrote Jefferson that although South Carolina was not as well prepared for manufacturing as some of the Northern states, excellent homespun goods were being produced. Great numbers of the white and Negro population of the upper and middle parts of the state, where three fourths of the white people lived, were clothed in homespun. More than half of the members of the house of representatives had been so clothed. Jefferson Papers, December 18, 1811. It is interesting to note that Jefferson, in replying to this letter, February 2, 1812, stated that at last he believed war was necessary. *Writings of Jefferson*, Def. Edition, XVIII, 271-272.

tives. "Vindex" insisted that the nation must prepare to defend herself. Particularly did she need a navy.[10] French sympathizers insisted that France had not wanted to violate the laws of nations. If she sought to overthrow the despotic powers of Europe and reform England's outworn constitution, Americans should praise not condemn.[11] When the Federalists charged the Republicans with exaggerating the injuries inflicted by the British and trumping up new offenses for electioneering purposes, "Gracchus" asserted that the people would not believe such ridiculous accusations. Immoral methods were not necessary to keep "democrats" in power.[12]

When time passed and no news came of vigorous action by Congress, the people of Charleston became restless. On May 18, a large group composed of both Federalists and Republicans met and appointed a bi-partisan committee to draw up resolutions and recommendations which were to be acted upon at a second meeting two days later.[13] On the appointed day an overwhelming majority of the large group present voted that the aggressions and hostile conduct of Great Britain and France justified war, that the energetic measures advocated by the South Carolina members of Congress should be approved, that these representatives be urged to strive for such addition to the defense as would be necessary for the adequate protection of Charleston and the coast of South Carolina, and that the governor should be requested to arrange and organize the militia of Charleston District so that the exposed parts might be most adequately defended from attack.[14]

[10] *City Gazette,* January 17, 1812.
[11] A series of articles defending the French began in the *City Gazette,* March 30, 1812.   [12] *Ibid.,* April 1, 1812.
[13] *Ibid.,* May 19, 1812. Among the Federalists on the committee were Charles Cotesworth Pinckney, K. L. Simons, and David Ramsay. John Geddes, a Republican, was called to the chair. Thomas Lehre, Thomas Bennett, Geddes and other Republicans were on the committee.
[14] *City Gazette,* May 21, 1812. John Geddes to Madison, May 18; Thomas Lehre to Madison, May 20, 21, 1812; Madison Papers. Lehre reported that the meetings were orderly except for the hissing of a young Federalist who tried to speak against vigorous action. K. L. Simons presented a minority report but got little support, the vast majority being in favor of the recommendations adopted. See also *City Gazette,* May 23, 25.

In a series of letters in June addressed "To the President of the United States," "A Mountaineer" urged Madison to emulate the firmness of Washington. According to him, the present chief executive was not equal to the first but was the ablest and most honest of his contemporaries. The writer thought that a majority of the members of Congress would support the President in redressing the grievances against Great Britain and France. If they did not, the electorate would dismiss them from office at the next election. Great Britain should be blamed more for her jealousy of the United States than for her violation of international law. She feared that the new American nation would develop a strong navy that would rival hers. The conduct of France had been just as reprehensible, but she could interfere with only the commerce going to her own ports, while Great Britain could ruin our whole carrying trade. "A Mountaineer" called for war against Great Britain and *Letters of Marque* against France.[15] As evidence of the need for immediate protection, E. S. Thomas, editor of the *City Gazette,* stated that two ships and brigs of the blockade had recently approached the harbor to observe their future prey.[16] Another writer opposed conscription on the ground that no force was needed to compel citizens to defend their country.[17]

While the Republicans were thus engaged the Federalists were busy. In fact, Thomas Lehre, one of the leading Charleston Republicans, complained to Madison that they received information concerning the actions of the federal government before the Republicans did and so distorted the facts that the friends of the administration found it difficult to make the proper corrections.[18] The *Charleston Courier* printed with hearty approval the speech of Josiah Quincy on the Embargo.[19] The editor ridiculed the estimates of Gallatin as to the federal income for the coming year, and with an effort at biting sarcasm, remarked, "We have the greatest financier in the world at the head of the treasury department, and we have a most

[15] *Ibid.*, June 1, 3, 4, 5, 10, 1812.
[16] *Ibid.*, May 22, 1812.   [17] *Ibid.*, June 17, 1812.
[18] Lehre to Madison, March 30, 1812, Madison Papers.
[19] *Charleston Courier,* April 29, 1812.

redoubtable President to back him—War is certain and inevitable."[20] A few days later the same writer again called attention to the opposition that was being aroused in the New England states because of the "threatened measures of folly, imbecility and oppression which an intoxicated administration have fancied the people would submit to." These disturbances reminded him of the prophecy of a former South Carolina representative in Congress that the Federalists would be returned to power when the people discovered the dangers of permitting the Republicans to govern.[21]

In the meantime Calhoun, Cheves, Lowndes and Williams vigorously argued for preparedness. Public opinion, Calhoun said, would not continue to support Congress if the conduct of the members did not inspire confidence. Already doubts were arising as to whether they were really in earnest. If the gentlemen in the house continued to offer amendments to the bills before them, he feared that the nation would be forced into a war before she was ready.[22] Williams declared that the time had come when indifference or delay was criminal. There was no use hoping that Great Britain would modify her Orders in Council in any way that would be of material assistance to the United States. He had no patience with those who asked why war should be declared but attempted to mention a few reasons. Some of the objects that should be gained by armed hostility were "the liberation of our unfortunate, incarcerated seamen," the establishment of the "right (not a restricted permission from Great Britain) to a free and common use of the ocean," the "renunciation of a principle which exercises foreign jurisdiction over us," and the "reacknowledgment, not in form, but in fact, of independence—practical sovereignty." The principles at stake were greater than those of the Revolution. In advocating war, Williams insisted that he kept in mind the interests of the East as well as the South. If the interests of either were forgotten, the ties of the Union would be weaker. The situation had changed since 1798, when the people were afraid of an army because they feared that those in power

[20] *Ibid.*, May 15, 1812. [21] *Ibid.*, May 20, 1812.
[22] *Annals of Congress,* 12th Cong., 1st Sess. (January 2, 1812), p. 616.

would change the form of government. The argument that Great Britain was fighting for freedom, Williams asserted, was utterly without foundation. To say that the Devil had espoused the cause of Christianity would be just as worthy of acceptance. "So far from fighting for the liberties of the world, the standard of freedom had never been raised in any country without her attempting to pull it down." "For whose fell cupidity were so many humble hecatombs sacrificed in India? For whose more fell ambition did she wage war on infancy and innocence in the West? For whom does the savage yell now wake the sleep of the cradle? England, indisputably, to extend the blessings of liberty to the world." The people knew that the administration had done even more than could have been expected in its attempt to avoid war. The whole South Carolina delegation showed its attitude toward preparedness by voting to increase the military strength of the nation.[23]

In discussing the question as to whether the general government could use the militia anywhere it might be needed, Cheves went into the national and federal nature of the central government. It was national for the purpose of making war. The government under the Constitution differed from that under the Articles of Confederation. "The last, unlike the former, was not in itself a sovereignty." Instead, it had represented the sovereignty of many individual sovereignties. The government under the Confederation had not been able to act upon individual citizens. "This, then, is a definition of a National Government, or a Government of the people. It acts immediately on the person and property of the citizen, and such, as to the power of declaring and making war, is the nature of the Government of the United States." It was the right to declare war that made it possible to use the militia but it could not be used except in time of war. The President, Cheves said, had no doubt as to the power of the federal government to send the militia beyond the bounds of the United States. It might not be expedient, however, to employ the militia in seizing the

[23] *Annals of Congress,* 12th Cong., 1st Sess. (January 6, 1812), pp. 678-691. Lowndes had advocated war on January 4, pp. 648-652.

JEFFERSONIAN DEMOCRACY IN S. C. 251

open country of Canada until after a regular army had captured Quebec and held the region around the town.[24]

As chairman of the Naval Committee, Cheves led the fight for a stronger navy. There was much opposition, he said, especially within his own party. Because of the necessity for organized action, he generally worked with a party, but party loyalty could not force him to change his views on the navy. If the infant navy were abandoned, the party in power would become a minority in Congress and in the country. Besides, naval defense was cheap. The argument that it was anti-Republican was a misconception. Republicans had objected to the navy in 1798 because they believed it was to be used for "improper objects," not because it was against their principles.[25]

In his speech supporting the navy bill, Lowndes asked whether Canada could be held, which some insisted would be captured and kept, unless the nation had a strong navy. Furthermore, the United States must have sea power in order to maintain her commerce. Without commerce the nation would be weak. Would Great Britain close the war if she were not persuaded that its continuation meant greater loss?[26] Williams, however, radically disagreed with Cheves and Lowndes. According to him navies had deceived the hopes of all nations that had relied on them. One smaller than that of the British would be of little value in the approaching conflict. Building a navy would merely burden the people with taxes and provide the President additional patronage. The people desired to provide commerce all the protection possible, but they could not furnish a navy for that purpose.[27]

[24] *Annals of Congress*, 12th Cong., 1st Sess., January 11, 1812, pp. 733-739. On January 17 (pp. 800-801), all of the South Carolina representatives except Winn, who was absent, voted for the bill authorizing the President to accept the services of voluntary groups organized in the various states.

[25] *Ibid.* (January 17, 18, 1812), pp. 803-823.

[26] *Ibid.* (January 21, 1812), pp. 884-895.

[27] *Ibid.* (January 24, 1812), pp. 938-939. Butler and Earle and the majority of the house were on the side of Williams in striking out the section providing for new frigates, on January 27 (p. 999). In other votes one or more of the South Carolina representatives supported Williams in his fight against naval measures. *Ibid.* (January 27, 28, 1812), pp. 999-1003. But on the final passage of the Naval Bill itself, Williams

Although he opposed increasing the navy, Williams favored strengthening the military forces, especially the militia.[28] All the South Carolina representatives except Calhoun voted to arm the militia. In fact, his opposition was to the distribution of the arms by the state governments instead of to the arming of the militia itself.[29] On the passage of such war preparatory measures as the laying of an embargo on all ships and vessels in the ports and harbors of the United States, providing for additional military forces, and prohibiting the exportation of certain goods for a limited time, not a South Carolina representative voted in the negative.[30]

---

was the only South Carolinian to vote against it. Earle was absent. *Ibid.* (January 30, 1812), p. 1005.

[28] *Ibid.* (February 4, 1812), pp. 1030-1031.

[29] *Ibid.* (February 20, 21, 1812), p. 1080. Williams and Winn were absent at the time of voting, on final passage.

[30] *Annals of Congress*, 12th Cong., 1st Sess., Secret Journal (April 1, 2, 9, 1812), pp. 1598, 1599-1600, 1622. Moore was absent when the first was voted on, Moore and Winn on the second and Moore on the third. An extremely interesting letter written by William Lowndes to Mrs. Lowndes from Washington, March 23, 1812, is worthy of mention here in view of the attitude of the South Carolina representatives toward war. "We hear from all quarters that the people do not expect war; I look forward with great uneasiness to the shock which an unexpected declaration will give to the mercantile class. Nothing is more true than that, in the political as in private life, popularity should be the result, and not the object of our measures. No artificial excitement should be resorted to; yet I am much afraid that in the present state of the public mind the slow but steady approach of our government to war is unnoticed, and without an embargo, which I fear will not be resorted to, the war at its commencement must be necessarily disastrous—my politics are too hastily expressed for any ear but your own. There is much to disappoint us at Washington; many follies which we cannot conceal from ourselves, and which in the present state of the country we cannot with prudence publicly censure." Quoted in Ravenel, *Life of Lowndes,* pp. 102-103.

The impatience of John C. Calhoun with the executive department is well shown in a letter to James MacBride, April 18, 1812. "Our President tho a man of amiable manners and great talents, has not those commanding talents, which are necessary to control those about him. He permits division in his cabinet. He reluctantly gives up the system of peace. It is to be hoped, that as war is now seriously determined on, the Executive department will move with more vigor. Without it, it is impossible for Congress to proceed." Quoted in Julius W. Pratt, *Ex-*

JEFFERSONIAN DEMOCRACY IN S. C. 253
3. The Declaration of War

The South Carolina representatives showed by their speeches and votes that they were becoming more and more impatient with those who opposed war or preparedness. All except Cheves favored refusing to consider petitions asking the repeal of the Embargo. Calhoun argued that such a procedure would not be treating the petitioners with contempt and seized the opportunity to make one of his ultra-patriotic speeches.

> I assert, and gentlemen know it, if we submit to the pretensions of England, now openly avowed, the independence of this nation is lost—we will be, as our commerce, recolonized. This is the second struggle for our liberty; and if we but do justice to ourselves, it will be no less glorious and successful than the first. Let us but exert ourselves, and we must meet with the prospering smile of Heaven. Sir, I assert with confidence, a war, just and necessary in its origin, wisely and vigorously carried on, and honorably terminated, would establish the integrity and prosperity of our country for centuries.[31]

Likewise did most of the South Carolinians in Congress oppose considering John Randolph's resolution that "under existing circumstances it is inexpedient to resort to war against Great Britain."[32]

Finally on June 4, 1812, the house of representatives voted to declare war upon Great Britain. Every South Carolina representative was present and voted for war.[33] Likewise, in the

---
pansionists of 1812 (New York: MacMillan, 1925), p. 155, from the James MacBride Papers.

[31] *Annals of Congress,* 12th Cong., 1st Sess. (May 6, 11, 1812), pp. 1395-1414, 1419.

[32] *Ibid.* (May 29, 1812), pp. 1467-1478. Williams voted to consider the resolution but did not favor its adoption. Cheves and Moore were absent.

In the senate, both Taylor and Gaillard supported the preparedness measures. *Ibid.,* Senate (April 3, 13, 1812), pp. 189, 203. Taylor did favor considering the petitions of certain New York merchants and bankers requesting the continuance of the Embargo and Non-intercourse measures as a substitute for war. He thought that they ought to be considered merely out of respect for the importance of the petitioners.

[33] *Ibid.* (June 4, 1812), p. 1637. The vote was 79 to 49. Several years later, on September 9, 1825, Calhoun wrote Virgil Maxcy that a majority of those "in our ranks . . . anticipated anything rather than the successful termination of the war. . . . It does not seem to me

senate, both Taylor and Gaillard voted for war.[34] Armed hostilities having been determined upon by both houses of Congress Calhoun thought that some of the pre-war measures, particularly the Non-importation Act, should be repealed. He said that some were laboring under the false hope that continuation of non-importation would result in a speedy peace.

Let us strike away this false hope; let us call out the resources of the nation for its protection. England will soon find that millions of freemen, with every material of war in abundance are not to be despised with impunity. I would be full of hope, if I saw our sole reliance on the vigor of war; but if we are to paralyze it; if we are to trust, in the moment of danger, to the operation of a system of peace, I greatly fear. If such is to be our course, I see not that we have bettered our condition. We have had a peace like a war; in the name of Heaven let us not have the only thing that is worse, a war like a peace.[35]

The news of the declaration of war was welcomed by the Republicans and patriotically accepted by most Federalists of

---

possible that any who then took a part could now doubt, that there was the deepest distrust, as to the capacity of our government to sustain the shocks of war; or in other words, whether the virtue and intelligence of the people were sufficient for self-government under the sure trials incident to war. . . . Almost all, friends and foes, expected that the war party would be turned out; not because the cause was not just, or that in the abstract it was not right to resist; but because the people would not bear its burdens." Quoted in Pratt, *Expansionists of* 1812, pp. 155-156, from "Galloway-Markoe Papers."

Cheves and Lowndes showed that they were not expansionists by opposing the bill authorizing the President to take possession of East Florida. Butler, Calhoun, Moore and Williams favored it. Earle and Winn were absent. *Annals of Congress*, 12th Cong., 1st Sess. (June 25, 1812), pp. 1684-1685.

[34] *Ibid.*, Senate (June 17, 1812), p. 297. Pratt has shown that the vote on the declaration of war was along sectional lines in both the house and the senate, indicating a drift of sentiment in the Northeast among Republicans as well as Federalists against the war. "The war was plainly a sectional war, and the strength of the opposition vote—the declaration was carried by a vote of 79 to 49 in the House, 19 to 13 in the Senate—was ominous of an enterprise which would need the country's undivided support." *Expansionists of* 1812, pp. 162-163.

[35] *Annals of Congress*, 12th Cong., 1st Sess. (June 24, 1812), p. 1541. The majority of the house differed with Calhoun as to the advisability of repealing the Non-importation Act. In the South Carolina delegation, Cheves and Lowndes were the only ones to join him in favoring repeal.

South Carolina. The *City Gazette* declared that Congress had "only met the wishes of their constituents, an infinite majority of whom have long considered this as the only alternative; and the Eighteenth of June, 1812, will rank with the Fourth of July '76; the latter having only declared while the former will establish our independence." In the same issue was a communication headed "The Immortal Twelfth Congress!!!"[36] The *Times* proclaimed that

At length the Representatives of the People have met the feelings and wishes of the great majority of their constituents, by a Declaration of War against England. This interesting and important event, we presume will unite all good men; and the bitter contentions of party will be sacrificed at the shrine of Universal Patriotism. The energies and resources of our country will be called into action; and the war which a faithless nation has waged against us for ten years past, will no longer be on one side only; and, however we may suffer some privations in the conflict, we shall avenge our wrongs and long borne injuries; and the contest will terminate in glory, and the permanent security of our just rights.[37]

The Federalist *Charleston Courier* asserted that the time for argument as to whether the war could have been avoided had passed. Now all must "carry it on with vigor, with unanimity, and, we must sincerely pray with glory and success." "If a change of measures is, at any time, deemed to be essential to the welfare of the Nation, that change must be produced by our elections, & not by opposition to laws. This is federal doctrine. These are American principles."[38]

The coming of the Fourth of July soon after the declaration of war gave opportunities for outbursts of patriotism and statements in regard to the war itself. The *City Gazette* affirmed that not since the "never to be forgotten 4th of July '76" had there been a return of the anniversary "calculated to excite such sentiments and feelings as the one so recently passed." July 4, 1812, would be looked upon "by the future American patriot as the day when political animosities were merged in the love of country, and one undivided sentiment of

[36] *City Gazette*, June 25, 1812.　　[37] *Times*, June 24, 1812.
[38] *Charleston Courier*, June 25, 1812.

patriotic ardour animated every American bosom."[39] The most popular subjects for toasts throughout the state were "the President," "the Majority in Congress," "the 18th of June, 1812" and "the American Republic."[40] In Newberry District the President was described as a man who had "exercised the meekness of Moses, and the patience of Job; may he now, in the wisdom of Solomon, put forth the strength of Samson."[41] One group showed its interest in Canada by calling it the "den of corruption, the nursery of spies, and the Indian intriguer, the smugglers' resort, the refugee's asylum, and the British footstool." Let the Eagle find a roost in Quebec and the Lion be driven out.[42] Even when regret for the necessity of the war was expressed, the declaration itself was approved on the theory that Great Britain had forced it.[43] A group in Newberry District expressed animosity against France as well as Great Britain.[44]

A large proportion of the officers in the War of 1812 came from South Carolina.[45] Even before the declaration of war, President Madison surprised Southern Republicans by appointing Thomas Pinckney, a Federalist, commander of the Southeast or the Sixth Military District.[46]

Soon after the citizens of Charleston and other parts of the state learned that the nation was at war, public meetings were held to discuss methods of aiding in the prosecution of the con-

[39] *City Gazette*, June 7, 1812.
[40] *Ibid.*, July 8, 10, 14, 30, 1812.   [41] *Ibid.*, July 14, 1812.
[42] *Ibid.*, July 14, 1812, from Robertville (Black Swamp).
[43] *Ibid.*, July 30, 1812.   [44] *Ibid.*, July 14, 1812.
[45] Madison appointed South Carolinians to fill one-sixth of the new generalships created by Congress. Cook, *Life and Legacy of Williams*, p. 99; Wallace, *History of S. C.*, II, 394.
[46] The appointment of her father gave Mrs. William Lowndes an opportunity to chide her husband as to the scarcity of capable Republicans. He replied that though he would not approve the exclusion of Federalists he thought there were enough Republicans if the administration knew how to select and employ them. "There is certainly something to be dissatisfied with here." Ravenel, *Life of Lowndes*, pp. 104-105. Thomas Pinckney himself is said to have hesitated about accepting until he was assured that the appointment was an act of conciliation on the part of the President toward the Federalists. Pinckney, *Life of Thomas Pinckney*, p. 189.

JEFFERSONIAN DEMOCRACY IN S. C.   257

flict.[47] When persons in other states became hostile to the war, writers to the Republican newspapers in South Carolina called them Federalists. "Marion" laid the responsibility for the opposition upon the Federalists but asserted that they would not be able to influence the people of the Southern and Middle states.[48] Perhaps the statement most indicative of the attitude of South Carolinians was that found in the resolutions passed by the unanimous votes of both houses of the state legislature. The President, the majority in Congress and the South Carolina delegation in Congress were praised for their decision that the United States should go to war with Great Britain. Parts of the preamble seem extremely bombastic today, but possibly the words had real meaning to the members of the South Carolina legislature in 1812.[49]

[47] There was a meeting in Charleston on June 27, *City Gazette*, June 30, 1812. On the same day in the same town another group discussed the immediate problem of protecting the harbor. *Ibid.*, July 1. The young men formed an organization called the "Charleston United Blues." They pledged that they would be as valiant in the present war as their fathers had been in the Revolution. *Ibid.*, July 8. On July 12, a group in Union District pledged its allegiance to the President in a poem which expressed the hope that Madison would be a "second Washington." *Ibid.*, July 24. In the Madison Papers is an interesting letter from Eli Simpson Davis of Abbeville District. With the letter is a record of the proceedings of a meeting in that district at which those present promised their support in the war. They stated that though they might not actually take part in the war they would support those who did. Perhaps many others who were so ready to go to war were like these in not expecting to fight.

It may be of interest to record here also the statement of Thomas Lehre, one of the Republican leaders in the South Carolina legislature, in a letter to Jefferson, July 14, 1812. He wrote that it was now admitted that if the "salutary measure, the Embargo" had been rigidly adhered to it "would have been the means of bringing the British Government to a sense of the injustice of her conduct to us, long before this." Jefferson Papers. In reply Jefferson wrote August 8, that those opposing the war were the same group as the Tories of the Revolution. He believed that if the repeal of the Orders in Council had come earlier war could have been avoided. Jefferson thought that "indemnification for the past, & security for the future should be the motto of the war."

[48] *City Gazette*, August 26, 1812.

[49] "Influenced by no lust of dominion, no unjust spirit of encroachment; but impelled to arms by wanton and continued violations of our best rights and our vital interests—if ever a war deserved to be denominated Holy, it is this. It is a war of right against lawless aggression, of

In order to help alleviate the economic stress that faced all groups in 1812, the South Carolina legislature established the Bank of the State of South Carolina. Although the immediate purpose was to loan money to businessmen and planters so that they might withstand the unusual conditions of the day, the bank set up was more than a loan office. It was a complete commercial bank with a charter of twenty-three years duration. Unlike the other four South Carolina banks already established, it was owned by the state and was designed to operate through-

---

justice against perfidy and violence. Thus driven to hostilities, it is vain that faction would repress the energy and the spirit of the nation, or disaffection depreciate the resources of our country. The glory of the issue will be commensurate with the righteousness of our cause. If we cannot at this moment contend with our enemy for the empire of the ocean, individual valour and enterprize at length permitted to be exerted will ensure our citizens no inconsiderable indemnity for the spoliations so long practised upon their fair and peaceful commerce. If the acquisition of Canada be of little value in a territorial point of view, in other respects it will not be unimportant. It will remove from us a treacherous and barbarous neighbor, who at the very moment her Envoys were loudest in protestations of conciliation & friendship, were secretly fomenting, by her Emissaries, divisions and factions among us: and who has at no time ceased to direct the Tomahawks and scalping knives of her fellow Savages, the Indians, against the defenceless women and children of our frontier. From the inconveniences and privations incident to a state of war, we affect not to expect an exemption; but we are willing and able to support them. We shall support them with the more cheerfulness, as they will not fail to be accompanied with more than correspondent advantages. A commercial as well as political independence, predicated upon the improvement and advancement of domestic manufactures; the extermination of the spirit of faction, a cordial union of all parties for the common welfare: a happy amalgamation of the various, and in some instances, discordant materials, which to a certain degree, compose our population; in a word the formation of a national character —these are some of the benefits confidently anticipated from the present contest. When to these, on the one hand, are added on the other, the accumulated insults and wrongs sustained from Great Britain,—wrongs which if tamely submitted to, must have reduced us to worse than Colonial Slavery; we do not hesitate to believe the war in which we have engaged wise, necessary and just. Under this conviction, Sir, the Legislature of South Carolina have deemed it expedient and wise not to withhold the full expression of their feelings and opinions." S. C. House Journal, August 28, 1812. During the same session the legislature not only gave verbal approval of the war but also passed liberal appropriations for the purchase of arms and equipment for the militia that might be raised by draft or enlistment. *S. C. Statutes at Large*, V, 670-671.

out the whole state. The new bank aided materially in the period of bad economic conditions and continued to operate even through the Civil War.[50]

4. THE ELECTION OF 1812

Several months before the election of 1812, members of both parties began discussing the issues. An early charge of the Federalists, stoutly refuted by the Republicans, was that the latter were fabricating stories of British outrages for election purposes.[51]

Many Republicans were dissatisfied with the method used by their party to choose candidates for President and Vice-President.[52] On May 30, the *Charleston Courier* reported that Williams, Cheves and Lowndes had refused to attend the Congressional caucus on the grounds that it was "improper, inexpedient, indelicate, unconstitutional and a monstrous usurpation of the rights of the people."[53] After the nominations had been made, "Polybius" argued that the people should refuse to accept the nominees, for submission might establish a dangerous principle.[54]

As early as May the South Carolina Republicans took it for granted that the Federalists would support De Witt Clinton. In a newspaper article, "Lucius" gave as evidence of Clinton's artful intrigue the fact that he had gained the support of many persons throughout the country who had never seen him and who knew nothing about his public record. He had promised the Federalists peace with Great Britain and a big navy. He had assured Gallatin's enemies that there would be a new Secretary of the Treasury. So many officers and other rewards had been pledged that Clinton had raised a formidable party in support of his candidacy.[55]

The Republicans were strengthened in the summer by the

[50] *S. C. Statutes at Large,* VII, 24-33. Wallace, *History of S. C.,* II, 396-398. Clark, *History of Banking in S. C.,* pp. 74-96.
[51] *City Gazette,* April 1, 1812.
[52] During the months of April, May and June, 1812, several articles appeared in the *City Gazette* in opposition to the caucus.
[53] Quoted in Ravenel, *Life of Lowndes,* p. 111.
[54] *City Gazette,* June 3, 1812.
[55] *Ibid.,* May 26, June 1, 10, 1812.

establishment in Charleston of a new organ of expression, the *Investigator,* under the management of John Mackey and John Lyde Wilson.[56] On August 22, the editors called upon the Republicans of Charleston to meet the following Monday to choose worthy nominees for the approaching election. "Support those who have been firm in the *cause,* and promptly put down those who have abused your confidence." Federalists were told that they were not wanted at the meeting and Quids that they would not be admitted.[57]

Although the Republicans had already begun attacking De Witt Clinton as the Federalist candidate, the Federalists themselves found it difficult to choose a nominee. On August 24, Charles Cotesworth Pinckney wrote John B. Wallace of Philadelphia that the South was so "Democratic" that the Federalists should expect no votes there. If they could not find a Federalist strong enough to defeat Madison in the Middle and Northern states, they should support some "Democrat" whose views were acceptable. To be acceptable, the candidate must promise to end the war with an honorable peace, save the country from a French alliance, remove the restrictions from commerce and strengthen the nation's military and naval forces. Pinckney offered his services in every way possible but regretted that the Federalists had waited so late to begin activity.[58]

During the summer and fall opponents of Madison flooded the state with pamphlets, papers and letters in the interest of Clinton.[59] The Republicans, thereupon, renewed their attack

[56] The Investigator began publication August 1, 1812. It was strongly Republican and was considered of great use to the party in the election of 1812. Thomas Lehre to Jefferson, August 28, 29, 1812. Jefferson Papers.

[57] *Investigator,* August 22, 1812. On September 17, a communication signed "Many Citizens" deplored the lack of interest shown in the recent ward meetings. Some of the members of the legislature with irreproachable records had been left off the ticket. All Republicans might not feel bound to support the nominees. The letter urged every voter to be certain that he voted for a friend of Madison.

[58] Personal Papers, Miscellaneous, Library of Congress.

[59] On September 20, John Geddes wrote Madison that the friends of Clinton were trying to turn the Republicans against their nominee. The address of the New York correspondent committee had been widely distributed. An answer had been prepared and would be submitted to the members of the legislature before they chose the Presidential electors.

JEFFERSONIAN DEMOCRACY IN S. C. 261

upon Clinton with increasing vigor.[60] War conditions and political fervor developed unusual intolerance in both parties. Professing belief in the freedom of the press, the *Investigator* did not think that that privilege should furnish protection for "British, Indians and Tories." "Let these imposters then cease their attempts to aid the British under the flimsy pretense of supporting the freedom of the press."[61] The *City Gazette* accused the *Charleston Courier* of a false statement in claiming that it was not aiding the British when it denounced the President. Such freedom would not be permitted in England.[62] The Federalists were charged with carrying partisanship so far as to discriminate against their political opponents in the election of members to the Charleston Library Society.[63] Professing to love the patriotic Federalists, the *Times,* nevertheless, advised Republicans not to vote for them so long as there were candidates of their party. Regardless of their good intentions, these patriotic Federalists would seek to change the policy of the government. The most despicable men living were the Quids, who pretended to be fair to both parties. The Tories were those who rejoiced at American reverses. The Quids and Tories were aiding the Federalists because of their desire for a change in government. The Tories wanted civil war. If the Federalists should happen to win, they would soon despise the Tories. The Republicans already abhorred them.[64] "Lycurgus" held that rotation in office was necessary under a free government but that if the Federalists won there would not be another President as long as Clinton lived.[65]

Madison Papers. Thomas Lehre wrote Jefferson, September 21, 1812, that the mails were bringing abundant supplies of pamphlets, papers and letters "teeming with the greatest abuse, and the most palpable falsehoods against Mr. Madison and his administration." The purpose, he thought, was to influence the Republicans and destroy "our happy form of government;" but his knowledge of South Carolina caused him to know that they would fail. Jefferson Papers.

[60] *City Gazette*, September 5, 8, 14, 18, 25.
[61] *Investigator*, September 1, 1812.
[62] *City Gazette,* October 9, 1812.
[63] *Investigator,* September 19, 1812.
[64] *Times,* September 11, 1812.
[65] *Investigator,* September 23, 1812. On November 23, the editor of the *Investigator* asserted that there was no reason why the Federalists

A particularly heated campaign preceded the elections in the town and district of Charleston. An indication of the trend was shown by the difficulty with which Robert Bennett, Jr., a Republican, was elected intendant of Charleston over the Federalist candidate, Peter Smith.[66] During the interval before the election of members of the legislature and the representative in Congress neither side was certain of the outcome. The Federalists brought forward John Rutledge against Langdon Cheves, whose advocacy of the war and support of the Madison administration were bitterly attacked.[67] On the election day, however, Cheves easily defeated Rutledge, and all of the Republican candidates for the legislature in Charleston were elected.[68] In the other Congressional districts Republicans were also chosen.[69] For a time it seemed that John Gaillard

should not be called Tories. "We cannot see the propriety of calling men *Federalists,* whose principles and practices have a direct tendency to unfederalize the states; nor of calling men *Friends of Peace,* who are well known to be the authors of the war, in which we are engaged, and whose conduct is evidently calculated to drive their country into a ten times worse dilemma, a *civil war.* We shall therefore still continue to call them *Tories!* their objection notwithstanding." On November 28, the same writer said that those who hindered the war under the pretense of being "Friends of Peace" deserved the fate of traitors. "A war like a peace" was declared to be as unnatural as a "peace like a war."

[66] *City Gazette,* September 22, 1812. The vote was 522 to 390.

[67] Governor Middleton was charged with aiding Rutledge and other Federalists by appointing them to high positions in the militia. "Cassius" in the *Investigator,* October 2, 6; and "Causidicus" in the same paper, November 21, 1812. In the *City Gazette,* October 1, "Cato" argued that any party in power would have been forced to declare war and that the real issue between Cheves and Rutledge was whether the United States would pursue an honorable war. A letter from John Geddes to Madison, September 26, 1812, also tells of the contest between Rutledge and Cheves. Madison Papers.

[68] The votes for the Republican legislative candidates varied from 857 to 1182, the Federalist from 163 to 823. *City Gazette,* October 16, 1812. The Federalists, though, were not without leaders in the next legislature. For instance, Benjamin Huger was elected from Georgetown. *Investigator,* December 3, 19, 1812.

[69] A reapportionment had given South Carolina nine representatives in Congress instead of eight. The members elected to the Twelfth Congress were John C. Calhoun, John Joel Chappell, Langdon Cheves, Elias Earle, David R. Evans, Samuel Farrow, Theodore Gourdin, John Kershaw and William Lowndes.

would meet difficulty in securing reelection to the United States senate because of the opposition of Governor Middleton. Since he had appointed Federalists to offices in the militia, recommended reforms thought to be too expensive and associated with some Federalists as frequently as he had with Republicans, Middleton had become unpopular among members of his own party.[70] The final outcome was the overwhelming reelection of Gaillard.[71] This was taken as a decided victory for Madison and the war.[72]

The South Carolina legislature had trouble for a while in 1812 deciding who should be the next governor. The early trend was toward the choice of either Thomas Sumter or Andrew Pickens, both Revolutionary patriots.[73] After these two had eliminated themselves, the governorship went to Joseph Alston.[74] With a strong Republican majority in the legislature, the choosing of Presidential electors who would vote for Madison was certain and easy.[75]

[70] Correspondents to the newspapers criticized the governor for recommending that the state go to the "needless expense" of providing public schools when the majority of the people neither needed nor wanted to resort to the public treasury for such a purpose. He was accused of wanting a state penitentiary because Pennsylvania had one. His enemies asserted that he refused to sit at social gatherings with "Democrats" but courted the Federalists. *Investigator*, November 22, December 3, 5, 1812.

[71] The vote in the legislature was 118 for Gaillard to 37 for Middleton. *Investigator*, December 12, 1812.

[72] Thomas Lehre to Madison, December 4, 1812. Madison Papers. *Investigator*, December 12, 1812.

[73] A Columbia correspondent of the *Investigator* wrote November 29 (printed December 3, 1812), that General Pickens would likely be the next governor. Pickens was described as seventy-five years of age, in his second childhood and as not having been qualified for the office even in the vigor of his youth. Pickens, however, declined to be a candidate. *Ibid.*, December 9. A delegation was sent to Sumter to ask him to become a candidate. There is no record of his reply, but his health at that time would hardly have permitted him to serve if he had been elected. See Gregorie, *Thomas Sumter*, pp. 265-266.

[74] S. C. House Journal, December 10; *Investigator*, December 17, 1812.

[75] S. C. House Journal, December 2, 1812. The praise and criticism of Madison, however, continued in South Carolina. In a letter to the *City Gazette*, January 27, 1813, "Lucius" criticized the *Charleston Courier* for reprinting from the *Connecticut Mirror* a poem dealing with the reelection of Madison, in which were such statements as "Ye Vaga-

5. THE FIRST YEAR OF THE WAR

The Twelfth Congress, in its second session, attempted to cope with the problems of a nation at war. As chairman of the Military Committee, Williams had the responsibility of introducing and explaining military measures. When Josiah Quincy of Massachusetts referred to him as the introducer (into the house) of the "atrocious principle" of enlisting young men eighteen years of age, he replied that when anyone accused him of being actuated by an "atrocious principle" he would "throw it back in the teeth of the asserter as an atrocious falsehood." In 1798 the President had been given powers which "authorized him to send his recruiting sergeants into every family and take those who suited him best." What had not been considered atrocious in 1798 when used against France should not be called atrocious if employed against Great Britain in 1812. Williams was glad that Massachusetts had not yet come into conflict with the general government by resisting her laws as Quincy predicted she would do. But he was ready to assert that "if she shall, contrary to our mutual interest, array herself against the General Government, I for one, shall not hesitate to search for the proof that she is only a component part of the Union—not its arbitress." He was asking for the passage of the military measures, Williams said, to bring about an honorable peace which would benefit the representative from Massachusetts and his friends as much as any gentleman in the house.[76]

Much debate developed over the question as to what to do in regard to the ships that left Great Britain after the revocation of the Orders in Council. Although chairman of the committee on Ways and Means, Cheves opposed the report recommending that all petitions for the remission of the penalties of the Non-importation Act be referred to the Secretary of the Treasury. He feared that Gallatin might decline to remit

---

bonds of every land, cut-throats and knaves, . . . Mobs and Banditti!— all rejoice." In this way, said "Lucius," the President was being repaid for appointing Federalists to office.

[76] *Annals of Congress*, 12th Cong., 2nd Sess. (November 21, 1812), pp. 175-193. The military bill passed with the support of all from South Carolina except Moore, who was absent.

JEFFERSONIAN DEMOCRACY IN S. C. 265

some of the penalties on the ground that revenue was needed. In fighting against the report of the majority of his committee, Cheves received the support of Calhoun, Williams and Lowndes. Lowndes, in particular, showed no great admiration for a Secretary of the Treasury who would seek to have delegated to himself the authority to decide what penalties should be remitted.[77] The other members from South Carolina, however, were not sufficiently interested in commerce or distrustful of Gallatin to oppose the measure.[78]

The South Carolina members of the war party attributed early reverses in the war to treachery and incompetence.[79] Williams thought that immediate plans should be made to seize Canada and Florida. British power must be removed from the

[77] *Annals of Congress,* 12th Cong., 2nd Sess. December 2, 4, 8, 9, 1812), pp. 215-216, 241-256, 315-321, 339-349.

[78] A compromise was finally worked out which directed the Secretary of the Treasury to remit the penalties of those whom an investigation showed to have been innocent victims. *Ibid.* (December 15, 16, 1812), pp. 394-404, 450-451.

The speech of Cheves against the report of the committee was severely denounced by the editor of the *Investigator.* He wished that Cheves were soon to face the electorate. An election would show that Cheves was no longer representing the views of his constituents. The editor particularly resented Cheves's alignment with the commercial group. "If then Mr. Cheves has deserted the republican ranks, and on the floor of Congress openly acknowledged himself to be associated and connected with their political enemies, it is certainly time for them to forsake him." *Investigator,* December 22, 1812, January 19, 1813.

[79] Williams charged that the surrender of Detroit had resulted from the "treachery and cowardice" of an officer. *Annals of Congress,* 12th Cong., 2nd Sess. (December 29, 1812), pp. 460-466. Calhoun wrote James MacBride, December 25, "Our executive officers are most incompetent men, and will let the best of causes I fear perish in their hands. We are literally borne down under the effects of errors and mismanagement. . . . I do believe the executive will have to make a disgraceful peace." Quoted by Pratt, *Expansionists of 1812,* pp. 180-181, from James MacBride Papers. The criticism became so severe that Madison finally yielded and accepted the resignations of his Secretaries of War and Navy. Paul Hamilton, a former South Carolina governor, who had been Secretary of the Navy since 1809, resigned in December, 1812. Upon Hamilton's request, Madison gave him a letter describing his faithful service. The President spoke of the "faithful zeal, uniform exertions and unimpeachable integrity with which you have discharged that important trust." Paul Hamilton to Madison, December 30; Madison to Hamilton, December 31, 1812. Madison Papers.

borders, to be recovered only through negotiation. "The road to peace then lies through Canada. When we shall once be in possession of it, peace, honorable peace, the sole object of us all, is secured." To those who argued that the Canadians had not injured the United States, he replied that Canada was an agent of Great Britain and a place from which this country could be injured.[80]

Speaking for Williams because of his indisposition, Cheves ridiculed those who continued to ask why the United States had gone to war. The opponents of war reminded him of the character *Goldfinch* in one of Holcroft's plays, who, when he heard the name Roman, exclaimed, "Romans! Romans! who are they?" Likewise did the members of the opposition cry "national honor! what's that? what's that?" The causes of the war were "principally new and unheard of blockades—the Orders in Council, which have been generally so called, by way of pre-eminence; the spoliation of our commerce under various unfounded and insulting pretexts, and the impressment of our seamen." Public opinion had demanded war at the time of the declaration. If war fervor had moderated slightly, the fact remained that it had been desired. Cheves praised the naval activities during the war, but refrained from discussing the military record to any great extent on the ground that he was not very familiar with military affairs. When the bill providing for further increases in the military strength of the nation was voted upon, all South Carolinians present except Lowndes voted affirmatively.[81]

[80] *Annals of Congress,* 12th Cong., 2nd Sess. (December 29, 1812), pp. 460-466.

[81] Williams, the only South Carolina member absent, was of course in favor of the bill. *Annals of Congress,* 12th Cong., 2nd Sess. (January 14, 1813), pp. 827-844. Lowndes was not an expansionist and voted against the bill designed to provide troops for the invasion of Canada. On January 16, Lowndes wrote his father-in-law, General Thomas Pinckney, that the army bill had passed, but that he did not believe more than half a dozen men in Congress actually approved it. "Every one was sensible, however, that to deny to the Executive the means which he thought necessary to carry on the war would be a measure of doubtful propriety. . . . It was fortunate for the administration, or at least for their wishes in this particular measure, that the opposition selected it as the occasion of a general discussion of the war, its causes, and the necessity for its continuance. The vote was by many considered

By the beginning of 1813, many citizens of South Carolina began to have fears as to the outcome of the war. News of victories on the sea was anxiously awaited and ardently celebrated. However, throughout the days of gloom the bombastic, Republican *Investigator* attempted to make up for reverses by exaggerating the number and importance of victories. When the Federalists expressed surprise that American ships had been able to win victories, the *Investigator* appealed to history. "We beat them in the revolution; we beat them now; & if they do not indemnify us for the past, and secure us against future aggressions, we will beat them from the ocean!"[82] The attitude of Josiah Quincy toward the army bill was described as treasonable, and he himself was characterized as "a friend of disunion." The editor was happy that the administration would not be influenced "by the barking and howling of the whole New-England Pack in our present and necessary war."[83] When he learned that Frederick Dalcho, who had been connected with the *Charleston Courier,* was planning to change his vocation to that of a minister, the editor of the *Investigator* remarked that when other methods failed the British resorted to the pulpit. He hoped that Dalcho would not secure the pulpit of St. Paul's Church in Charleston. "No politician, but one that has made the Holy scripture his chief study, such a man will be agreeable to the people and no doubt would restore peace and harmony in the Parish."[84] So bitter against the Federalists had the editor become that he was ready to charge them with the responsibility for the recent delays in the arrival of the mail. A Peace Society organized in Charleston and composed largely of Federalists was said to have pledged itself to hinder the operation of the government in every way possible. The interference with the mail was thought to be one of its activities.[85] That all Federalists did not oppose the war or

---

a vote of approbation to the war rather than to the measure." Quoted in Ravenel, *Life of Lowndes,* p. 119.

[82] *Investigator,* January 12, 1813. [83] *Ibid.,* February 13, 15, 1813.

[84] *Ibid.,* February 16, 1813. Dalcho, however, did secure the pulpit of St. Paul's.

[85] *Ibid.,* March 12, 1813. A somewhat less partisan explanation of the delay in the arrival of the mail was given by the editor of the *City Gazette,* another Republican paper, several months later. On October

interfere with the operation of the government is evidenced by the fact that so influential a member of that party as Daniel Elliott Huger actually supported the war.[86] By March, 1813, some of the Federalists, as badly as they disliked to see Madison President, had come to believe that matters would have been still worse if Clinton had been elected in his stead.[87] The war, however, was never popular with the South Carolina Federalists.[88]

6. REPUBLICAN FACTIONALISM DURING THE ADMINISTRATION OF JOSEPH ALSTON

Although the Republicans were critical of the Federalists in 1813, they were at times even more critical of each other. Because of bitter factionalism, the administration of Governor Joseph Alston was one of the most dissentious in the history of the state.[89] Having for some time been on unfriendly rela-

---

16, 1813, he called upon the Postmaster General to do his duty by employing efficient contractors or resign.

[86] O'Neall, *Bench and Bar in S. C.*, I, 180-181. In fact, Huger was preparing to take charge of a brigade of state troops when the war ended. His experiences, however, were not happy. "Judge Huger, though a Federalist, was denounced by the Republicans as a Federalist, and by the Federalists as an apostate. His friends passed him in the streets without speaking." Benjamin Franklin Perry, *Reminiscences of Public Men, with Speeches and Addresses*, Second Series (Greenville, S. C.: 1889), pp. 96-97.

[87] It is hard to imagine a more bitter castigation of a President than that given Madison by "An American" in the *Charleston Courier*, March 24, 1813. But his conclusion was that conditions would have been worse under Clinton.

[88] Printed in his own column, June 18, 1813, by the editor of the *Charleston Courier*, was the article signed "a friend of Peace." The views of this writer were similar to those of others appearing about this time. It was stated that the forces of the enemy were increasing along the coast. Commerce was being destroyed. "The rich are impoverished —the poor are ruined—the industrious are rendered idle—the idle dissolute—and the dissolute desperate." If the nation should increase its territory, the writer argued that such expansion would merely weaken a country, "overgrown in youth." A long war would be disastrous even if the American forces were finally successful. On the other hand peace might restore former conditions to some extent. "War, how deserving of honest indignation and censure are those who embark in it without cause and without hope."

[89] Alston's private life was no less unhappy than his public life. During the first month of his administration he lost his wife, the beautiful and brilliant Theodosia Burr. Six months earlier his only child died.

JEFFERSONIAN DEMOCRACY IN S. C. 269

tions with Alston, E. S. Thomas, editor of the *City Gazette,* soon became one of the severest critics of the governor's conduct.[90] The approach of the division among the Republicans was foreshadowed by the criticism of Cheves by the editor of the *Investigator,* already mentioned. On April 5, 1813, Thomas stated that he had evidence indicating that Langdon Cheves, John C. Calhoun, Elias Earle, William Lowndes and Thomas Moore had vacated their seats in Congress because of their failure to notify the governor of their acceptance of election within the period required by law.[91] This announcement gave rise to many articles attacking the governor for withholding the commissions of those representatives. On the other hand, the *Investigator* defended Alston for not forwarding the commissions without the notification from the five members of Congress. To have done so, declared the editor, would have made the governor liable to impeachment. Besides, it was very fortunate that Cheves would so soon return to his constituents for their decision as to the propriety of his recent conduct.[92] In the *City Gazette,* Thomas, writing under the pseudonym of "Argus," contended that the question should have been raised earlier. Four months had elapsed since election, whereas the legal period for notification of acceptance was twenty days. If the governor had not intended to commission them without the formal notification, he should have ordered a new election.[93] The real purpose back of the proceedings, he thought, was to void the election of Cheves, whom the governor and his satellites called a "political Jesuit."[94] The contest continued unabated for weeks. The secretary of state denied that Alston had given specific orders that the commission of Cheves should not be delivered but did admit that a general order had been

[90] Thomas says that the bad relations began years before and were largely the result of the effort of Alston to dominate the "Moot Society," of which both were members. Thomas finally withdrew from the society. Thereafter they were unfriendly privately and politically. "We were never on speaking terms after he was defeated in his first attempt to gain the gubernatorial chair; he succeeded in the second, by his own vote, if my memory is correct, and became my implacable foe." Thomas, *Reminiscences,* II, 69-71. Unfortunately the legislative journals and the newspapers do not afford an opportunity to check the majority by which Alston was elected governor.

[91] *City Gazette,* April 5, 1813. [92] *Investigator,* April 6, 1813.
[93] *City Gazette,* April 9, 1813. [94] *Ibid.,* April 12, 1813.

issued in January that none of them should be presented without authorization from the governor.[95] Thomas was accused by Alston's friends of trying to undermine the confidence of the people in the state government and attempting to split the Republican party.[96]

Although Governor Alston finally delivered the commissions to the five representatives, factional bitterness continued. Thomas charged that the governor had been elected as the result of intrigue and expressed the opinion that he would serve the state by causing the adoption of a radical amendment providing for the popular election of the governor.[97] He virtually accused the governor of lying in regard to the withholding of the commissions, asserted that his election had been a source of great displeasure to the state and recommended that he resign immediately.[98] The governor sued Thomas for libel be-

[95] *Investigator*, April 12, 1813. In the same paper on April 13, "Causidicus" stated that it was he instead of the governor who had called Cheves a "political Jesuit." "Causidicus" thought it would be wise to force Cheves to face election again.

In the *Investigator* on August 14, "Polyphemus" addressed a letter to "Argus." "I do not believe you are a lawyer, but a *wandering* vagabond, who originally came here and offered 25,000 dollars for the City-Gazette Establishment, to make Clinton President, and finally ended, by writing for Madison. . . . A word as to trusting Governors with commissions. It is said that an ill effect has been produced by it in one instance in Pennsylvania, from which circumstance, your paper dubs you *major*. I wonder if it be true, that Governor Snyder did sign your commission, or whether you found it in a deceased friend's closet, and made it answer your purpose. What has become of your Riga consulship commission? If you ever had that you would have shown it with your *major's* commission, no doubt. Your paper recommended you sometime since as consul to Tunis—have you received that appointment, pray? Do you think that the Government would trust you? Oh! Thou Laughing Stock and Fool! good bye to you!" Thomas says in his *Reminiscences*, II, 69, that he received the appointment as consul to Tunis.

[96] "The Owl and Owlet Club," *Investigator*, April 23, 1813. It was also charged that Thomas was influenced by his failure to be elected director of the State Bank. On April 27, the same writer asked Thomas if he had ever been of value to the Republicans. Again he was accused of having favored Clinton for a time. It was stated that he had refused to print strong Republican letters. The writer asserted that the society he represented planned to reveal all such delinquencies.

[97] *City Gazette*, April 27, 1813. [98] *Ibid.*, April 27, 1813.

JEFFERSONIAN DEMOCRACY IN S. C. 271

cause of his publication of the charge that he had bought his election to the legislature as a step toward the governorship. Considering it hardly fair for the pardoning power to be in the hand of the accuser, the court postponed the trial till the close of Alston's term. At that time the jury, being legally permitted to decide only on the fact of publication, involuntarily found Thomas guilty, but he served only four days of his month's imprisonment, the time required to send a messenger to David R. Williams, the new governor, for a pardon. That the conduct of Thomas met the approval of many was shown by the attitude of the jury, his entertainment during the few days of confinement, the ready issuance of a pardon by the new governor and his triumphal escort home by his fellow townsmen.[99]

Even more vexing to the general public than the controversy over the withholding of the commissions was the conduct of Governor Alston in regard to the military defense of the state. Being greatly exposed because of its numerous inlets, the coast of South Carolina was difficult to defend from British vessels. The panic that usually seizes inhabitants of coast towns was well exemplified in Charleston in 1813. The fear had been increased by the withdrawal of the federal barges from the inlets.[100] In February, the people of Charleston believed the

[99] The law did not permit the jury to decide the truth of statements, said to be libelous; but the accused could inform the judge himself of the basis for them. The chief evidence furnished by Thomas was that Alston's father had told him that his son spent $9,000 and his opponent $7,000 in the contest for election to the legislature in the small and thinly populated All Saint's Parish. The sentence of a $200 fine and a month's imprisonment was light. Of course other developments which will be recorded below made Alston even more unpopular by the time of the trial of Thomas. So bitter had political feeling become that during the interval between the charges and the trial someone fired at Thomas through his window. Governor Williams offered a reward for the arrest of the would-be assassin but he was never apprehended. Thomas exonerated Alston but stated that he suspected the identity of the one who fired at him. However, he mentions no name. Thomas, *Reminiscences*, II, 69-82.

[100] *Ibid.*, II, 62-68. Thomas says that it was largely through his own firm manner in dealing with the Secretary of the Navy that the latter returned the barges. He, of course, had the support of other influential citizens.

harbor blockaded.[101] Considering the city in danger, citizens gathered to discuss methods of defense.[102] The "Owl and Owlet Club" addressed a letter to the Secretary of the Navy criticizing the withdrawal of the barges as "highly impolitic" and "highly injurious."[103]

In order to protect the military magazines from possible danger from the British, Governor Alston called out the Charleston militia. In July some members of two of the four regiments declined to serve the short period of service of three days in five months. The governor, thereupon, announced that the militia, when called into war service, were under articles of war which stipulated death as the possible penalty for disobedience. Accordingly, he ordered that court-martial proceedings be brought against some forty members. The governor was thwarted, however, by *habeas corpus* action and a hostile court decision rendered by Judge Bay.[104]

In denying the claim of the *Charleston Courier* that "no decision was ever more satisfactory,"[105] Alston declared that

[101] *Times*, February 25, 1813.

[102] The *City Gazette* on March 26, 1813, tells of such a meeting. Resolutions were passed calling for the erection of six additional batteries and two new furnaces at sites "best calculated for that purpose." General Pinckney was requested to "deposit, within the limits of Charleston as many pieces of heavy ordnances, mounted on travelling carriages, as he can spare." The city council was asked to levy special taxes and contributions were requested. The governor was urged to employ the militia in the defense of the city. The city council was further asked to request the Secretary of the Navy to return the ships formerly used to protect the harbor. A committee of twenty-one was appointed to aid in prosecuting the program outlined in the resolutions.

That new means of defense were being sought is evident from the publication in the *City Gazette*, March 31, 1813, of an article taken from the New York *Western Star* telling how to construct a floating battery. The attention of the committee of twenty-one was called to this method.

[103] *Investigator*, June 10, 1813.

[104] In the proceedings Alston, as usual, had the opposition of Editor Thomas of the *City Gazette*, in whose paper were printed hostile sentiments. In this case, the Charleston public was angered by the governor's actions against fellow townsmen. For once the Federalist *Charleston Courier* agreed with the *City Gazette*. The decision of Judge Bay, given on August 23, declared that the articles of war applied only to the one third of the militia which the governor might send out of the state and that there was no legal penalty prescribed for the failure to serve in the defense of the state.

[105] *Charleston Courier*, August 24, 1813.

JEFFERSONIAN DEMOCRACY IN S. C. 273

the court had placed the militia in a state of anarchy. He forthwith dismissed the loyal as well as the disobedient regiments, in spite of the presence of sixteen British vessels on the coasts. The governor's zeal for order and protection of the magazines was commendable, but his summary release of all the militiamen in a time of danger could hardly have been approved by even his supporters. However, Alston did summon the legislature; and upon the landing of the British on St. Helena Island he again used the militia. Soon the legislature revised the law so as to make the militia, when in actual service, subject to the articles of war and passed other measures to aid in the protection of the coast.[106] Some of the gloom of the summer disappeared when news of victories on the Great Lakes arrived in the fall.[107]

7. EFFORTS OF THE WAR PARTY TO JUSTIFY THE WAR AND STIMULATE CONFIDENCE, 1813-1814

In the first session of the Thirteenth Congress, Calhoun, as chairman of the Committee on Foreign Relations and as one of the chief advocates of war, spent much of his time justifying the beginning of armed hostilities against Great Britain and defending the foreign policy of the Executive Department. With particular vigor did he attempt to refute the charges that Madison had withheld information concerning the French emperor's revocation of decrees and had thereby been partially responsible for the delay of the British in repealing their Orders in Council.[108] Samuel Farrow, a new member from South Carolina, thought the existence of war should be accepted as a fact. The representatives had been elected to prosecute the war, not to argue about its causes.[109] Most of the South Carolina members, however, were willing to vote for the resolution of Daniel

[106] *S. C. Statutes at Large*, VIII, 518. The whole proceedings are reviewed in articles in the *City Gazette*, September 2, 3, 6, 7, 8, 1813.

[107] In the *City Gazette* on October 22, was the letter of a correspondent who stated that he had never seen the people in better spirits than upon the receipt of the good news from the Great Lakes. Three days later the editor of the same paper referred to similar rejoicing over the news of another victory.

[108] *Annals of Congress*, 13th Cong., 1st Sess. (June 16, 1813), pp. 174-178.

[109] *Ibid.* (June 17, 1813), pp. 185-186.

Webster asking the President, if it were not against public interest, to inform the house when and how he learned of the alleged repeal of the Berlin and Milan decrees.[110] After an examination of the material sent by Madison, the Committee on Foreign Relations reported that the pressure of American measures and not the repeal of the French decrees brought about the revocation of the British Orders in Council.[111]

However much Calhoun might defend the President when charges were brought against him in regard to the origin of the war, he did not always follow his suggestions as to methods of prosecuting the conflict. In July, Madison sent a confidential message stating that there was sufficient evidence to show that the British were combining with the blockade of our ports the licensing of neutral ships or British ships in neutral disguise to get goods from our ports. As a remedy he suggested the prohibition of exports till some time during the next session of Congress. Upon the passage of a measure laying an embargo on all ships in American ports, Calhoun, Cheves and Lowndes voted negatively, but all other South Carolina representatives voted affirmatively.[112]

The division among the Republicans showed up in the few scattered elections held in South Carolina in the fall of 1813. In the contest for the position of intendant of Charleston, the Federalist candidate received 465 votes to 468 for his three Republican opponents.[113] In Beaufort, however, a Republi-

---

[110] At first Calhoun tried to soften the tone of the resolution, but finally withdrew his amendment. Evans and Kershaw voted against the resolution; Farrow was absent; but Calhoun and the other South Carolinians voted for it. *Annals of Congress,* 13th Cong., 1st Sess. (June 21, 1813), pp. 302-303. [111] *Ibid.* (July 13, 1813), p. 435.

[112] *Annals of Congress,* 13th Cong., 1st Sess. (July 20, 1813), pp. 503-504. In the senate there was divided support of the President on another matter. When Madison nominated Gallatin as one of those to treat with Great Britain regarding peace, Gaillard voted for and Taylor against the resolutions stating that the powers and duties of the Secretary of the Treasury were incompatible with those of an envoy extraordinary to a foreign power. *Ibid., Senate* (June 14, 16, 1813), pp. 86-87.

[113] *City Gazette,* September 21, 1813. In the same paper on the following day, a correspondent denounced the *Charleston Courier* for claiming an actual Federalist victory. According to him there was merely a division among the "Democrats." The division, said the writer, did not

can defeated the Federalist candidate for the state senate by eighteen votes, despite skillful campaigning on the part of the latter, who was described as "a very respectable Federalist."[114]

In December, 1813, the South Carolina legislature again expressed its approval of the declaration of war. Resolutions were passed stating that the President had "by his energetic prosecution of the war furnished a new claim to the confidence of his fellow citizens," and that "indemnity for our wrongs and satisfactory security for our rights as a nation are the only terms on which an honorable peace can be bottomed." Perhaps the strongest statement in the document was in the preamble. After asserting that an honorable peace would be a desirable event, the legislature stated, "but if it cannot be procured without a surrender of our rights as a sovereign and independent people, we are ready to say—Let the war be perpetual—it is an evil it is true—but it is an evil more tolerable than national humiliation."[115]

During the winter and spring of 1813-1814 the most loquacious of the South Carolina Congressmen took advantage of many opportunities to correct the opinions of fellow members as to the origin and nature of the war they had aided materially in bringing about.[116] Naturally, they were also peculiarly interested in the successful prosecution of the conflict.[117] Cal-

---

extend to other parts of the state and before the next election there would be unity in Charleston.

[114] *City Gazette,* November 1, 1813.

[115] S. C. House Journal, December 17; Senate Journal, December 18, 1813. In his letter transmitting the resolutions to Madison, John Geddes assured the President that the whole people of South Carolina were united in the support of the general government in the prosecution of the war.

[116] The influence of the South Carolina members, already clearly recognized by their committee appointments, was further emphasized by the election of Langdon Cheves to succeed Henry Clay as speaker, following the latter's resignation. *Annals of Congress,* 13th Cong., 2nd Sess. (January 19, 1814), p. 1057. The election of John Gaillard as president *pro tempore* of the senate, now becoming a custom, took place again. *Ibid.,* Senate (April 18, 1814), p. 778.

[117] Lowndes advocated encouraging re-enlistment, so as to take advantage of experience. The other South Carolina representatives except Farrow, who was absent, joined him in voting for the passage of such

houn severely condemned the defeatist attitude of the opposition. The coast, particularly New York harbor, was not as defenseless as some thought. If the country would remain united, all the objects of the war could be accomplished. The seamen could be protected and the commerce made secure. As to the conquest of Canada, Calhoun "hoped" that the United States possessed ample means to conquer all the British provinces on this side of the ocean "if necessary."[118] In his defense of the war itself, Cheves stated that, since he had not been an indiscriminate supporter of the administration, he would not be an indiscriminate apologist for its conduct of the war. He was willing to admit the difficulties confronted in changing a peaceful nation to a warring one, and in bringing people with the democratic spirit under military authority. Furthermore, Cheves declared, the reverses of the war had been magnified. Actually there had been only two "signal instances" of discomfiture of which the nation should complain—the surrender of Detroit and the failure of the expedition against Montreal. Against these, the United States could place the "destruction of Proctor's army, and the successful attack and capture of York." These defeats had been of such consequence that the British commanders on these occasions had not since been employed. In regard to the successes at sea, Cheves felt that they should not all be credited to his political friends, many of whom had been willing to neglect the navy. As to Canada, he had little expectation that Great Britain would be willing to surrender a region to which she was attached not only because of commercial interests but also because of historical memories. Attacks upon Canada were valuable on account of their effect upon England's willingness to make

---

a bill. *Annals of Congress,* 13th Cong., 2nd Sess. (December 15, 1813; January 14, 1814), pp. 791-792, 979.

Particular approval of the Embargo was voiced by Samuel Farrow, who was serving his first term in Congress. He wished it enforced to the extent of chaining the ships to the wharves. Although recognizing the severity of the measure upon the American citizens, he thought it operated more heavily upon the enemy. "It was similar to a parent's giving his child medicine which was disagreeable at first, but would operate beneficially in the end." *Ibid.* (January 22, 1814), pp. 1115-1116.

[118] *Ibid.* (February 8, 1814), pp. 1262-1263.

peace. If the United States took Canada, it did not mean that she must keep it. While the importance of the American trade as a means of coercion had been over-estimated, it too would be a force in bringing the war to a successful conclusion.[119]

In discussing the repeal of the Embargo and Non-importation Acts, Calhoun again reviewed the nature of the war. He declared that it had been emphatically and correctly called "a war for Free Trade and Sailors Rights." He had been of the opinion that the restrictive measures should have ended with the beginning of the war; but such a motion had been lost by one vote. Certainly the time had come when trade with the neutral nations should be resumed. As to the possible effect upon the American manufacturing industry of the repeal of the restrictions Calhoun believed that tariffs already voted would prevent a dangerous influx of competing goods. He himself hoped that at all times and under every policy manufacturing would be protected with "due care." On the passage of the repeal measure all of the South Carolina representatives voted affirmatively.[120]

Several times during the session Calhoun felt called upon to deny that the war was an offensive one. Recalling that during the previous session the gentlemen on the other side of the house had argued that the knowledge of the revocation of the Berlin and Milan decrees would have brought about the repeal of the Orders in Council, Calhoun asserted that they did not think then that the desire for Canada was the cause of the war. It would have been idle, he thought, to inquire

[119] *Annals of Congress*, 13th Cong., 2nd Sess. (February 24, 1814), pp. 1632-1650.

[120] *Ibid.*, 13th Cong., 2nd Sess. (April 6, 7, 1814), pp. 1962-1965, 2001-2002. The editor of the *City Gazette*, on April 8, and 18, disagreed with Madison in regard to the desirability of repealing the Embargo. According to him, no measure of the federal government in the last six years had met such general approbation as the Embargo. He felt that it had gone far toward relieving the coast of the British blockade and the unpleasant occurrences connected with privateers. The editor had hoped that it would continue till peace. However, on April 18, he refused to publish the letter of "Eugenius," who attributed base motives to Madison in recommending the repeal of the Embargo. The editor did not believe that the restrictive measures should have been removed, he said, but he was not willing to attribute base motives to the President for making such recommendations.

whether resistance to the Orders in Council were offensive or defensive. Equally idle would it be to ask whether protecting our seamen from impressment was offensive or defensive. Canada was incidental. If the United States took that province and kept it, she would be indemnified for her defensive exertions.[121] In his emphasis on the influence of impressment and interference with American commerce as causes of the war, Calhoun was heartily supported by Cheves. The latter thought that it was "the daily continuance of the injuries, the incessant infliction, and the absence of all hope that these injuries were to end, that drove the nation necessarily and unavoidably to resistance." Submission would have meant loss of prestige among nations and would have gained "the everlasting contempt of the world." However, Cheves was willing to admit that, had he known of the repeal of the Orders in Council, he would not have voted for war. Although he knew of others with similar views, he was aware that there were some who would have favored war even if they had been informed of the repeal of the obnoxious British measures.[122]

In South Carolina the leading Republican newspaper tried to encourage its readers by reporting that recruiting officers all over the country had been successful in enlisting volunteers. There was, the editor said, no longer any doubt that the ranks would be filled even to overflowing before the opening of the spring campaigns.[123] Toward the middle of the summer, however, Thomas Lehre wrote Jefferson that the outlook was gloomy. He still thought, though, that the war would be successful.[124] On the Fourth of July, there were the usual parades, speeches and toasts. The toasts generally expressed confidence in the President and advocated the prosecution of the war until a successful peace had been won.[125] Party feeling was manifest in the resentment by the Republicans of the claims of the Federalists that officers belonging to their party deserved

[121] *Annals of Congress*, 13th Cong., 2nd Sess. (January 15, 1814), 994-1002.
[122] *Ibid.* (February 24, 1814), pp. 1628-1631.
[123] *City Gazette*, March 14, 1814.
[124] Lehre to Jefferson, July 7, 1814. Jefferson Papers.
[125] *City Gazette*, July 6, 1814.

credit for the naval victories.[126] After the capture of Washington by the British, Federalists and Republicans competed with each other in their efforts to defend Charleston from a similar fate.[127] The *City Gazette* reported that the citizens of Barnwell and adjacent districts were desirous of being called out for the defense of the seacoast.[128] Men and women of both parties co-operated in building fortifications which British officers later described as the "best put together field work they had ever seen."[129]

In the elections of 1814, the war was of course one of the main issues. The Federalists gained some hope after the election of their candidate as intendant of Charleston.[130] In this contest both candidates pointed to their defensive activities; but the Federalist contender was able to persuade most of the voters that he could promote the safety of the city more successfully than his opponent. When the voters of Charleston elected members of the legislature, however, they chose Republicans for all the places.[131] Likewise did Charleston District elect the Republican candidate, Henry Middleton, as its representative in Congress.[132] All other South Carolina Congress-

[126] "Junius Brutus" denounced the Federalists for claiming credit that did not belong to them. If they believed as they claimed that the war was unjust, he could not understand how there could be any Federalist officers left in the navy. *City Gazette*, August 26, 1814.

[127] The Republicans accused the Federalists of calling a public meeting, through the city council then controlled by their party, at the same time that they themselves were to assemble for the same purpose. The Republicans, however, met an hour earlier and transacted their business in time to attend the meeting with the council. Both parties then discussed means of defending Charleston. *City Gazette*, September 17, 1814, *Charleston Courier*, September 12, 1814.

[128] *City Gazette*, September 23, 1814.

[129] Wallace, *History of S. C.*, II, 393.

[130] The vote was—Thomas Rhett Smith (Federalist), 611 and Thomas Lee (Republican) 517, *City Gazette*, September 20, 1814.

[131] The votes of the Republican candidates in Charleston varied from 1078 to 1205, those of the Federalists from 707 to 833. *City Gazette*, October 13, 14, 1814. The campaign had been heated. The Federalists charged the Republicans with incompetence in carrying on the war and pledged themselves to restore order and efficiency. *Ibid.*, October 7, 10, 1814.

[132] *Ibid.*, October 13, 1814. Cheves had returned to the practice of law and was not a candidate for re-election. He had declined the appointment of Secretary of the Treasury to succeed Gallatin. In 1816

men were Republicans also, except Benjamin Huger, who defeated Theodore Gourdin in Georgetown District.[133] For governor the South Carolina legislature chose David R. Williams, who had served in Congress and for a few months as Brigadier-General in the regular army, but who had recently been engaged in agricultural pursuits.[134]

After the destruction of the public buildings in Washington by the British in the summer of 1814, Congress was called upon to decide whether the seat of government should be removed. In voting on this question the South Carolina representatives lacked unanimity. Perhaps the one most hotly opposed to removal was Farrow. For his part, he wished the enemy would try to return to Washington. It would be time enough to move when the British were in sight. Farrow declared that he "would rather sit under canvas in the city than remove one mile out of it to a palace."[135] When the committee appointed to study the question made its report, the house divided equally on whether the word "expedient" should be substituted for "inexpedient." All the South Carolina repre-

---

he was elected an associate justice of the South Carolina court of appeals. Three years later he became president of the Bank of the United States. Cheves was told by Senator Middleton that Monroe was ready to appoint him to a vacancy on the United States Supreme Court, a position which he would have found more to his liking, but he was prevailed upon to accept the presidency of the bank. Haskell, "Langdon Cheves and the United States Bank," p. 364.

[133] Chappell, Calhoun, Lowndes and Moore were re-elected. The other members were William Mayrant, Stephen D. Miller, John Taylor of Pendleton, and William Woodward. John Taylor of Columbia and John Gaillard continued to be the United States senators.

[134] S. C. Senate Journal, December 10, 1814. Williams did not wish to be governor but felt that he should not decline if elected. He had been appointed Brigadier-General by Madison and served till December 8, 1813. The reasons for his resignation appear to have been private or personal. Cook, *Life and Legacy of Williams*, pp. 98-105. Later correspondence with Madison shows that they remained on very friendly terms. Williams to Madison, May 29, June 13, 1815; December 6, 1816. Madison Papers.

[135] *Annals of Congress*, 13th Cong., 3rd Sess. (September 26, 1814), pp. 316-323. Gourdin was the only South Carolinian who voted to appoint a committee to report on the expediency of moving the seat of government. Calhoun and Evans were absent. Cheves, as speaker, did not vote on this question.

JEFFERSONIAN DEMOCRACY IN S. C. 281

sentatives whose votes are recorded opposed the substitution. As speaker, Cheves cast the deciding vote. Declaring that this duty was "as unexpected as painful," he stated that he would nevertheless give that vote which he thought the interests, safety and honor of the nation required. Believing that the District of Columbia could not be defended except at a very great expense in a time when money was needed for the war, he voted for removal.[136]

After the coming of peace in Europe, Calhoun believed that Great Britain would concentrate on the war in America. Speaking on the question of increasing the direct taxes by one hundred per cent for war purposes, he asserted that if any body of men had ever held the destinies of a country in their hands Congress did at that time. Immediate and effective measures were absolutely necessary in order to meet the enemy, who could be expected to prosecute the war vigorously and try "to crush us if possible by one mighty effort." He went into the plans of campaign he thought should be followed the next season. On the coast, the United States should be on the defensive; but on the Canadian frontier the action "must be wholly offensive." He had hoped, Calhoun said, that "the miserably stale and absurd objections against offensive operations in Canada" had ceased until he heard them again the day before from the representative from New Hampshire (Daniel Webster). Such a campaign, he thought, was the cheapest and most effective method of operating upon the enemy. If the British defended Canada, they would have to divide their forces. If they chose to neglect the region, Canada would fall into our possession. Either alternative would be desirable. A force of at least 50,000 should be sent against Canada not later than May or June. "With skillful officers, and with the aptitude of the Americans to acquire the military art, the finest army in a few months might be formed." The progress already made was "not short of wonderful." Never had a country under such circumstances in so short a time "developed so much military talent." If a sufficient force, "well appointed," were put under able officers, the nation would find itself "in the road

[136] *Annals of Congress*, 13th Cong., 3rd Sess. (October 3, 1814), p. 341. Calhoun and Gourdin were absent.

to honor and secure peace." But this could not be achieved by arguing the causes of the war or disputing about the relative contributions of the two political parties. It was the Revolution over again. They were again "struggling for liberty and independence." If the members of the opposition could not support, he hoped they would at least not hinder. All of the South Carolina representatives except Gourdin, who was absent, joined Calhoun in voting for the increase in revenue for war purposes.[137] Likewise did all of them vote for the measure authorizing the President to call upon the several states for their respective quotas of militia for the defense of the frontier from invasion.[138]

Although Calhoun was evolving grandiose plans for the coming military campaigns and attempting to paint a picture of hopefulness for the future, all South Carolinians were not so optimistic. Surveying the recent developments with anxious interest, the editor of the *Southern Patriot,* a new South Carolina Republican newspaper, hardly dared to predict what results the new year would bring.

The Bank bill has been *negatived*—the draft bill has received its *quietus.* We are now comparatively without an army, and actually without *money.* The wheels of government of a *nation at war,* must now be carried on by the *mere forces of genius.* How far this will progress without either men or means, is an experiment in legislation never before attempted.[139]

[137] *Annals of Congress,* 13th Cong., 3rd Sess. (October 25, 1814), pp. 465-469, 478. Cheves, as speaker, did not vote.

[138] *Ibid.* (December 14, 1814), pp. 921-929. Farrow made a speech in which he denied that the bill was unconstitutional, arguing that it came under the part of the Constitution giving Congress the power to "make rules for the government and regulation of the land and naval forces; to provide for calling forth the militia to execute the laws of the Union, suppress insurrections, and repel invasions."

[139] *Southern Patriot* (Charleston), January 9, 1815. The reference to the bank is to the bill passed but vetoed by Madison. The large majority of the representatives from South Carolina, at one time or another during the long discussion of the measure, had expressed themselves as favoring a bank; but it was difficult to agree as to the type of bank; *Annals of Congress,* 13th Cong., 2nd Sess. (April 4, 1814), p. 1956. 3rd Sess. (November 16, 17, 18, 21, 25, 28, December 23, 28, 1814; January 2, 3, 7, 18, February 3, 11, 16, 1815), pp. 587-589, 613-632, 643-644, 651, 976, 997, 1025, 1031-1032, 1044-1045, 1083, 1148, 1167-1168. *Ibid.,* Senate, 13th Cong., 3rd Sess. (December 9, 1814; January 30,

The news of the Hartford Convention was further disquieting.

What the Convention have done is *nothing*. What the *Principles* they publish may do—is everything. We laugh at their self-importance—we despise their folly—but we tremble at the influence of State prejudice, wielded by the arm of personal ambition. . . . We abhor a civil war—even in prospective. We abhor all doctrines, that tend to separate those, whose interest, whose glory, whose existence, is union. . . . Increase the powers of the National Congress—amend your constitution where it is too weak for the purpose of *National Defense;* and give your Executive a discretionary power, for which he can always be responsible. This is the key stone that binds the arch.

If these policies were followed, the editor thought that the nation would become more firm. "But, if interest, and speculation, and paltry considerations, and vile passions, nourished and directed by designing men should cause any of the States to *retire from our embrace*—alas! the example will be Contagious."[140]

8. Peace at Last

The news of the victory at New Orleans revived hope;[141] and before Calhoun's military plans could be attempted or the editor's fears be realized, the "joyful tidings of Peace" came.[142] "Peace, honorable peace," was the announcement of the *City Gazette*.[143] From the editor of the *Southern Patriot* came a burst of enthusiasm that appeared to be *painfully* pleasant.

" 'Tis done—the agony is over!"

A war of glory has been concluded with a peace of honor. An experiment has been made of the *energies* of the Republic, and they have been found adequate to the *security* of the nation. We have established for ourselves a lofty National

---

February 2, 12, 1815), pp. 126-127, 214. In the senate, Gaillard consistently opposed and Taylor favored the bank.

[140] *Southern Patriot,* January 28, 1815.

[141] On February 10, 1815, the editor of the *City Gazette* stated that the Lynchburg mail had just brought the news of the victory at New Orleans. "Ye have triumphed over the brave soldiers who have stormed the works of St. Sebastian's, and the batteries of Bayonne. But over you, they could not triumph."

[142] These are the words used by the *Charleston Courier,* February 22, 1815.

[143] *City Gazette,* February 22, 1815.

Character. We have preserved our independence from external insult, without one infringement upon our civil liberty. We have subdued by land and wave the self stiled conquerors of Europe's peace—the boasted mistress of the ocean.

Whether the Congress of Vienna have hastened an event, which *our own conduct* would have produced;—whether the clamours of the manufacturers, the enormous expense or the continuous disgrace of the British arms, have brought it about— we shall enquire on some other occasion. The peace comes upon us in the acme of our glory, at the moment of National triumph. "Britain (says a ministerial print) yet bleeds from the lashes America has inflicted." We shall not dispute the justness of the allusion. It only now remains for the signature of our government, to unlock the sluices of commerce, and to renew the intercourses of civilized states.[144]

But perhaps the most expressive comment was the statement that thereafter *"Britain will presume less, and America will bear less."*[145] "Thus came through the War of 1812, South Carolina patriotic and nationalistic."[146]

The armed conflict had ceased; but the results were not yet clearly discernible. Would South Carolina remain nationalistic? A mere perusal of the votes of her representatives in Congress soon after the close of the War of 1812 gives an affirmative indication. Eight representatives and one senator voted to establish the Second Bank of the United States.[147] Of the seven representatives present on final passage, four favored and three opposed the tariff of 1816.[148] Early in 1817, six

[144] *Southern Patriot*, February 21, 1815.
[145] *Ibid.*, March 13, 1815.
[146] Wallace, *History of S. C.*, II, 395.
[147] Mayrant was the representative and Gaillard the senator who opposed the passage of the Bank Bill. *Annals of Congress*, 14th Cong., 1st Sess. (March 14, 1816), p. 1219. Senate, April 3, 1816. Gaillard and Taylor had been in the senate in 1811 and had opposed and favored, respectively, the rechartering of the First Bank of the United States; *ibid.*, 11th Cong., 3rd Sess. (February 19, 20, 21, 1811), pp. 294-297, 346-347. On July 24, 1816, the *City Gazette* boasted that Charleston had already subscribed "upwards of" $2,600,000 to the capital of the bank and on August 3, the same newspaper stated that Charleston had subscribed more than New York.
[148] Calhoun, Lowndes, Mayrant and Woodward supported, Huger, Moore and Taylor opposed the tariff of 1816. Chappell and Middleton were absent. *Annals of Congress*, 14th Cong., 1st Sess. (April 8, 1816), p. 1352. The senate votes are not given individually on final passage,

JEFFERSONIAN DEMOCRACY IN S. C. 285

of South Carolina's representatives supported and three opposed the bill providing for national internal improvements.[149]

These votes do not show unanimous sentiment in support of nationalism among South Carolina's representatives in Congress, but they do indicate a possible trend in that direction. This potential trend, though, had begun under abnormal war conditions; and sufficient time had not elapsed to demonstrate how firm it might be. With the coming of peace and with the growth of the idea that South Carolina was destined to remain agricultural, the people of the state soon questioned the notion that their interests could best be served by nationalism, a doctrine with which they had recently toyed and toward which the young Republicans had led them far. The abandonment of this incipient trend, however, occurred in a later period, and, therefore, will not be treated further in this study.

In 1816 the Federalists, for the last time, nominated a Presidential candidate. South Carolina in that year, as had long been her custom, gave her electoral votes to the Republican nominee. Of the same party, too, were all her representatives and senators in the next Congress. The Federalist party was not dead in South Carolina; but its members had already come to realize that they had little in common with the Federalists in other sections of the country.

In his recent monograph, *The Jeffersonian Tradition in American Democracy,* Charles Maurice Wiltse aptly wrote: "To understand Jefferson we must appreciate what preceded him; to evaluate him we must consider what has followed."[150] In order to find the sources and the influences of Jeffersonian Democracy in South Carolina, one must go far back of 1800

---

but on the second reading Gaillard voted affirmatively. Taylor was absent. *Ibid.,* Senate (April 19, 20, 1816), pp. 331, 334.

[149] Lowndes, Miller and Woodward opposed. All others favored the bill for national internal improvements. *Ibid.,* House, 2nd Sess. (February 8, 1817), p. 934. In the senate, both Gaillard and William Smith, who had succeeded Taylor, voted against the measure. *Ibid.,* Senate (February 27, 28, 1817), pp. 187, 191.

[150] Charles Maurice Wiltse, *The Jeffersonian Tradition in American Democracy* (Chapel Hill: University of North Carolina Press, 1935), p. 5.

and far beyond 1816. But the limitations of time and space as well as the academic practice of writing history in periods, necessitates a beginning and an ending of every study.

Since the Jeffersonian movement in South Carolina gained its immediate impulse from the conditions which existed during the Revolutionary epoch and the formative years of the new nation, it has been necessary to devote some attention to the culture of the state and to the events which preceded the formation of clearly defined political parties. Throughout the study an effort has been made to show how Jeffersonian Democracy affected South Carolina; but, in order to maintain a proper perspective, a large portion of the discussion has centered around the part that South Carolinians played in the developments which concerned the whole nation.

The evaluation of Jeffersonian Democracy through the consideration of "what has followed" in South Carolina must be the task of another, one who will carefully gather and interpret the evidence relating to the succeeding years. No serious student of history will dare to base his appraisal upon speculation or even general knowledge. It can be said, however, that, while the Republican party was evolving into the Democratic party of a later day, less immediate evolution took place in South Carolina than in the nation at large, for her particular economic system had already developed over most of her area and was fast becoming mature and solidified. After the state had gone far toward the erection of what might have served as the political, social and educational framework of a democratic structure, economic forces delayed the work of the builders. In truth, South Carolina was inclined to return to the form, if not the spirit, of early Jeffersonian Republicanism, which for the time was more to her liking than the new Democratic impulses. The democratic structure in South Carolina has never been completed. But no higher testimonial to the lasting influence of Jeffersonian ideals upon the people of the state can be written than the simple statement that men still struggle for their fulfillment.

BIBLIOGRAPHY

Primary Materials

Manuscripts

(A) Manuscripts in the Library of Congress:

Ralph Izard Papers. Letters between Izard and his wife, Alice Delancey Izard, and the correspondence of Mrs. Izard after her husband's death, 388 pieces, 1792-1814.

Robert Goodloe Harper Papers. Letters of public leaders to Harper and photostatic copies of his letters to his constituents, 1796-1801.

Thomas Jefferson Papers. Letters between Jefferson and most of the South Carolina public leaders.

James Madison Papers. The correspondence between Madison and South Carolina political leaders.

Robert Mills Papers. Miscellaneous letters, some of which are to Jefferson and to South Carolinians, 1807-1857.

James Monroe Papers. The correspondence between Monroe and South Carolina officials and leaders.

Charles Pinckney to Matthew Carey, August 10, 1788. A letter in regard to the "Pinckney Plan."

Charles Cotesworth Pinckney to John B. Wallace of Philadelphia, August 24, 1812. A letter dealing with the approaching Presidential election.

A Memoir of the Pinckney Family of South Carolina drawn from the Family Records and Communicated by William Gilmore Simms, 13 pp. Incomplete, dealing largely with Charles Cotesworth and Thomas Pinckney.

William Loughton Smith Papers. Letters from important men 1793-1806.

Thomas Sumter Papers. Largely letters to Sumter and a few broadsides issued to his constituents.

Thomas Tudor Tucker Papers. Letters to John Page, 1791-1808.

(B) Manuscript Collections of the South Carolina Historical Commission:

Journals of the House of Representatives of the State of South Carolina, 1787-1817.

Journals of the Senate of South Carolina, 1787-1817.

Contemporary Newspapers[1]

Carolina Gazette (Charleston), 1801-1816, the weekly edition of the *City Gazette*.
Charleston Courier, 1803-1817.
City Gazette (Charleston), 1788-1817.
Columbian Herald (Charleston), 1787-1796.
Georgetown Gazette, 1798-1800.
Investigator (Charleston), 1810-1813.
Niles' Weekly Register (Baltimore), 1811-1817.
Southern Patriot (Charleston), 1815-1817.
State Gazette of South Carolina (Charleston), 1788-1794.
South Carolina State Gazette (Charleston), 1795-1802.
Strength of the People (Charleston), June 24, 1809.
Telescope (Columbia), 1815-1816.
Times (Charleston), 1800-1813; 1816.

Official Reports, Debates, Proceedings, and Public Documents

American State Papers, Foreign Relations, Washington: Gales and Seaton, 1833, vols. I-III.
Biographical Directory of the American Congress 1774-1927.
House Document No. 783, Sixty-ninth Congress, Second Session. Washington: Government Printing Office, 1928.
Cooper, Thomas and McCord, D. J., ed., *Statutes at Large of South Carolina,* Columbia: A. S. Johnston, 1836-1841, 10 vols.
Debates and Proceedings In The Congress of the United States; with an Appendix Containing Important State Papers and Public Documents, and all the Laws of a Public Nature; With a Copious Index, Washington: Gales and Seaton, 1834-1854.
Debates Which arose in the House of Representatives of South Carolina on the Constitution Framed for the United States By a Convention of Delegates Assembled at Philadelphia Together with Such notices of the Convention as Could be Procured, Charleston: A. C. Miller, 1831.
Salley, A. S., Jr., ed., *Journal of the Convention of South Carolina Which Ratified the Constitution of the United States,* May 23, 1788, Atlanta: Foote and Davies, 1928.

Contemporary Speeches, Addresses, Sermons, Newspaper Articles, and Pamphlets

Charleston Library Society Collection:
Beresford, Richard, *Aristocracy the Bane of Liberty; Learning the Antidote Designed to Recommend The General Estab-*

---
[1] Dates of newspapers indicate the files used.

lishment of Free Schools and Colleges in Republicks, Charleston: W. P. Young, 1797. Series I, vol. XII, no. 7½.

[DeSaussure, Henry W.], *Address To The Citizens of South Carolina on the Approaching Election of President and Vice-President of The United States,* Charleston: W. P. Young, 1800. Series 5, vol. I, no. 6.

DeSaussure, Henry William, *Letters on the Questions of The Expediency of Going into Alterations of the Representation in the Legislature of South Carolina, as Fixed by The Constitution,* Charleston: Markland & McIver, 1795. Series 3, vol. VI.

Fourth of July Orations 1812-1824. Series 4, vol. XVIII.

[Ford, Timothy], *The Constitutionalist, or an Enquiry How Far It is Expedient and Proper to Alter The Constitution of South Carolina,* Charleston: Markland & McIver, 1794. Series 3, vol. VI, no. 8.

Furman, Richard, *A Sermon Occasioned by the Death of the Honorable Major General Alexander Hamilton; Preached at Charleston, South Carolina, the Fifteenth Day of August, 1804, Before the State Society of the Cincinnati, the American Revolution Society and a Numerous Assemblage of Other Citizens,* Charleston: W. P. Young, 1804. Series 1, vol. I, no. 3.

[Harper, R. G.], *An Address To the People of South Carolina by the General Committee of the Representative Reform Association at Columbia,* Charleston: W. P. Young, 1794. Series 3, vol. XI, no. 1.

M'Leod, Donald, *A Sermon Preached in the Presbyterian Church of Edisto-Island, on the Eleventh of March, 1812. Being the Day Appointed For Religious Reflection, Humiliation and Prayer By the Proclamation of His Excellency Henry Middleton, Governor of South Carolina,* Charleston: E. Morford, Willington & Co., 1812. Series 1, vol. I, no. 7.

Member of Old Congress, *Sketches of French and English Politics in America in May 1797,* Charleston: W. P. Young, 1797. Series 3, vol. XIII, no. 2.

Moultrie, Alexander, *An Appeal to the People on the Conduct of a Certain Public Body in South Carolina Respecting Col. Drayton and Col. Moultrie,* Charleston: Markland, McIver & Co., 1794. Series 3, vol. XI, no. 2.

"A Native of South Carolina," *The Tocsin: or The Call To Arms! An Essay; Being an Enquiry into the Late Proceedings of Great Britain, In Her Unjustifiable Attack Upon the Liberty and Independence of the United States of America,* Charleston: J. Hoff, 1807. Series 3, vol. XII, no. 19.

Pinckney, Charles, *Three Letters, Written, and Originally Published under the Signature of a South Carolina Planter. The First, on the Case of Jonathan Robbins; the Second, on the Recent Capture of American Vessels by British Cruisers; the Third, on the Right of Expatriation,* Philadelphia: Aurora-Office, 1799. Series 3, vol. XII, no. 6.

[Smith, William Loughton], *The Numbers of Phocian, Which Were Originally Published in the Charleston Courier, in 1800 on the Subject of Neutral Rights,* Charleston: Courier Office, 1806. Series 3, vol. IV, no. 8.

Published Works—Correspondence, Speeches, Memoirs, Travel Accounts, and Histories

Adams, Charles Francis, ed., *The Works of John Adams, Second President of the United States; with A Life of the Author, Notes and Illustrations by His Grandson,* Little, Brown and Co., 1856, 10 vols.

Adams, Henry, ed., *The Writings of Albert Gallatin,* Philadelphia: J. B. Lippincott & Co., 1879, 3 vols.

American Remembrancer or an Impartial Collection of Essays, Resolves, Speeches, &c., Relative, or Having Affinity to the Treaty with Great Britain, edited by Henry Tuckniss, Philadelphia: Mathew Carey, 1795.

Asbury, Francis, *The Journal of The Rev. Francis Asbury, Bishop of the Methodist Episcopal Church, From Aug. 7, 1771, to December 7, 1815,* New York: N. Bangs and T. Mason, 1821, 3 vols.

Bartram, William, *Travels Through North & South Carolina, Georgia, East & West Florida, The Cherockee County, the Extensive Territories of the Muscogulges, or Creek Confederacy, and the Choctaws,* Philadelphia: James & Johnson, 1791.

Bergh, Albert Ellery, ed., *The Writings of Thomas Jefferson Definitive Edition,* Washington: 1907, 20 vols.

Ford, Paul Leicester, ed., *Essays on the Constitution of The United States Published During Its Discussion By the People 1787-1788,* Brooklyn, N. Y., Historical Printing Club, 1892.

Ford, Paul Leicester, ed., *The Writings of Thomas Jefferson,* New York: G. P. Putnam's Sons, 1892-1899, 10 vols.

Ford, Timothy, "Diary of Timothy Ford 1785-1786," in *South Carolina Historical and Genealogical Magazine,* Vol. XIII, 1912.

Ford, Worthington Chauncey, ed., *Writings of John Quincy Adams,* New York: Macmillan, 1913, vols. I-VII.

JEFFERSONIAN DEMOCRACY IN S. C.

Ford, Worthington Chauncey, ed., *The Writings of George Washington*, New York: G. P. Putnam's Sons, 1889-1893, 14 vols.
Fraser, Charles, *Reminiscences of Charleston, 1785-1854*, Charleston: John Russel, 1854.
Gibbs, George, ed., *Memoirs of the Administration of Washington and John Adams*, New York: William Van Norden, 1846, 2 vols.
Hamilton, John C., ed., *The Works of Alexander Hamilton*, New Work: Charles C. Francis & Co., 1851, 7 vols.
Hamilton, J. G. de Roulhac, ed., *The Best Letters of Thomas Jefferson*, Boston and New York: Houghton Mifflin, 1926.
Hamilton, Stanislaus Murray, ed., *The Writings of James Monroe*, New York: G. P. Putnam's Sons, 1898-1903, 7 vols.
Harper, Robert Goodloe, *Select Works of Robert Goodloe Harper: Consisting of Speeches on Political and Forensic Subjects with the Answer Drawn up by Him to the Articles of Impeachment Against Judge Chase, and Sundry Political Tracts Collated from the Original and Carefully revised*, Baltimore: O. H. Neilson, 1814.
Hunt, Gaillard, ed., *The Writings of James Madison*, New York: G. P. Putnam's Sons, 1900-1910, 9 vols.
Lodge, Henry Cabot, ed., *The Works of Alexander Hamilton*, New York: G. P. Putnam's Sons, 12 vols.
Maclay, William, *Journal of*, edited by Edgar S. Maclay, New York: D. Appleton and Co., 1890.
Phillips, U. B., ed., "South Carolina Federalist Correspondence, 1789-1797," *American Historical Review*, vol. XIV, (1900).
Plumer, William, *Memorandum of the Proceedings in the United States Senate, 1803-1807*, edited by E. S. Brown, New York: Macmillan, 1923.
Ramsay, David, *The History of South Carolina from its First Settlement in 1670 to the Year 1808*, Charleston: David Longworth, 1809, 2 vols.
Smith, William Loughton, *Journal of*, edited by Albert Matthews, Cambridge, Mass.: the University Press, 1917.
Smyth, J. F. D., *A Tour in the United States of America*, Dublin: G. Perrin, 1784. 2 vols.
Sparks, Jared, ed., *The Writings of George Washington*, Boston: American Stationer's Co., 1837, 12 vols.
Thomas, E. S., *Reminiscences of the Last Sixty-Five Years*, Hartford: Case, Tiffany and Burnham, 1840, 2 vols.
Turner, Frederick J., ed., "The Mangourit Correspondence in Respect to Genêt's Projected Attack upon the Floridas, 1793-94," *Annual Report of the American Historical Association, 1897.*

Warden, D. B., *A Statistical, Political, and Historical Account of the United States of North America; from the Period of Their First Colonization to the Present Day,* Edinburgh: Archibald Constable and Co., 1819.

Van Doren, Mark, ed., *Correspondence of Aaron Burr and His Daughter Theodosia,* New York: Covici-Friede, 1929.

Winterbotham, W., *An Historical, Geographical, Commercial, and Philosophical View of the American United States, and of the European Settlements in America and the West-Indies,* London: I. Ridgway, 1795, 4 vols.

SECONDARY MATERIALS

Monographs, Biographies, Special Studies and General Works Consulted in This Study:

Anderson, D. R., "The Insurgents of 1811," *Annual Report of the American Historical Association,* 1911.

Bacot, D. Huger, "Constitutional Progress and the Struggle for Democracy in South Carolina Following the Revolution," *South Atlantic Quarterly,* vol. XXIV, (Jan., 1925).

Beard, Charles A., *Economic Origins of Jeffersonian Democracy,* New York: Macmillan, 1915.

Bemis, Samuel Flagg, ed., *The American Secretaries of State and Their Diplomacy,* New York: Alfred A. Knopf, 1927-1929, 10 vols.

Bemis, Samuel Flagg, "The London Mission of Thomas Pinckney," *American Historical Review,* XXVIII, 228-247, (January, 1923).

Bemis, Samuel Flagg, *Pinckney's Treaty A Study of America's Advantage from Europe's Distress 1783-1800,* Baltimore: Johns Hopkins Press, 1926.

Bernheim, G. D., *History of The German Settlements and the Lutheran Church in North and South Carolina,* Philadelphia: Lutheran Book Store, 1872.

Boucher, Chauncey Samuel, "Sectionalism, Representation, and the Electoral Question in Ante-Bellum South Carolina," *Washington University Studies,* vol. IV, Part II, no. 1 (October, 1916).

Bowen, W. E., *Charles Pinckney a Forgotten Statesman,* Greenville, S. C., W. E. Bowen, 1928. A copy is in *Pamphlets South Carolina, Biography,* vol. XLIV, University of S. C. Library.

Bowers, Claude G., *Jefferson and Hamilton, the Struggle for Democracy in America,* Boston & New York: Houghton Mifflin, 1925.

JEFFERSONIAN DEMOCRACY IN S. C.   293

Channing, Edward, *A History of the United States,* New York: Macmillan, 1905-1925, 6 vols.

Chinard, Gilbert, *Thomas Jefferson, the Apostle of Americanism,* Boston: Little, Brown and Co., 1929.

Clark, W. A., *The History of the Banking Institutions Organized in South Carolina Prior to 1860,* Columbia, S. C.: the State Co., 1922.

Cook, Harvey Toliver, *The Life and Legacy of David Rogerson Williams,* New York: Country Life Press, 1916.

Chreitzberg, Rev. A. M., *Early Methodism in The Carolinas,* Nashville: Publishing House of the Methodist Episcopal Church, 1897.

Easterby, J. H., *History of the St. Andrew's Society of Charleston South Carolina,* 1729-1929, Charleston: Walker, Evans & Cogswell, 1929.

Elliott, W. S., *Hon. Charles Pinckney, Lld., of South Carolina,* a copy in *Pamphlets, 5th Series,* vol. XI, no. XI. Charleston Library Society.

Elzas, Barnett A., *The Jews of South Carolina from their Earliest Times to the Present Day,* Philadelphia: J. B. Lippincott, 1905.

French, Carrie Isabel, "The Early Political, Economic and Social Philosophy of Thomas Jefferson," M.A. thesis, University of Chicago, 1932.

Gilpatrick, Delbert Harold, *Jeffersonian Democracy in North Carolina 1789-1816,* New York: Columbia University Press, 1931.

Gregg, Alexander, *History of the Old Cheraws,* Columbia: the State Co., 1905, reprint of 1867 edition.

Gregorie, Anne King, *Thomas Sumter,* Columbia: R. L. Bryan Co., 1931.

Guilday, Peter, *The Life and Times of John English First Bishop of Charleston 1786-1842,* New York: The American Press, 1927, 2 vols.

Green, Fletcher M., *Constitutional Development in the South Atlantic States, 1776-1860. A Study in the Evolution of Democracy,* Chapel Hill: The University of North Carolina Press, 1930.

Hamilton, J. G. de Roulhac, "Jefferson's Americanism," *Virginia Quarterly Review,* 117-122 (January, 1930).

Hamilton, J. G. de Roulhac, "Jefferson and Religion," *The Reviewer,* 5-15 (October, 1925).

Harper, William, *Memoir of the Life, Character, and Public Service of the Late Hon. Henry Wm. DeSaussure, Prepared and Read on 15th February, 1841 at the Circular Church, Charleston, by Appointment of the South Carolina Bar Association,* Charleston: W. Riley, 1841, a copy in Pamphlets of Charleston Library Society, series 2, vol. V, no. 7.

Haskell, Louisa P., "Langdon Cheves and the United States Bank: A Study from Neglected Sources," *Annual Report of the American Historical Association,* 1896, I, 361-371.

Henry, H. M., *The Police Control of the Slave in South Carolina,* Emory, Virginia: 1914.

Jameson, J. Franklin, "The Federal Convention of 1787," *Annual Report of the American Historical Association 1912,* I, 87-167.

Jameson, J. Franklin, "Portions of Charles Pinckney's Plan for a Constitution, 1787," *American Historical Review,* VIII, 509-511 (April, 1903).

Jennings, Walter Wilson, *The American Embargo 1807-1809,* Iowa City: the University of Iowa, 1921.

Jervey, Theodore D., *The Slave Trade, Slavery and Color,* Columbia: the State Co., 1925.

Johnson, Guion Griffis, *A Social History of The Sea Islands with Special Reference to St. Helena Island, South Carolina,* Chapel Hill: University of North Carolina Press, 1930.

Jones, F. D., and Mills, W. H., eds., *History of the Presbyterian Church in South Carolina since 1850,* Columbia: R. L. Bryan, 1926.

Kirkland, Thomas J., and Kennedy, Robert M., *Historic Camden,* Columbia: the State Co., 1905 and 1906, 2 vols.

La Borde, M., *History of the South Carolina College from Its Incorporation December 19, 1801, to Nov. 25, 1857, Including Sketches of Its Presidents and Professors,* Columbia: Peter B. Gloss, 1859.

Lesesne, Thomas Petigru, *History of Charleston County South Carolina, Narrative and Biographical,* Charleston: A. H. Cawston, 1931.

Libby, Orin Grant, "The Geographical Distribution of the vote of the Thirteen States on the Federal Constitution, 1787-8," *Bulletin of the University of Wisconsin, Economics, Political Science and History Series,* vol. I, no. 1.

McGlothlin, W. J., *Baptist Beginning in Education: A History of Furman University,* Nashville: Sunday School Board of the Southern Baptist Convention, 1926.

McLaughlin, A. C., "Sketch of Pinckney's Plan for a Constitution, 1787," *American Historical Review*, IX, 735-747 (July, 1904).

McMaster, J. B., *History of the People of the United States from the Revolution to the Civil War*, New York: D. Appleton & Co., 1883-1913, 8 vols.

Mills, Robert, *Statistics of South Carolina, Including a View of Its Natural, Civil, and Military History, General and Particular*, Charleston: Hurlbut and Lloyd, 1826.

Mood, Rev. F. A., *Methodism in Charleston: A Narrative of the Chief Events Relating to the Rise and Progress of the Methodist Episcopal Church in Charleston, S. C. with Brief Notices of the Early Ministers who Labored in That City*, Nashville: A. H. Raeford, 1875.

Morrison, Samuel Eliot, *The Life and Letters of Harrison Gray Otis, Federalist 1765-1848*, Boston & New York: Houghton Mifflin, 1913, 2 vols.

Muzzey, David Saville, *Thomas Jefferson*, New York: Charles Scribner's Sons, 1918.

Nott, Charles C., *The Mystery of the Pinckney Draught*, New York: Century, 1908.

O'Neall, John Belton, *Biographical Sketches of The Bench and Bar of South Carolina*, Charleston: S. G. Courtenay & Co., 1859, 2 vols.

Perry, Benjamin Franklin, *Reminiscences of Public Men*, Philadelphia: John D. Avil & Co., 1883.

Perry, Benjamin Franklin, *Reminiscences of Public Men, with Speeches and Addresses Second Series*, Greenville, S. C.: Shannon & Co., 1889.

Phillips, U. B., "The South Carolina Federalists," *American Historical Review (1901)*, XIV, 529-543, 731-745.

Pierson, W. W., Jr., "The Sovereign State of North Carolina 1787-1789," *Proceedings of the Seventeenth Annual Session of the State Literary and Historical Association of North Carolina*, 1916, pp. 58-69, Raleigh: Edwards & Broughton Printing Co., 1917.

Pinckney, Rev. Charles Cotesworth, *Life of General Thomas Pinckney*, Boston and New York: Houghton Mifflin, 1895.

Pratt, Julius W., *Expansionists of 1812*, New York: Macmillan, 1925.

Randall, Henry Stephens, *The Life of Thomas Jefferson*, New York: Derby and Jackson, 1858, 3 vols.

Ravenel, Mrs. St. Julien, *Charleston the Place and the People*, New York: Macmillan, 1912.

Ravenel, Mrs. St. Julien, *Life and Times of William Lowndes of South Carolina 1782-1822*, Boston & New York: Houghton Mifflin, 1901.
Salley, A. S., Jr., "A Century of The Courier," *Centennial Edition of the News and Courier*, Charleston: 1903.
Schaper, William A., "Sectionalism and Representation in South Carolina," *American Historical Association Annual Report 1900*, I, 237-463.
Sears, Louis Martin, *A History of American Foreign Relations*, New York: Thomas Y. Crowell, 1927.
Sears, Louis Martin, *Jefferson and the Embargo*, Durham: Duke University Press, 1927.
Sears, Louis Martin, "The South and the Embargo," *South Atlantic Quarterly*, XX, 254-275 (July, 1921).
Shipp, Rev. Albert M., *The History of Methodism in South Carolina*, Nashville: Southern Methodist Publishing House, 1883.
Stephenson, N. W., "Calhoun, 1812, and After," *American Historical Review*, XXI, 701-707 (1926).
Townsend, Leah, "South Carolina Baptists 1670-1800," doctoral dissertation, University of S. C., 1929.
Tuomey, M., *Report on the Geology of South Carolina*, Columbia: 1848.
Walker, C. Irvine, *History of the Agricultural Society of South Carolina Founded Aug. 24th 1785 at Charles Town, S. C.*, n.p. (1919).
Wagstaff, Henry McGilbert, "State Rights and Political Parties in North Carolina 1776-1861," *John Hopkins University Studies in Historical and Political Sciences*, Series XXIV, nos. 7-8, Baltimore: the Johns Hopkins Press, 1906.
Wallace, David Duncan, *The Historical Background of Religion in South Carolina, 1916*, copy is in *Pamphlets South Carolina*, vol. 27, University of South Carolina Library.
Wallace, David Duncan, *History of South Carolina*, New York: American Historical Society, Inc., 1934, 4 vols.
Wallace, David Duncan, *Life of Henry Laurens*, New York: G. P. Putnam's Sons, 1915.
Wallace, David Duncan, "The South Carolina Constitution of 1895," *Bulletin of the University of South Carolina no. 197*, Columbia: 1927.
Wauchope, George Armstrong, "Literary South Carolina, a Short Account of the Progress of Literature and the Principal Writers and Books from 1700 to 1923," *Bulletin of the University of South Carolina no. 133*, Columbia: 1923.

Whitaker, Arthur Preston, *The Spanish-American Frontier: 1783-1795, the Westward Movement and the Spanish Retreat in the Mississippi Valley,* Boston and New York: Houghton Mifflin, 1927.
Wightman, William M., *Life of William Capers, D.D., One of the Bishops of the Methodist Episcopal Church, South; Including an Autobiography,* Nashville: Publishing House of the M. E. Church, South, Barbee & Smith, Agents, 1896.
Willis, Eola, *The Charleston Stage in the XVIII Century,* Columbia: the State Co., 1924.
Wiltse, Charles Maurice, *The Jeffersonian Tradition in American Democracy,* Chapel Hill: University of North Carolina Press, 1935.

INDEX

Adams, John, Vice-President, 55; incensed at support of Thomas Pinckney for President, 99; becomes President, 102; proposes preparedness measures, 104-105; opposes war, 107; informs Congress of "X.Y.Z." affair, 109; criticized by Hamilton, 146-147.

Adams, John Quincy, minister to Berlin, 110 n.

Agricultural Society of South Carolina, formation and early work, 18-19.

Alien Act, passage, 116-117; effects of discussed in Congress, 124-126; negative reaction to in South Carolina, 128.

Alston, Joseph, elected speaker of South Carolina house of representatives, 211; alleged connection with Burr conspiracy, 212; favors reform in basis of representation, 218; elected governor, 263; personal misfortunes, 268 n.; intense factionalism of his administration, 268-273.

Alston, Lemuel J., elected to Congress, accused of Federalist tendencies, 210-211; defeated by Earle, 241.

Andrews, Loring, editor of *Charleston Courier*, 182 n.

Anderson, Robert, investigates Genêt affair, 74-75; active in election of 1800, 155-159.

Aristocracy, controls state government, 6, 13, 49; approved by William Loughton Smith, 81-82.

Aurora, editor of summoned by senate, 133-134.

Bank of the State of South Carolina, established, 258-259.

Bank of South Carolina, established, 66-67.

Bank of the United States, First, votes of South Carolina representatives on, 65-66 n.; branch established in Charleston, 66-67; opposition to its policies, 66.

Bank of the United States, Second, established, 284.

Benton, Lemuel, elected to Congress, 70; habit of appearing late, 103 n.; attacked by Federalists, defeated, 122-123.

Barnwell, Robert, favors ratification of federal Constitution, 30.

Burke, Aedanus, describes economic conditions, 13; opposes ratification of federal Constitution, 36, 38; writes against Society of Cincinnati, 41; sketch of early life, 41 n.; favors low tariff, 58; opposes early action on amendments, 59-60; opposes bank, 66 n.; advises Jefferson through Madison on appointments, 169-170.

Burr, Aaron, candidate for Vice-President, 136; supported by some Federalists for President, 161-162; alleged conspiracy, 212.

Burr, Theodosia, marries Joseph Alston, 211-212; lost at sea, 268 n.

Butler, Pierce, delegate to federal convention, 22; favors ratification of Constitution, 27; takes senate seat late, 54; opposes high tariff and tonnage duties, 59; sends Madison copy of Jay Treaty secretly, 83; opposes ratification of Jay Treaty, 83; eulogized, 85-86; regrets letter introducing Harper to Madison, 87-88 n.; warns Madison of political plot against him, 94; resigns from senate, 98; advises Jefferson on appointments, 169-170.

Butler, William, elected to Congress, 156.

[299]

Calhoun, John C., elected to Congress, 241; early career, 244 n.; emphasizes patriotism and American rights, 245; insists upon preparedness, 249; criticizes Madison, 252 n., 265 n.; hopes United States can capture all British provinces in America, 276; reviews nature of the war, 277; evolves extensive plans for the prosecution of the war, 282.

Camden, as seen by foreign visitor in 1784, 9; conditions in during Confederation, 17; school established, 48.

Canada, seizure of suggested by John Taylor, 234; by Williams, 265; by Calhoun, 276; by Cheves for temporary military advantages, 276; declared not to be cause of war by Calhoun, 277.

Carpenter, Stephen Cullen, connection with *Charleston Courier*, 183 n.; attacked by Republicans, 198, 199.

Caucus, opposed as method of nominating candidates, 259.

Charleston, as seen by a foreign visitor in 1784, 9; description of by Timothy Ford in 1785-1786, 10-11; chosen as meeting place for ratifying convention, 33; called Jacobinical, 233; citizens of demand preparedness, 247-248.

Charleston Courier, Federalist newspaper, established, 182; general policy, 183-184; favors purchase of Louisiana, 184-185, 186; less favorable to purchase, 188; advocates public schools, 175.

Chase, Judge Samuel, impeachment and trial, 178-179.

Chesapeake, attacked by *Leopard,* 215-216.

Cheves, Langdon, elected to Congress, 241; early career, 243 n.; insists upon preparedness, 249; explains nature of federal government, 250-251; favors large navy, 251; criticizes Gallatin, 264-265; ridicules opponents of the war, 266; called "political Jesuit," 269; favors attacking Canada for military advantages, 276; speaker of federal house of representatives, 281.

Cincinnati, Society of, opposition to, 41.

City Gazette, Republican newspaper, friendly to France, 102.

Coastal region, physical features of, 2.

Columbia, becomes Capital, 45; description of town in 1790, 45 n.

Confederation, economic disorganization during, 15-19; as possible agency in economic improvement, 19; praised by Rawlins Lowndes, 31.

Constitution of 1776, South Carolina, general character of, 43.

Constitution of 1778, South Carolina, general character of, 43-44.

Constitution of 1790, South Carolina, a summary of, 44-47.

Constitution of the United States, delegates to convention elected, 22; contributions of South Carolinians to, 22-24; discussion of in newspapers, 24-26; debate in legislature, 26-33; ratified, 36-37; amendments proposed, 37; opposition to Constitution, 38; early action on amendments favored and opposed, 59-60.

Constitutional reform, dominant issue after 1790, 5-6.

Cooper, Thomas, criticizes Federalists, 195.

Colhoun, John Ewing, elected to senate, 157; opposes repeal of Judiciary Act of 1801, 176.

Crafts, William, supports public schools, 176.

Culture, South Carolina, varying elements of, 4-13; societies in up country and low country, 8-13. *See* population, sectionalism, up country, and low country.

INDEX 301

Democracy, early strivings in South Carolina, 40; opposition to aristocracy, 49; Jeffersonian principles, 166-168; not realized but still sought, 288. *See* suffrage, Republican Party, Federalist Party, party politics.

Democratic societies, formed, 75 n.

DeSaussure, Henry William, opposes change in basis of representation in state legislature, 6 n., 51-52; writes pamphlet in support of John Adams, 149-151; thinks compromise with Republicans in election of 1800 possible, 158 n.; "inaccuracy of memory" as to opposition to South Carolina College, 173 n.

Dollard, Patrick, opposes ratification of federal constitution, 36.

Drayton, John, elected governor, 171; recommends establishment of schools and colleges, 172; South Carolina College established, 173.

Earle, Elias, member of Congress, defeated by Lemuel J. Alston, 210-211; defeats Alston, 241.

Economic conditions, after Revolution, 15-19; during War of 1812, 258-259. *See* Embargo.

Education, early schools, 48-49; arguments for public schools, 171-172; "free school system" begun, 175-176. *See* South Carolina College.

Election, of 1789, 43, 43 n.; of 1792, 69-70; of 1796, 95-99; of 1798, 121-124; of 1800, 135-165; of 1802, 181-182; of 1804, 197-198; of 1806, 210-212; of 1808, 227-232; of 1810, 240-241; of 1812, 259-263; of 1814, 279-280; of 1816, 285.

Elliot, Stephen, favors public schools, 175.

Embargo, passage of, 217-218; economic effect upon South Carolina, 220-221; described by Wade Hampton, 222; approved by South Carolina house of representatives, 224; condemned by *Charleston Courier*, 231-232; special efforts to enforce it, 232-233; difficult to enforce, 237-238.

Excise Act, opposed in South Carolina, 67; repealed by Republicans, 177.

Farrow, Samuel, member of Congress, opposes moving government from Washington, 280.

Federalist Party, slight gains in 1798, 121-124; sponsors defense measures, 129-130; division in party, 145-148; losses in 1800, 156-157; opposes repeal of Judiciary Act, 176; members of ask Jefferson for information concerning Louisiana, 185; denounced for claiming credit for military and naval victories, 279 n.; nominates its last Presidential candidate, 285.

Florida, acquisition favored by *Charleston Courier*, 188; opposed by Sumter, 204-205; seizure advocated by Williams, 265.

Ford, Timothy, describes South Carolina culture in 1785-1786, 10-13; opposes constitutional changes, 50.

Foreign affairs, early state inclinations, 20-21; influence upon American politics, 71. *See* Great Britain, France, French Revolution.

France, sympathy for, 71 ff.; French theatre established, 78; reaction against, 119-120. *See* French Revolution, Genêt.

French Revolution, early approval of, 71; supporting societies formed, 72; general approval, 76; "X. Y. Z." affair, 108-116. *See* Genêt.

Freneau, Peter, co-publisher of *City Gazette*, 182 n.

Freneau, Phillip, recommended for appointment by Burke, 169 n.

INDEX

Gadsden, Christopher, opinion of federal Constitution, 25; opposes state constitutional changes, 46-47; favors a positive commercial policy, 120-121; pessimistic about general conditions, 165.

Gaillard, John, senator, opposes conviction of Judge Chase, 179; votes for Non-Intercourse Act, 206.

Gaillard, Theodore, considered for Supreme Court, 196.

Gallatin, Albert, defends French against attacks of South Carolina Federalists, 105; opinion of Charles Pinckney, 223 n.; estimates of ridiculed by *Charleston Courier*, 248-249; criticized by Cheves, 264-265.

"Geffroy Letters," said to have been written by John Rutledge, Jr., 179-181.

Genêt, Citizen, reception in South Carolina, 73; plans for expeditions thwarted, 74-75.

Gillon, Commodore, favors ratification of federal Constitution, 30-31; opposes stamp duties, 77.

Governor, powers of, 45-46.

Great Britain, early opposition to, 20-21; educational and commercial ties with, 71; friendly demonstrations toward, 76; defended by William Loughton Smith in *Phocian Letters*, 206-209; severely denounced by David R. Williams, 250.

Hamilton, Alexander, Secretary of the Treasury, report of on debts, 56; secures appointment as second in command of army, 115; advises Federalists to encourage Burr but vote for Jefferson, 162, 162 n.

Hamilton, Paul, elected governor, 197; resigns as Secretary of the Navy, 265 n.

Hampton, Wade, forbidden permission to carry slaves through South Carolina, 189 n.; gives Jefferson advice on patronage, 196; describes effects of Embargo, 222.

Harper, Robert Goodloe, favors reform in basis of representation in state legislature, 6 n.; sponsors constitutional reform, 49; approves Jay Treaty, 87-89; denies early Jacobinism, 87 n., 111-112; given letter of introduction to Madison by Pierce Butler, 87 n.; ablest debater and pamphleteer in house of representatives, 104; denounces French, 105; arrogant and intolerant attitude, 110-111, 112-113; insists that war already exists with France, 114-115; urges Hamilton to become Secretary of War, 115; fails to get military appointment, 116; obsessed with opposition to foreign born, 116; favors Sedition Act, 117-118; changes residence to Maryland, 129; valedictory to constituents, 164-165.

Hartford Convention, reception of news of in South Carolina, 283.

High Hills of Santee, location of and origin of term, 3 n.

Huger, Benjamin, Federalist, member of Congress, 123; opposes repeal of Judiciary Act, 176; joins Republicans in repealing Excise Act, 177; part in election of 1800, 162.

Huger, Daniel Elliot, Federalist, supports War of 1812, 268.

Hunter, John, opposes censure of "self-created" societies, 81; disapproves of Adams administration, 105; favors defense of American commerce, 118; part in election of 1800, 158, 158 n.

Inflation, as means of improving economic conditions during Confederation, 15-19.

Inhabitants. *See* population.

Internal improvements, 1817, supported, 284-285.

INDEX 303

Investigator, Republican newspaper, established, 259-260.

Izard, Ralph, opposes democracy, 13, 13 n.; senator, 54; discusses titles and ceremonies, 55-56; criticized by Jefferson, 69; favors confirmation of John Rutledge as Chief Justice, 91 n.

Jay, John, plans for temporary surrender of commercial rights on Mississippi opposed by Southerners, 20; appointment as special minister to Great Britain criticized, 82-83. *See* Jay Treaty.

Jay Treaty, storm of protest in South Carolina, 82-92; copy sent Madison secretly by Pierce Butler, 83; ratified, 83 n.

Jefferson, Thomas, early letters to South Carolinians, 14 n.; views on ratification of federal Constitution, 33, 37 n.; early reception of Jeffersonian doctrines in South Carolina, 41; urges Edward Rutledge to accept federal appointment, 61-62; criticizes William Loughton Smith and Ralph Izard, 67-68; friendly correspondence with Thomas Pinckney, 106; nominated for President, 136; secures electoral vote of South Carolina, 158; elected President, 162; congratulated by groups in Charleston and Columbia, 162-164; appointments in South Carolina, 168-171; policies of approved by South Carolina house of representatives, 187; policies opposed by *Charleston Courier,* 195. *See* Jeffersonian Democracy, Federalist Party, Republican Party, Party Politics, Election of 1800.

Jeffersonian Democracy, principles of, 166-168; men still strive for its accomplishment, 288.

John Adams, sloop-of-war, built in South Carolina, 121.

Johnson, William, Republican, speaker of state house of representatives, 123; appointed Associate Justice of Supreme Court by Jefferson, 196.

Judiciary Act of 1801, supported by South Carolina Federalists, 164; repealed, 176-177.

Kentucky Resolutions, negative reaction to in South Carolina, 128 n.

Laurens, Henry, favors federal constitutional convention, 21; declines to act as delegate to the convention, 22 n.; opinion of the new Constitution, 24.

Leopard, attacks *Chesapeake,* 215-216.

Lincoln, James, opposes ratification of federal Constitution, 32.

Livingston, Edward, Republican member of Congress, leads discussion of Jonathan Robbins case, 132-133.

Lotteries, prizes offered, 235-236.

Louisiana, purchase of, 184-188; approved by state house of representatives and various groups, 187-188.

Low country, South Carolina, society of in 1785, 11-13; opposes constitutional changes, 44-47; considers up country not educated enough for political power, 171; loses control of house of representatives, 219-220.

Lowndes, Rawlins, most persistent opponent of ratification of federal Constitution, 28, 29, 30, 31-32.

Lowndes, Thomas, Federalist, opposes changes sought by Republicans, 177-178.

Lowndes, Williams, Republican, elected to Congress, 241; early career of, 243 n.; insists upon preparedness, 249; favors large navy, 251; pessimistic as to condition of country, 252 n.; opposes expansion, 266.

Lower pine belt, physical features of, 2.

Maclay, William, quoted on first Congress, 55 n., 59.
Macon's Bill No. 2, passed, 238.
Madison, James, societies bearing his name formed, 80; receives copy of Jay Treaty secretly from Pierce Butler, 83; warned by Butler of political plot against him, 94; receives electoral vote of South Carolina, 231; policies approved at public meetings, 236-237; loses support in South Carolina, 242-243.
Mangourit, A. B., French consul in Charleston during Genêt episode, 72-73.
Manufacturing, encouraged by war, 246 n.
Marion, Robert, Republican, member of Congress, opposes duties on slaves, 190; reelected, 230; retires from Congress, 241.
Middleton, Henry, elected governor, 241; recommends free schools, 175; becomes member of Congress, 279.
Moultrie, William, governor, alleged approval of Genêt's plans, 73; proclamation against Genêt's proposed expeditions, 74.
Monroe, James, minister to France, recalled, 100-101.
Moore, Thomas, Republican, elected to Congress, 156.
Moser, Philip, supports public schools, 176.
Mountains, South Carolina, location and elevation, 4.

Nationalism, apparent tendency toward, 284-285.
Naturalization Act, modified, 177-178.
Non-Importation Act, passed, 205-206.
Nott, Abraham, Federalist, member of Congress, 123; defeated, 156.

Paper money, during Confederation, 15-19.
Parishes, few voters in, 42.
Party politics, background of, 38-39; affiliation af first Congressional delegation, 43 n.; Jay Treaty as issue, 92, 94. *See* election, Federalist Party, Republican Party.
Pendleton, Judge, opposes ratification of federal Constitution, 27, 36.
Phocian Letters, strongest case for Federalist commercial policy, 206-209.
Physiography, South Carolina, geographical features, divisions, 1-4.
Pickens, Andrew, Republican, member of Congress, opposes censure of "self-created" societies, 81; mentioned in 1812 for governor, 263, 263 n.
Pickering, Judge John, impeachment and trial, 178-179.
Piedmont, South Carolina, physical features, 3-4. *See* up country.
Pinckney, Charles, opposes surrender of commercial rights on Missisippi, 20; favors amending Articles, 21; contributions of to federal Constitution, 22-24; favors ratification, 26-27, 34-35, 35-36; first election to legislature, 42; favors state constitutional changes, 44; recommends public education, 48; fails to secure federal appointment under Washington, 62-63; formulation of his political views, 63-65; lack of adequate source material concerning his life, 64 n.; speaks against Jay Treaty, 84-86; elected to United States senate, 123; writes on Jonathan Robbins case, 127-128; presents views of planters, 129; advocates reform of federal judiciary system, 130-131; opposes appointment of Chief Justice to any other office, 131; played up by Republicans, 138-

INDEX

139; attacked by Federalists, 139; principles of, 139 n.; most active Republican in South Carolina, 148; writes pamphlet in support of Jefferson's election, 151-152; debts and personal habits of, 154 n.; consulted by Jefferson on patronage, appointed minister to Spain, 161; returns from Spain, 199; general account of his Spanish mission, 199-201 n.; general characterization of, 201-202 n.; elected governor for fourth term, 211; supports Embargo enforcement, 221, 222-223.

Pinckney, Charles Cotesworth, delegate to federal convention, 22; favors ratification of new Constitution, 27, 33, 36; declines appointment as Supreme Court Justice, 62; declines offer of positions of Secretary of State, Secretary of War, 94; becomes minister plenipotentiary to France, 100; moderate Federalist, 101 n.; refuses to pay French government for recognition, 108-109; agrees to serve under Hamilton in army, 115; welcomed upon his return from France, 126-127; on ticket with Adams, 136; supported by Hamilton for President, 136-137; opposes any connection with Republicans, 139-140; candidate for President, 197 n., 228; thinks Federalists should nominate "satisfactory Democrat," 260.

Pinckney Draught, 23 n., 24 n.

Pinckney, Thomas, governor, 26; declines appointment as federal judge, 61; becomes minister to Great Britain, 63; temporarily superseded by Jay, 82; special minister to Spain, 92; negotiates treaty, 92-93; candidate for Vice-President, favored by Hamilton for President, 95-99; succeeds William Loughton Smith in Congress, 110; not permitted by Congress to accept gifts from Spain, 119; appointed commander of Sixth Military District in War of 1812 by Madison, 256.

Planters' and Mechanics' Bank, established, 239.

Population, South Carolina, national origins, 4-5; in 1790, 5; different interests in up country and low country, 6-14. See up country, low country, sectionalism.

Primogeniture, abolished, 46.

Pringle, John Julius, favors ratification of federal Constitution, 28, 36; considered for Supreme Court, 196; declines position of Attorney General, 197 n.

Ramsay, David, asks Jefferson's aid in publishing French edition of his history, 14 n.; opinion of federal Constitution, 24; contests Congressional seat of William Loughton Smith, 54 n.; opposes British commercial practices, 77; approves purchase of Louisiana, 188.

Randolph, Edmond, Secretary of State, 80.

Read, Jacob, opposes French, 78; favors ratification of Jay Treaty, 83; criticized and hung in effigy, 85-86; supports Adams administration, 105; continues support of Adams, 118; defeated for reelection to senate, 157; fails to secure judgeship offered by Adams, 164 n.

Red hill region, physical features of, 3.

Religion, democratic tendencies in churches, 40-41; disestablishment of Episcopal Church, 44, 46.

Republican Party, connection with "anti-federalists" of 1787-1788, 38-39; makes Jay Treaty a party issue, 92; victories in 1796 of, 95-99; slight losses, 121-124; Jonathan Robbins case as an issue, 127-128; opposes Federalist program of defense, 129; gains in 1800 of, 156-157; opposition of to compromise in 1800 with Federalists, 157 n., 158 n.; repeals Judiciary Act, 176-177; repeals Excise Act, 177; modifies Naturalization Act, 177. *See* Federalist Party, party politics.

Republican societies, formed, 75 n., 79-80.

Robbins, Jonathan, case of, 127-128; reviewed in Congress, 132-133.

Rutledge, Edward, warm friend of Jefferson, 14 n.; favors ratification of federal Constitution, 29-30; declines federal appointments, 61-62; opposes Jay Treaty, 84; supports Jefferson ticket, 96, 98 n.; elected governor, 123-124; death of, 135; political influence of, 135-136.

Rutledge, John, delegate to federal convention, 22; favors ratification of new Constitution, 32; resigns as Supreme Court Judge, 61; appointed Chief Justice of Supreme Court by Washington, 90; opposes Jay Treaty, alleged insanity, rejected by senate, 90-92.

Rutledge, John, Jr., tour of Europe by, 33; correspondence with Jefferson on ratification of Constitution, 33; early sympathy for French Revolution, 71-72; Jefferson elector, 98 n.; becomes Federalist in Congress, 103; favors Adams administration, 105; expects war with France, 110; opposes foreigners, 117; favors Sedition Act, 118; toasted in Orangeburg, 127; supports Judiciary Act of 1801, 176; connection with "Geffroy Letters" and retirement from Congress, 179-181; opposes purchase of Louisiana, 186-188; thinks war with Great Britain probable, 216; delegate to Federalist convention, 228; defeated by Cheves for Congress, 262.

Sand hills, physical features of, 3.

Sectionalism, beginning of in South Carolina, 5; intensification of, 47; decreases after change in basis of representation, 219-220; alleged promotion of in United States by Young Republicans, 244 n.

Sedition Act, passed, 118; effects of discussed in Congress, 124-126; negative reaction in South Carolina, 128.

"Self-Created" Societies, formed in South Carolina, 79-80; condemned by Washington, 80-82; censure of opposed, 81.

Slavery, slave trade reopened, 188-189; carrying slaves through state prohibited, 189 n.; import duty on opposed, 190; extent of trade, 192; slight opposition to slavery, 193-194.

Smith, William, Republican, member of Congress, 103; attacked by Federalists, defeated, 122-123.

Smith, William Loughton, Congressional seat contested by Ramsay, 54 n.; connection of with government securities, 56; opposes salt tax, 58; opposes tax on slaves, 59; favors Bank of the United States, 65-66; advocates extensive powers for federal government and liberal interpretation of Constitution, 66; criticized by Jefferson, 68; supported by Hamilton, 69; becomes staunch defender of British, 76-77, 105; approves aristocracy, 81-82; his life threatened, 82 n.; approves Jay Treaty, 86-87; suggested by Hamilton as possible Secretary of State, 94-95; adds "Loughton" to his name, 103 n.; minister to Portugal and to Spain, 110 n.; writes *Phocian Letters* in support of British

INDEX

commercial policy, 206-209; breaks with Federalists and supports Marion for Congress, 230.

Soil. *See* physiography.

South Carolina, physiography of, 1-4; inhabitants and culture of, 4-13; conditions in during Confederation, 14-21; surrenders tariff rights and claims to Western lands, 21; work of delegates in federal convention, 22-24; ratifies Constitution, 36-37; constitution of 1776, 43; constitution of 1778, 43-44; constitution of 1790, 44-47; education in, 171-176; approves purchase of Louisiana and Jefferson's policies in general, 187; reforms basis of representation in state legislature, 218-220; adopts manhood suffrage, 240; still strives for principles of Jeffersonian democracy, 286.

South Carolina College, establishment of and its early history, 171-174.

South Carolina State Gazette, supports French Revolution, 78-79; opposes Jay and Jay Treaty, 82-83; becomes anti-French, 102.

Stay-laws, during Confederation, 15 n., 16.

State rights, impost right surrendered, 19; claim to Western lands given up, 21; discussion of in first Congress, 59-60; apparent tendency toward nationalism, away from state rights, 284-285.

Suffrage, South Carolina, under constitution of 1790, 46; plural voting, 54; manhood suffrage established, 240.

Sumter, Thomas, opposes ratification of federal Constitution, 36; alleged connection with government securities, 57; favors early action on amendments, 59-60; defeated in 1792, 69-70; defends militia against attacks of Harper, 113-114; attacked by Federalists, reelected, 122-123; opposes Federalist program of defense, 129; elected to senate, 170; favors repeal of Judiciary Act, 176; gives information on patronage, 196; opposes acquisition of Florida, 204-205; opposes Non-Intercourse Act, 206; retires from senate because of illness, 241.

Tariff of 1789, attitude of South Carolinians toward, 57-61.

Tariff of 1816, vote in Congress on, 284.

Taylor, John, favors seizing Canada, 234; denounces Non-Intercourse Act, 237.

Thomas, E. S., bookdealer, 192; aids in establishment of Planters' and Mechanics' Bank, 239; editor of *City Gazette,* warns against British ships, 248; has difficulties with Governor Alston, 269-273.

Times, Republican newspaper, established, 170.

Trezevant, Judge Lewis C., considered by Jefferson for Supreme Court, 196.

Tucker, Thomas Tudor, only South Carolina representative present at opening of first Congress, 54; opposes high tariff, 57-59; opposes Bank of the United States, 66 n.

Tweed, Alexander, professes an open mind on the ratification of the federal Constitution, 35.

Twelfth Amendment, opposed by Pierce Butler, ratified, 194.

Ugly Club, formation and practices of, 41-42.

Up country, description of by foreign visitor in 1784, 9-10; favors constitutional changes, 44-47; interest of in public affairs, 107; seeks free public schools, 171-172; gains control of house of representatives, 219-220. *See* sectionalism, low country.

Upper pine belt, physical features of, 3.

War of 1812, declared, 253-254; welcomed by Republicans, patriotically accepted by Federalists in South Carolina, 254-255; South Carolina officers in, 256; approved by both houses of legislature, 257; early defeats in attributed to treachery, 265; causes of given by Cheves, 266; outcome of feared in South Carolina, 267; again approved by state legislature, 275; nature of reviewed by Calhoun, 277; increasing pessimism concerning in South Carolina, 282; great rejoicing over victory at New Orleans and peace, 283-284.

Washington, George, offers appointments to South Carolinians, 61-62; visits South Carolina, 67-68; becomes head of the army again, 115-116; news of his death causes sorrow in Charleston, 135.

Waties, Thomas, considered by Jefferson for Supreme Court, 196.

Williams, David R., co-publisher of *City Gazette,* 182 n.; opposes import duty on slaves, 190; declines dinner with Jefferson, 203; opposes "contingent expenses" appropriation, 204; objects to breaking commercial relations with Great Britain, 205; prefers war to Embargo, 218; denounces New England for disloyalty, 234-235; insists upon preparedness, 249; opposes a large navy, 251; favors strong policy toward New England, 264; advocates immediate seizure of Canada and Florida, 265; elected governor, 280, 280 n.

Willington, A. S., publisher of *Charleston Courier,* 182 n.

Winn, Richard, defeats Sumter for Congress, 69; loses to Sumter, 98, 98 n.; succeeds Sumter, 177 n.

"X. Y. Z." affair, 108-116.

www.ingramcontent.com/pod-product-compliance
Lightning Source LLC
Chambersburg PA
CBHW021354290426
44108CB00010B/238